The Social Technology Of Organization Development

W. Warner Burke
and
Harvey A. Hornstein

UNIVERSITY ASSOCIATES, INC.

7596 Eads Avenue
La Jolla, California 92037

(THE SOCIAL TECHNOLOGY OF
ORGANIZATION DEVELOPMENT) December 1, 1971

DESIGN AND USE OF THIS BOOK

Three different audiences may find benefits in this book:

1. Organization development practitioners
2. Organization managers
3. Students of organization behavior and change.

For OD practitioners new OD techniques and new knowledge in the effective use of OD techniques are provided.

Managers are provided with information that may help them answer two questions: "What is OD?" and "Just what do you do when you do OD?" Commonly, in answer to the first question professionals say "OD is a process" and add, as an answer to the second question, "I do team building"—to which managers then respond, "What or when is process and what is team building?" More complete answers to these questions are contained throughout this book. Managers and others who can't afford the time to read the entire book can get answers to their questions by reading only the chapters by Weisbord, Burke and Hornstein (the Introduction), Crockett, Schmidt and Tannenbaum, Seashore and Bowers, and possibly the Editors' Overview for each section. This "short course" in OD would probably be more effective if read in the order in which these articles are listed.

For students, the purpose is to provide (a) a conceptual overview of OD, with particular attention paid to the technology, and (b) some understanding as to how some current principles of OD are put into practice. Our bias is that effective use of OD practices requires the understanding of underlying OD principles, and the development of useful principles depends on familiarity with practices. The two are interdependent.

We want to emphasize that this book does not deserve the title, "The complete book about OD technology." In fact, one frustration in making decisions about articles to include in the book was that just as soon as a decision was made, it seemed outdated—even more recent technology should have been included. Thus, as stated in the Preface, this book is only one in a series. OD is in flux and change. The OD ship is definitely out to sea, and it is headed in a general direction (applying behavioral science principles for the improvement of organizations), but its specific course is unknown. We invite you to help us chart that course.

W. Warner Burke
Harvey A. Hornstein

CONTENTS

v

PREFACE

"Organization development" as an approach to changing social systems has a short history, only a decade or so long by some accounts. But it is a history already replete with folk heroes, myths, and epic events. Beckhard, Bennis, Blake, Shepard, Schein, Davis, Schmidt, and Tannenbaum are just a few of the names that command attention and respect from students and practitioners of organization development. "The events at Union Carbide," "the TRW story," and others are viewed as landmarks in the rapid development of this approach.

The history of organization development is unsystematically chronicled in the relevant professional literature. *The Journal of Applied Behavioral Science*, the *Harvard Business Review*, and a number of periodicals frequently publish articles describing the technology of organization development as well as related theory and research. In the past decade we have witnessed publication of Schein, Bennis, and Beckhard's *Organization Development* series, G. Lippett's *Organizational Renewal*, Herzberg's *Work and the Nature of Man*, McGregor's *The Human Side of Enterprise*, Schein and Bennis' *Personal and Organizational Growth through Group Methods*, and Hornstein et al.'s *Social Intervention: A Behavioral Science Approach*. The approach to changing social systems represented by this burgeoning group of publications has proven itself to be fertile. Ideas and innovative techniques are flourishing. However, too often they fail to reach an interested public.

This book represents the editors' attempt to provide a brief but comprehensive overview of organization development technology through a selection of good representative articles from the literature. Most often the articles are case studies and research reports describing successful and unsuccessful organization development efforts. Theoretical pieces are included when they provide useful conceptual schemes for organizing the literature.

Although this volume is billed as the first in a series, no commitment is being made to a specific time schedule for the publication of subsequent volumes. At the moment, maintaining the freedom to be responsive to the growth and quality of the literature seems wisest. A cautious projection into the future, however, suggests that the next volume will be published within two years.

An invitation is extended to all readers: Please call our attention to articles you see as appropriate and necessary additions to this series. If you have no suggestions but feel a need for information about a particular technique, please let us know that too. If the need is at all widespread, we will try to be responsive.

We hope both scholars and practitioners of organization development will find this series to be of interest. Changing organizations in our society is a task too urgent to be left only to scholars and too important to be left only to practitioners.

W. Warner Burke
Harvey A. Hornstein

CONTRIBUTORS

CLAYTON P. ALDERFER
Department of
Administrative Sciences
Yale University

JAMES D. ANDERSON
Episcopal Diocese
Washington, D.C.

ROBERT R. BLAKE
Scientific Methods, Inc.
Austin, Texas

DAVID G. BOWERS
Institute for Social Research
University of Michigan

LELAND P. BRADFORD
Executive Director (Retired)
NTL Institute

BHOPINDER S. BOLARIA
University of Maine

W. WARNER BURKE
Director, Center for
Organization Studies
NTL Institute

WILLIAM J. CROCKETT
Vice-President, Human Relations
Saga Administrative Corporation
Menlo Park, California

LOUIS E. DAVIS
Graduate School of Business Administration
and Institute of Industrial Relations
UCLA

C. BROOKLYN DERR
School of Education
Harvard University

WILLIAM G. DYER
Department of Organization Behavior
Brigham Young University

RAY FERRISS
Education Department
Polaroid Corporation

FRANK FRIEDLANDER
School of Management
Case Western Reserve University

ROBERT T. GOLEMBIEWSKI
Departments of Political Science
and Management
University of Georgia

ROGER HARRISON
Development Research Associates
London, England

JERRY B. HARVEY
George Washington University
Washington, D.C.

HARVEY A. HORNSTEIN
Department of Psychology
Teachers College
Columbia University

R. STEPHEN JENKS
Whittemore School of Business
and Economics
University of New Hampshire

H. ROY KAPLAN
University of Massachusetts

DANIEL LANGMEYER
Department of Psychology
University of Cincinnati

EDWARD E. LAWLER, III
Department of Administrative Sciences
Yale University

SEYMOUR LEVY
Manager, Personnel Research and
Manpower Development
The Pillsbury Company
Minneapolis, Minnesota

ROBERT F. MADDOCKS
RCA
N.Y., N.Y.

J. WELDON MOFFITT
Department of Psychology
Brigham Young University

JANE S. MOUTON
Scientific Methods, Inc.
Austin, Texas

LYMAN W. PORTER
Graduate School of Administration
University of California, Irvine

PHILIP J. RUNKEL
Center for the Advanced Study of
Educational Administration
University of Oregon

WARREN H. SCHMIDT
Assistant Dean
Graduate School of Business Administration
UCLA

RICHARD A. SCHMUCK
Center for the Advanced Study of
Educational Administration
University of Oregon

STANLEY E. SEASHORE
Institute for Social Research
University of Michigan

RICHARD L. SLOMA
Scientific Methods, Inc.
Austin, Texas

ROBERT TANNENBAUM
Graduate School of Business Administration
UCLA

CURT TAUSKY
University of Massachusetts

WILLIAM J. UNDERWOOD
Training and Applied Behavioral Science
RCA
Camden, N.J.

ERNST S. VALFER
Management Sciences Staff
U.S. Forest Service
Berkeley, California

RICHARD E. WALTON
Graduate School of Business Administration
Harvard University

MARVIN R. WEISBORD
Consultant Organization Research and
Development

INTRODUCTION

Practitioners of organization development (OD) generally agree about their ultimate goal: to create a self-renewing organization. They are in less agreement about how this goal is to be achieved—that is, about the *technology* of OD. The purpose of the present volume and of the series to follow is to collect and conceptualize this technology as it is currently understood. In this introduction we want to provide readers with a frame of reference by defining OD, discussing ways of categorizing OD technology, and describing the various OD techniques currently in use.

DEFINITION

Organization development is a process of planned change—change of an organization's culture from one which avoids an examination of social processes (especially decision making, planning, and communication) to one which institutionalizes and legitimizes this examination, and from one which resists change to one which promotes the planning and use of procedures for adapting to needed changes on a day-to-day basis. As previously defined (Hornstein, Bunker, Burke, Gindes and Lewicki, 1971), the *culture* of an organization is a set of learned and shared assumptions about the norms (standards, rules) that regulate member behavior. OD is a process of continually examining these norms and planning and executing social interventions to alter dysfunctional ones.

Underlying this process is Lewin's (1958) notion that individual and group change is most effective when norms or standards regulating behavior are changed. When a norm is changed, group members change their behavior as a function of social pressures and their desire to conform to the new norm. Attempts to change group or organizational behavior by changing individual behavior often result in resistance to change, particularly when an individual perceives that the change is not endorsed by his peers. Thus, the primary focus in OD is normative change; individual change is simply a by-product. But how does normative change occur at the group or organizational level, and how can the social functioning of organizations be enhanced? Through the social technology of OD!

OD TECHNOLOGY

OD technology has two phases: *diagnosis* and planned *intervention*. The primary component of the diagnostic phase is the gathering of data about critical social processes in an organization. Data-gathering techniques include (a) surveys, (b) interviews (of an organization, or every organizational member), and (c) observations of members' behavior as they go about their work. The data collected are categorized into problem areas, and consultants and/or organizational members, collaboratively or individually, attempt to discern the difficulties that exist. Interventions are then planned to alter dysfunctional conditions and enhance members' abilities to cope with the problems they face. Figure 1 shows the major types of intervention currently in use. The various slices of the figure 1 "pie" should be conceived as overlapping, and differing in size depending on the extent of their use by an organization. Note that when data are collected from people in an organization, an intervention is occurring. Thus it is often academic to distinguish between diagnosis and intervention.

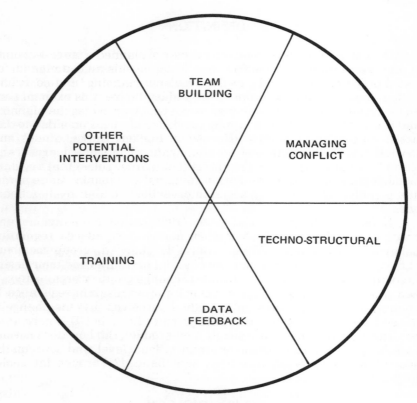

Figure 1. Types of OD intervention

TEAM BUILDING

Many organization members, especially managers, it seems, consider work in groups to be a waste of time. Indeed, the processes characteristic of work groups—problem solving, decision making, conflict resolution, and communication—often *are* inefficient and costly. Even when a group does succeed in achieving some goal, a successful end does not justify an inefficient means. Unilateral decision making, for example, can sometimes cause resistance by subordinates, which may lead to inefficiency and high costs.

Team building is a continuing process of diagnosing the effectiveness of a group's work procedures and interpersonal relationships. Work procedures include such things as

1. *Team organization for task accomplishment.* Does the group remain together throughout the task or does it subdivide for certain segments of the work? Does the team leader function in an active member role or is he aloof?

2. *Team decision-making procedures.* Do the members vote or is consensual decision making practiced? Does the leader reserve the right to make the final decision, or does he "live with" a team decision?

3. *Team agenda building.* Should the meeting be designed for communicating information or for making a decision? Should future action steps be planned as a part of the meeting? If so, have provisions been made to identify which members will assume responsibility for various steps? How long should it take the team to accomplish its purpose for a particular meeting, and has enough time been allotted? Does the team tend to waste time on discussion of irrelevant matters?

Diagnosing the effects of team member relationships on task accomplishment does not necessarily imply T-grouping in the usual sense. Team building is not T-grouping for the sake of accomplishing personal growth or a "group spirit," although these are desirable by-products. The real aim of team building is to build a group norm that encourages examination and open discussion of the effects of team members' relationships on task accomplishment. For example, if two team members' continual bickering is adversely affecting the team's work, this matter should be legitimate team business. Members should feel free to explore the reasons for the bickering and to take steps to ameliorate the problem. Feelings and attitudes should be legitimate data.

One of the most important facets of team building is discerning how the team handles internal conflicts. The notion that an effective team is one which "runs smoothly," with no conflict is a mistaken one. High quality decisions depend on the extent to which teams *surface* member conflicts and attempt to resolve them. As Hall and Watson (1970) have demonstrated, groups that treat differences of opinion as a help rather than hindrance and work toward consensus on decisions tend to make higher quality decisions than groups that ignore disagreements or decide by the traditional majority rule.

Team management requires different skills from those needed in the more commonplace patterns of management, such as one-to-one boss-subordinate relationships, or situations in which all authority is vested in a leader. As Blake and Mouton (1964) and McGregor (1967) have stressed, the skills of team management have to be learned. Effective team management requires a team leader to delegate more expeditiously and trustingly. He must share power and learn to manage shared power by becoming less of a director and more of a consultative manager or coordinator or resource person.

During team meetings the distribution of authority and responsibility must be continually clarified. Team managers should take a leading role in this clarification. They must be willing to deal with their subordinates' feelings about them as superiors and as people.

Training in team management skills constitutes the second phase of Blake and Mouton's (1968) grid approach to OD. Team training for more effective interpersonal relationships is also explored in the NTL Institute's Selected Reading No. 5, *Issues in Training* (Blake, Mouton, and Blansfield, 1962). These sources are recommended for further reading.

MANAGING CONFLICT

Individuals who work together interdependently over a period of time inevitably experience conflict. So do work groups in an organization. Intergroup conflicts are often destructive rather than constructive and prevent an organization from reaching its objectives. In his study of constructive approaches to dealing with intergroup conflict, Sherif (1951; Sherif and Sherif, 1956) found that once initiated, competition between groups tends toward stability, but collaborative behavior often remains unstable. Collaborative relationships between groups, especially when there has been previous conflict, require considerable intergroup trust. The slightest sign that this trust is being violated is likely to lead to a rearousal of conflict. For two groups to work collaboratively, they must have a superordinate goal, i.e., a goal which one group alone cannot reach. Following Sherif's experimental work, Blake and Mouton (1961) developed the approach further by designing laboratory training sessions for resolving intergroup conflict. Eventually they applied this laboratory approach to actual organizational problems (Blake, Mouton, and Sloma, 1965*). This early work led to some standard ways of conducting intergroup problem-solving sessions. Beckhard's approach (1969) is to separate the two conflicting groups and have each generate two lists of descriptive statements, one about itself and one about the other group. Then each group develops a third list, speculating about how it has been described by the other group. The groups are brought together, perceptions are shared, and issues are identified and ranked in order of importance by each group. Then the consultant helps to develop temporary teams composed of members from both groups work to generate solutions and action steps to alleviate the problems that have been identified.

Since most organizational units have interface with more than one other unit, intergroup problems may involve three or more groups. OD

*Also a chapter in this book, see pp. 101-126.

specialists at TRW Systems have extended the usual intergroup session to involve three or more units. In organizational "mirroring," as they call it, one group receives feedback from two or more other groups concerning interface problems they have with the "central" group. If most of the problem areas exist between two of the groups, the third group may serve as a consultant or mediator—an objective third party which "mirrors" the conflicts between the other two groups. The role of a third party in conflict situations has been explored by Walton (1969). Hornstein and Johnson (1966) have investigated the use of data feedback as a mediator of intergroup conflict. Harrison (1968) has discussed some useful approaches to intergroup collaboration even when a prior behavioral set of competition has been created.

In order to function, an organization must have groups which work together interdependently. It must continually examine the effectiveness of relationships between its work groups, surface unproductive conflict, and search for ways to maintain collaboration.

TECHNO-STRUCTURAL INTERVENTIONS

Techno-structural interventions are not commonly used by behavioral scientists. They involve changes which are more "technical" than social or psychological. Such changes, however, may have far-reaching effects on human behavior.

Techno-structural interventions are based on the assumption that since organizational life and functioning are regulated by forms of organizational structure and by technological and environmental constraints, organizational change may be mediated by such factors as patterns of work flow, hierarchial relationships, formal communication systems, division of labor, and inventory systems. Techno-structural interventions attempt to improve organizational functioning by changing formal organizational structure or some technical or environmental feature of a system. For example, Trist (1960) in his work with the British coal mines changed the organizational structure and the organization of work from a "conventional" system developed according to accepted industrial-engineering practice (work being minute, routine, repetitive, and individualistic) to a "composite" system in which individuals worked on a variety of tasks instead of a simple task, and were themselves responsible for the quality of work, instead of having outside inspectors responsible. In addition, Trist established a pay system based on a team's performance rather than an individual's. As a result of these changes, absenteeism, accidents, and costs were reduced. These interventions and their underlying assumptions are discussed at length by Hornstein et al. (1971).

Two prominent examples of the techno-structural approach are Herzberg (1968) and Beckhard (1967). Herzberg, applying the basic tenets of his theory or work motivation, has proposed a system of structural change which involves "enriching" a person's day-to-day job by modifying the content of his work. The principle followed in the change is one of giving the individual more responsibility for and authority over his job, for example, letting a salesman negotiate a discount for a client on his own rather than making him defer to his superior for the decision.

Beckhard's "confrontation meeting" (1967) may also be classified as techno-structural, since the intervention constitutes a temporary *reorganization* of some organizational unit. The reorganization affects primarily the communication patterns of the unit, by allowing rapid communication across all levels. Beckhard suggests that this intervention is particularly useful in conditions of crisis, when rapid problem solving is required.

A change in the organizational structure, or in the content of work, has often been the outcome of research and consultation by the Tavistock group (Rice, 1958; Trist, Higgin, Murray, and Pollock, 1963). Their change objective has been that of improving the fit between the technical and social subsystems of an organization. Katz and Kahn (1966) summarize an ideal sociotechnical system as "one in which the technical aspects of the work could be organized in such a manner that the immediate work group would have a meaningful unit of activity, some degree of responsibility for its task, and a satisfactory set of interpersonal relationships." (p. 435). Their sociotechnical approach is similar to Herzberg's job enrichment approach except that the structural change is more at the group than at the individual level. An example of a sociotechnical change would be a work group's performing a complete task—assembling an entire radio—rather than a part of it.

Chapple and Sayles (1961) approach organizational change similarly, modifying organizational structure and work patterns rather than modifying individual behavior. Behavioral change, they contend, will be a result of structural changes.

OD specialists who come from a "people approach" background tend to overlook such technical approaches to change. The point here is not to argue for a single technique of organizational change but rather to emphasize that the goals of OD can most usefully be attained through a *variety* of techniques.

DATA FEEDBACK

As noted earlier, data about an organization's culture and the problems faced by its managers may be gathered via interviews, questionnaires, or observations. Problems may range from boss-subordinate relationships to lack of clarity regarding the overall goals of the organization. Organizations frequently collect huge volumes of information about the current status of their climate, health, or potential for future markets but do little with it. The critical matter is *how* to best use this wealth of information.

For data to be used as an effective intervention for change, they must be fed back to the persons who generated them, and action planning should follow. Mann (1957) in his survey feedback procedure helped to ensure action by having organizational family groups discuss the data in a task-oriented atmosphere. Members analyzed the problems identified in the survey, searched for probable causes, and generated possible solutions.

Although their methods are not as elaborate as Mann's, Beckhard (1967, 1969) and Shepard (1968) likewise use data as an intervention for change. Beckhard collects data by conducting informal interviews. He categorizes the data by problem areas, convenes a meeting of the persons interviewed (usually an organizational family group), leads a group discussion of the data, and helps the group to plan action steps for meeting some of the needs that are identified and discussed. Shepard interviews several key organizational personnel and helps them to diagnose the needs and problems of their organization. He then facilitates the forming of a planning group made up of those persons most ready to cosider the action implications of the diagnosis. This group typically becomes a temporary task force for organizational change and makes plans for including others in its change efforts as quickly as possible. Using this procedure Shepard helps to "multiply" his own effectiveness as a change agent and provides a model for the way organizational members may work together in everyday situations. The model is based on the norm of collecting data rapidly, seeing that the information is shared, and taking the action that is needed.

A more comprehensive discussion of the use of data as an intervention for change may be found in Hornstein et al. (1971).

TRAINING

Training interventions are based on the assumption that organizations are improved when their members are trained to perform their work proficiently. But research evidence suggests that the degree of success depends on the type of training. Training programs designed to improve skills and motor activity frequently demonstrate positive effects (Crawford, 1962; Wolfe, 1951). There is also evidence that leadership training (Shartle, 1956) and laboratory education (Bunker and Knowles, 1967; Dunnette, 1969; Hall and Williams, 1966; Rubin, 1967; Schein and Bennis, 1965) result in some behavioral and attitudinal change.

These results are equivocal, however. See, for example, Campbell and Dunnette (1968); Fleishman, Harris, and Burtt (1955); House (1967). Most of the studies suggest that training may lead to individual change, but there is very little evidence that it has any impact on organization.[1] Fleishman (1955) found that as a result of a leadership training program foremen were more sensitive to and considerate of the feelings of their subordinates than before. His measurements were based on the foremen's self-perceptions and on ratings by their superiors and subordi-

1. Some possible exceptions include studies by Argyris (1962); Blake, Mouton, Barnes, and Greiner (1964); and White (1967). However, Dunnette and Campbell (1968) raise doubts about these.

nates. After a long time interval, however, these foremen reverted to their pretraining mode of leadership and were even *less* considerate of their subordinates' feelings than a control group who had received no training. Additional data demonstrated that foremen who remained considerate of their subordinates had supervisors who were themselves highly considerate. Schein (1965) succinctly clarifies the issue in his discussion of the Fleishman study:

. . . The effects of training were intimately related to the culture, or climate, of the departments from which the men came. These climates had as much of an effect on the trainee as did the training. Consequently, the training was effective, in terms of its own goals, only in those departments in which the climate from the outset supported the training goals. (p. 38)

The Fleishman study and others (e.g., Sykes, 1962) thus suggest that if training is to be an effective intervention, it must be coupled with a change in the organization's culture which will support and facilitate the objectives of the training effort. This notion is a fundamental in organization development.

OTHER POTENTIAL INTERVENTIONS

Team building, managing conflict, techno-structural interventions, data feedback, and training are the *major* types of interventions currently practiced in OD, but there are others. For example, the technique of management by objectives as developed by Drucker (1964) can easily become an integral part of an OD effort. Similarly, Herzberg's (1968) technique of job enrichment, mentioned earlier, may be a useful OD intervention, especially when motivation seems to be a fundamental problem. It is important to remember, however, that these techniques are part of a process, not an end in themselves. The process is one in which the diagnosis and change of social conditions is a regular feature of organizational life.

There is a risk that OD specialists may try any and all techniques for change without having a systematic change plan in mind, or without an organizational culture that supports the values and philosophy of OD. To support these values and philosophy, an intervention should be a *planned* activity that—

—Responds to a felt need on the part of the client group.
—Initiates or supports normative change in the organization's culture.
—Involves the client group in the planning and implementing of the change effort.

NEW AREAS IN NEED OF OD EXPERTISE

If we may hazard a guess as to the contents of the next volume in this series, it seems likely that many, if not all, of the interventions discussed in the present volume will be covered again. OD is still embryonic; considerable refinement of existing change techniques is needed and will undoubtedly be forthcoming. But new ideas are needed as well. OD specialists are not currently involved to any great extent in acquisitions and mergers, career development, or the management of creativity, but these areas of organizational life need their kind of expertise. Business and industrial organizations are more and more in the habit of acquiring smaller companies and merging with other organizations to form larger companies. After a merger or acquisition the financial picture for the resultant organization is often bright, but the human problems that arise can darken that picture. Unfortunately the people who plan these acquisitions and mergers usually come only from the finance and legal departments. Afterward, executives cannot understand why the acquired company's personnel are not happy with the new situation. After all, they say, "everyone is making more money." But "we-they" feelings linger and often interfere with needed collaborative efforts. OD expertise is needed to deal with these problems.

An implicit, if not explicit, objective of OD is to integrate individual goals with organizational goals. Central to this integration is career development. Employees often wonder, "What plans is the organization making for me?" They feel they have little opportunity to formulate goals for their future and act as though things happen to them but are not caused by them. Giving employees an opportunity to plan significant segments of their career with organizational support can lead to greater self-actualization for employees and more effective use of their talents for organizations. Relatively few organizations are currently providing these opportunities in career planning. One exception is TRW Systems, where Herb Shepard and Frank Jasinski are working.

Finally, organizations are going to be faced with the need to create conditions to elicit the creativity that now lies dormant within the organizational membership. How can people be "freed up" to develop new ideas and take bold steps that will help both organizations and individuals? We need to be "creative about the management of creativity."

Farson (1969) has said that a major problem facing our society is that "modern man seems unable to redesign his institutions fast enough to accommodate the new demands, the new intelligence, the abilities of segments of society which heretofore have not been taken seriously." (p. 20) Farson is referring to such "segments" as blacks, students, and women, who will undoubtedly have more influence on organizational life in the future. Organizations of today can begin preparing for this new influence by making more effective use of their present talent. The role of the OD specialist is to create organizational conditions that allow this talent to be tapped effectively.

Although Farson (1969) is not discussing OD, he does capture the essence of this strategy for change:

People who *have* the problems often have a better understanding of their situation and what must be done to change it. What professionals (Eds.: OD specialists) have to do is learn to cooperate with that resource, to design the conditions which evoke that intelligence. (p. 48.)

OVERVIEW

The format of this volume corresponds to the one used for this introductory chapter. Sections II through VI are each concerned with a different category of OD intervention: team building, managing conflict, techno-structural intervention, data feedback, and training.

The 15 articles in these sections comprise the "technology" of the book. The guidelines for allocating the articles the way we have are not precise. For example, the article by Jenks is included in the section on data feedback, but we could have logically made it a team-building article. Our allocation usually depended on what we viewed as the salient feature of the technique being described.

Section I, which contains four papers, is concerned with the general application of OD in different organizations. Weisbord gets to the heart of the matter by explaining OD so that any nonbehavioral scientist can understand it. Since most of the growth of OD has been in industrial organizations, an obvious question is whether the social technology developed in these organizations is more generally applicable. There is some evidence that it is, but with some important exceptions as we move into the world of nonprofit organizations. The articles by Golembiewski and Anderson illustrate some constraints on the application of OD in government agencies and the church, respectively. Derr's paper provides a case example of how OD was attempted in a large public school system. It is a story of some success and a lot of failure.

In the final section of the book, Seashore and Bowers provide one of the few quantitatively documented examples of the long-term success of an OD effort.

REFERENCES

ARGYRIS, C. *Interpersonal competence and organizational effectiveness.* Homewood, Illinois: Dorsey Press, 1962.

BECKHARD, R. *Organization development - strategies and models.* Cambridge, Massachusetts: Addison-Wesley, 1969.

BECKHARD, R. The confrontation meeting. *Harvard Business Review,* 1967, 45, No. 2, 149-155.

BLAKE, R. R., and Mouton, J. S. *Group Dynamics - Key to decision making.* Houston: Gulf Publishing Co., 1961.

BLAKE, R. R., and MOUTON, J. S. *The managerial grid.* Houston: Gulf Publishing Co., 1964.

BLAKE, R. R., and MOUTON, J. S. *Corporate excellence through grid organization development.* Houston: Gulf Publishing Co., 1968.

BLAKE, R. R., MOUTON, J. S., BARNES, L. B., and GREINER, L. E. Breakthrough in organizational development. *Harvard Business Review,* 1964, 42, 133-155.

BLAKE, R. R., MOUTON, J. S., and BLANSFIELD, M. G. The logic of team training. In I. R. Weschler and E. H. Schein (Eds.) *Issues in training.* Washington, D.C.: NTL Institute for Applied Behavioral Science, 1962, Pp. 77-85.

BLAKE, R. R., MOUTON, J. S., and SLOMA, R. The union-management intergroup laboratory. *Journal of Applied Behavioral Science,* 1965, 1, 25-57.

BLAKE, R. R., SHEPARD, H. A. and MOUTON, J. S. *Managing intergroup conflict in industry.* Houston: Gulf Puublishing Co., 1964.

BUNKER, D. R., and KNOWLES, E. S. Comparison of behavioral changes resulting from human relations training laboratories of different lengths. *Journal of applied Behavioral Science,* 1967, 3, 505-524.

CAMPBELL, J. P., and DUNNETTE, M. D. Effectiveness of T group experiences in managerial training and development. *Psychological Bulletin,* 1968, 70, 73-104.

CHAPPLE, E. D., and SAYLES, L. R. *The measure of management.* New York: Crowell-Collier and MacMillan, Inc., 1961.

CRAWFORD, M. P. Concepts of training. In Gagne, R. M. (Ed.), *Psychological principles in system development.* New York: Holt, Rinehart and Winston, 162, Ch. 9.

DRUCKER, P. *Managing for results.* New York: Harper and Row, 1964.

DUNNETTE, M. D. People feeling: Joy, more joy, and the "slough of despond." *Journal of Applied Behavioral Science,* 1969, 5, 25-44.

DUNNETTE, M. D., and CAMPBELL, J. P. Laboratory education: impact on people and organizations. *Industrial Relations,* 1968, 8, 1-45.

FARSON, R. E. How could anything that feels so bad be so good? *The Saturday Review,* 1969, Sept. 6, 20-21, 48.

FLEISHMAN, E. A. Leadership climate, human relations training, and supervisory behavior. *Personnel Psychology,* 1953, 6, 205-222.

FLEISHMAN, E. A., HARRIS, E. H., and BRUTT, H. E. Leadership and supervision in industry. *Ohio State Business Educational Research Monograph,* 1955, No. 33.

HALL, E. J., and WATSON, W. H. The Effects of a normative intervention on group decision making performance. *Human Relations,* 1970, 23, 299-317.

HALL, J., and WILLIAMS, M. S. A comparison of decision-making performances in established and ad hoc groups. *Journal of Personality and Social Psychology.* 1966, 3, 214-222.

HARRISON, R. Training designs for intergroup collaboration. *Human Relations Training News,* 1967, 11, No. 1, 1-3.

HERZBERG, F. One more time: How do you motivate employees. *Harvard Busines Review,* 1968, 46, 53-62.

HORNSTEIN, H. A., BUNKER, B. A., BURKE, W. W., GINDES, M. G., LEWICKI, R. J. *Social intervention: A behavioral science approach.* New York: Free Press, 1971.

HORNSTEIN, H. A., and JOHNSON, D. W. The effects of process analysis and ties to his group upon the negotiator's attitudes toward the outcome of negotiations. *Journal of Applied Behavioral Science,* 1966, 2, 449-463.

HOUSE, R. J. T Group education and leadership effectiveness: A review of the empirical literature and a critical evaluation. *Personnel Psychology,* 1967, 20, 1-32.

KATZ, P., and KAHN, R. L. *The social psychology of organizations.* New York: Wiley, 1966.

LEWIN, K. Group decision and social change. In E. E. Maccoby, T. M. Newcomb and E. L. Hartley (Eds.) *Readings in Social Psychology.* New York: Holt, Rinehart and Winston, 1958. Pp. 197-211.

McGREGOR, D. *The professional manager.* New York: McGraw-Hill, 1967.

MANN, F. C. Studying and creating change: A means to understanding social organization. In C. M. Arensburg *et al.* (Eds.) *Research in industrial human relations.* New York: Harper, 1957.

RICE, A. K. *Productivity and social organization: The Ahmedabad experiment.* London: Tavistock Publications, 1958.

RUBIN, I. Increasing self-acceptance: A means of reducing prejudice. *Journal of Personality and Social Psychology,* 1967, 5, 233-238.

SCHEIN, E. H. *Organizational psychology.* Englewood Cliffs, N.J.: Prentice-Hall, 1965.

SCHEIN, E. H., and BENNIS, W. G. *Personal and organizational change through group methods: The laboratory approach.* New York: Wiley, 1965.

SHARTLE, C. L. *Executive performance and leadership.* Englewood Cliffs, N. J.: Prentice-Hall, 1956.

SHEPARD, H. A. Changing interpersonal and intergroup relationships in organizations. In J. G. March (Ed.) *Handbook of Organizations.* Chicago: Rand McNally, 1965.

SHERIF, M. A preliminary study of intergroup relations. In J. H. Rohrer and M. Sherif (Eds.), *Social psychology at the crossroads: The University of Oklahoma lectures in social psychology.* New York: Harper, 1951. Pp. 388-424.

SHERIF, M. and SHERIF, C. W. *An outline of social psychology.* (Rev. Ed.) New York: Harper, 1956.

SYKES, A. J. M. The effect of a supervisory training course in changing supervisors' perceptions and expectations of the role of management. *Human Relations,* 1962, 15, 227-243.

TRIST, E. L. *Socio-technical systems.* London: Tavistock Institute of Human Relations, 1960.

TRIST, E. L., HIGGIN, G. W., MURRAY, H., and POLLOCK, A. B. *Organizational choice.* London: Tavistock Publications, 1963.

WALTON, R. E. *Interpersonal peacemaking: Confrontation and third party consultation.* Reading, Massachusetts: Addison-Wesley, 1969.

WHITE, S. T. *Evaluation of an analytic trouble shooting program: A preliminary report.* (research memo Kepner-Tregoe and Associates, July 28, 1967), 14 pp.

WOLFE, D. Training. In S. S. Stevens (Ed.) *Handbook of experimental psychology.* New York: Wiley, 1951. Pp. 1267-1286.

SECTION I

OVERVIEW

WHAT, NOT AGAIN! MANAGE PEOPLE BETTER?

Marvin R. Weisbord

A former executive argues that everyone talks about the importance of managing people, but very few companies have created the kind of organizations in which people can, or want to produce up to their maximum capabilities. Now the theory and technology exist to do that, but who will have the fortitude to try?

This past fall 12 executives of a "big board" corporation sat around a conference table analyzing turnover costs, trying to understand behavioral scientist Rensis Likert's ideas about measuring how much people are worth. When the final dollar figure—based on recruiting, hiring and training costs—emerged on the blackboard, several mouths went slack. The amount equaled 75 percent of the company's net profit before taxes a year earlier.

This cost was hidden in the company's books, and did not show up in any one place on the profit and loss statement. There was no account called "turnover." In consequence, nobody had been managing the problem. Indeed, it had not even been *identified* as a managerial problem, much less a human problem.

The 12 executives, however, responded in an all-too-human way. They began attacking their own figures, looking for ways to knock down the estimates.

They never once considered whether the costs could be cut. Implicit in their discussions was the notion that the nature of the job, the company and the employees was fixed, immutable, in the right relationship, and based on holy writ. The company might logically invest a million dollars to acquire a subsidiary with annual earnings of $100,000 (a 10 percent return); that would be considered astute financial management. It was hard for the executives to conceive, however, that even a 2 percent reduction in turnover would save the company much more than $100,000 each year, and with a much smaller investment.

Many of this company's top executives had read behavioral scientists McGregor and Likert, and served their time in T-groups. They understood Theory Y, and were nice to their secretaries. But when inflation began eating into profits in 1969, the order came down from on high—as it did in 1953 and 1957 and 1966—to start "tightening up" on costs, which meant to cut payroll and get people to turn out more, although the company already was undermanned nearly everywhere but at the top.

Any behavioral scientist, knowledgeable about organizations, would almost certainly point to high turnover costs as the most produc-

This chapter is a more expanded version of an article previously published in THINK Magazine and is reprinted here by permission from THINK Magazine, published by IBM, Copyright 1970 by International Business Machines Corporation.

tive place to tighten up. But rather than face the obvious complexities of that problem and, possibly flaws in their *management system*, these sophisticated executives—expert at managing cash, computers, plant layout, product quality and sales—looked instead for flaws in their *data.*

This real-life incident illuminates one of the formidable paradoxes facing business on the threshold of the '70s. It is the fact that while thousands of managers have been exposed to behavioral science over the past decade, very few companies have moved beyond the talking stage.

The effort to manage *all* of a company's resources, *including its management style and behavior,* in relationship to each other is called "organization development" (or O.D.), a new discipline which may have a profound impact on management in the '70s.

The key word is "may." Although the big names in behavioral science, whose contributions are indicated on page 4, draw ritual obeisance at every management seminar, while their theories and research have been digested into hundreds if not thousands of "units" in management development courses, the evidence suggests that the implications of behavioral science for management are simply not well understood or widely practiced. In a recent survey by the National Industrial Conference Board, for example, cited also on page 4, only one manager of every four queried listed Douglas McGregor as having personally influenced him; and McGregor, one of the most influential men of his time, was named far and away more often than the runners-up. ("Oh sure," said one personnel training man recently, "We do a unit on McGregor. Theory X, Theory Y. All our managers know about him." Asked what they were *doing* "about him," besides talk, the man smiled sheepishly. "Damned if I know," he replied.)

Statistics in this field are hard to come by. But if you drew up a list of companies which had made *significant* breakthroughs in organization structure, policy and behavior leading to greater job satisfaction and/or higher production, it would be a short list indeed, judging from the paucity of published case histories. It is doubtful the roll would include three dozen names.

THE "O.D. NETWORK"

Of the "Fortune 500" corporations, only 30 (6 percent) are represented in the 'O.D. Network," a loose association of applied behavioral science professionals. In these companies, interest in O.D. may be limited to the man on the list, or his department, or one plant. The network includes about 30-40 smaller firms, too, and there are perhaps dozens of other non-member companies doing important O.D. work. But even if the number ran to the hundreds, it still would be a tiny fraction of the 1.5 million-plus business firms in the United States.

The overwhelming majority of companies—despite 40 years of behavioral research—continue to manage the daylights out of half their assets (physical and financial), while thinking of the other half (the human side) as a luxury or frill. A vast gap exists between the glib use of names like McGregor, Likert and Herzberg in seminars and the paeans of praise to "our people" in annual reports, and the creative use of science-based theories to improve the way companies are managed.

The time for testing and perfecting new organization structures, policies and rewards based on conditions under which people are known to do their best has never been more propitious. But the resistance seems formidable. Why? One way to understand this paradox is to analyze the pressures pushing for and resisting change.

Among the "driving forces" which will impel companies toward creative experimentation with behavioral science in the 1970s are these:

• *Inflation and the threat of recession, which raise costs and squeeze profits, push management toward the use of any new knowledge which might increase effectiveness*—especially greater output at lower cost, but also flexibility in responding to new market opportunities.

• *Recognition is growing that improved technology requires better human capabilities.*

This is best illustrated by a new awareness among systems analysts that the most technically-perfect work system is no better than the willingness (and not just the ability) of people to make it go. "Implementation" cannot be accomplised by pushing buttons from behind a desk. Nor is "retraining" in new motor or intellectual skills enough. Both implementation and retraining require new interpersonal and group skills—how to surface and use conflict creatively, how to define and systematically solve problems, how to seek innovative "third" solutions, how to involve people in the design of their own work process so they will be highly-motivated to succeed.

A growing body of research supports the conviction (sometimes felt as despair) of many managers that as technology becomes more complex employees balk more at traditional efforts to "direct, control, reward, and punish." Everybody, it seems, wants a piece of the action, not just money, but also the psychic pay-off that comes from sharing in control over the job.

THE VALUE OF HUMAN RESOURCES

• *There is relatively much less room for improvement in the highly-rationalized and sophisticated systems we have for managing physical assets like equipment, land, buildings and cash, than in the still primitive area of organizing people for work, giving them the necessary tools, and rewarding them for their contributions.* Like the 12 executives struggling with turnover, management has considerably more to gain from improved organizational capability than in areas already well managed.

How much are people really worth? "Management says all the time that people are the company's most valuable asset," says Likert. "But I've asked a great many managers to be more specific than that—how much they think it would cost to build their present human organization from scratch. They consistently put the figure at about 3-4 times payroll. Since payrolls these days are averaging about eight times earnings, that means the human organization is worth, conservatively, at least 24-25 times earnings. That's the size asset management is dealing with. An able president who could increase the productive capacity, hence the value, of his human organization by only 5 percent would be achieving earnings double the figure on the balance sheet."

There are other considerations in trying to assess the value of human resources. For example, what does it mean when they increase in value through growth, experience, commitment, or interaction with each other? What does it cost when people leave, or—much worse— lose involvement, motivation and loyalty as a result of some management practice, *without* actually leaving (what Robert N. Ford, AT&T's job enrichment advocate, calls "on-the-job retirement")? Quite a large part of a man's value to a company disappears the day he starts scanning the want ads.

One company, the R. G. Barry Corporation (Columbus, Ohio), is working on what is believed to be the first "human resource accounting" system. Barry is trying to place accurate values not only on its employees but also on good customer and supplier relations. At Barry, every manager must account not only for profits and solvency, but also for the physical, organization and customer assets in his care. Barry checks results in all five areas, aware that an executive who is expected only to maximize profits may well do it at the expense of customer or employee resources, a short-term gain injurious to long-range company health.

"We are talking about a tool," says Barry's president, Gordon Zacks, "which can revolutionize the whole style of management in our companies."

BANISHMENT FOR ABSENTEEISM

● *In the last decade we have developed much improved ways of studying and measuring the human organization and its internal changes.* The sophisticated work of Rensis Likert in this area is still largely unappreciated and unapplied. Likert has shown, for example, that there are *three* kinds of things going on in a company ("variables"): its management structure and behavior, which establish the basic climate; employee attitudes and motivation, which evolve from and maintain the climate; and productivity and earnings, which are the result.

Most managers only measure the end product—profits. They tend to leave human resources, which gain or lose value based on management behavior and its impact, to chance. Yet, as research at Michigan and elsewhere has begun to show, by measuring the first two sets of variables, management can predict what costs and profits *will* be—two, three or four years later. Companies which integrate data about the condition of the organization with cost, production and profit figures can develop an extraordinary ability to be self-regulating; they might even, conceivably, banish turnover and absenteeism forever when they know how to detect, in advance, the deterioration in managerial capability that makes human loss inevitable.

Motivaton to do so is found mainly among companies which have experimented successfully with O.D. "I think we have reached the point," says George Raymond, Jr., president of The Raymond Corporation, who tried "scientific management" in the 1950s and turned to behavioral science-based strategies in 1963, "where we can now begin to develop in-house a five-year plan for development of human resources, just as we now plan and forecast our production output and marketing strategies."

● *In addition to better measuring rods, there is an evolving, and increasingly-effective "technology" of organization development.* It has grown, in part, from the T-group movement of the last 20 years. Nobody but a few diehards believes any more that "turning people on" to openness and trust in T-groups will revitalize organizational life. The T-group is not a management structure and never was intended to be. Trust is a norm, not a policy. Nevertheless, T-groups have pioneered in teaching human skills essential to better organizations: how to tell people what's *really* bugging you without alienating them; how to listen and act creatively when others say things you'd rather not hear; how to behave as if leadership meant acting effectively, which anybody can learn to do, rather than a set of fixed traits for a chosen few; how to use the committee, butt of so many jokes, as a powerful problem-solving instrument by encouraging its members to learn and play the same game by the same rules.

The T-group remains a basic tool, but only one, in a fast-expanding and apparently infinite kit. Another is "team-building," a powerful management technology in which a work group experiences new ways to deal with work-related problems based on information supplied by themselves. Often groups emerge from a team workshop with a set of norms and commitment to the task which other groups fail to achieve in 10 or 20 years of working together.

The technoloy for these and other O.D. activities includes paper and pencil exercises, group task experiences, role playing, and simulation games. It is growing daily.

● *The wedding of measurement to technology has made possible a set of coherent strategies for organization development.* These incorporate a diagnosis of organization problems and power realities, and a notion that the organization is a system in which each part affects every other. Strategies tend to be long-range, flexible, experimental, but built firmly on theories which hold that it is possible to change human behavior for the better.

Some strategies use T-groups, others the "feedback" of survey data to work groups which then decide what they want to change and how to change it; still others employ Blake's Grid O.D., a six-phase program in which the stouthearted, ultimately, rewrite company goals, policies and structure.

Results from the handful of firms which have kept at it doggedly for five years or more suggest that significant cuts in absenteeism, turnover and costs, and increased profitability may reward those who persevere.

TEMPORARY TEAMS

● *Many managers already feel uneasy with the rigid, army-type organizational form which dominates our society.* "Channels" often appear to defeat the tasks they're supposed to facilitate. A few innovative firms are experimenting with "temporary systems," the work team built around a problem and picked for relevance, not job titles.

Other firms have added "cross-function" management teams, in which line and staff people make decisions together, report to two bosses, and turn usual notions about "delegation" and "authority" upside down and inside out.

Behavioral scientists Warren G. Bennis and Philip E. Slater see temporary systems and democratic decision-making as essential features of "post-bureaucratic" management. "Democracy," they write in THE TEMPORARY SOCIETY (1968), "becomes a functional necessity whenever a social system is competing for survival under conditions of chronic change."

The human skills we will need to operate well in the loose, free-flowing companies of the future are the same ones we will need to develop the companies we already have. Far-sighted managers seek not only for new company structures but also for the behavior needed to make them click.

Companies which have strategies for using creatively both the group process and the conflict it engenders can afford to try radical new organizational forms. Dynamic, rather than static structures may liberate creativity in ways we cannot yet fully understand.

● *At last, everybody feels pushed to the wall by inexorable, fast, and sometimes incomprehensible social change, what author Alvin Toffler calls "future shock."* Blacks, women, young people—all are looking to get a better break from society, or to re-make society in ways they believe will be more humane. Whatever his feelings about the various "revolutions" we are undergoing, no manager can afford to ignore what may happen to his company if he doesn't accept certain social responsibilities once considered out of bounds for management.

How to do this and still avoid loss remains a developmental problem. It will be done, it is being done, by companies redefining their missions and seeking new ways to live out those missions. None of us can foresee where this may lead, but there is a strong urge to build organizations that can handle the future, whatever it brings.

These are just a few of the forces pushing for change. The opportunities appear to be unlimited. We are, as American Airlines President George A. Spater put it, "still in the stone age when it comes to applying the behavioral sciences." The most exciting discoveries about how to organize work so that people obtain growth and satisfaction from it lie ahead. Who will make them? How? When?

Many formidable "restraining forces" impede the use of behavioral research in businesses.*

● *We have no precedent for organizing in new ways.* From public school on, as Chris Argyris has pointed out, we experience a world which talks a lot about "responsibility" and "self-control," but offers few chances to use or be rewarded for those qualities. We have learned to be expert talkers about building a better world, but we have hardly begun to develop the kind of school system that could teach it.

As a rule, schools teach competition as the only road to success. Cooperative effort is called "cheating," and indeed, the way the school sees it, it is. Learning goes one way, if it goes at all, from teacher to pupil. Few schools have made any moves to tap into the most powerful of all educational discoveries, our extraordinary capability to help each other learn. Schools, like most other organizations, tend to be bureaucracies encased in cement. They tend to define for us what is possible.

Hence we can talk Theory Y (or System 4, or 9,9) management far into the night, drunk with enthusiasm for the dawn; but few of us know what it looks, feels, smells and tastes like to actually manage or be managed that way.

● *Behavioral science jargon badly garbles efforts to communicate important new knowledge to managers.* Apart from McGregor, who was the Ernest Hemingway of social science, few professors write and talk in a way that instantly engages executives. Likert, whose writings, however honored, receive nowhere near the close attention they deserve, speaks of "interaction-influence systems," and "causal, intervening, and end-result variables." Argyris advocates "interpersonal competence." Herzberg talks of "hygiene factors," and Maslow named his vision of a better organization "Eupsychian management." Such language might cause even the most open mind to slam shut like a bear trap.

● *The field is and always will be highly experimental.* There is no iron-clad guarantee of results. Businessmen have anxiety fits over the word "experiment," especially when the laboratory is their office, not a building full of scientists.

Moreover, each manager must repeat the experiments for himself. Executives speak of "Theory Y techniques," or "System 4 techniques," as if there were a compendium of universal rules which anybody can memorize and use. But Theory Y is a set of *assumptions*, and each

---

*Business, however, is light years ahead of public schools, universities, hospitals, foundations and other "nonprofit" entities, which have a hard time setting performance goals and incentives, and shy away from measuring results.

manager must discover anew which *practices* these assumptions, if he held them, would lead to in *his* situation.

Trial and error learning is essential to organization development. Managers hate the thought of "error," which has always triggered punishment of one form or another. Those who wonder what magic feats coordinated the efforts of the thousands of people to put men on the moon might ponder the comment of the Space Agency's Dr. Al Siepert, "In NASA, we never punish error. We only punish the *concealment* of error." How many executives can say that?

• *Management information and accounting systems are inadequate to the job of measuring the results of organization development.* If you must experiment to develop, it is essential that you measure the effects. Are you getting change for better or worse? Management information now means production, output, cost and money data. A great many top executives today came up through finance or engineering, and feel right at home with symbols. They understand figures on the books which change instantly if they reduce inventory, sell buildings, or lay off employees.

Most do *not* understand human value or how to measure it, nor is there any good place to hook such data into conventional information systems. Those who would experiment with "human resource accounting," for instance, need a new theory of what management information is before they can begin.

Rensis Likert, for example, recently described how one giant corporation which decentralized after World War II rewarded its location managers with bonuses based on current earnings, giving them authority to do whatever they felt necessary to increase those earnings. The managers went like a house afire, most of them by putting the screws on their people, pushing them to maximum effort without commensurate rewards. Then came a recession in the mid-1950s. Now the company demanded a 5 percent profit or else. Within two years, Likert recalls, more than 50 of the top managers were gone. "They couldn't make it." he said. They had liquidated rather than invested in the human assets in their organization to get short-term earnings and big bonuses; they hadn't built the kind of organization which could respond quickly to cost pressure and belt tightening.

Until their efforts can be measured, evaluated and rewarded, it is unrealistic to expect managers to try to enhance the value of their human assets.

• *Even when executives have new data about their company, they tend to disbelieve it if it contradicts habit, tradition, or current management practice.* Almost any personnel researcher can tell tales of studies and surveys locked in bottom desk drawers because their implementation might seem like an admission of previous poor management practices.

THE DATA SEEM TOO UNREAL

Recently the Institute for Social Research studied a chemical plant before and after a "cost reduction" program reduced the payroll by one man in four. The company's figures showed a saving of $250,000. ISR's data revealed severe deterioration in an already-ineffective management system. "There was a drastic decline in communications, for instance," says ISR's Dr. David Bowers, "which in this plant forecast a rise in costs of at least a million dollars two years hence." What has the company done with this information? Nothing. It goes right on improving profits its own way. The data just seem too unreal, unbelievable. Says Bowers: "They're already paying in terms of reduced productivity."

● *The payoff comes slowly in O.D. work.* Often it takes three to five years or more to build a strong, well-integrated, flexible and highly-motivated organization. The bigger the company, the longer it takes. Production may drop before it rises, while people invent and learn to play by new ground rules. Three years is much too long for the "results-oriented" manager. Indeed, it is probably too long for his stockholders, too.

Consider, for example, this case, described to a group of organizational development executives at a recent Foundation for Research on Human Behavior conference in Ann Arbor. The company got into a profit bind a few years back and decided on total O.D. as the way out. During the first three years, anxiety rose as the company underwent dramatic changes. But profits stayed disappointingly low.

"It was a traumatic experience for many in top management," reported one executive. "Many of us had worked together for years without openly discussing some of the really hard issues."

But the men kept doggedly at it, senior executives mastering the O.D. strategy, then teaching it in four- or five-day workshops to subordinates, and so on down the line. Toward the end, the company reorganized. A task force prepared a new total business plan, staff functions were shucked, policies rewritten.

Five years after the effort began, despite a 3 percent decline in gross sales, earnings rose 91 percent in a year. And the company has kept it up since. It took extraordinary faith and firm commitment from the man at the top to stick it out. For every story like this one there are 10 others—of companies which took step one and panicked when they didn't get instant success, and blamed behavioral science for their troubles. Nobody knows a way around the time lag.

● *Those most interested in and capable of changing an organization tend to be those with the least power to do it.* Even in companies which hire behavioral scientists, the O.D. specialist is an anomaly, a staff man who would like to shake up practices and policies but can't do it unless a line manager invites him. Moreover, to the extent that the O.D. man is denied access to the chief executive officer in a company, he will be ineffective. There can be no important organization change unless men at the top believe enough in its potential.

Often the O.D. man pushes for a redistribution of power and influence to make the organization work better. Chief executives who see power as a scarce resource (for them to have more, others must have less) will rightly feel threatened. Organization development is not a "program." It is a way of life. No company can live it without commitment from the boss.

Can Work Be Fun?

• *We come at last to the deep-seated belief in the incompatibility of people and production.* This force, while not rational, may be the most severe restraint on action. At bottom, most of us feel uneasy about changing organizations in the direction of making work fun. Playfulness, joy, excitement are what you work *toward* during the week, but experience only on weekends. Indeed, for many of us, tension, pressure, suppressed conflict and exasperation are the essence of work.

Everybody knows some executive, wildly hedonistic on vacation, who goes rigid with anxiety at the sight of a couple of secretaries engaging in horseplay in the office—a clear example of self-indulgence on company time.

Can work be fun? Can it even be deeply and continually satisfying? The "evidence" says no. Most of our policies, practices and job designs are such that the rare man in the rare company gets any fun out of organizational life.

Perhaps the only important trait of the Theory Y, or System 4, or 9,9 manager is that he tends not to see any contradiction between work and satisfaction. Most of his energy goes into figuring out how to make company and personal goals compatible. In this, he draws on a whole repertoire of personal behavior—from participative to authoritarian—as the situation requires. He is not hung up on a system or an ideology, but shows a great deal of flexibility in driving towards his goal.

Nevertheless, he is constantly swimming upstream. There are legendary stories of high-producing Theory Y managers who conceal how much they involve others in decisions for fear they will be ordered to stop doing it. Often they are believed by others to be some sort of managerial mutant, men who get results *despite* their eccentric hang-up on people, not because of it.

One high-producing manager, for example, got extraordinary results by involving employees in such diverse matters as plant layout, changes in work procedures and even day-to-day policy. Fundamentally, it was group problem-solving and decision-making. Says Likert, who observed this situation: "When we tried to describe his leadership style at his company's executive development school, everybody said, 'Well, it's okay for him. That's his personality. Nothing here I can use.' To this day, top management doesn't realize this man's management principles are worth at least 5 percent of the company's total payroll, because virtually every one of its thousands of managers could improve his performance by using them. Instead, he'll retire, and the firm will never know what a great asset slipped through its fingers."

Faced with a genuine Theory Y manager, live and in color, most executives simply refuse to accept the obvious. Why?

There is no good research on this.

Maybe we're all victims of Western theology, perpetually doomed to pay off Adam's sin for having ruined a good arrangement by eating the forbidden apple. Work was Adam's punishment, not his reward, and men have resisted mightily all efforts to set things up so they might toil within the Garden of Eden, not outside of it. Some physiologists speculate that there is a "work gene," perhaps a carryover from the days when survival was a fulltime job.

Whatever the reason, sin, work and guilt seem inextricably linked to our attitudes toward behavioral science. O.D. holds out a terrifying prospect—the chance to design organizations so that the thing which needs doing is the very thing people like, need, want and are rewarded to do. Perhaps God is dead and religion dying; but guilt over mixing work and pleasure is alive and well everywhere.

What can be done to break the equipment between forces pushing for and resisting organizational change? "Rational argument and intellectual persuasion," Douglas McGregor pointed out eight years ago, "are frail tools for the purposes of changing these emotional forces. Confronting management with facts, research findings, and behavioral science theory often amounts to little more than applying force to human objects, thus increasing tension in the system. . . ."

An All-Consuming Experience

Why should an article like this one do any better? Certainly it is not possible to give people six easy rules for planned change.

How, indeed, would you organize work, set goals and rewards in a company truly committed to the notion that human satisfaction and high standards need not be in conflict?

Anybody who wants to experiment with this question might try this simple 5-minute exercise: Take a few subordinates aside and ask them what's going on in the company that keeps them from doing as good a job as they know how. If you get an honest answer, that's a good sign; and you can go to work on it. Almost invariably, you will soon find yourself managing problems you didn't know you had. You're off and running on organization development, and whose theory you run with doesn't make much difference, if you're willing to experiment with what turns people on. Sooner or later you will hit and question every part of the system—work methods, vacation policies, plant layout, fights between production and marketing, whether it makes sense to have people report to time clocks, and last (though you may well do this first) the extent to which your own management behavior has been getting in the way of what you're trying to do.

To let people in on managing their own work situation is a powerful and all-consuming experience. It is much harder to manage people and production together than to play one against the other. The rewards may be much greater too; but it would be foolish and futile to advise anybody to try it who really believes, deep inside, that Theory X is a better predictor of the nature of man.

Maybe behavioral scientists are off the scent. Perhaps Theory X really does tell it like it is, and Theory Y is a form of wishful thinking. If so, we should know for sure before the 1970s are out. Though few companies are going the O.D. route, there are enough on the road now to provide, within 5 to 10 years, some conclusive evidence about what does and does not make organizations more effective and satisfying.

Companies which feel they can afford to wait may talk McGregor a while longer, and send a few more people off to T-groups. Change, especially now, with the economy shaky, is sure to be troublesome. It might well be put off for later. Those willing to meet trouble sooner in hopes of avoiding it later, however, if they start now (and if McGregor was right about Theory Y) may know by 1975 what it's like to face an uncertain future with a self-renewing organization.

THESE SIX THEORISTS HAVE INFLUENCED
MANAGEMENT MOST*

ABRAHAM MASLOW, unlike the others here, did not base his major work on studies of business organizations. A theoretical psychologist, he described in *Motivation and Personality* (1954) a "need hierarchy," suggesting that motivation proceeds up a ladder of human need. His ideas seem to suggest that "a satisfied need is not a motivator," and that people do their best only in situations offering more than good pay and benefits—a chance for growth and involvement. Maslow, a former professor of psychology at Brandeis University, is now a resident fellow with the W. P. Laughlin Foundation.

CHRIS ARGYRIS has been a prodigious writer and researcher on the effects of organization life on individuals and an advocate of efforts to build consistency between individual and organization goals. He is widely known for his work with T (for training)-groups and for developing new designs for organizational structures and administrative controls. A professor of administrative sciences at Yale University, Argyris is best known for *Interpersonal Competence and Organizational Effectiveness* (1962) and *Integrating the Individual and the Organization* (1964).

ROBERT BLAKE, who with JANE S. MOUTON wrote *The Managerial Grid* (1964), neatly integrated the research of Likert, Argyris, McGregor and many others into an easily-understood tool for analyzing

---

*The National Industrial Conference board queried 500 companies, got 302 replies, found 241 companies "interested" in behavioral science. Influential behavioral scientists most often named, and frequency: McGregor (134); Herzberg (96); Likert (88); Argyris (85); Maslow (54); Blake and/or Mouton (52). From: "Behavioral Science Concepts and Management Application" (Studies in Personnel Policy, No. 216), by NICB's Harold M. F. Rush, 1969.

and attempting to change organization and management styles, based on the balance between one's concern for production and conern for people. In Blake terminology, a "9,1" manager (low on people, high on output) looks much like a System 1 or Theory X type, while a "9,9" (high on people and output both) parallels System 4 or Theory Y. Blake, a former University of Texas psychology professor, now heads a multi-million-dollar consulting firm.

The late DOUGLAS McGREGOR's The Human Side of Enterprise (1960) is probably the most widely-read book in its field in this century. McGregor, a psychologist, college president (Antioch), and management professor at MIT, cut through jargon to describe two sets of contrasting "assumptions" about man and his relation to work. In consequence, "Theory X" (men are willful, lazy, capricious and in need of constant watching), and "Theory Y" (men like work, seek responsibility, are capable of self-control) have become part of management language. The latter theory, McGregor argued, more nearly corresponded to the evidence derived from research into human capability. Before his death in 1964, McGregor often lamented that Theory Y was commonly mistaken to mean "soft" management, when he in fact believed that high management standards and goals were implicit.

RENSIS LIKERT showed that an organization is a complex system in which leadership, motivation, decision-making, communication and control tend to vary together. Likert maintains that these can be measured, and over a stretch of time related closely to production and profit. He described four organizational model systems.

Likert's "System 1" manager, a dictatorial type, might be said to hold Theory X assumptions; his "System 4" manager, who seeks group consensus, would probably believe in Theory Y. In New Patterns of Management (1961) and The Human Organization (1967), Likert suggested radical changes in structure, behavior, and the collection and use of management data by those who would tap the full potential of their employees. His proposal that the value of people be measured and managed as carefully as land, buildings and machinery has led to work, now in progress, on a revolutionary human asset accounting system. A psychologist and sociologist, Likert directs the University of Michigan's Institute for Social Research, where important work in changing business and other organizations is being done.

FREDERICK HERZBERG in Work and the Nature of Man (1966) confirmed and elaborated upon his earlier Motivation-Hygiene theory. Fringe benefits, working conditions, etc., are "hygiene factors," essential but not motivating. Responsibility, achievement, recognition and growth opportunities are the factors which motivate people to perform better. Herzberg is professor of psychology at Case Western Reserve University.

ORGANIZATION DEVELOPMENT IN PUBLIC AGENCIES: PERSPECTIVES ON THEORY AND PRACTICE

Robert T. Golembiewski, *University of Georgia*

This article is adapted from a paper prepared for delivery at the Annual Meeting of the Southern Political Science Association, held November 6-7, 1968, in Gatlinburg, Tennessee.

The special genius of each age is reflected in distinctive ways of organizing work. If the preceding age stressed stability and consistency, roughly, the emphasis today is on organizing for change and variability. The specific implications are diverse and still obscure, but the general point is overwhelming. John W. Gardner reflects both the certainty and the caution. "What may be most in need of innovation is the corporation itself," he notes. "Perhaps what every corporation (and every other organization) needs is a department of continuous renewal that could view the whole organization as a system in need of continuing innovation."[1]

The major recent response to the need for planned organizational change is the burgeoning emphasis on organization development, or OD. Three themes constitute the core of typical OD concepts. As Winn explains:[2]

The term "organization development" . . . implies a normative, re-education strategy intended to affect systems of beliefs, values and attitudes within the organization so that it can adapt better to the accelerated rate of change in technology, in our industrial environment and society in general. It also includes formal organizational restructuring which is frequently initiated, facilitated and reinforced by the normative and behavioral changes.

Changing attitudes or values, modifying behavior, and inducing change in structure and policies, then, are the three core-objectives of OD programs. In contrast, the reorganization literature in political science is concept-oriented and gives little attention to changes in attitudes and behavior necessary to implement its guiding concept.

This article provides a variety of perspectives on the characteristics of OD programs, and also summarizes experience from a number of OD efforts in public agencies at federal and local levels. Not all these agencies can be identified here, unfortunately, but the database consists of seven cases. No attempt will be made to evaluate the effectiveness of any particular OD application; and even less is the purpose here to assess the specific technology of OD programs such as the use of sensitivity training.[3]

The motivation of this piece derives from the following propositions. First, government agencies have begun experimenting with various OD approaches, if less bullishly so than business and service

Reprinted from Public Administration Review, Vol. XXIX, No. 4 July/August 1969 bimonthly publication of the American Society for Public Administration 1225 Connecticut Avenue, N.W., Washington, D.C. 20036.

organizations. Second, the public sector has a variety of distinctive features that provide special challenges to achieving typical OD objectives. Third, these distinctive features have received inadequate attention in the literature and in the design of OD programs in public agencies. Fourth, applications of OD programs in public agencies probably will become more common. The need to tailor OD programs in public agencies more closely to the distinctive constraints of their environment should consequently increase sharply. Finally, students of public administration can play useful and distinct roles in such OD programs, providing they develop appropriate competencies.

A TYPICAL OD PROGRAM: AND THE UNDERLYING NETWORK OF FINDINGS AND HYPOTHESES

Despite their variety, OD programs rest on similar conceptual foundations. These foundations are a mixed bag, including relatively "hard" empirical findings and plausible hypotheses. These foundations of OD programs also prescribe how organizations ought to be so as to be effective, "healthy," or morally acceptable.

Figure 1 simplifies the web of findings/hypotheses/values that underlies the typical OD program. The figure focuses strictly on the "front-load" of OD programs; that is, on how sensitivity training or related techniques can induce greater openness, trust, and shared responsibility. Based on such social and psychological preparation, OD programs can flower diversely. For example, early exposure to sensitivity training might encourage greater openness in an organization, which in turn might highlight critical needs for changes in policies, procedures, structure, or technology. An OD program then would be appropriately expanded to meet such needs, as by additions of training programs, etc.[4]

A TYPICAL OD PROGRAM: MAJOR OBJECTIVES

The findings/hypotheses/values underlying OD programs imply several common objectives. Overall, the goal is to release the human potential within an organization. Specifically, a typical OD program emphasizes major objectives such as these:[5]
1. To create an open, problem-solving climate throughout the organization.
2. To supplement the authority associated with role or status with the authority of knowledge and competence.
3. To locate decision-making and problem-solving responsibilities as close to the information sources as possible.
4. To build trust among individuals and groups throughout the organization.
5. To make competition more relevant to work goals and to maximize collaborative efforts.

6. To develop a reward system which recognizes both the achievement of the organization's mission (profits or service) and organization development (growth of people).
7. To increase the sense of "ownership" of organization objectives throughout the work force.
8. To help managers to manage according to relevant objectives rather than according to "past practices" or according to objectives which do not make sense for one's area of responsibility.
9. To increase self-control and self-direction for people within the organization.

Basically, the organization is seen "as a system in need of continuing innovation," and an OD program begins by stressing the development of attitudes, behaviors, and skills that will support such continuing innovation.

The list of OD objectives does double duty here. In addition to providing additional content for the concept "organization development," the list of objectives helps highlight some of the special difficulties facing OD programs in public (and especially federal) agencies. The discussion below focuses on one major question: What specific properties of public agencies make it especially difficult to approach specific objectives such as those above? Evidence comes primarily from seven OD programs at the federal and local levels in which this author has participated.

CHARACTER OF THE INSTITUTIONAL ENVIRONMENT: CONSTRAINTS ON APPROACHING OD OBJECTIVES

Public agencies present some distinctive challenge to OD programs, as compared with business organizations where most experience with OD programs has been accumulated. Four properties of the public institutional environment particularly complicate achieving the common goals of OD programs.

Multiple Access

1. As compared to even the largest of international businesses, the public environment in this country is characterized by what might be called, following David Truman, unusual opportunities for *multiple access to multiple authoritative decision makers*. Multiple access is, in intention if not always in effect, a major way of helping to assure that public business gets looked at from a variety of perspectives. Hence the purpose here is to look at the effects of multiple access rather than to deprecate it. Figure 2 details some major points of multiple access relevant to OD programs in four interacting "systems": the executive, legislative, "special interests," and mass media systems.

Multiple access has its attractive features in beginning OD programs in public agencies. For example, one large OD program was inaugurated in an economical way: a top departmental career official

FIGURE 1
A Simplified Model of Findings/Hypotheses
Underlying the Typical OD Program

Basic Premise: When individuals can meet their own needs while meeting organizational needs, output will be qualitatively and quantitatively best.

An individual's basic needs center around *self-realization* and *self-actualization.* The former involves a person seeing himself as he is in interaction with others, with the goal of increasing the congruence between his intentions and his impact on others. Self-actualization refers to the processes of growth by which an individual realizes his potential.

An individual whose basic needs are satisfied does not seek comfort and security; rather, he *searches for work, challenge, and responsibility.*

An efficient organization will develop an appropriately shifting balance between *institutionalization* and *risk-taking.* The former refers to *infusing with values* the activities of the organization, so as to elicit member support, identification, and collaboration. Risk-taking is necessary in *innovating* more effective ways to deal with existing activities, and in *adapting* to environmental changes in society, market technology, and so on.

An organization's successful balancing of institutionalization and risk-taking will depend upon
— the increasingly complete *use of people* as well as nonhuman resources
— the development and maintenance of a viable balance between *central control* and local initiative
— fluid lines of *communication,* vertically, horizontally, and diagonally —
— *decision-making* processes that solve problems that stay solved without creating other problems.

Satisfaction of both individual and organization needs will be facilitated by, if such satisfaction does not in fact crucially depend upon, *skill and competence in interpersonal and intergroup situations.*

An individual's growth and self-realization are facilitated by interpersonal relations that are *honest, caring, and nonmanipulative.* Hence the reliance on "stranger" experiences in sensitivity training groups composed of individuals with no past relationships. Such training is a managed process of gaining experience with attitudes and skills for inducing greater openness about positive and negative feelings, attitudes, or beliefs. Such openness leads to greater trust and reduced risk in communicating in the "stranger" group, and is intended to suggest possible transfers into other environments.

Organizational "family" teams are exposed to sensitivity training, with the intention of *increasing trust and responsibility* that can be applied directly to solving organizational issues, and with the intention of *decreasing the risk* in being open in interpersonal and group situations. Skill and competence in interpersonal and intergroup situations can be increased in sensitivity training groups composed of strangers, but the real test is the application of such learning in life-relevant situations. Such application will require that substantial numbers of organization members learn appropriate interpersonal skills, as well as that they internalize a set of values which support and reinforce such learning.*

FIGURE 1 Continued

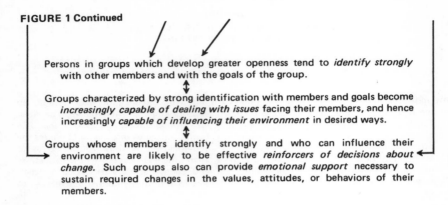

Persons in groups which develop greater openness tend to *identify strongly* with other members and with the goals of the group.

Groups characterized by strong identification with members and goals become *increasingly capable of dealing with issues* facing their members, and hence increasingly *capable of influencing their environment* in desired ways.

Groups whose members identify strongly and who can influence their environment are likely to be effective *reinforcers of decisions about change.* Such groups also can provide *emotional support* necessary to sustain required changes in the values, attitudes, or behaviors of their members.

*Robert T. Golembiewski, "The Laboratory Approach to Organization Development: The Schema of A Method," Public Administration Review, Vol. 27 (September 1967), p. 217.

FIGURE 2

Some Critical Publics Relevant to Federal OD Programs

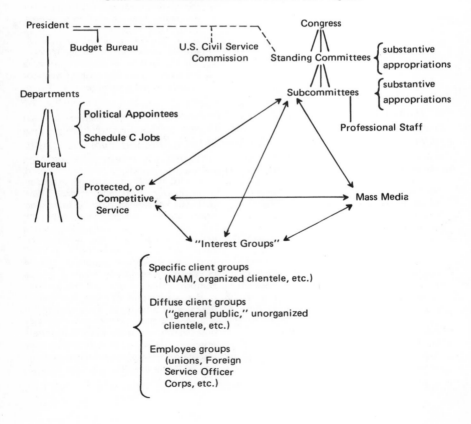

sponsoring an OD program had developed a relation of deep trust with the chairman and the professional staff of a congressional appropriations subcommitee, and that relation quickly, even mercurially, triumphed over lukewarm support or even opposition from the department head, the Bureau of the Budget, and the U.S. Civil Service Commission.

But multiple access can cut two ways. Funds for that very OD program "became unavailable" after its inception, despite strong support from both career and political officers at the top levels. In short, the successful counter-attack was launched by agency personnel in the protected/competitive service, an interest group representing these employees, members of a concerned substantive committee of Congress, and the media. The two themes of the counterattack were common to several reactions against OD programs of which I know. First, ordinary decency required allowing the dedicated civil servants affected to complete their careers in peace and in the traditional ways, rather than being subjected to an unwanted program that was seen as having problematic value.[6] Second, the use of sensitivity training in the OD program was disparaged as violating the privacy of organization members, or worse.[7]

Viewed from the perspective of top-level political and career officials intent on inaugurating a public OD program, the "iron quadrangle" in Figure 2 inspires substantial pessimism about a fair trial, in the general case. Specific conditions may raise or lower the odds, since the several links in the counterattacking forces above can be variously strong or weak. For example, a public agency may have a very positive constitutional image, which gives its top officials an important edge in presenting their case to congressional committees, the mass media, or the general public. Similarly, top political and career officials can induce—or capitalize on—organized clientele opposition to policies and procedures and use it to force changes at the protected levels. Or political resources and professional skills may provide agency executives with substantial power to control their environment.[8]

Whether the iron quadrangle is more or less integral, the design and implementation of OD programs in public agencies has given that constellation short shift. Perhaps this is because most experience with OD programs has been gained in business organizations, where nothing even remotely like the iron quadrangle exists at managerial levels.

Greater Variety

2. Again as compared to business organizations, the public arena involves in all OD programs a greater variety of individuals and groups with *different and often mutually exclusive sets of interests, reward structures, and values.* In the case outlined above, for example, the appropriations subcommittee was interested in improved operations and reduced costs. But the substantive subcommittee was concerned more with safeguarding program and personnel with which they had

developed a strong identification. And never the twain did meet. Role conflicts between legislators and administrators also seem to have been significant. For example, one congressman explained his opposition to an OD program in these terms: "Improvement of efficiency is O.K., but messing with people's attitudes sounds subversive to my constituents." The agency's top administrators felt no such constituency pressure, and their view was that attitudes toward work had to be changed.

Such incongruencies of expectations, rewards, and values also occur in business organizations, of course, as in labor-management issues. In my experience, however, they occur there in less intense and exotic forms.

A conclusion need not be forced. All OD programs have to stress the development of viable "interfaces," that is, relations between individuals or groups with different values and interests. This problem is enormously complicated in public agencies undertaking OD programs, and has received little explicit attention in concept or in practice. For example, in no case that I know of has the development of an explicit interface between legislative and administrative interests been attempted as part of an OD program, apparently in part because of the constitutional separation of powers.

The failure to build such interfaces was a major contributor to the death of a major recent urban OD program. Departmental officers rejected the idea of attempting to build an explicit interface between a substantive subcommittee, an appropriations subcommittee, and the agency as part of an OD program. Tradition, jealousy over prerogatives, and separation of powers were blamed, and with good reason. But it also seemed that departmental officials preferred things as they were. The lack of integration between subcommittees, perhaps, provided alternative routes of access and gave departmental officials some room to operate.

Command Linkages

3. The "line of command" within public agencies, as compared to business and service organizations, is more likely to be characterized by *competing identifications and affiliations*. Again the difference is one of degree, but it approaches one of a kind. Consider only one aspect of the integrity of command linkages common in business organizations. In them, typically, "management" is separated from "labor" only very far down the hierarchy, at or near the level of the first-line supervisor. Moreover, the common identification of all levels of management often is stressed. "Management," moreover, commonly does not enjoy the kind of job security that can come from union contracts. One of the effects of such carrots and sticks, without question, is the more facile implementation of policy changes at all levels of organization.

Hierarchy has its effects in public agencies as well as businesses, but the line of command seems less integral in the former. Thus a unique family of identifications alternative to the hierarchy exists at levels both low and high in public agencies, the apparent underlying motivation being to maximize the probability that evil will not occur, or at least will be found out. That is, the chain of command at the federal level is subject to strong fragmenting forces even up to the highest levels, where political and career strata blend into one another. For example, the ideal of a wall-to-wall civil service is approached closely in practice, and it provides a strong countervailing identification to the executive chain of command. Career officials are "out of politics," but their commitments to programs may be so strong as to inhibit or even thwart executive direction.[9]

That the public institutional environment permits (indeed, encourages) a fragmenting of the management hierarchy at points well up in the higher levels may be illustrated in three ways. First, the "neutrality" of civil servants has been a major defensive issue in at least two federal OD programs in which I have participated, the OD efforts having been painted by many career people as sophisticated but lustful raids on a chaste protected service. Second, Congress is an old hand at creating similar countervailing identifications so as to enhance its control over administration,[10] for which the Constitution and tradition provide a solid rationale. Third, the executive has also played the game, sometimes unwittingly. Consider the presidential-inspired Federal Executive Boards. Basically, these Boards were intended to be a horizontal link between field units of federal agencies and vertically between the presidency and top career field officialdom. The FEB's provide career field managers with a potential way to supplement or even bypass departmental reporting relations, both career employees and political appointees. Indeed, President Kennedy may have intended them as just such a bypass around "the feudal barons of the pemanent government" whom he saw as obstacles to change.[11]

A conclusion flows easily. Congress often encourages slack in the executive chain of command to facilitate its oversight of the President and his major appointees; and the executive as well as the protected service itself often uses the same strategy. The integrity of the executive chain of command suffers. Although the consequences are mixed, public executives are limited in initiating[12] (for example) OD programs. Witness the furor over the mere handful of Schedule C jobs removed from the protected service during Eisenhower's first term to permit greater executive leverage. Any corporation president would have an immensely broader field to act upon. The motivation to avoid "spoils politics" is recognized, but managerial rigidity is the other side of the coin. Herbert Kaufman concludes that although extensions of the civil service were intended to provide upper-level political administrators with capable help, the latter have often been driven to "pray for deliverance from their guardians."[13]

Weak Linkages

4. Exacerbating the point above, the *linkages between political and career levels* are weak as a consequence of a variety of features of

the public institutional environment.[14] This slippage between managerial levels significantly complicates beginning and implementing OD programs, and severely challenges the linkage of executive management with operating management.

The generalization concerning weak linkages in the managerial chain of command is meant to apply in four distinct senses. First, political and career levels often are weakly linked due to the brief tenure of the former. Second, the job of linking the political leadership and the permanent bureaucracy must be handled by a tiny group of executives—political appointees and occupants of Schedule C jobs—who owe diverse allegiance to the chief executive. Third, there is reason to suspect significant slippage between the top career officialdom and lower levels. For example, what lower-level careerists see as necessary protections of tenure, top career officials perceive as cumbersome limitations on managerial flexibility. Fourth, the executive often weakens its own managerial linkages, as it seeks sometimes-unreconcilable political and administrative goals. Thus the unionization of public employees which has been encouraged by presidential executive order hardly discourages labor unions looking for new fields to conquer. But one of the groups of federal employees to organize were inspectors in the U.S. Civil Service Commission who, if anybody, would be seen as "management" in most business organizations.

OD programs consequently must face the issue of somehow intefacing political and career linkages which powerful forces—constitutional, political, and historic—tend to pull apart. Consider only one dilemma facing OD programs. The general rule of thumb is that OD programs should begin "at the top" of organizational hierarchies, or as close to the top as possible. The rationale is obvious: that is where the power usually is in business organizations. Respecting this rule of thumb in public agencies raises a multidimensional dilemma. Basically, "the top" in public agencies is more complex than in most businesses. Initiating an OD program at the level of the political leadership maximizes formal executive support, but it may also raise complex problems. Support of the OD program is problematic because of frequent personnel changes at that level,[15] because of possible well-entrenched resistance from the permanent service, because legislators may fear that any strengthening of the executive chain of command would only mean fewer points of access and sources of information, and because employee associations may resist executive direction. Relying more on support from those in the competitive/protected service maximizes the chances of permanent support, and it may raise congressional and CSC trust in the program. But this approach may encourage executive resistance from such vantage points as the Bureau of the Budget.

The OD specialist faces real dilemmas, then, in choosing the "top" of the hierarchy at which to direct his interventions. I have participated in change programs that have taken both approaches to seeking a power base, and they show only that avoiding Scylla seems to imply meeting Charybdis. The ideal is to appeal to both the political officialdom and to the permanent service, of course, but that is a demanding ideal indeed.

In summary, four properties of the institutional environment of public agencies complicate attaining the objectives of typical OD programs. Consider the objective of building trust among individuals and groups throughout the organization. Technically, viable interfaces should be created between political officials, the permanent bureaucracy, congressional committees and their staffs, and so on and on. Practically, this is a very tall order, especially because the critical publics tend to have mutually exclusive interests, values, and reward systems. Indeed, although it is easy to caricature the point, Congress has a definite interest in cultivating a certain level of distrust within and between government agencies so as to encourage a flow of information. This may seem a primitive approach but, in the absence of valid and reliable measures of performance, it may be a necessary approach. No OD program in a business organization will face such an array of hurdles, that much is certain.

CHARACTER OF THE HABIT BACKGROUND: CONSTRAINTS ON APPROACHING OD OBJECTIVES

The "habit background" of public agencies also implies serious obstacles to approaching OD objectives. Five aspects of this habit background are considered below by way of illustrating their impact on OD objectives. These five aspects do not comprise an exclusive list, and they are conceived of only as general patterns and behaviors which give a definite flavor to the broad institutional environment sketched above.

Patterns of Delegation

"Habit background" is perhaps better illustrated than defined. First, in my experience, public officials tend to favor patterns of delegation that maximize their sources of information and minimize the control exercised by subordinates. Specifically, the goal is to have decisions brought to their level for action or review. The most common concrete concomitants of the tendency are functional specialization and a narrow span of control, one of whose major consequences is a large number of replicative levels of review.[16]

"Layering" of multiple levels of review is not unique to public administration, indeed it inheres in generally accepted organization theory; but it is supported by forces more or less unique to public agencies that have been powerful enough to substantially curtail innovation of ways to centralize policy and to decentralize operations.[17] The protection of the "public interest" is one such unique factor, for example. The rationale is familiar. Political officials of short tenure often cannot rely on established relations of confidence with personnel at lower levels, nor do they exercise as much control over career rewards and punishments as is common in business organizations or in the military.

However, the legislature will hold the political officials responsible. Consequently, political officials seek to maximize information sources and minimize the control exercisable by subordinates. This tendency is reinforced by law and tradition so that it permeates down the hierarchy throughout the permanent bureaucracy. The tendency is often referred to as "keeping short lines of command."

Keeping chains of command short implies constraints on approaching OD objectives in public organizations, based on my experience as well as the logic of the situation. Consider only two of the OD objectives above—three and nine:

—to locate decision-making and problem-solving responsibilities as close to the information sources as possible; and
—to increase self-control and self-direction for people within the organization.

To the degree that the rough distinction above is accurate, public agencies will experience difficulties in approaching both objectives. The prevailing habit pattern in public agencies patently constitutes a tide to swim against in these two particulars, although there are outstanding exceptions to this generalization.

Legal Habit

Second, and again only as a description of what exists, legal patterns make approaching OD objectives severely more difficult in public agencies than in business organizations.[18] The point applies in two major senses. Thus patterns of administrative delegation are often specified in minute detail in legislation, basically so as to facilitate oversight by the legislature. To be sure, we are a considerable distance beyond the first Morgan case, which seemed to argue that only administrative actions personally taken by, or under the direct supervision of, a department head were constitutionally defensible. But flexibility in delegation is still a major problem. Perhaps more important, a corpus of law and standard practice exists which also makes it difficult to achieve OD objectives. For example, considering only those employees on the General Schedule, salary and duties are tied to a position classification system whose underlying model emphasizes transdepartmental uniformity and compensation for individual work.[19]

This legal habit background complicates approaching OD values. Thus efforts to achieve OD objective three above may run afoul of the possibility that relocating responsibilities in one agency is considered to have systemwide implications, with consequences that complicate the making of local adjustments. As one official noted of an OD effort in such straits: "I feel like I have to raise the whole civil service by my bootstraps." Relatedly, OD objective two above seeks:

—to supplement the authority associated with role or status with the authority of knowledge and competence.

This is hard to do to the degree that a pattern of delegation is specified in law. The same point applies to any rigidities due to the duties classification common in public agencies in the United States, and especially to the concepts for assigning authority and for organizing work underlying the duties classification. Job enlargement begun as part of OD programs has run afoul of such concepts, for example.

At the bread-and-butter level, existing legal patterns also inhibit approaching OD objectives. Consider objective six which proposes:

—to develop a reward system which recognizes both the achievement of the organization's mission and organization development.

Existing law and practice severely limit the search for such a reward system. Thus rewards for exceptional performance—in money payments or in higher-than-normal GS levels for personnel in the civil service—are now possible, but they still are exceptional in practice. Equal pay for equal work, in sum, still practically means that exceptional work is not rewarded exceptionally. Management in business organizations typically has far greater control over reward systems, and especially at managerial levels. More of a problem, neither existing law nor practice promise much in the way of support for various group compensation plans. Experiments in industry with some such plans have yielded attractive results.

Need for Security

Third, the need for security or even secrecy in public agencies as against business organizations is more likely to be strong enough to present obstacles to approaching OD objectives. Military and defense agencies come to mind first, but they hardly exhaust the list. The "need for security" as used here can concern national security, it can be induced by a general anxiety born of a need to make significant decisions whose results will not be manifest for a very long time, or it can derive from felt needs for protection from such outside forces as a congressman with fire in his eye. [20] The need can also be real, exaggerated, or even imagined in various combinations.

Consider one case, which seemed to reflect some of all of these components. Agency personnel were exposed to sensitivity training, one of whose major purposes is to increase skills in being open about both positive and negative emotions or reactions. The training staff provided several settings in which these intentions might be approached, one of which was a "park bench." During one week of sensitivity training some time was set aside each evening for a meeting of all participants in a large room which was the locus of the "park bench." But agency personnel seldom used the arena, although there was a good deal of nervous laughter from the periphery of the "park." After some three abortive tries of an hour each, one participant approached me. "I see the point of the thing," he said, "but a park bench is all wrong." Suddenly, the dawn came. "Park benches," were seen as stereotypic sites for sexual assignations and/or for exchanging secrets with enemy agents. Without doubt, some participants thought the "park bench" a silly notion, and hence did not participate. For most participants, however, the symbolism was so compelling that they could not use the "park bench." Moreover, many agency personnel were so closed, distrustful, and fearful of taking a risk that they could not talk about their guiding symbolism, even if they were aware of it.

This greater need for security cannot be established concretely, to be sure, and all that may be said definitely is that to the degree this need exists so are OD objectives more difficult to reach. Consider only OD objective one above:

—to create an open, problem-solving climate throughout the organization.

An open climate and a great need for security or for secrecy do not mix well.

Procedural Regularity and Caution

Fourth, for a variety of reasons, government personnel are rather more likely to stress procedural regularity and caution. Perhaps better said, even if agency personnel are convinced that certain heuristics provide solutions that are "good enough," this conviction may conflict with other (and especially congressional) needs for external control. For example, sample checking of vouchers was widely accepted as an efficient enough administrative approach long before relevant publics in Congress and the General Accounting Office recognized it as appropriate for their control purposes.

Good reasons support this bias toward procedural regularity and caution in public agencies, of course, and so much the worse for OD objectives. For example, the bias patently runs against the grain of OD objective eight above, which seeks:

—to help managers to manage according to relevant objectives rather than according to "past practices" or according to objectives that do not make sense for one's area of responsibility.

The underlying rub, of course, is that a "past practice" making little or no sense administratively may seem an utter necessity from the legislative point of view. To be sure, the dictum "where you sit determines what you see" applies to all organizations. But the needs and identifications of administrators and legislators are likely to differ more than is the case for (let us say) the executives and middle managers of a business organization.

"Professional Manager"

Fifth, the concept "professional manager" is less developed in the public versus the business arena, in rough but useful contrast. The relative incidence of business schools and schools of public administration suggests the conclusion, [21] as do the Jacksonian notions deep at the roots of our basic public personnel policies. For example, the "career system" notion has been a difficult one to develop in this country at the federal level. No small part of the difficulty derives from the value we place on an "open service" with lateral entry. Hence the tendency of our public personnel policies to emphasize hiring for a specific position rather than for long-run potential.

Derivations from these taproots have had profound impact. For example, to simplify a little, massive federal attention to training was long delayed by the wrigglesworthian legislative notion that, since the federal service was hiring people who already had the abilities to do the specific job for which they were hired, there was little need to spend money on training. [22] The relative attractiveness of public employment at the federal level at least through World War II provided the proverbial finger in the dike, but conditions changed much faster than did public policy. Instructively, also, the system of regional executive development centers manned by the U.S. Civil Service Commission began as late as 1964, and then only with a miniscule budget and against substantial congressional opposition. Roughly, business has a 10-20 year lead over government in acting on the need for training. Not very long ago, in contrast, the federal government was considered *the* model employer.

The relatively lesser stress on the "public professional manager" implies significant problems for approaching OD objectives. Thus OD objective seven proposes:

—to increase the sense of "ownership" of organization objectives throughout the work force.

No sharp contrast is appropriate. But a definite bias of public personnel policy limits such a sense of identification with, and commitment to, public agencies. If there is one thing most civil services reformers did not want, it was a public work force who "owned" the objectives of their agency. The only "owner" was the public; the model employee was a politically neutral technician who repressed his own values in return for guaranteed tenure. Only thus could an elite and unresponsive bureaucracy be avoided, goes a major theme shot through our public personnel policies and institutions.

Conclusion

The body of this paper can be summarized tersely. Organization Development programs are appearing with increasing frequency in both business and public agencies. Moreover, applications of OD programs in government agencies face some unique problems. However, these unique problems tend to go unrecognized or underrecognized by OD teams in part because students of public administration have tended to be underrepresented on such teams. Hence this paper.

Some derivative implications seem appropriate, in addition. First, "poaching" in the public sector by OD teams composed basically of psychologists and sociologists will continue to grow, if only because (as

William F. Whyte noted in another connection) such poaching is necessary. Second, students of public administration can play a useful and partially distinct role in such OD programs. But, third, students of public administration are likely to play such a role only as substantial numbers of them develop competencies that complement their special interests in public administration. Such competency enlargement for "change-agents" or organization consultants is provided by the NTL Institute of Applied Behavioral Science and by such university-based programs as those at UCLA and Boston University.

NOTES

1. John W. Gardner, *Self-Renewal* (New York: Harper & Row, 1965).
2. Alexander Winn, "The Laboratory Approach to Organization Development: A Tentative Model of Planned Change," paper read at the Annual Conference, British Psychological Society, Oxford, September 1968, p. 1. More broadly, see Edgar H. Schein and Warren G. Bennis, *Personal and Organization Change Through Group Methods: The Laboratory Method* (New York: McGraw-Hill, 1966).
3. For an overview of the technique, see Robert T. Golembiewski, "The Laboratory Approach to Organization Development: The Schema of a Method," Public Administration Review, Vol. 27 (September 1967), pp. 211-220.
4. Sheldon Davis, "An Organic Problem-Solving Method of Organizational Change," *Journal of Applied Behavioral Science*, Vol. 3 (January 1967), pp. 3-21.
5. NTL Institute, "What Is OD?" *News and Reports*, Vol. 2 (June 1968), p. 1.
6. The theme also appeared in mass-circulation news stories and editorials which argued against Project ACORD in the U.S. Department of State, for example. Stewart Alsop, "Let the Poor Old Foreign Service Alone," *Saturday Evening Post*, (June 1966), p. 14.
7. For example, sensitivity training has been criticized as "amateur group therapy," For an incisive distinction between training and therapy, see Chris Argyris, "Conditions for Competence Acquisition and Therapy," *Journal of Applied Behavioral Science*, Vol. 4 (June 1968), pp. 147-178.
8. See, generally, Francis E. Rourke, *Bureaucracy, Politics, and Public Policy* (Boston: Little, Brown, 1969).
9. For a sensitive summary of the programmatic commitments of career personnel, see John J. Corson and R. Shale Paul, *Men Near the Top* (Baltimore, Md.: Johns Hopkins Press, 1966), pp. 23-51.
10. Joseph P. Harris, *Congressional Control of Administration* (Washington, D.C.: The Brookings Institution, 1964).
11. Arthur Schlesinger, *A Thousand Days* (Boston: Houghton Mifflin, 1965), p. 681.
12. President Truman expressed the point directly in contemplating the problems that General Eisenhower would experience as President Eisenhower, without the discipline and definite career patterns and established ways of doing things he knew in the military. "He'll sit here," Truman predicted, "and he'll say, 'Do this!' 'Do that!' *And nothing will happen.* Poor Ike—it won't be a bit like the Army. He'll find it very frustrating." Richard E. Neustadt, *Presidential Power* (New York: Wiley, 1960), p. 9. His emphases.
13. Herbert Kaufman, "The Rise of A New Politics," p. 58, in Wallace S. Sayre (ed.), *The Federal Government Service* (Englewood Cliffs, N.J.: Prentice-Hall, 1965).
14. Dean E. Mann, "The Selection of Federal Political Executives," *American Political Science Review*, Vol. 58 (March 1964), pp. 81-99.
15. One ambitious OD program, for example, was unable to overcome the rumor that several political appointees were negotiating terms of private employment. Agency personnel were encouraged to inaction, since these officials would "soon be riding their OD hobbyhorse" someplace else. These officials did leave. But all claim that

the stories were seeded by career personnel who opposed the OD program, nd that it was only the intensity of such "dirty fighting" that encouraged the political appointees to seek private employ after the rumors began.

16. Before a reorganization inspired by an OD program in the Department of State, some review layers were so numerous that "it could take as long as six months for an important problem to reach the Deputy Under Secretary. Now it takes an average of two days." Alfred J. Marrow, "Managerial Revolution in the State Department," *Personnel*, Vol. 43 (December 1966), p. 13.

17. Such innovation has been the major trend in large businesses over the last three or four decades. See Robert T. Golembiewski, *Men, Management, and Morality* (New York: McGraw-Hill, 1965); and *Organizing Men and Power* (Chicago: Rand McNally, 1967). Strong pressures for just such innovation are now being widely felt in public administration. Aaron Wildavsky provides a case in point in his "Black Rebellion and White Reaction," *The Public Interest*, No. 11 (Spring 1968), especially pp. 9-12.

18. A very useful discussion of the antimanagerial thrust of much legislation is provided by Harris, *Congressional Oversight of Administration*.

19. Robert T. Golembiewski, "Civil Service and Managing Work," *American Political Science Review*, Vol. 56 (December 1962), pp. 961-974.

20. Great needs for "security" as here broadly defined can rigidify an organization and curb the effectiveness of its members. To the point, see Chris Argyris, "Some Causes of Organizational Ineffectiveness Within the Department of State," Center for International System Research, *Occasional Papers*, No. 2 (1967).

21. Revealingly, it was not until 1946 that Cornell developed the first two-year master of public administration program comparable to the MBA long given by schools of commerce or business administration.

22. Paul P. Van Riper, *History of the United States Civil Service* (Evanston, Ill.: Row, Peterson, 1958), pp. 429-434.

SOME REFLECTIONS ON THE ORGANIZATION DEVELOPMENT AND CONSULTATION PROCESS WITHIN RELIGIOUS ORGANIZATIONS *

James D. Anderson, *Episcopal Diocese of Washington, D.C.*

---

*This paper is a revision of an informal article previously written by the author.

The increasing flood of articles and research on organizational change, planned change, and the consultant's role in an organization development process contains very little material on the application of these processes to religious and volunteer organizations. For the past five years I have been engaged, first as a parish priest and now as a diocesan consultant, in the practice and application of the principles of organization development within a wide variety of church structures. In the last two years I have become particularly involved in three different levels of church organizations and the application of planned change principles. As an outside consultant, I am now working on a parish or congregational level, the diocesan or regional level, and with para-institutional structures such as a Trappist religious community and a theological seminary.

It is now possible on the basis of this experience to provide some reflection on a consultant's role in religious organizations, particular organizational problems of religious bodies, and the relevance of an organizational development approach within the church. In this paper, I wish to address myself to what I regard to be some distinctive aspects of the development process as it applies to the church.

PART I

THE CRITICAL ROLE OF A CLERGYMAN

The church is perhaps the only institution in society in which the leadership by both structure and belief is imbued with mythical dimensions of power. As I consult with local congregations in the application of such standard organization development interventions as the confrontation meeting and team building for the session or vestry, I am continually struck by the centrality of the minister's role in congregational life. In the last decade the Christian church throughout the world has given serious ideological attention to enhancing the role of the layman in church life. The theology of the laity has, indeed, brought change and reform moving towards a broader base of participation and, particularly, two-way communication between laity and clergy within the Christian church as a whole. Nevertheless, the truth remains that the minister, priest, or rabbi stands and will continue to stand at the center of religious life within the community he serves. The church leadership is beginning to recognize that the ministerial role has an importance which the reforms of the theology of the laity will neither change nor diminish. The Rev. Myron Bloy, executive director of the Episcopal Church Society for College Work, makes the following comments on the role of the college chaplain which I see to be also illustrative of a ministerial role in a local congregation.

"The peculiar ministry which the Chaplain can offer—which no other adult no matter how structurally marginal and dedicated, can—is a symbolic one. He focuses in himself and brings to subconsciousness for the young, by virtue largely of his ordination and his leadership in liturgical functions, the religious quest which is such a deep part of the counter culture. In recent years especially under the influence of Bonhoeffer most Chaplains have tried to escape this symbolic identity."

The importance of this fact for the organizational consultant is manifold. Church groups are highly inexperienced at talking honestly about their reactions to the minister in charge. A clergyman is not just a boss, or coach, or team leader, or friend, or counselor, or confidant, or teacher, or holy man of God. He may be any or all of these things to the congregation. In a congregation with which I have been working for some time the clergyman is a very gentle, kind man who lacks initiative and the ability to take firm leadership. It was extremely difficult for this vestry to develop its trust and insight to a point where they could talk openly about the problems caused by the leadership style of the minister.

In a business organization it is difficult for individuals to level with the boss because of the fear of being fired or not promoted; in the Church it is difficult for people to tell the clergyman what is on their minds because in a sense he is God.

Another major dimension of the complexity surrounding the clergyman's role and of the difficulty of organizational diagnosis within the church is the problem of the psychological contract. By this I mean what the members of a congregation expect to receive psychologically for their commitment of time, energy, and money to the parish. The psychological contract in church organization is highly intangible. Some people wish to exchange their presence on Sunday morning and a dollar or two in the collection for a renewal of their hope and an underpinning of some of the securities of their life to ritual, prayer, and sermon. Other persons wish to exchange the commitment of their energy and time for a sense of involvement and excitement in relevant community issues. Through his sermons and conduct of public worship it is the clergyman who has the primary say as to which of these two contrasting contracts a Sunday morning service will fulfill. For a sizeable group of people in any congregation the psychological contract involves receiving something from the minister in person. This may be his attention, or his friendship, his advice, or his communication of an attitude of care and concern. But whatever people may be asking from him it constitutes an enormously powerful influence on the organization as a whole.

A prime example was furnished by the minister of a small, marginal middle-class Negro congregation who gave a major share of his time to the development of work in the surrounding neighborhood and the founding of a community center. His congregation had risen above the econimic level of the immediate neighborhood of the parish buildings. They were commuters to the church who felt few real ties to the actual neighborhood. The congregation aspired to middle-class values and wished the rector to be the kind of person they would like their children to emulate and to provide solidarity of conviction for their values and hopes. Thus, they were dissatisfied with what they called his "hippie" hairdo (the minister was a white man) and his involvement in what they considered to be militant black power organizations. But they were pleased to have as their minister a white clergyman who had status and influence within the diocese. As consultant, I helped the clergyman to become aware of the way he was violating the psychological contract of the congregation and suggested some ways of responding to them by adding to the "religious content" of his leadership and being more attentive in some small ways to his congregation. These were tried and with good results.

Many of today's younger clergy have reacted to what they now discern as the ills of a previous generation of stern, authoritarian, "treat-the-congregation-like-children" clergy by withdrawing almost completely from their legitimate exercise of authority and responsibility. What this clergyman wanted from the congregation was that they grow up enough to see the necessity for the church's involvement in the affairs of the neighborhood. What he had to be helped to see was his own crucial role in assisting them to mature from their present childish ways. The development process demanded that a number of hours be spent counseling with the clergyman around the question of his own blindness to the possibility of being a good father to some of the congregation—the kind of father who did not create dependency but rather helped people to mature to a greater degree of personal autonomy.

The centrality of the clergyman's role and his personal involvement in the contract with his parishioners makes the problem of the succession of ministers in a congregation particularly difficult. By concentrating directly on the importance of the selection process of a new clergyman it has been possible to offer to congregations an organization development process oriented directly to this crucial problem. The departure of the clergyman is a natural moment of thaw for the frozen patterns of communication and authority within a parish. Moreover, it is a time when the leadership find it easy to ask for assistance due to their sense of urgency and general unfamiliarity with the selection process. By keying his help to this problem the organization development consultant can offer the aid of a process which will involve the entire congregation in an assessment of strengths and weaknesses and in the formulation of criteria for the selection of the kind of man who can respond best to the problems and opportunities uncovered. By a combination of process consultation and team building sessions the calling committee can be helped to discover the benefit of open communication among themselves and with prospective candidates. The tremendous value conflicts present in Church people today over the role of the Church in relation to political and social issues make it crucial for them to face with trust and candor their differences with regard to future leadership and direction. The external consultant can help the congregation to adequately solve problems in the organizational dynamics of the vacancy period and moment of transition. What often seems to happen is that the ghost of a departed clergyman remains to haunt and confuse the new man in his leadership. I believe that it is necessary to face and expose this problem quite directly. Interventions which have helped alleviate it include collaborative role analysis between the minister and the designated congregational leadership, setting up procedures for evaluation of the new minister on an annual basis to ensure the surfacing of expectations and criticism, and inviting the departed clergyman back for a Sunday service intended to bury his ghost through an open facing of the grief over his departure.

I find in most congregations that a rapid reading of the vitality of both the clergyman and the parish can be obtained by discussing with the clergyman the degree of his own job satisfaction. Clergy who are dissatisfied with their role in the parish, who get their "kicks" from extraparochial activities, and who have a narrow base of informal relationships with members of the congregation are generally in trouble. For years the Church has recognized the necessity for indigenous clergy in overseas missions, but many clergy are as alien to the environment they find themselves serving in the United States as they would be to a mission abroad. By failing to appreciate the importance of this informal system of relationships in a parish, a clergyman who enjoys Philip Roth, French cooking, and art films will probably not recognize and never hear directly of the depth of his unconscious estrangement from a TV, baseball, and bowling league-oriented congregation.

A clergyman must be helped to assess more accurately the impact of his behavior on the congregation, to see his own strengths and weaknesses, and to increase his own job satisfaction. A developing major resource toward this end is the provision of career counseling services especially directed toward ministers, priests, and rabbis. I have referred clergymen to one such center in Princeton, New Jersey, on several occasions. By assessing a minister's aptitudes, psychological make-up, achievement pattern, experience, and values, this center helps him to sort out the patterns of his life and begin to approach the chaos of an unsatisfactory job experience in a careful step-by-step problem-solving approach.

LEADERSHIP INSTITUTE OF SPOKANE

SOUTH 3220 GRAND BLVD.   PHONE: (509) 624-8437

SPOKANE, WASHINGTON 99203   P. O. BOX 8005

PART II

THE VALIDITY OF AND NECESSITY FOR A SOCIO-THEOLOGICAL SYSTEMS APPROACH

Successful planned change requires the active involvement and support of those at the top of an organization and involves the total system in working on the solution of actual organizational problems. Trying to deal with the clergyman in isolation from the context of his work situation is a weak approach. Certainly the central role of the clergyman in religious life provides a particularly fruitful point of entry into the system problems of the psychological contract and the exercise of authority, as well as highlighting the potential of interventions geared to career planning, placement, and selection procedures.

The pioneering study of organizational change documented in the Harwood-Weldon industrial plant merger graphically illustrated the necessity of taking a socio-technological approach to the problems of the system involved.[1] In this case the consultants had to consider the technical questions of the manufacture and marketing of pajamas as well as the human problems involved in the introduction of more effective technological procedures. A similar comprehensive approach is needed in work with religious organizations. It is my experience that it is quite easy for the behavioral scientist working with religious groups to avoid the technical aspects of the form and content of Sunday worship and the message communicated from the pulpit. This is fully as great an oversight as would be an avoidance of technical production questions in a manufacturing plant. My hypothesis is that it may be an even greater oversight, because of the complex way the beliefs, values, and attitudes of church members are commingled with the rites of worship and key symbols of the religion.

In a team-building two-day conference with the vestry (elected lay leadership) of a parish, it soon became apparent that this group contained some highly creative individuals whose training and daily work experience indicated a measure of competence and ability which they were not contributing to the work of the vestry. The key that unlocked this puzzle was a short theory presentation by one of the consultants correlating spiritual growth with the type of professional career development work one of the men performed for his space-age firm. This intervention, based on informal conversations outside the working hours of the conference and on observation of the rector's religious style, was designed to correct and reinterpret the narrow definition of spiritual growth prevalent in the vestry. Only when the vestry heard their leadership in the area of spiritual growth described as setting a climate in which the individuals of the congregation could work toward the release of their creative potential, as providing learning situations which could help persons to grow and mature, and as providing professionally competent help to assist families through crises, were they able to begin to see connections between their everyday skills and their positions of leadership in the congregation.

Another intervention used with this parish was a two-evening meeting of the entire active congregation. The design of the two evenings was an adaptation of Beckhard's "confrontation meeting."[2] People in small groups were asked to share freely, without having to debate or defend, their answers to the questions, "What prevents life in this congregation from being more satisfying to me? What would make life in this congregation more rewarding to me?"

It is my experience that both the clergy and the elected lay leadership usually have very poor information concerning the sources of satisfaction and dissatisfaction within the congregation at large. Church leadership seems invariably to lapse into a guilt-inducing, exhortative, "it's-your-duty-to-volunteer" style of leadership. The designated and elected leadership tend to dissipate their management power overworking the motivated few by attempting to generate programs that will engage the unmotivated many.

The confrontation meeting is a structured intervention which, as the accompanying table idicates, represents a step in a new direction for the exercise of management power in the Church. The genius of the design is that in a very short space of time it sets up new procedures and opportunities for problem solving based on the felt needs, aspirations, and talents of a large percentage of the congregation.

MANAGEMENT POWER IN THE CHURCH

	Where It Resides	How It Characteristically Functions	How It Sees Other People in the Organization
As Usually Found	At the top in the hands of a few All initiation at the top	Thinks up "good" ideas so that the few can be directed to lead programs to engage the many Exhorts and communicates positions, teachings, and information to others	As pool of volunteers to be *utilized* As group who *need to be motivated* or hooked by the use of the proper bait
As Intended in OD	Persons are recognized for their competence as well as their designated role Initiation wherever there is interest	Is diagnostic and inquisitive concerning what is preventing people from turning on, receiving help, doing their thing Facilitates candid communication laterally as well as vertically concerning what people in the entire organization are thinking, doing, and feeling Sets a climate of inquiry and interpersonal trust	As people with needs and feelings like one's own As persons seeking to grow, to find help, to contribute their talent As highly differentiated individuals, all of whom cannot be suited by any one response

In a major organization development project with one of the dioceses of the Anglican Communion, the consultants identified two norms within the diocese illustrative of the interaction between the human and technical (theological) problems of the system:

1. The problem of authority is dealt with by a norm which values and expects dependent behavior,
2. Despite verbal support for the idea of the witness of the laity in society, the actual behavior valued and supported is attendance at mass, with no practical supports for ministry in the world.

The consultants had originally been called in to help the diocese design a scheme to train laity for Christian ministry or mission in their daily life. The bishop and clergy of the diocese were excited over the theological beliefs connected with the mission of the laity and were concerned with their inability to bring change in this area. They had heard of sensitivity training and thought it might be of help. By identifying these two norms and the sanctions which supported them, the consultants were able to change the original request for help with a short-term training event into a long-term contract for a development process involving the entire diocese.

Some of the sanctions exposed struck close to the center of the system of beliefs and sentiments in the diocese. A common practice was the communion record cards kept for each lay person. The cards had to be picked up at the parish church on Saturday and given to an usher on Sunday morning in order to be admitted to communion. The custom of both government and business was to ask for references from a job applicant's clergyman. It was common knowledge that the clergyman used the communion record cards as the primary basis for their recommendations. Thus, while the theology of the pulpit was for involvement in the world, this far stronger theology of actual practice was for strict obedience to the norm of priestly obedience and regular Sunday worship.

The identification through group interviews and feedback of the data which highlighted these norms constituted the first major intervention. Later interventions included the training of regional change-agent teams, training in management by objectives for the key members of the hierarchy, action research efforts in several of the congregations, and a demonstration community organization and development project in a crucial industrial area.

The last three decades have seen a wave of proposed remedies for the organizational ills of the institutional Church. Curriculum reform, sensitivity training, long-range planning, social action involvement, and the conference-retreat movement—all have been eagerly tried and found wanting. The residue of these movements is a polarization of opinion regarding the worth of each "solution" and a great lack of experience and ability in moving beyond a symptomatic response.

The organization development consultant who is attempting to work with the problems of a total religious system needs to be aware of this history and some of the associated difficulties. Church organizations generally have trouble understanding the concept of a systems approach and tend to regard persons who have been associated with sensitivity training as being solely interested in interpersonal process. A recent major conference of the Episcopal Church illustrates the manner in which the Church still searches for an answer, a cure, for ailing congregations. The conference assembled a number of clergy whose parishes represented centers of renewal, hoping to distill from their experience the answers to the question of what it takes to build a healthy, vital parish. The conference was based on the same kind of thinking that says that if you get a group of 90-year old men together and ask them what they have done to stay so healthy, you will get some valuable information. Just as the complexity of the system of the human body renders such information almost valueless, so the complexity of the organizational systems involved quite naturally foreclosed any knowledge gain from the conference.

The tendency of Church clients and Church people to lapse readily into dealing solely with interpersonal issues is illustrated by a series of events stemming from a request to assist with a team development conference for the large staff of an ecumenical religious organization. During the course of the conference, several persons on the staff voiced their apprehension that the weekend's long-term results might be as disappointing as those from two similar short-term events in the last two years. As a result of these comments and the nature of the problems the conference exposed, the consultants made repeated efforts to point out the widespread and complex nature of the difficulties facing this organization and the necessity for a continuing, long-term, total systems approach if anything was really going to improve. The last decision of the conference was that if this staff elected to pursue this line of action they would contact the coordinator to arrange a meeting to discuss the contract. They did decide to go ahead and did contact the coordinator. Unfortunately, the call was a request to have the consultants be present for several staff meetings and to hold a 24-hour conference with the staff. Rather than arranging a meeting to discuss a contract which would have more clearly defined the terms of the help needed, the coordinator agreed to their suggestion as presented. Unable to be a part of the original series of staff meetings, I discovered only prior to the 24-hour conference that the total focus of the help given had been related to the interpersonal process of the staff team. This vignette is illustrative of the difficulty of establishing a clear OD contract between consultant and client, particularly when the major experience of the consultant stems from sensitivity training. An organization development consultant walks a tightrope between the two contrasting roles of technical expert and process facilitator. In the continuum between task and process he must be able to move with flexibility in response to the actual problems and goals of the client group. The application of this principle to work with religious organizations involves building a contract with the leadership which assures them that you are interested in a mutual working together for the best solutions to the wide range of problems which will be confronting the organization. It means communicating a willingness to understand the values and goals of the people involved and a refusal to apply wholesale patent medicine solutions to specific and discriminate problems. It means the adoption by the consultant of a wide and flexible range of interventions to help the organization see its problems more clearly, solve them more adequately, and move closer to human experience approximating the divine promise.

NOTES

1. Marrow, A.J., Bowers, D.G. and Seashore, S.E., *Management by Participation*, N.Y.: Harper and Row, 1967.
2. Beckhard, R. "The confrontation meeting." *Harvard Business Review*, 1967, 45, 149-155.

SUCCESSFUL ENTRY AS A KEY TO SUCCESSFUL ORGANIZATION DEVELOPMENT IN BIG CITY SCHOOL SYSTEMS

C. Brooklyn Derr, *Assistant Professor,*
The Harvard Graduate School of Education

Entry for Organization Development

Successful entry into an organization for the purpose of engaging in organizational change activities does not mean getting into the organization at any cost. Rather it means establishing the ground rules, the expectations, and the kind of relationships that will give the entering person or team every opportunity necessary to accomplish the change objectives and will ultimately permit those coming in to leave an organization that "owns" the changes and the methods used for changing.[1]

Most people in academic life have experienced a research entry model. Researchers often enter the organization with hidden agendas. They say they will examine one set of variables agreeable to those in the organization while they are really looking for other more secret information which, if exposed, would be more threatening to the organization. They use participant-observation methods and other forms of spying. Sometimes presenting such research forces change, and often the research data of this kind can be useful to the organization. However, researchers have an obligation not to use the information in ways that will assure organizational change. Organization developers are obliged to use the data they collect to intervene in the ongoing processes of the organization for the purpose of changing it in the desired direction.

The author recently did a study of the relationship between six neighboring universities and one big city school system. One overall impression held by the administrators in the school system was that the university researchers had "used" the system. The administrators believed that persons from the university had entered the system by making promises for giving feedback on their research, by raising certain expectations for some future payoff, by appearing to want to collaborate, and, in some instances, by lying about the purpose of the research. In very few cases had the university people actually completed their part of the agreement and delivered anything in return for the opportunity of doing the research. In many cases, the information was used to argue against the survival of the system. As a result, those in the system are very distrustful of university people and reluctant to collaborate with them.

Some consultants confuse the collaboration concept to mean capitulating to or unquestionably serving the interests of the client without due regard for the change process. Such consultants, seeing themselves as support staff to the organizations they serve, allow themselves to be used by the client and accept at face value his own concerns for more dollars, more staff, or more influence. Many consultants allow their names to be used as rubber stamps for a program desired by their client. Organization developers, on the other hand, use the entry period to determine the sincerity of the client, to ascertain whether or not they have the skills and knowledge to be helpful to the client, and to make decisions about whether they will agree to act as a consultant to the organization. Entry means hammering out a contract that is acceptable to both parties and that allows the OD practitioner to accomplish his goals.

One goal of most OD specialists is to withdraw from the organization as soon as it has its own capacity for implementing the particular change and for spotting, diagnosing, and intervening to implement other needed organizational changes. The entry process is important in light of this goal. During the entry period, the consultant and the client normally establish an open, trustful, and collaborative relationship, define the roles and expectations of both parties, define the parameters of the client system or systems on which the change will focus, discuss their motives, needs, problems, goals, and reservations, define the rules for data collection, and discuss the client's perceptions about the nature of the problem, the desirable outcomes, and the organizational constraints.

The following are some of the questions normally going through the mind of the organization developer at entry: How do I "connect" with this client? Why did he call me in? Where is he? How do I establish a personal relationship with the client? How can I get the client's conditional trust and confidence? How will I establish a problem-solving climate without being too threatening? How do we define the joint ventures? On what pieces of work will we collaborate? How do I avoid being seen as "the great healer"? How can I communicate a desire to get the client's initial perceptions of the problem while not necessarily accepting those hunches? How can I get into a position where the client will also listen to the other data I collect about the nature of the problem? How do I get the "hidden agendas" out on the table? How do I establish my own independence, ethics, and integrity? Who do I tell people in the organization I am?

Among the questions typically going through the client's head at entry are these: What are the consultant's motives? How much information can I divulge to an outsider? Is the consultant competent? Will he try to change the organization in a way that is unfavorable to me? If I make a mistake, will the consultant think of me as incompetent? Does he like me? Can this guy handle our particular problem? Is he generally interested in us? Does he have integrity? Will the consultant try to take over and control the organization? Am I comfortable working with this person?

One important aspect of the entry process is that it is continuous. A broken contract or a misunderstood agreement is grounds for renegotiation—even for termination of the former agreement by one of the parties. New dimensions of the relationship emerge and are cycled through the entry process. It is important to continuously reinterpret, model, and reinforce the nature of the relationship and the terms agreed upon at entry.

Organization Development and Entry in a Big City School System: A Case Study

During the 1968-69 school year, a team of six advanced doctoral students taking a practicum course in the organization development method at the Sloan School of Management, MIT,[2] undertook to use the OD method in a big city school system. The team, known as the MIT Management Survey Team, was asked to consider the problems of 14 departments known collectively as the Special Services departments, and to suggest ways to reorganize them to make them more effective.

Entry was very difficult in this case. The school system was defensive about outsiders coming in at all, evidence by two months of deliberation and delay before the exploratory meeting between the two parties took place. Also, those at the top of the school organization, at the associate superintendent level, were somewhat skeptical of the team's ideas about collaboration. Other university researches had also promised but never delivered such help. Most of those at the top simply wanted the report.

It was not possible for the MIT team to make direct contact with those at the top of the organization regarding their proposal. Instead, they decided to use a third party (a professor from Harvard who knew several associate superintendents) to make contact. Although there is no reason to be suspicious of the initial conversations between the third party and those in the upper echelons of the administrative hierarchy, their expectations, motives, and commitments for the proposal remained unknown.

The MIT team, on the other hand, was anxious to get into the school system and begin collecting data after such a long delay, and they were unwilling to risk the learning experience by insisting on the collaborative work method at entry. The team also felt that the best way to implement the method would be simply to model it, that is, to collaborate as part of the process during the study. For all of these reasons, data collection began without the MIT team members being convinced that the city school system authorities understood the OD work method that they would be using.

The data collection phase comprised 30- to 90-minute interviews with a cross-section diagonal slice[3] of Special Services personnel and with those outside special services who had some knowledge about it. Twenty-four people in all were interviewed. Respondents were asked open-ended questions about their perception of the positive and negative features of the special services area as it was constituted. They were also asked to make suggestions for possible changes. Respondents were told how the data would be used and were assured that no names would be identified with statements made.

A diagnosis of the data collected revealed four common problem areas which were perceived by the respondents as hindering the work process: coordination, communication and information flow, adaptive capacity, and authority/power issues.

It was discovered that the area known as Special Services was very differentiated and was both geographically disperse (i.e., housed in different buildings throughout the city) and organizationally disperse (i.e., under the direction of three associate superintendents and one assistant superintendent). As one associate superintendent put it, "Special Services is an area that has just added on and on." While differentiation is an encouraging bureaucratic phenomenon because it shows a willingness to meet the diverse needs of the environment, no accompanying integrating force was present here to help coordinate such diversity.

It was discovered that there was little vertical communication between superiors and subordinates and that official horizontal communication (from peer to peer across departmental lines) was almost nonexistent. Communication was mainly "folkway" in nature, taking place informally and socially in nonwork or pseudowork settings.

The information exchanged, it was revealed, was of generally poor quality. Subordinates told superiors what they wanted to hear so as to gain their favor. Peers perceived information as power and tended to distort it and use it resourcefully in political ways. The quantity of information exchanged was also found wanting. Information was frequently hoarded as a future power resource, and that which was exchanged took a great deal of time to get from sender to receiver.

The data collected substantiated that the Special Services area was generally nonadaptive to its environment. While it is true that departments were added to handle new demands, these new departments were usually initiated in response to offers for financial and programmatic assistance made by the State of Massachusetts. Within departments already established, little was done to meet the needs of a changing environment. In general, the norm perceived by members of Special Services was that it is generally risky to be too innovative and adaptive. A person interested in advancement within the school system does not make waves. Planned organizational change happens periodically—especially in response to crisis—not on a continuing basis. On the other hand, the fact that the MIT study was initiated by the system was evidence that it could change and that it was making some attempt to adapt.

Finally, the data revealed the prevalence of rather dysfunctional power struggles. Information exchange as power has already been cited as one example. Instances were also discovered of both noncompliance with directives coming from very high administrative levels, and limited compliance with such directives in politically helpful ways, that is, compliance according to how it would affect one's potential for influence. A pronounced status and pay differentiation between the various department heads added to the struggle.

Data feedback meetings were held with all department directors and other representatives to confirm the above diagnosis and to try to obtain some consensus among the directors about alternatives for improving the system. The use of the laboratory method enabled the MIT team to maximize participation and information exchange by those who attended the workshop. (See the appendix for the workshop design.) The diagnosis was confirmed. In addition, it became obvious from observing the group that the sharing of information (with whom and how much), was a major issue that the norms of the system made it very difficult to disagree, that reverting to "professional standards" was a way to escape from and detour confrontive issues, and that official communication prior to the sessions had been almost nonexistent (some participants met others for the first time at the data feedback sessions).

The participants in the sessions were generally enthusiastic about the method of working together. A number of those interviewed stated that the data feedback sessions were one of the few times they could remember when they had had an opportunity to influence decisions made above. They enjoyed participating in the meetings rather than just listening to directives from above. Several participants mentioned that they were surprised at the accuracy of the data fed back to them.

The MIT team had originally refused to present a final report to those at the top of the organization unless they would agree to work collaboratively with the team on a blueprint for change. However, communication and collaboration with the top were less than satisfactory throughout the project. Attempts to collaborate were rejected by the top school administrators as too time-consuming and unnecessary ("just tell us what we should do"). The team finally agreed to write a report that would signal the problems, incorporate the feelings and ideas of the workshop participants, and be general enough so that those in authority would still have to decide what to do, hopefully in collaboration with the MIT team.

This report was prepared and presented to the superintendent of schools and the four interested associated superintendents. The MIT team requested that copies of the report be sent to the workshop participants and that all concerned meet to discuss some action-planning phases based on the data. This request was not granted. The team then met with three associate superintendents, explained the report to them, fed back additional data, and offered to help them plan further action steps. This offer was not accepted.

In May 1969 a meeting was called at which the deputy superintendent presented an organizational chart which departed from the real message of the MIT report. The team generally felt that their work was both distorted and ignored.

In February 1970 the participants in the original workshop feedback sessions were again interviewed. It was discovered that (a) most of them had never seen the MIT report (while they had been told they could read the report at the deputy superintendent's office, they had not been encouraged to do so) and were unaware of its contents; (b) they felt that their activity at the feedback sessions was a useless exercise and that they had really exerted no influence on the reorganization decisions; and (c) the organizational problems which had existed the year before had not been rectified or even modified by the work of the MIT team.

During April-May 1970, questionnaires were distributed to the department directors of Special Services as part of another study. Some of the data collected reveal that vertical and horizontal coordination and communication had not improved as a result of the OD intervention a year earlier. For example, on the average they meet with their supervisor "less than monthly as needed." This data was based on a four-point Likert-type scale where (1) means "daily meetings," (2) "weekly meetings," (3) "monthly meetings," and (4) "less than monthly as needed." The average score for the directors of Special Services was 3.65. It was also discovered that other than preparing a budget request one year in advance, the directors were doing no formal long-range planning. Using the same scale cited above, it was determined that the directors meet "less than monthly as needed" with their supervisors for purposes of reviewing the performance of their unit. The average score was 3.67.

However, in the fall of 1970, the organizational responsibilities were shifted to comply with recommendations of another report recommending structural changes. Thus, there is an attempt at the present time to improve the coordination of Special Services. They are currently under one supervisor.

One question on the spring 1970 questionnaire asked for the amount of time the directors normally spent working with other directors of Special Services. The choices were 0 percent, 5 percent, 10 percent, 25 percent, 50 percent, 75 percent or more. The average answer was 10 percent.

When asked to rank-order the importance of various modes of communication from most important (1) to least important (8), the directors responded as follows:

(1) Official memos
(2) Formal appointments
(3) The telephone
(4) Officially called meetings
(5) Informal visits
(6) Bulletins
(7) The grapevine
(8) Social gatherings

The fact that more informal and interactive modes of communication are not ranked as most important leads one to believe that communication has not greatly improved in the school system.

Some of the interviews helped the author to discover that there is a small group in Special Services who meet informally and exchange information in the form of gossip. Many of the other directors are still hoping for improved communication. One stated, "There is a total lack of communication between us and the rest of the system." Another asked, "If we got together, what would we have to say to one another?" Another remarked, "I have complete autonomy. One great thing about the _____ schools is that nobody questions you. If I want to make a decision, I talk it over with myself."

Were the Special Services more adaptive to the environment in 1970 than they appeared to be in 1969? This particular big city school system does exist in an environment that demands adaptation. The respondents to the questionnaire estimated that sixty to one hundred percent of their work tasks were new or different from what they were five years earlier. On the other hand, the feedback mechanisms which signal the system's adaptiveness (i.e., how it corrects itself based on feedback) are not good in Special Services. The questionnaire asked for the rate of feedback response on a seven-point Likert-type scale: one day (1), one week (2), one month (3), six months (4), one year (5), five years (6), longer (7). The directors indicated an average of one year to get feedback on job performance.

Also, using the Lawrence and Lorsch methodology to measure the amount of differentiation and integration in the organization as compared to the amount required by the external environment, it was determined that the Special Service departments had not adapted to their environmental requirements on these dimensions.[4]

There is no good 1970 data that would help us to determine if there had been a change in the nature of the power struggles in Special Services since the OD intervention.

From the interviews and the questionnaire data collected in the spring of 1970, one year after the MIT team's intervention, it can be inferred that little change had taken place as a result of the brief organization development activity. This research did not follow a pre- and post-test design with controls; therefore, it is impossible to make pointed arguments and conclusions from the data. We may conclude, however, that no significant improvements occurred on the four organizational problem areas outlined in the initial MIT report. These problems, recognized in 1969, continue to exist. The one exception to this general conclusion may be the attempts to streamline the structure as a result of another study and thereby to improve the coordination of the departments.

The MIT organization development effort had two positive effects which help to qualify it as partially successful. One is that a more extensive organization development project was later approved by the school committee and board of superintendents. Some of the associate superintendents felt that one of the reasons for its favorable reception was that it promised to use some of the same methods used by the MIT team. One associate superintendent remarked that "few university people around here have ever really worked with us and tried to help us like that before."

Secondly, those lower down in the organizational hierarchy, especially at the level of department director, were quite enthusiastic about the data feedback sessions and desired to do "more of that kind of thing in the future." One director remarked that "nobody has ever really listened to us like that before. Although it didn't go very far (in influencing those above), we at least felt like we were considered."

Analyses

In general, the MIT team's OD effort did not succeed. The OD method for effecting organizational change was never really understood by those at the top echelons of the school services hierarchy. There were no joint action-planning sessions between those at the top and the consultant team on intervention strategies. Data collected at a later date indicate that no attempt was made to deal with the organizational problems identified by the MIT team.

The team's failure to intervene successfully may be due to many factors, but it is the feeling of this author that the primary factor was an unsuccessful entry. Too much emphasis was placed by the MIT team on getting into the system to practice their OD skills. Many of the issues normally associated with the entry process were left unexplored. The team wrongly assumed that once in the system, they would be able to renegotiate the contract and teach the clients the OD method.

One major problem with this organization development effort was that the relationships and roles of those at the top of the client system and of the consultants were never clearly defined. Those at the top did not initially understand that they were expected to play an active role in helping to diagnose the system and plan the interventions. When requested to participate later on, they said they didn't have enough time. Some preferred not to work together. They asked the team to "just give us the report and tell us what to do." Although members of the MIT team felt that they invited and modeled a collaborative kind of relationship, this relationship never seemed to materialize. It is the author's feeling that more time should have been spent establishing trust and defining the nature of the working relationship.

Another fault of the MIT team at entry is that they did not establish a norm for openly confronting differences of opinion. For example, the team should have insisted that more time be alloted by top administrators for collaboration. Some provision should have been made for a follow-up and for leaving behind an internal OD capacity in Special Services. Later on, the team should have refused to submit the report without the active participation of those at the top in the data feedback workshops, without some commitment by those in authority that the plans of the directors would receive attention, and without some assurance that the report would be interpreted correctly.

The "hidden agendas" of the two parties were never really disclosed. In a sense, the MIT team wanted to practice using OD in the school system and to teach the clients OD methods. It was later discovered that those at the top of the school organization wanted an outside report which could be used to support their request for more staffing, especially for an administrative assistant or coordinator for Special Services. Lack of open disclosure about the needs of the two groups resulted in a client-consultant power struggle where each side spent a good deal of time trying to second-guess the motives and next moves of the other side.

The student status and youthful appearance of the MIT team was another reason for failure. School systems tend to be very status conscious. Also, the average age for a top-level administrator in this city school system was about fifty-five at the time the intervention was made. The team was frequently referred to as "kiddos" or "young people." Team members were regarded as students using the school system for practice (and that assessment was somewhat merited, because their effort *was* an assignment for a practicum course in OD methods).

Finally, the original motivations and agreements made by the third party and the associate superintendent he contacted were never disclosed. They may have established some expectations that affected the working relationship of the MIT team.

Some of the questions normally posed at entry were answered by both parties. The parameters of the intervention were defined (i.e., the 14 departments were identified). The perceptions of the problems in Special Services were outlined by those at the top of the hierarchy, those with whom the consultants first came into contact. The question of "who are we" was answered when it was decided that the team would be called the MIT Management Survey Team and when those in authority legitimized the team's work by writing supporting introductory memos and by voicing support. (Perhaps the team should have used the time of decision making on its name as an opportunity to explore its real purpose.) The rules for data collection were also defined at entry. However, these things all taken together do not seem to be enough to support a successful entry.

Conclusion

The key to a successful entry into a large urban school organization is that the client and consultant define a working relationship that really permits collaboration on the changes such that those changes can be implemented, owned, and then revised by the clients (i.e., the system must have its own internal OD capacity for continuing the change). The contract should be favorably defined so that both sides are clear about the expectations of the other. Entry should also be a continuous process. Most important, however, is the establishment of a relationship that allows for mutual understanding and respect, that permits active collaboration between the parties, and that allows for an open exploration of motives, misunderstandings, and alternatives.

Program 30, "Strategies for Organizational Change," at the Center for the Advanced Study of Educational Administration (CASEA), and Program 100 at the Northwest Regional Educational Laboratory (NWREL) have together devised an entry strategy for school systems that might solve some of the problems encountered by the MIT team.[5] This strategy may be called the entry workshop. It is a two-day demonstration laboratory that helps administrators and teachers in a school system to understand and to experience organizational development methods.

After initial entry takes place and a tentative contract is negotiated between the clients and the consultants, the two-day entry workshop is scheduled to introduce a large segment of the system (e.g., top-level administrators, a representative group of principals, department heads, teachers, union representatives) to the organizational development method. The agreement is made that the client does not have to agree to participate in the organizational change program until after he experiences the demonstration workshop.

Goals for the workshop may be to develop enthusiasm among participants for what this kind of intervention may mean for the organization; to articulate a vision about a better (more "self-renewing") organization for the future; to help the participants understand how they could tackle some really concrete current problems if they had an OD capability; to help the participants understand OD in contrast to traditional consulting or sensitivity training; to give the participants a feeling for some of the new skills they could obtain by learning organizational development methods; and to establish a collaborative relationship between the clients and the consultants—that is, to make the participants feel that they are expected to influence the change program and eventually to own it, and that they are encouraged to be open, confrontive, and honest about their opinions as to what is best for the system.

Participants in the two-day workshop are asked to suspend judgments until the end of the event. A learning sequence is developed for each event wherein the participants do an exercise or participate in a new procedure or simulation for each aspect of the OD method to be learned. Second, they debrief the exercise with the help of observers. They comment on how the experience itself went, what some of the dynamics were, and how they felt during the event. Third, the participants relate the exercise to "back home" in the organization and comment on how the learning is actually relevant to their organizational life. Fourth, the trainers make a presentation on the subject matter being discussed. They give a brief lecturette or other form of presentation that helps the participants to get a theoretical handle which generally explains the subject matter for complex organizations. Finally, the trainers hand out readings that explain the subject in more detail.

The entry workshop grid shows some of the methods used and the organizational issues explored. The reader can complete the boxes according to the exercises, simulations, feedback methods, skills, and procedures he prefers. The experience should be geared to the particular organizational issue and the particular needs of the organization with which he is working. It is also possible to change the organizational issues explored, but the author feels that these are issues relevant to big city school system personnel.

THE ENTRY WORKSHOP GRID

Organizational Issues   OD Training Methods

	Skill Training	Group Exercises	Survey Feedback	Intergroup Exercises	Procedures
Decision Making					
Communication					
Norms (Culture)					
Group Effectiveness					
Surfacing and Resolving Conflicts					

Some way is needed to help organization developers achieve a successful entry into organizations as suspicious of and estranged from OD methods as are big city school systems. The normal entry techniques must be used and improved. In addition, a brief organization development kind of experience, such as the entry workshop, may be needed to help the client organization to really understand the OD method so that they can use it successfully for organizational change. The key to engaging in successful organization development activities in large urban school systems may well depend on a successful entry.

NOTES

1. See Schein, Edgar H., *Process Consultation: Its Role in Organization Development* (Reading, Mass.: Addison-Wesley, 1969), and Sofer, Cyril, *The Organization from Within* (Chicago: Quadrangle Books, 1961).
2. This practicum is part of the OD Track at the Sloan School under the direction of Professors David Kolb and Richard Beckhard.
3. A "cross-section diagonal slice" interview sample, as used here, is one which is randomly selected according to role. That is, relevant (according to the problem) organizational members at all levels of the system are identified (e.g., associate and assistant superintendents, department directors, teachers, nurses, counselors,

principals) and at least two in each role are chosen. This sample covers both the vertical and horizontal levels of the organization.

4. See Lawrence, Paul R., and Lorsch, Jay W., *Organization and Environment* (Boston: Harvard Business School, 1967); and *Developing Organizations: Diagnosis and Action* (Reading, Mass.: Addison-Wesley, 1969); C. Brooklyn Derr, "Organizational Adaptation to Forces for Change in a Big City School System," an unpublished paper presented at the American Educational Research Association Annual Meeting, February, 1971.

5. The author was a visiting research associate in Program 30 at CASEA during the 1970-71 academic year. Other members of the team designing the entry workshop were Richard Schmuck, Chic Jung, Philip Runkel, Ruth Emory and Rene Pino.

SECTION II

TEAM BUILDING

EDITORS' OVERVIEW

Modern technology divides the knowledge and skill needed to do a job among a relatively large number of people. One social consequence of this technological advance is an increased reliance on the use of teams. In order to facilitate team efforts a new social technology called team building has evolved, which aims to allow group members to work on *how* they are working together. In the course of their work, groups develop regular patterns of behavior. For example, group members often have a tacit agreement about who will *really* make their decisions and how conflict is to be handled. Sometimes such regularities in individual member and group behavior are functional; for example, people may feel at ease in a work group because they know what to expect from other members. Too often, however, routine procedures are unwittingly dysfunctional and cause team efforts to fail. The social technology for altering dysfunctional member and group behavior and for developing team potential can be grouped into three categories: *process consultation, process skills development,* and *substantive interventions.*

Process consultation in turn subsumes at least three different kinds of interventions:

1. Interventions that deal with process issues concerning a team task, such as, How is the leadership function implemented? What are the consequences of the decision-making procedure that the team employs? How are power and influence distributed?

2. Interventions that deal with problems of group maintenance, such as, To what extent are members open and trusting? How are feelings of anger, joy, sorrow, and enthusiasm expressed? What are the procedures for handling intragroup conflict?

3. Interventions that occur in response to "cultural" issues. These issues reflect the relationship between a team and the larger social context in which it is located. The central focus is on the ways in which organizational and community norms and values influence team activities—for example, does the team conform to organizational or community norms in dealing with minority group members?

In practice, process consultation interventions include:

Data feedback (Team members are questioned about crucial issues, the data are fed back, preserving anonymity, and the team is helped to organize for effective problem solving.)

Ideal vs. actual (Team members identify where they are and where they would like to be along some critical dimensions. They then develop plans for reducing the discrepancies, where they are relatively large but malleable.)

Training (In response to a felt need, a team plans two or three days of agenda-free meetings and uses the time to study itself as a group.)

The second category of team building interventions, *process skills development,* is aimed at developing durable group skills. There is less attention to exploring and understanding current process than there is in process consultation interventions. An assumption underlying the use of process skills development is that current behavior is a consequence of maladaptive learning, but that it is not serving any unconscious needs; hence, there is no need to explore the behavior and its roots. To produce behavior change it is only necessary to provide a team with more productive alternatives. This is done through skill exercises on decision making, problem solving, long-range planning, and communication.

Substantive interventions are used in response to urgent team needs that arise from specific work problems. For example, a work team may be floundering because it lacks an organized agenda, or progress may be blocked because members are misunderstanding one another or are unable to invent compromise solutions. Team members are often too involved in a task to provide these interventions. Hence, it is sometimes incumbent upon OD practitioners to be "the good group member."

The three articles in this section all contain examples of process consultation. The Crockett article discusses how Charles Ferguson and Charles Seashore used both data feedback and current observations of teamwork to facilitate team building. (Note that the article's author was the team's "boss" when this successful intervention occurred.) Friedlander's article presents data on the effectiveness of process consultations and process skills development laboratories with armed forces research and development work groups. Harrison's paper describes another type of process skills development. His is one of the newer, less frequently used approaches: he has team members systematically examine the nature and consequences of their present teamwork, and then negotiate with each other for behavioral changes which will lead to more effective work ("If you do X, I will do Y.") All negotiated agreements are made known to the entire team. The focus is on power and influence, not on probing team members' feelings about each other.

There are no clear examples of the third category of team-building technology, *substantive interventions,* among the articles that follow. The work represented in each of the three articles may imply elements of this category, however.

Unfortunately, it is not possible to specify rules for determining when one or another of these three groups of interventions should be used. In order to develop an understanding of the contingencies that regulate success and failure of these various interventions, readers are urged to read the articles in this section with an eye toward analysing the social settings in which the successful interventions occurred.

TEAM BUILDING-ONE APPROACH TO ORGANIZATION DEVELOPMENT

William J. Crockett

William J. Crockett is vice president, Human Relations, Saga Administrative Corporation, Menlo Park, California.

The following article is a description of the first team-building meeting [between boss and subordinates] ever held in the Department of State and perhaps in any organization of the federal government throughout the United States.

The article describes the serious doubts that were in the mind of the leader at the start of the meeting, how the premeeting interviews were conducted, and how the interview data were handled. The inhibitions felt by boss and subordinates upon leveling in front of one another are revealed, and the methods used by the consultants in enabling the group to confront the data and work them through are fully described.

As the author shares his own fears and experiences, one can see how a team is created by the individual members in working through the data which they themselves have had available all the time.

After a description of the back-home results of these efforts there is the conclusion that it is indeed a worthwhile experience for a workgroup.

THE TEAM MEETS

They could have been any business or professional group, these ten men around the luncheon table. There was the usual banter and kidding; the good-natured poking of fun and the quick retort. There was the obvious story and the laughter of men at ease with one another. I tried to detect signs of strain among them but saw none, except for my own nervousness. For this group of ten were my men, men whom I had picked—men with whom I had worked and achieved. They were all good men. Some had worked for me as long as six years, from the time that I was first appointed by President Kennedy to be Assistant Secretary of State for Administration early in 1961. In fact, some of the relationships went beyond that, back to the time when I was one of them, a fellow employee in the Department of State.

Now five years later I, the Boss, and my ten key subordinates were having lunch together before starting a series of meetings which were called "Organizational Development." The meetings would run for a day and a half or two days. During this time we would explore our feelings and our problems of working together. In addition to the eleven of us, there were also Charles Ferguson of U.C.L.A. and Charles Seashore of the NTL Institute for Applied Behavioral Science, Washington, D.C. Dr. Ferguson and Dr. Seashore would meet with us and help us with the problems we would encounter.

As the luncheon drew to an end and the time for work approached, I found myself questioning the whole activity.

Could there, I wondered, be any real problems beneath the surface of our relationships that would be worth two days of our busy time away from the State Department? After all, were these men not all well adjusted, well acquainted, and quite at ease with one another? This seemed obvious from the way they had enjoyed their luncheon together. Would this kind of confrontation fracture the well-being of this group? I wondered. Would we ever have this kind of friendly, jovial, easy feeling again if we went ahead with this "team-building" exercise? And yet, I knew that there were some personal animosities among us that surfaced occasionally and, when they did, made us all uncomfortable and edgy until they were again safely tucked away from sight. Could we, I wondered, deliberately surface these feelings and then be able to handle them as a group?

HOW MUCH RISK?

I was also concerned about the other risks that a meeting like this might hold. These men were good. I needed them all. I could ill afford to lose any of them, for they did work together as well as any group with which I had ever been associated. And if, as a result of this meeting, some persons were to leave me, the price would have been too great!

I questioned also whether or not it were proper to expose the group's problems in front of two outsiders. Would these two men be trusted enough by the group for us to talk frankly and openly about our problems in front of them? Was it not true that we should not wash our dirty linen in public? Should we not try to work our problems through together without these outside consultants?

In anticipating what to follow, I was troubled with the thought that I would be called upon to share my feelings about each of these fellows in front of the others, and later on, we would expose each of these persons before his peers. I had been taught as a manager that the boss does not discuss a man's performance, capabilities, and weaknesses in front of his peers. It just is not done. Now I suddenly realized that I would surely be called upon to do just that before the day was finished. Another strain to cause the group to fracture? Perhaps. Even more distressing to me was the thought of the honest, face-to-face evaluation which I would be expected to give on each of them. That kind of open confrontation would be the most difficult problem I personally had to face.

I also wondered about the validity of our concept of forming an Executive Group. Could I share my responsibilities and my authority with them in a group situation? We had recently reorganized my area of responsibility by eliminating, in some cases, as many as five layers of hierarchy between me and the basic program managers (personnel, budget, building, finance, accounting, audit, and so on). We must now find a means of strengthening my office, stretching it laterally rather than deepening it vertically, to enable me to cope with the many new demands that these 30 or 40 new managers, who now reported directly to me, would make upon my time. How could we organize an Executive Group that would somehow be an extention—an elongation—of "me," so that these new managers would not feel that we had freed them of an old and established bureaucracy on the one hand only to put them into a new and strange hierarchical structure on the other?[1] Could we talk openly and honestly about the issues involved? Of course, there would be opposition and hurt and doubt and questions posed for everyone. Could we really work this through at such a meeting, or would it not be easier, simpler, and better for me just to direct things to be done? After all, I did have the authority. I might even be able to "manipulate" the organization into being as I had so often done in the past when I wanted to accomplish something difficult. Why waste all this time on such an issue when I already knew the answer I wanted?

COULD WE REALLY LEVEL?

I wondered whether we would have the nerve—the guts—to confront one another with the personal problems (feelings) that were bothering us. Or would we slip off the issues and try to cover up the difficulties as we had so often done in the past? This group had been meeting together for years in a staff capacity. Our practice was to go around the table each morning, talk about the problems of the day, and discuss the issues. Some of those ten would always be silent. Some would have ideas on almost any subject. Some would talk superficially about the problems which were in another's area of responsibility. But in the end, all would give way to me, the boss, to make the final decision and determine what to do. They did not as a group, nor were they much interested as a group in the total problems I faced. Each problem, no matter how complex for me, was for each of them very simple. It was either his to handle or it was someone else's. And if it was someone else's the others had no interest; nor did one man want anyone else involved if it was his. Would they, could they, really become deeply involved with complex issues that cut across the lines of each one's responsibility? Could these individuals help me perform the complex integrative process of management? And, more importantly, would each one be able to take criticism and suggestions and ideas from the others on problems which each considered to be within his own responsibility? If anything was apparent to me about the group it was their lack of commitment to the entire Organizational Development program we had mounted some months before.[2] Each person in the group fiercely defended his own piece of the program, even at the expense of the others. Could they gain commitment to the whole from such a meeting as this?

I also wondered about the data that my good friend Chuck Ferguson had collected from the group. He had maintained that we needed a method of "deep sensing" within this group to discover the subsurface feelings that might be different from those on the surface. Some of these men had come to me privately, saying, "Do you really want him to dredge into the depths of all our feelings about one another and about you? Isn't it being disloyal for us to tell him of our problems and of our feelings for you? Does it serve any purpose for these problems to be brought out into the open and exposed? In fact, is he not *creating* problems for us when he digs as deeply as he has done into the problems we have as a group together?" And, of course, while assuring them they would not be disloyal to talk honestly and that these were things that we wanted to get out onto the table, I had my secret doubts about whether this were really the way to develop an organization. Now I had the sinking feeling that these two days could really end up in "group destruction" rather than in "group growth."

These were some of the feelings and questions that went 'round and 'round within me as we were finishing our lunch. And yet I knew that, according to the Theory at least, it would come out all right in the end, and something good would be the result.

Finally, the lunch ended and we filed into the conference room away from telephones and papers to confront the evidence that Chuck Ferguson and Charlie Seashore had gathered about us. We were ready to start our first session of "Organizational Development" or "Team Building."

THE GROUP HAS THE DATA

In accord with the design for the meeting, the two behavioral scientists interviewed all the persons who reported directly to me in order to get data that we would use in our off-site conference together. Interviews were conducted informally and in a friendly atmosphere, but they probed very deeply into each person's relationships and feelings for each of the others in the group and with me. Searching questions were asked. What are the real problems of getting the job done? What problems do each of the members cause you in getting your job done? What are the problems that the boss has caused in the group? What are the personal problems, the personality problems, and the real life business problems that are destructive to the group? What are the deep interpersonal feelings? Is there confrontation? How are differences handled in the group when they come up? Is there conflict? Are you interested in participating in others' areas of responsibility? Is there any feedback to members who get out of line or who have problems? Is there a spirit of help and coaching within the group? Is there a spirit of trust and caring in the group? What are the group norms; what will the group tolerate? And there were many, many other questions as well.

When the meeting started, Chuck put all of us in a large circle—a common shape within T Groups—and talked to us about the agenda and the procedures for the next two days. He said that he would present the data that he had developed about each of us, then each person would have a chance to comment or to talk about them, and finally others would be asked to join the discussion. Since the data were to be presented anonymously, we could start the process of seeing ourselves without creating embarrássment and animosity. This would give us the first opportunity for coaching and feedback, we were told. In this way the group would have an opportunity to work, for the very first time, on problems within the group in a non-threatening atmosphere.

Chuck explained that we would work upon the real issues, such as how we might form the new "Executive Group," how we might make policy, and so on, as well as dealing with the specific issues identified in the data. He assured us that in all cases he and Charlie Seashore would be there to help us to work through the data that we now had about ourselves and one another. He told us that he would stop us occasionally to talk to us about Organizational Development, to ask us to look at ourselves and what we were doing to one another or what we were doing as a group, or what we were not doing as a group.

Dr. Ferguson had coded the data by number so that the various kinds of data that were similar were given the same number. One number would represent one kind of data gathered from numerous sources (persons), and another number would represent another kind of data, and so on. Thus, if more than one of us had a problem in common with others, that problem would have a common number for us all. In a group of ten there might be 20 common items—things that everyone felt about some of the others—and several individual items about various persons which no one else had felt.

THE BOSS IS THE HANG-UP

The consultant put each of our names on a large board and around each one he accumulated the numbers that related to the problems others had said that they had with that particular person. I remember seeing names going up with five or six numbers encircling them, but I certainly was not prepared to see the large cluster of numbers that went up around my name! Dr. Ferguson explained what each number meant, and I can still remember some of the ones around my name. For example: "He doesn't delegate properly." "He gives the same assignment to two or three people." "He gives contradictory instructions to different people so that there are binds within the group." He makes unilateral decisions relating to our responsibilities without first talking them over with us." "He takes action in our areas without telling us." "We are not generally informed about what's happening in the whole group." "We are kept ignorant about one another's activities." "He doesn't like confrontation and conflict." "He can't make tough (people) decisions." "We can't get in to see him." "He sees the wrong people." "He doesn't give us his attention when we do see him." "He has too many irons in the fire at one time." "He confuses us about priorities." "He is manipulative." And more. In each case that "He" was myself! I could feel my anger rising. My feelings were really hurt at this point because I still was not convinced that any of these things were actually true despite their perception by these now not-so-loyal "friends." Further, I rationalized that in their dredging for feelings and in trying to discover problems, probably these people had stretched their imaginations just to come up with something to talk about. In my first throes of resentment, I could hardly refrain from saying, "If I'm so bad, pack up and get out and I'll find others who not only can do the job but will be glad for the chance!"

But it was not all bad. Chuck drew two big symbolic climates on the board, one of sunshine and one of rain. And he wisely pointed out that the evidence on each of us was not totally rain nor totally sunshine. There was some of both for each of us.

OUR SELF-IMAGES

About this time, after the session had run for an hour or more, Chuck eased the situation with a lecture. This lecture was about "the perception of self-image" as opposed to how we might be seen by others. He explained how our own perceptions might actually have little to do with reality. For example, a person could feel as right and as righteous as he wished and have absolutely pure motives when he was doing something—starting a policy or making a decision or taking a stand. But it was also true that others might see his motives and acts in an entirely different light. Thus, what really mattered was not what he thought and felt but how he appeared to others.

We came to realize that a person need not admit that anything he was doing was necessarily wrong, but that it was the wise man who could understand the way he made other people feel. If the reasons for what a person was doing and the way he was doing it were both misunderstood by his staff, and if it could be revealed to him why they were being misunderstood, then it might be easier for him to face the problem and talk about it and work it through and learn how to avoid being misunderstood in the future. This understanding was especially helpful to all of us in dealing with our own "self-images." For example, it came out that one of the men in the group was very resentful of me because I had singled him out in a public meeting to give him credit for a new program. I had thought that I was doing him great honor and favor, and my motives were pure and generous. But he had felt that I was trying to say to the group that if the project turned out to be wrong or did not work or somehow failed, that it was his idea and, therefore, he would have to bear the blame. I was making him the scapegoat! And while I did not have to admit to any wrongdoing in dealing with him, because my motives were pure, I did have to admit to a better understanding of the way he felt after seeing it through his eyes. We both perceived that our mutual failure to talk about this at the time had permitted our relationship to fester for no real reason. This was the spirit in which Chuck led us into the discussion of the problems we would face in our relationships with one another.

GIVING AND RECEIVING FEEDBACK

After these kinds of discussions, we had a deeper understanding of what we could achieve. Chuck then asked me to go around the room and tell each person how I felt about him and what my problems were with each one. The moment I dreaded had come! I was to confront, in public, each of these persons and reveal my feelings for them. This was to be my most difficult hour. But here again the consultants tried to give us an understanding of the deep difference between a cold, hard, objective, critical "appraisal" by the boss on the one hand a legitimate (even if critical) "feedback" that is given in a climate of trust and warmth and caring, on the other. We discussed the obligations which were imposed upon all who opted into such a group; specifically, we were reminded of the obligation of "caring" for other group members. Members who "cared" had obligations both individually and collectively to help the others to understand how they "came through" and "were seen," how they were "felt" and "perceived," how they "looked," and how their actions and conduct and attitudes were helpful or were hurtful in their communications. Each had an obligation to give and to receive feedback, and to give coaching to the others.

Since Chuck had also interviewed me prior to the meeting, I knew that he had my candid observations on each of the individuals. All of them were my friends but, nevertheless, all of them had a few human weaknesses in their relationships among one another and in their relationships to me. I knew that I had revealed these in my data. I also knew that I had never liked or felt easy with such confrontation. I found it very difficult to express my feelings and my thoughts about each of my men. But I had the choice of giving them honest data about themselves or doing half a job, sliding off the issues as easily as possible despite what I had already told Dr. Ferguson.

As I went through the difficult task of discussing with each one of them the way he came across to me, there was not so much hurt as I had expected; strangely enough, there was no anger but genuine curiosity and interest. There was a great deal of group support, disagreement, and participation in what I was saying about each person. The discussions were animated in a give-and-take way, and my data were then often related to those which Chuck had collected from each subordinate. Caring and sharing became an exciting new game.

WORKING THE DATA

After we had gone around the room like this for a while, we decided to come back to those problems which related to me. We worked on them one by one.

For example, where one had said I did not delegate, I denied it by saying, "I am the best delegator in the Department. You all have authority. You have responsibilities in your area. And it is up to you to get them done." And then the anonymity would disappear because the person who had put this item on the list would come in hard to justify his stand. And so with illustration of time and place and circumstance he would prove when I had not delegated properly or how I would fall back after I had given them authority, or how I had made a decision unknown to them or how, before evidence had come in, I had changed their decision, and so on. This kind of confrontation only started the conversation. Chuck would not let any of us off so easily. He probed deeply. How did my action make them feel? How did they see me? What were my motives? How did this affect the group's work together? This and many more questions that he asked would give me the opportunity to reply, "Yes, but you don't realize the pressure I am under from the White House . . . or from the Congress . . . or from the Secretary. . . ." And the whole complexity of relationships, the pressures upon me, and explanations for my seemingly erratic behavior would come out. From such explanations and probings came understanding and a sense of sharing that had never before existed in the group.

After they had worked with me for awhile, someone else would say, "Well, I would like to talk about [such and such] a problem around my name because I really am not this way, either." Here again the anonymity would be dropped, because the person who had put up that item would say, "Now Mr. X, don't you remember when you did that? Don't you remember when we had this kind of problem with you in your shop? Don't you remember how you wouldn't give us the funds to get the job done? Don't you recall how you changed policies while we were in midstream and then we had to scrap all the efforts we had made to that date?" And then the general discussion would start—'round and 'round—with new appreciation for people, new insights into the problems the others faced, and a new understanding of the interlocking relationships of all the functions.

There were many job-related problems that were put on top of the table for discussion for the first time, as well as many personal relationship problems. Why do you act this way? Why don't you like me? Why do you mistrust me? What do I do that annoys you so? How can I gain your confidence? Why are you so rigid? And the amazing thing to me was that the group members were actually eagerly working on their own problems without getting angry—almost urging us, "Get on to mine. I would like to talk about the cluster around my name; and while I don't really believe it, if it's true let's talk about it and I'll try to do something about it." I could see the group, hour by hour, literally growing in trust, growing in solidity, growing in caring. They were somehow involved here with one another as they had never been involved before. In the old meetings they were just individuals attending a not too interesting discussion of another person's function. But here they were a real group facing a world of problems together.

The first night we worked until very late. No one really wanted to stop. We decided that we would come back early the next day and go on with the process which in reality had just started.

A TEAM SPIRIT IS BORN

The next day's activity was interspersed with lectures and with other techniques to make the group grow in trust and in confidence, in its ability to give and receive feedback, and in its confidence to deal with confrontation and conflict. For example, we would pair off in twos or threes to discuss the interpersonal problems we faced as they appeared on the board. We would then come back and tell the others about our findings and what we thought we could do to overcome these problems. The whole group would then be brought into the discussion, and the group members would talk about these things together. We talked about how we could work better as a group, how we could make group decisions, how we could share the problems that were coming to me, and how each member in the group could broaden his interest beyond his own specialty and responsibility so that he could accept a share in the whole group's problem. We discussed how the group could rid itself of its own individual parochialism and start a process of enlarging its interest and responsiblity by working together as an extension of me. There was confrontation and conflict in the group and this was handled. There was feedback and caring, disagreements and frustrations, and these were handled. Personal animosities were probed and discussed and often settled, or at least understood. There was also creativity, and risk, and in the end there was a real sense of commitment to the principles which I at one time had thought that I might achieve more quickly by directive or more easily by manipulation.

I also realized that I had not fooled them about the real me. The group had had the data all along. But due to the climate of the group—its norms—we had not been able to be open with one another; we had not been able to face confrontation, and so the group could not share the data with me earlier. It would have hurt me too much at the time. It would have asked them to risk too much at the time. As "tough minded" as we thought our own management to have been, we soon learned that it had not been tough enough to deal with real conflict, deep personal feelings, or confrontation. Instead of this kind of confrontation's causing my leadership to dissipate, I saw a new excitement born of involvement emerging within the group. There could be no question of their total commitment to me as their leader and to the concept of the "Executive Group" which we had been discussing. Out of this meeting we all saw the phenomenon of a new group come into being before our very eyes! We were a united group—trusting and caring and sharing as never before.

These were a tough, exhausting, exciting, and fulfilling two days! But we were a team at the end and felt that we had the start of a capability of functioning as an effective Executive Group.

ACTION ITEMS FOR THE BACK-HOME SITUATION

Before breaking up for the weekend, we decided on several courses of action.

We decided that we would meet every morning to talk about the issues of the day, to decide how we would deal with them, what our actions would be, how we would proceed, and who would have the responsibility for handling each problem. In these meetings everyone would have an opportunity for input and discussion before decisions were made. In this way problems were made the responsibility of the whole group, with the whole group's having knowledge and input and commitment to the decisions that were made.

We decided to continue having a behavioral scientist (Charles Seashore) meet with us occasionally in our regular staff meetings and other work sessions so that he could observe what was going on among us, and so that he could stop the group occassionally to let us observe our own process. Certainly we knew that we would need his expertise, at least for some time.

We decided that we would come back together again at some future date to have another off-site session to review our group health and our new-found spirit of trust and caring. We came to realize that the relationships between people need maintenance to keep them working smoothly and that it cannot be something done only occasionally. We came to realize that we were embarking on a new management style, a new method of handling every day's problems, which would require a great deal from each of us—a new toughness of mind but dispensed with a great deal of "heart." Therefore we would need a continuing process of growth and understanding if we were to succeed.

We determined that we would like to have Dr. Seashore do continuing research with members of the group and go deeper into our organization so that there would be a continuous sensing of how employees felt. By this we could have a better understanding of the attitudes of our members and of how people "down below" saw us and were reacting to us. Thus we would be able to take steps within the system to handle the problems.[3]

Several of the members of this group decided that they would like to take their own subordinate staff off-site for the same kind of Organizational Development meeting. This was courageous on their part because they had seen how difficult it had been for me, the boss; and when they went off-site with their staff they realized that they would assume "the boss" role. Yet they were willing to take the risks because of the obvious vitality of the process in bringing people together, in opening people up so that they could make contributions, in actually reducing conflict by facing it, and because of the commitment that results when people participate and become deeply involved in the management process.

We decided to explore the possibility of having other off-site Organizational Development conferences with other major areas of the Department of State for whom our group was responsible for service and with whom we interfaced. For example, we provided administrative support to all the Bureaus and Offices; and if we could take them off-site with us we might be able to learn how we looked to our clients, how they felt about us, and what, if any, the problems might be in working together.

We discussed how we could be helpful to one another in the future in the way we worked together in the organization. For example, what were the coaching opportunities we had; how could each one help the other see himself and understand how he was coming through? How could we give feedback in the future that would not hurt but would be helpful and reinforcing? We determined that we would try to receive such feedback without defensiveness. We agreed that we would not "put off" all of our process discussions for some future get-together but that we would feed this kind of information into our regular meetings so that we could deal with it on the spot since the data were there for all to see. In other words, we agreed that the group must police and reinforce and maintain the group and its members if what we had started to learn at this meeting would indeed be continued within the group. We agreed that if I did something they did not like or understand the others would bring it up for discussion.

The first attempt ever made in the State Department of bringing together a manager and his own staff to talk about their individual and group problems had come to an end. It accomplished many of the positive hopes that we had had for it. It had not gone aground. We had not risked so much as I had feared in those doubt-filled moments just before the meeting started. In other words, I believe that all of us felt that it was a worthwhile, constructive two days.

WHAT WERE THE RESULTS?

A story such as this requires a sequel—some description of what happened after the group went back to work in its real life situation. Certainly it would be erroneous to say that there were no continuing problems, because there were. The process did not guarantee an end to problems. All the old animosities were not forgotten. The process did not promise that, either. Conflicts and disagreements were still with us. But in the weeks and months that followed, the group showed a highly increased capability for getting issues out into the open, of surfacing the hidden problems, and in exposing personal animosities so that we could deal with them—in short, an increased capability to work together as a group.

It did break down the fragmentation that had previously existed. The process of welding ourselves into a total integrated management team was started. As a result, I believe there came to be a great deal more understanding of points of view, understanding of the total issues, understanding of the total problems and programs, and a greater commitment on the part of everyone to the total goals.

Also, the process did move downward in the organization and horizontally, to include other parts of the State Department. As proposed in our meetings, some of the members did take their own staffs off-site for similar meetings with similar positive results. The Assistant Secretary of State for African Affairs at this time used this same technique of going off-site with his staff to better the management and decision-making process in his bureau. The same kind of program was planned for the Latin American Bureau and other areas. Our group did meet together in a similar off-site meeting with our client organizations and gained insights into how we were creating many of our own problems.

CONCLUSION

The lesson that was most impressive to us all was that the so-called Theory Y style of management—management by participation—is neither soft-headed nor "easy." It is much easier to sit in the big office and issue directives. It is much easier to avoid confrontation by issuing orders. It is easier to avoid personal involvement and conflict by smoothing over the surface. Theory Y management is not for the executive who likes surface serenity and obsequiousness. Theory Y management is for those managers who are willing to take the gut punishment of a truly tough-minded approach to management. It is for those who believe that conflict can be handled best by confronting it openly and for those who understand that real commitment of their people can be secured only by their continuing participation in making plans and setting objectives.

Organizational Development is not a panacea but a style—a tough-minded management style—and it works!

NOTES

1. Part of the State Department's reorganization called "Management by Programs and Objectives" (MOP).
2. A multi-action development program called "Action for Organizational Development" (ACORD). A major part of the program was the extensive use of laboratory training and behavioral scientist consultants provided under a contract with NTL.
3. Mr. Crockett resigned from the Department of State on January 31, 1960, and the ACORD program was soon discontinued by his successor. The reasons for his action were varied but included cost, style of management, failure of the Secretary to be personally involved, and so on. The discontinuance of the program should not be interpreted as the result of an evaluative judgment of its efficacy.

THE IMPACT OF ORGANIZATIONAL TRAINING LABORATORIES UPON THE EFFECTIVENESS AND INTERACTION OF ONGOING WORK GROUPS

Frank Friedlander, *School of Management*
Case Western Reserve University

SUMMARY

The impact upon four work groups ($N = 31$) which participated in organizational training laboratory sessions is evaluated in comparison with eight similar groups ($N = 60$) which did not participate. Criteria were six-factored dimensions, each composed of items gathered from earlier interviews which group members perceived as problems. Significant changes occurred in training groups in the following dimensions: group effectiveness, mutual influence, and personal involvement. No significant changes occurred in leader approachability, intragroup trust, or in the evaluation of group meetings. The relevance of a work unit participating in training as a total group, rather than each member participating in a separate session, is discussed.

INTRODUCTION

Action taken to resolve problems which hinder the effectiveness of work groups is a topic touched upon only occasionally in the research literature. For the most part, innovations in group training efforts, such as group problem-solving and sensitivity training, have fallen apparently outside the boundaries of industrial psychology, despite the fact that much of this training currently occurs in industrial settings. On the other hand, a number of studies have been reported in such journals as *Human Relations* and the *Journal of Applied Behavioral Research*. In part, this may be because group training programs deal with the social and environmental factors, and not merely with individual differences in characteristics. It may also be because group training involves efforts toward change, and not merely acceptance and measurement of a status quo situation. In an article relevant to these issues, Sanford (1965) strongly advocates programs and studies aimed toward understanding the conditions and processes of developmental change, the social settings in which these changes occur and, in particular, the settings that have been designed to modify people in some way.

This article is concerned with an evaluation of the impact of change programs which will be called here *organizational training laboratories*. The nature of this training quite naturally varies among groups in some ways. In general, however, the laboratory sessions last approximately four to five days and are attended by *all* members of a particular work group. The purposes of the sessions generally are a) to identify problems facing the work-group system and the reasons for their existence, b) to invent possible solutions to the problems in the form of needed system changes, and c) to plan implementation of these solutions through regular and newly-constructed channels. Within this problem-solving context, the group explores numerous inadequacies in interpersonal and intergroup processes which directly or indirectly influence the total work system.

It is important to note that these training sessions deal with the intact work group as an integrated system into which is introduced procedural and interpersonal change, rather than with a collection of strangers representing different organizations—or unrelated components of the same organization. This difference is relevant to the expected training impact and, therefore, to the research design and criteria.

Much of the previous emphasis in training seems to have been upon evoking changes in the *individual* primarily in the isolated island of his training context. The organizational training laboratory is directed at helping the individual bridge the hazardous, yet critical transition from his trainee role to the "real life" role of his back-home environment, and at preventing dissipation of the training effects. Since much of the discussion centers upon the relevant work problems which the group actually faces, and since the members of the training group are also the members of the organizational work group, ideally there is a perfect consolidation of the training and organizational membership roles. The back-home and the here-and-now are one and the same.

To the researcher, this shift in emphasis implies not only a criterion of more enduring change, but perhaps a qualitatively different one. Research emphasis is not only upon behavioral change in the individual, but also upon change of the individual within his organizational context, and changes in the organizational context or organic system of which the individual is one interacting part.

Although back-home criterion for evaluating laboratory training is frequently an implicit assumption made by both the consultant and the researcher, it is seldom made explicit in the design of the training or in the design of the research. "Change process," as Mann (1962) points out, "needs to be concerned with altering both the forces within an individual and the forces in the organizational situation surrounding the individual." This point is dramatically emphasized by Bennis, Benne, and Chin (1962) in their discussion of programs and technologies of planned change:

> Isolating the individual from his organizational context, his normative structure which rewards him and represents a significant reference group, makes no sense. In fact, if it sets up countervailing norms and expectations, it may be deleterious to both the organization and to the individual.

It is usually assumed that changes in individual behavior "will lead to increased effectiveness in the back-home situation; and this, rather than change per se, is the *raison d'etre* for the training group" (Stock & Thelan, 1958).

Those who have concerned themselves with back-home impact have reported mixed results. Trainees attending as a team have been found to change more than trainees attending as individuals (Lippett, 1949). Similarly, Riecken (1952) found that those who attended work camp, and who had continuing contact with others from developmental experiences, were most likely to retain attitude changes. On the other hand, Bennis (1963) uses the term "fade-out" to describe the disturbing lack of durability of training results when participants return to their company. Shepard (1960) reports that the impact of laboratory experience was greater on personal and interpersonal learning than in changing the organization. Harrison (1962) reports that trainees increased their use of emotional and interpersonal descriptions of each other, but did not increase such descriptions of their fellow employees back home. The thorough and extensive study by Fleishman *et al.* (1955) lends further disturbing evidence—that although training resulted in immediate changes in self-perception, this impact soon gave way to the leadership style of the trainee's supervisor once the trainee returned to his organizational context. Mann (1962) summarizes these disappointing results as follows: "At best, these studies suggest that this type of training has little or no general effect. . . . Training which does not take the trainee's regular social environment into account will probably have little chance of modifying behavior. It may very well be that human relations training—as a procedure for initiating social change—is most successful when it is designed to *remold the whole system of role relationships. . . .*"

In a parallel manner research, which ignores the impact of training upon the organization or the ongoing work groups of which it is composed, may be utilizing a criterion of low and temporary relevance. The appropriate research criteria for training that deals with the work groups within an organizational is *group change within the organizational context.*

In light of the above assumptions, the purposes of this research project were to study the impact of several organizational training laboratories upon problems that were of most relevance and utility to the group members of intact organizational work groups who had participated as a group in training laboratories. The data which evolved from this study are also utilized to shed further light on several additional issues concerning potential changes in organizational work groups.

BACKGROUND

The organizational context in which this project was embedded consists of one of the armed services' largest research and development stations, employing approximately 6,000 personnel. Eighty percent of the employees are civilians, including about 1,200 scientists and engineers. The organization's mission covers the complete research and development spectrum from basic research through applied research: design, development, test, engineering, evaluation, and limited production. Its products are in all fields of ordnance: rockets, guided missiles, underwater ordnance, propellants, explosives, and aircraft fire-control systems.

In early 1962, a series of individual interviews was held with the members of the Policy Board, the highest level group in the organization. The proposed topic did not concern the Board or its meetings as such. However, it soon became evident that the members were not content merely to discuss the "planned" topic; instead they dwelled rather consistently and concertedly upon the Board membership and leadership, and the interactions and effectiveness of the Board meetings.

The series of interviews resulted in two decisions—one action-oriented and one research-oriented. In view of the perceived inadequacies that members expressed of the group and its meetings, and in view of the willingness on the part of both group members and the internal consulting staff to do something about these inadequacies, a decision was made to bring in an outside trainer-consultant to work with the group. The second, and parallel decision, was to initiate a research study which might provide an evaluation and an increased understanding of the entire training phenomenon as it would occur in its original context.

It became apparent to the initial stage of the research study that at least one group which did *not* participate in the training experience (a comparison group) would be needed with which to compare any changes that might occur in the Policy Board. Over a two-year period the participation of 11 additional organizational work groups was obtained, making a total of 12 groups involved in the study. These 12 groups, described in more detail elsewhere (Friedlander, 1966), represent four levels in the organizational hierarchy. The groups are composed of from five to 15 members, who meet (usually weekly or biweekly) and work together regularly for a variety of purposes, including problem discussion and resolution, general coordination, information dissemination, decision-making, policy formulation, future planning, etc. As such, the 12 groups represent traditional, task-oriented work groups which use typical lateral and hierarchical interaction patterns toward their task accomplishment. Four of the groups eventually participated in organizational training laboratories; the others did not, thus providing the project with four training groups and eight comparison groups.[1]

RESEARCH DESIGN

The previously-mentioned series of interviews with members of various work groups resulted in the collection of an extensive amount of material dealing with the problems and the issues which members perceived as important in their work groups. The content of the material concerned such issues as cooperation, competition, openness, initiative, self-awareness, participation, spontaneity, creativity, intimacy, effectiveness, conflict, communication, divergency of ideas, procedural adequacy, authority relations, exploitation, mutual influence, and consensus. Detailed notes were taken during the interviews and the verbatim comments made by group members were rephrased into questions to form the main body of a questionnaire. Additional group-descriptive variables were obtained through discussions with members of several different groups. Relevant group-descriptive dimensions, issues, and hypotheses recurrent in the professional literature provided a third source of information. In addition to evaluations of adequacy and effectiveness of the group and its meetings, the variables encompassed perceptions of the actual network of feelings—both in terms of the perceptions of one's own position in the network as a member, and of the perceptions by members of relationships existing between other members of the group.

Directly quantifiable data were also collected for each individual concerning the number of meetings he had previously attended, the number of topics he had submitted for the agenda, the number of problems he felt needed discussion at the next meeting, the percentage of time he had talked, and his estimate of the percentage of time the chairman had talked. A nine-adjective semantic differential of the concept "X Department Staff Meetings" was also included.

In an effort to reduce these items to a comprehensive set of dimensions, a factor analysis was performed from which six underlying dimensions of group phenomena evolved. A detailed account of the construction, development, and factor analysis of the items is described elsewhere (Friedlander, 1966). However, since these six dimensions were utilized as principle variables in the current research, a brief description of each is provided.

I. *Group Effectiveness:* This dimension describes group effectiveness in solving problems and in formulating policy through a creative, realistic team effort.

II. *Approach to vs Withdrawal from Leader:* At the positive pole of this dimension are groups in which members can establish an unconstrained and comfortable relationship with their leader—the leader is approachable.

III. *Mutual Influence:* This dimension describes groups in which members see themselves and others as having influence with other group members and the leader.

IV. *Personal Involvement and Participation:* Individuals who want, expect, and achieve active participation in group meetings are described by this dimension.

V. *Intragroup Trust vs. Intragroup Competitiveness:* At the positive pole, this dimension depicts a group in which the members hold trust and confidence in each other.

VI. *General Evaluation of Meetings:* This dimension is a measure of a generalized feeling about the meetings of one's group as good, valuable, strong, pleasant, or as bad, worthless, weak, unpleasant.

The questionnaire from which this data was obtained is described here as the Group Behavior Inventory (GBI). Group members were introduced to the study at one of their regular meetings. After a discussion period where questions were answered, a copy of the GBI was distributed to each member of the group to be completed at his leisure in the privacy of his own office. Each member was asked to affix an identification code number of his own choice to the GBI so results of a planned second administration of the questionnaire might be compared to the first one. The GBI was administered twice to each of the 12 groups. For the four training groups, the second administration followed the training by six months. For the eight comparison groups, the second administration followed the first administration by six months.

INQUIRIES, METHODS, AND RESULTS

The remainder of this paper will incorporate selected issues which the research project attempted to explore, the methodologies used to explore each issue, the results of the analyses, and a brief discussion of the possible relevance of the results.

Issue 1—General Impact of Organizational Training Laboratories.

What changes took place within the four work groups which participated in organizational laboratory training relative to any changes that took place within the eight work groups which did not participate in organizational training laboratories—for each of the six group dimensions?

In order to shed light on this question, analyses of covariance (ANCOVA) were performed. In a statistical sense, the procedure tests whether, after training, differences between training groups and non-training groups remain after a statistical adjustment has been made for differences before training. In a sense, the ANCOVA attempts to approximate a situation in which each of the 12 groups is equated before training has occurred (Winer, 1962).

Two separate ANCOVA's were performed on each of the six group dimensions. In the first set, the four training groups were compared with the eight comparison groups. In the second set, the groupings were ignored and changes in the mean of the 31 individuals who participated in training were compared with the changes in the mean of the 60 individuals who did not participate. The results of the two analyses were similar. The extent and direction of change in the four training groups vs. the eight comparison groups are depicted in Figure 1.

It is immediately apparent from Table 1 that group dimensions in which a significant change occurred involved team effectiveness in problem solving (I), mutual influence among group members (III), and member's sense of personal involvement and participation in group meetings (IV). Dimensions where no significant improvement occurred included feelings of approachability toward the chairman (II), intragroup trust and confidence (V), and the general evaluation of group meetings (VI). Thus, a random group which had participated in laboratory training might phrase its perceptions as (1) we now expect and achieve greater participation in group meetings, (2) we now have

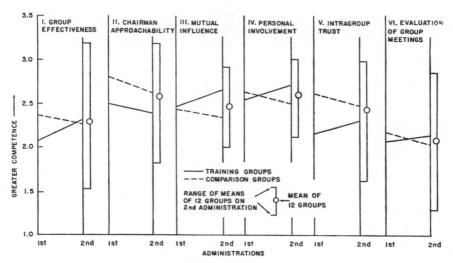

Fig. 1. First and Second Administration Scores on Six Group Dimensions.

greater influence with each other, and (3) we now are a more effective team in solving problems; but (4) our chairman is no more approachable than he was, (5) we are just as much a collection of competitive individuals as we were, and (6) our group meetings are no more worthwhile than they were.

This pattern of change represents some interesting interdimensional relationships. Group effectiveness (I) and evaluation of meetings (VI) might well be considered syntality dimensions in that they are measures of the group acting as a whole. Yet, in only group effectiveness (I) did members of training groups perceive significant change. This might be considered as a change in effective synergy (Cattell, Saunders & Stice, 1953), which is that portion of group energy devoted to attaining group goals. The change also represents perceived improvement in productive performance. As a function of laboratory training, greater team effectiveness was evidently achieved without concomitant increases in evaluation of group meetings (VI). Furthermore, these increases in effective synergy were not supported by similar increases in the maintenance synergy of increased trust and reduced competition (V).

In accordance with the literature in the area of group change and group dynamics, changes in all six of the group dimensions might have been hypothesized. For example, durable modifications in group ideology and social practice are frequently considered in terms of increased mutual influence (III), heightened involvement and participation (IV), and increased trust (or decreased competition) (V) among group members (Lewin, 1947, pp. 330-344; Coch & French, 1948). While the laboratory experience did result in significant increases in mutual influence and participation, no parallel gains in trust were found. The implication

TABLE 1

Comparisons of Relative Gains for Training Members (T) vs. Comparison
Members (C) in Each of Six Group Dimensions by Analysis of Covariance

Group Dimension	Relative Gain[a]		Difference in Gain (T − C)	F-Level[b]	
	Trainees	Comparisons		Individuals	Groups[c]
I. Group Effectiveness	2.40	2.14	.26	5.01*	3.98*
II. Leader Approachability	2.51	2.47	.04	.14	.21
III. Mutual Influence	2.55	2.32	.23	6.53*	4.94*
IV. Personal Involvement	2.64	2.44	.20	7.15**	6.76**
V. Intragroup Trust	2.36	2.34	.02	.03	.00
VI. Evaluation of Meetings	2.09	1.93	.16	1.15	.79

[a]Relative gains are represented by the adjusted means in the ANCOVA. All signs are necessarily positive as a result of the computational method rather than indicating that no decrement occurred.

[b]The F-levels for the column marked "Individuals" indicate the significance of the ANCOVA in which the 31 trainees were compared to the 60 comparison members as *individuals*. The column marked "Groups" indicates the significance of the ANCOVA in which the four training groups were compared to the eight comparison groups. In the latter method, all groups received the same weight regardless of differences in size of membership.

[c]Relative gains for the four training groups and the eight comparison groups are not shown. These were highly similar to relative gains by individuals.

*$p < .05$.

**$p < .01$, $df = 1.88$.

that increased trust is correlated with gains in effectiveness, mutual influence, and participation is not upheld in this study. Similarly, in this study it was found that laboratory training can result in a heightened sense of involvement and participation (IV) despite no significant improvement in members' rapport with their leader (II). Among groups which have participated in training laboratories, the coaction of heightened involvement, participation, and expectations (IV) on the one hand, and reduced leader approachability (II) on the other hand, may lead to the eventual frustration of group members and a declination in their involvement.

The combination of increased mutual influence (III) and greater member involvement (IV) after training participation implies that there is far more interaction among members in the group setting. But this interaction without concurrent improvement in intragroup trust (V) suggests that members are tackling group problems more as a collection of competitive individuals—each utilizing his own skills, rather than an interaction of the unified group—typified by intragroup trust and confidence—drawing upon the total-group competence.

These results, in general, point to the complexity of the training impact upon group members. Concomitant changes in all dimensions do not seem to occur. In particular, group members who have participated in training laboratories perceive themselves as a more effective problem-solving team despite the finding that certain hypothesized changes in the interpersonal processes do not appear to be significantly modified.

Issue 2—Diversity of Impact of Training upon Individuals on Each of the Six Group Dimensions.

What is the impact of training in terms of changes in the ranking of individuals on each of the six group dimensions?
The previous analysis (*Issue 1*) indicated that laboratory experience resulted in significant improvements in group effectiveness (I), mutual influence (III), and personal involvement (IV). That analysis was concerned primarily with changes in *average* group competence in training and control members. However, it is also possible that the impact of laboratory experience has diverse impacts across *individuals* who participate. Hypothetically, if this diversity is such that gains and decrements in group competence (as perceived by each individual) cancel out each other, no *average* change across trainees will have occurred. Yet, it is possible that every individual has changed his perception of his group; i.e., half in a positive direction and half in a negative direction. In order to test this possibility, correlations between pre- and post-scores on each of the six dimensions were computed separately for those who participated in laboratory experience and those who did not.
Correlation coefficients for training members and comparison members, as well as the differences in coefficients for each dimension, are listed in Table 2. The magnitude of the correlation is indicative of the consistency of the rank order of individuals before training as compared to after training. The correlations for control members, in effect, are a measure of the (test-retest) reliabilities of the six dimensions.[2] It is immediately apparent from Table 2 that group members who participated in organizational training laboratories during the six-month period experienced a diversity of impacts, whereas group members who

TABLE 2

Pre- and Post-Correlation Coefficients for Trainee Members and Comparison Members

Group Dimension	Comparisons	Trainees	Difference in Correlation $(C - T)^a$
I. Group Effectiveness	.80	.55	.25*
II. Leader Approachability	.81	.50	.31*
III. Mutual Influence	.71	.54	.17
IV. Personal Involvement	.80	.43	.37**
V. Intragroup Trust	.68	.57	.11
VI. Evaluation of Meetings	.64	.42	.22

[a]Tests of significance were computed after r to z transformations of all correlation coefficients.
*$p < .05$.
**$p < .01$; Comparisons, $N = 60$; Trainees, $N = 31$.

did not participate in such training maintained an unusually stable ranking on the six dimensions. This difference in stability (or change) among individual rankings was significant in the case of group effectiveness (I), leader approachability (II), and personal involvement (IV). Trainees changed significantly more in relative perception of their group on these dimensions than did the comparison members. This diversity is understandable in that laboratory experience can be expected to affect different individuals in different ways; in part as a function of each person's specific needs, and also in his mode of interaction in the training experience. The impact of laboratory experience upon perceptions of mutual influence (III), intragroup trust (V), and evaluation of meetings (VI) was somewhat more consistent when compared to that of comparison members; but no significant differences between trainee and comparison members were found on these dimensions. This seems to be due to less consistency on these dimensions among comparison members rather than to significantly greater consistency among training participants.

In dimensions of group effectiveness (I), mutual influence (III), and personal involvement (IV), it will be remembered that the analysis of *Issue 1* indicated a significant training impact. The results of this section can now be incorporated with the previous analysis to indicate that, although the impacts of training in group effectiveness and mutual influence are diverse across individuals, they are definitely positive in direction. The impact upon mutual influence (III) was significantly positive and consistent.

Finally, in perception of leader approachability (II), no significant changes occurred in the *average* competence of trainees as a result of laboratory experience, but the training impact was significantly diverse to have resulted in a larger number of both positive and negative changes. The .81 correlation for comparison members in perception of leader approachability and the significant decrement in this dimension for comparison members (Figure 1) imply a *deterioration* which is disturbingly consistent across group members who did not participate in laboratory experience.

Issue 3—Possible Biases in the Selection of Training and Control Groups.

Prior to training, did the competence of training groups differ from that of comparison groups?

In a field study of this kind, the researcher obviously has little prerogative in selecting matched groups for training and control purposes. He must generally abide by the decisions of the organizational groups with which he deals. The question then arises as to the similarity of the training and comparison groups for prior to training.

To explore this question, analyses of variance were performed which indicated that the comparison groups had significantly greater competence than the pre-training groups on three of the six group dimensions: group effectiveness (I), approachability of the chairman (II), and intragroup trust (V). These data are indicated in the first three columns of Table 3. Statistical (covariance) methods were used to compensate for these initial differences. However, such methods are not equivalent to experimental methods in which all groups are matched on each dimension prior to training.

Perhaps the more relevant question concerns the reasons for greater competence in the comparison groups (and less competence in the pre-training groups) before training. Note the words "before training," rather than "before the research project"; the administration of the GBI to the comparison groups actually was part of the research project. Obviously it is impossible to measure group adequacy before measuring group adequacy—it would have been neat to have done so, for then some light would have been cast upon the effect of the administration of the GBI.

If the assumption can be made that comparison groups were, in fact, more competent than pre-training groups, then a bias in selection of groups did exist. Such a bias might well be attributed to a selection process in which groups that perceive themselves as less effective gravitate toward training as a mechanism to alleviate procedural and interpersonal inadequacies. If this is the case, then the questionnaire is merely validly reflecting these inadequacies.

An alternative explanation, which incorporates and builds upon the above concepts, suggests that differences between comparison and training groups are artifactual and are due to researcher-participant interactions. It is quite possible that the process of reading, considering,

TABLE 3

Mean Raw Scores in Six Group Dimensions Before and After Research Project
for Four Training Groups and Eight Comparison Groups

Group Dimension	Before Research Project			After Research Project			Changes	
	Train-ees	Com-parisons	T − C	Train-ees	Com-parisons	T − C	Train-ees	Com-parisons
I. Group Effectiveness	2.08	2.35	−.27*	2.31	2.28	.03	.23*	−.07
II. Leader Approachability	2.46	2.78	−.32*	2.37	2.62	−.25*	−.09	−.16**
III. Mutual Influence	2.44	2.40	.04	2.61	2.37	.24*	.17*	−.03
IV. Personal Involvement	2.53	2.57	−.04	2.68	2.51	.17	.15*	−.06
V. Intragroup Trust	2.13	2.58	−.45**	2.25	2.45	−.20	.12	−.13
VI. Evaluation of Meetings	2.04	2.13	−.09	2.08	2.02	.06	.04	−.11

*$p < .05$.
**$p < .01$; Comparisons, $N = 60$; Trainees, $N = 31$.

and responding to items in a questionnaire serves as important stimuli upon each group member, and that the nature of these stimuli differs for pretraining members as opposed to comparison members. For example, in this study pre-trainees (1) had already planned to participate in a training laboratory when they completed the GBI, (2) had therefore considered at least some of the issues raised by the items in the GBI, (3) had hopes that something was going to be done about these issues, and (4) had perhaps reacted with greater acceptance and realism, and with less defensiveness, to the GBI items. Comparison members on the other hand (1) had probably not considered the issues raised by the questionnaire, (2) were informed that they were participating as a comparison group (although the word comparison was not used), (3) had reacted to the lack of previous confrontation and to their label of "comparison group" with a desire and a need to demonstrate the competence of their group to themselves and to the researcher. Furthermore, since no training was planned—nor was any likely to be planned—increased dissonance of the comparison groups would have resulted from their admission to the researcher and to themselves of any inadequacies with no corresponding remedy (laboratory training).

Issue 4—Possible Artifacts in Measuring the Relative Changes of the Training Groups vs. the Comparison Groups.

What changes occurred in the comparison groups when considered separately from the training groups? Did these changes affect measurement of the training impact?

A casual glance at Figure 1 will show that the mean competence for the comparison groups declined on all six dimensions.

Did the significant relative improvements that were found in Issue 1 occur within the training groups only because of this "unfair" comparison with comparison group decrements?

Separate analysis indicates that the apparent decrements of the comparison groups did not differ significantly from a zero change for five of the six dimensions, but a significant decline did occur on the chairman approachability dimension (II) ($p < .01$). For the training groups, gains in dimensions I, III, and IV do differ significantly from zero and thus are of consequence whether compared to the decrement in comparison groups or compared to a zero change.

As mentioned, during the course of a six-month period, the comparison groups declined significantly in the extent to which they perceived their chairman as approachable. This decline presumably occurred as a result of events which took place during the six-month interval. Similar findings of an increase in competence for training groups and a corresponding *decrease* for comparison groups is not uncommon. Miner (1960) reports that supervisors attending a course in psychology showed significant gains in attitude toward the human relations aspects of their jobs, while a control (comparison) group from the same department *evidenced a significant decline.* The author reasons that "the training acted in such a way to ward off or minimize those factors operating to produce an increase in negative attitudes. . . ." In other words, he suggests that *all groups would have declined* in attitude had not training occurred for some groups. This explanation would seem to assume that some negative event had transpired within the context in which *both* training and comparison groups operated, and yet no such event is noted. It is also difficult to explain the decline in chairman approachability (II) in the current study as one which might also occur if divorced from the research project itself. To do so would imply that groups in their natural organizational settings undergo continual deterioration on at least one dimension; that of chairman approachability. Rather, this decline might be viewed as a function of participation by comparison groups in a research project—without their concurrent participation in the corresponding laboratory experience.

In *Issue 3* of this report, the suggestion was offered that the tendency for comparison groups to describe themselves as more adequate in the first administration of the GBI was a function of researcher-participant interactions and the realization that no laboratory training would be forthcoming. But what happened to these auspicious descriptions as the comparison groups reassembled continuously over a six-month period and were confronted recurrently with whatever inadequacies they gradually perceived? Our hypothesis is that the opportunity to express their reactions (concerning the group and its meetings) to the feelings that had been aroused over a six-month period materialized in *the form of the second administration of the GBI.* Prior to the research study, members had an unclear perception of the role of the group leader, or of their expectations of this role as it affected them in terms of chairman approachability. The first administration of the GBI queried comparison group members with blunt questions on sensitive issues which they were unprepared to confront at that time. But after six months of observing those inadequacies which did occur, expectations and standards of the leadership role became clearer. Since current leadership practice did not conform to these expectations, comparison group members now perceived significantly greater inadequacies in the rapport and approachability of their chairman.

DISCUSSION

This study has indicated that significant improvements in effectiveness and interaction processes of work groups do occur as a result of participation in organizational training laboratories. These improvements take place in areas which are of direct personal and organizational relevance to members of the ongoing work groups and endure for a period of at least six months beyond the training experience. The specific problem areas in which significant positive changes occurred were group effectiveness, mutual influence among members, and personal involvement and participation. Those areas which showed no significant changes were leader approachability, intragroup trust, and the evaluation of group meetings. In general, these findings point to the complexity of the impact of organizational training laboratories upon ongoing work groups.

A further analysis has indicated that training participation not only has an impact upon the work group as a unit, but also upon individuals (relative to each other) within the group. Changes in perceptions of those individuals who participated in training laboratories were more diverse over the six-month period than were the changes of perceptions of those who did not participate. Although the diversity in change was apparent on all six dimensions, it was statistically significant in group effectiveness, leader approachability, and personal involvement.

Several questions were raised as a result of some of the unforeseen findings of this study. It was noted that groups which did not participate in training were significantly more competent than training groups on several dimensions *prior to the training.* This difference may be attributed to the training selection process in which groups that perceive themselves as less competent gravitate toward training. An alternative hypothesis is that pre-training differences were due to researcher-subject interactions. It was suggested that comparison group members were not playing the role assigned to them by the researcher (Back, Hood & Brehm, 1964). Rather, they reacted to the first administration of the GBI with a need to demonstrate the competence of their group to themselves and to the researcher. Comparison and training groups differed in this respect in that the former experienced no previous confrontation of the issues raised in the GBI, nor could they expect any remedy for an admission to work group problems.

NOTES

1. The term "comparison group," rather than the experimental psychologist's term "control group," is used throughout this paper since there is virtually nothing controlled in these eight groups. While it is true that they did not participate in a planned training experience, it is also likely that many events occurred in the eight groups during this period which had a positive or negative impact upon characteristics relevant to this study. Perhaps the term "control group," as used by the field-researcher, is a soothing misnomer which tends to gloss over a myriad of variables that might otherwise be quite relevant.
2. Of the first six factors, the test-retest reliabilities of scales V and VI are somewhat low. However, since the six-month interval is longer than usual for test-retest reliabilities and since the internal consistency reliability of these scales is relatively high, the reliabilities are viewed as acceptable.

REFERENCES

BACK, K. W., HOOD, T. C., and BREHM, MARY L. *The Subject Role in Small Group Experiments.* Durham, N.C.: Duke University, 1964.

BENNIS, W. G. "A New Role for the Behavioral Sciences: Effecting Organizational Change." *Administrative Science Quarterly,* VIII (1963), 125-165.

BENNIS, W. G., BENNE, K. D., and CHIN, R. (Editors) *The Planning of Change.* New York: Holt, Rinehart, and Winston, 1962.

CATTELL, R. B., SAUNDERS, B. R., and STICE, G. F. "The Dimensions of Syntality in Small Groups." *Human Relations,* VI (1953), 331-356.

COCH, L. and FRENCH, J. R. P. "Overcoming Resistance to Change." *Human Relations,* I (1948), 512-532.

FLEISHMAN, E. A., HARRIS, E. F., and BURTT, H. E. *Leadership and Supervision in Industry.* Columbus: Bureau of Educational Reserch, Ohio State University, 1955.

FRIEDLANDER, F. "Performance and Interactional Dimensions of Organizational Work Groups." *Journal of Applied Psychology,* L (1966), 257-265.

HARRISON, R. "Evaluations and Conclusions." In C. Argyris, *Interpersonal Competence and Organizational Effectiveness.* Homewood, Ill.: Richard D. Irwin, Inc., 1962.

LEWIN, K. "Group Decision and Social Change." In T. Newcomb and E. Hartley (Editors), *Readings in Social Psychology.* New York: Henry Holt, 1947.

LIPPETT, R. *Training in Community Relations.* New York: Harper & Brothers, 1949.

MANN, F. C. "Study and Creating Change." In W. G. Bennis, K. D. Benne, and R. Chin (Editors), *The Planning of Change.* New York: Holt, Rinehart, and Winston, 1962.

MINER, J. B. "The Effect of a Course in Psychology on the Attitudes of Research and Development Supervisors." *Journal of Applied Psychology,* XLIV (1960), 224-232.

RIECKEN, H. *The Volunteer Work Camp: A Psychological Evaluation.* Cambridge, Mass.: Addison-Wesley Publishing Co., 1952.

SANFORD, N. "Will Psychologists Study Human Problems?" *American Psychologist,* XX (1965), 192-202.

SHEPARD, H. "An Action Research Model." In Esso Standard Oil Company. *An Action Research Program for Organizational Improvement.* Ann Arbor, Mich.: Esso Standard Oil Company, Foundation for Research on Human Behavior, 1960.

STOCK, DOROTHY and THELAN, H. *Emotional Dynamics and Group Culture.* Washington, D.C.: National Training Laboratories, 1958.

WINER, B. J. *Statistical Principles in Experimental Design.* New York; McGraw-Hill, 1962.

ROLE NEGOTIATION: A TOUGH MINDED APPROACH TO TEAM DEVELOPMENT

Roger Harrison

Behavioural science approaches to business have tended to focus on *alternatives* to power and politics in management and decision making, rather than directly upon the influence process. In the United States, for example, the sensitivity training approach has had quite a vogue. Managers are encouraged to abandon competitiveness and manipulation of one another in favour of open discussion of feelings, collaboration based on mutual trust, and egalitarian approaches to decision making. Various techniques (the T group, the Managerial Grid) have been developed to bring about these changes.

In other approaches managers have been urged to change the motivational system, moving from reliance upon monetary rewards and punishments towards the development of more internal motivation based upon intrinsic interest in the job, and personal commitment to meeting work objectives. Examples are programmes of job enrichment and Management by Objectives. Still other practitioners have developed purely rational approaches to group problem solving (for example, Kepner Tregoe in the United States, and Coverdale in Britain).

In these approaches competition, conflict and the struggle for power and influence tend to be explained away or ignored. They assume people will be collaborative and productive if they are taught how or if the barriers to their doing so are removed. These approaches may be called *tender minded* in that they see power struggle as a symptom or a managerial *mistake* rather than as a basic and ubiquitous process in organizations. The problem of organizational change is seen as one of *releasing* human potential for collaboration and productivity, rather than as one of controlling or checking competition for advantage and position.[1]

Consider some examples of problems with which I have met in my own consulting practice.

A product centered system has been installed by a company which is organized along traditional functional lines. The Product Group includes representatives from the relevant functional Divisions (Sales, Marketing, Production, Engineering, Research, etc.). One group meets under the chairmanship of a Product Manager to review the commercial performance of the product and to plan capital expenditure, cost and production targets, pricing and marketing strategy. In practice, however, some of the Product Managers call very few meetings and prepare the Product Plans without much input or consultation from the functional members of the Group. The latter feel they have insufficient influence over the final target figures which they are called upon to meet and that the figures are frequently "unrealistic". Their performance frequently falls short of the target.

The Production and Engineering Managers of a works have frequent disagreements over the work that is done by the latter for the former. The Production Manager complains that the Engineering Manager sets maintenance priorities to meet his own convenience and reduce his own costs, rather than to make sure production targets are met. The Engineering Manager maintains that the Production Manager gives insufficient notice of jobs which can be foreseen, and that the Production operators cause unnecessary breakdowns by failure to carry out preventive maintenance procedures faithfully. The two men have aired their dissatisfactions with one another's performance from time to time, but both agree that no significant change has occurred.

A scientist in a Development Department complains of overly close supervision by his Section Manager. The Manager is said by the scientist to intervene to change the priorities that he assigns to work, to interfere with his development of promising lines of enquiry, and to check up with insulting frequency to see that his is carrying out the Manager's instructions. The scientist is actively trying to get a transfer to another Section, because he feels he cannot do a proper job with so much hampering inter-ference from above. When interviewed, the Section Manager says the scientist does competent work but is secretive and unwilling to listen to advice. He fails to let the Manager know what he is doing and deviates without discussion from agreements the Manager thought they had about how the work would be carried out. The Manager feels he has to spend far too much time checking up on the scientist and is beginning to wonder when his otherwise good work is worth the trouble which is required to manage him.

Each of these examples describes a problem involving the power and influence of one person or group over the activities of another. In each one, the objective of one or both parties is to gain increased control over the actions of the other, reduce control by the other over his own activities, or both at once. What is more, the participants themselves see the problem as one of influence and power. A consultant might tell them that their trouble was one of communication, or objective setting, or rational problem solving, and they would listen politely and perhaps try the approach suggested by the expert. But in their hearts they would still feel it was a question of who was going to have the final say, who was going to be boss.

Although my own development as a consultant was very much in the tender minded tradition, I have increasingly come to feel that these managers are right. My growing conviction is that my clients have a more accurate mental map of the forces affecting them in their organizational lives than do my academic colleagues. This map usually charts power and influence, and whether people are on their side or against them. On the map are indications as to whom one can be open and honest with, and who will use the information against one. My clients do not chart an organizational world which is safe for openness, collaboration, creativity and personal growth.

I do not mean to imply that the more optimistic behavioural science approaches to business are so naive as to claim the world is quite safe for the processes they try to promote. What I am concerned about is the failure to work with the forces which *are* in ascendance. In this paper I shall present a modest programme for working with human problems in organizations which does work directly with issues of power, competitiveness and coercion. The use of this method also involved an attempt to work from the clients' views of their problems and situations without making assumptions in advance about what their "real" needs are. This programme is based on "Role Negotiation," a technique which I have found useful in resolving differences and conflicts between managers and subordinates, between coworkers, and between different groups in an organization.

The name of the technique describes the process, which involves changing by means of negotiation with other interested parties the *role* which an individual or group performs in the organization. By an individual or group's *role* I mean the work arrangements he has with the others: what activities he is supposed to perform, what decisions he can make, to whom he reports and about what and how often, who can legitimately tell him what to do and under what circumstances, and so on. Some people would say that a man's *job* is the same as what I have called his *role*, and I would partially agree with this. But what I mean by *role* includes not only the formal job description, but also all the informal understandings, agreements, expectations and arrangements with others which determine the way one person's or group's work affects or fits in with another's.

The basic approach of Role Negotiation has been successfully used with a wide variety of situations and clients: for example, a top management work team, a small teaching faculty, a large group of school administrators, superior/subordinate pairs, a special project team, etc. It has even proven useful in working with marital disagreements between husbands and wives, and I have come to regard it as a more or less universal tool for conflict resolution. The technique can be used with very small or quite large groups, although it is well to break down into subgroups if the size is over eight to ten. I have administered the technique with 50 or 60 people at one time, where they worked in smaller units which brought together those people who had the most to do with each other on the job.

The technique makes one basic assumption: *that most people prefer a FAIR NEGOTIATED SETTLEMENT TO A STATE OF UNRESOLVED CONFLICT*, and that they are willing to invest some time and make some concessions in order to achieve a solution. To operate the programme a modest but significant risk is called for from the participants: they must be open about what changes in behaviour, authority, responsibility, etc. they wish to obtain from others in the situation. If the participants take the risk asked of them and specify concretely the changes desired on the part of others, then significant changes in work effectiveness can usually be obtained. I shall describe below a series of steps in this programme. For the sake of illustration, we shall assume that a consultant is working with a work group of five to seven people which includes a manager and his subordinates, two levels in the formal organization.

Preparation

It goes almost without saying that no interference into the work relationships of a group or organization will be very successful unless the participants have confidence in the motives and competence of the consultant and are therefore willing at his behest to try something new and a bit strange. It also stands to reason that the consultant should know enough about the people, their work system and their relationship problems to satisfy himself that the members of the group are ready to make a real effort towards improvement. No technique will work if the clients don't trust the consultant enough to give it a fair try or if the members of the group (particularly the high influence members) devote most of their effort to maintaining the status quo. In what follows I am assuming that this confidence and readiness to work have been established. I realise that this is a rather large assumption, but these problems are universal in consulting and not peculiar to Role Negotiation. If anything, I have found that Role Negotiation requires somewhat less preparation than other team development techniques I have used.

Time and Place

If these basics are out of the way, then I try to get at least a day with the group away from the job location to get the role negotiation process under way. I have conducted half day exercises, but they were more in the nature of demonstrations than actual working sessions. A two day session with a commitment to follow up in three to four weeks is about optimum. If the group is not felt to be quite prepared to undertake serious work, the session may be made longer with some trust building and diagnostic activities in the beginning working into the Role Negotiation when and if the group is ready for it.

The Consulting Contract

The first step in the actual Role Negotiation is *contract setting*. Its purpose is to get clear between the group and the consultant what each may expect from the other. This is a critical step in the change process. It controls and channels everything which happens afterwards. I work towards a contract with the following provisions which it is helpful to get written down as a first practise step in the rather formal way of working which I try to establish.

1. It is not legitimate for the consultant to press or probe anyone's *feelings*. We are concerned about work: who does what, how and with whom. How people *feel* about their work or about others in the group is their own business, to be introduced or not according to their own judgment and desire. The expression or nonexpression of feelings is not part of the contract.
2. Openness and honesty about behaviour is expected and is essential for the achievement of results. This means that the consultant will probe for people to be specific and concrete in expressing their expections and demands for the behaviour of others. Each team member is expected to be open and specific about what he wants others to do *more* or *do better* or *do less* or *maintain unchanged*.
3. No expectation or demand is adequately communicated until it it has been *written down* and is clearly understood by both sender and

receiver, nor will any change process be engaged in until this has been done.

4. The full sharing of expectations and demands does not constitute a completed change process. It is only the precondition for change to be agreed through negotiation. It is unreasonable for anyone in the group, manager or subordinate, to expect that any change will take place merely as a result of communicating a demand or expectation. Unless a team member is willing to change his own behaviour in order to get what he wants from the other(s), he is likely to waste his and the group's time talking about the issue. When a member makes a request or demand for changed behaviour on the part of another, the consultant will always ask what *quid pro quo* (something for something) he is willing to give in order to get what he wants. This goes for the manager as well as for the subordinates. If the former can get what he wants simply by issuing orders or clarifying expectations from his position of authority, he probably does not need a consultant or a change process.

5. The change process is essentially one of bargaining and negotiation in which two or more members each agree to change behaviour in exchange for some desired change on the part of the other. This process is not complete until the agreement can be *written down* in terms which include the agreed changes in behaviour and make clear what each party is expected to give in return.

6. Threats and pressures are neither illegitimate nor excluded from the negotiation process. However, group members should realise that over-reliance on threats and punishment usually results in defensiveness, concealment, decreased communication and retaliation, and may lead to breakdown of the negotiation. The consultant will do his best to help members to accomplish their aims with positive incentives wherever possible.

During the discussion of the contract, I try to help participants see that each member has power and influence in the group, both positively to reward and collaborate with others, and negatively to resist, block or punish. Each uses his power and influence to create a desirable and satisfying work situation for himself. When this process takes place covertly, people often use a lot of time and energy in it unproductively. It is unproductive because people are unsure about others' desires and intentions. This makes it difficult to judge how a particular action will be responded to. We often judge others' wants and needs as though they were like our own. We "do unto others as we would would have them do unto us", and because they are not in all respects like us, our ignorance results in ineffectiveness. We make guesses about how others will respond to our attempts to influence their behaviour, and when the guesses are wrong, we have no option other than to continue the laborious process of trial and error, slowly building up our knowledge of what is and is not effective with each other person through a clumsy and not very systematic experimentation.

In stable, slowly changing organizational situations, this trial and error process may be satisfactory, because people do learn how to influence one another given a sufficient period of contact. When situations and personnel change more rapidly (over periods of months rather than years), then this most primitive learning process does not do the job fast enough. The more fluid the system, the more important it is to develop information rapidly which will permit people to influence one another effectively. I try to help my clients to see that if information about desires and intentions is equally shared, then they will *all* increase the effectiveness of their influence attempts. Then, when others try to influence them the proffered *quid pro quo* will be more likely to be one which they really want and need. The Role Negotiation is not only intended to have the effect of resolving current problems but also of increasing knowledge within the group of how effectively to influence one another. The intended effect is that the *total amount of influence of group members on one another should increase.* The consultant will so conduct himself that opportunities to increase one's influence within the system are as nearly equal as possible.

Diagnosis

The next stage is *issue diagnosis.* I ask each member to spend some time thinking about the way business is conducted between himself and the others in the group. What things would he change if he could? What things would he like to keep as they are? Who and what would have to change in order to improve things? In thinking about these things, I ask the members to focus especially on the things which might be changed to improve their *own effectiveness,* as these are the things I shall ask them to discuss and negotiate.

After they have spent twenty minutes or so thinking about these matters and perhaps making a few notes, I ask each member to take a set of Issue Diagnosis Forms like the one in Exhibit 1. He is to fill out one Issue Diagnosis Form for each other member, listing those things he would like to see the other person

1. do more or do better;
2. do less or stop doing;
3. keep on doing, maintain unchanged.

All of these messages are to be keyed to increasing the sender's own effectiveness in doing his own job.

These lists are exchanged so that each person has all the lists which pertain to his work behaviour. Each member makes a master list for himself on a large piece of (flip chart) paper on which he shows the behaviour which each other person desires him to do *more* or *better, less* or *continue unchanged* (Exhibit 2). These are posted so that the entire group can peruse and refer to each list. Each member is allowed to question the others who have sent messages about his behaviour, querying the what? why? and how? of their requests, but no one is allowed a rebuttal, defence or even a yes or no reply to the messages he has received. The consultant intervenes in the discussion to make sure that only clarification is taking place and that argument, discussion and decision making about issues is not engaged in at this stage.

The purpose of this rather rigid and formal control on communication by the consultant is to make sure that the group does not have a negative problem solving experience and that members do not get polarized on issues or take up extreme positions which they will feel impelled to defend in order to save face. Communication is controlled in order to prevent escalation of actual or potential conflicts. The strategy is to channel the energy which has been generated or released by the sharing of demands and expectations into successful problem solving and mutual influence. The consultant intervenes to inhibit hostile and destructive expression at this point and later to facilitate constructive bargaining and negotiation of mutually beneficial agreements. This initial sharing of desires and change goals leads to a point at which the team development process is most vulnerable, because if sufficient anger and defensiveness are generated by the problem sharing, the consultant will not be able to hold the negative processes in check long enough for the development of the positive problem solving spiral on which the process depends for its effectiveness. It is true that such an uncontrollable breakthrough of hostility has not yet occurred in my experience with the method. Nevertheless, concern over the negative posibilities is in part responsible for my slow, deliberate and rather formal development of the confrontation of issues within the group.

Negotiation

After each member has had an opportunity to clarify the messages he has received, the group proceeds to the selection of issues for negotiation. The consultant begins this phase by reemphasizing that unless a *quid pro quo* can be offered in return for a desired behaviour change, there is little point in having a discussion about it: *unless behaviour changes on both sides the most likely prediction is that the status quo will continue.* (It can be argued that this is an extremely conservative point of view and that behaviour does in fact change between men of good will simply as a result of an exchange of views. While I do not deny that this occurs, I do not assume it in my practice and I allow myself to be pleasantly surprised when it happens!)

Each participant is asked to indicate one or more issues on which he particularly wants to get some change on the part of another. He is also asked to select one or more issues on which he feels it may be possible for him to move in the direction desired by others. He does this by marking his own flip chart and those of the other members. In effect, each person is indicating the issues upon which he most wants to exert influence and those on which he is most willing to accept influence. With the help of the consultant the group then goes through the lists to select the "most negotiable issues", those where there is a combination of a high desire for change on the part of an initiator and a willingness to negotiate on the part of the person whose behaviour is the target of the change attempt. The consultant asks for a group of two or more persons who are involved in one such issue to volunteer for a negotiation demonstration before the rest of the group.

The negotiation process consists of the parties making contingent offers to one another of the form, "if you do X, I will do Y." The negotiation ends when all parties are satisfied that they will receive a reasonable return for whatever they are agreeing to give. The consultant asks that the agreement be formalized by writing down specifically and concretely what each party is going to give and receive in the bargain (Exhibit 3). He also asks the participants to discuss openly what sanctions can be applied in the case of nonfulfilment of the bargain by one or another party. Often this involves no more than reversion to the status quo, but it may involve the application of pressures and penalties as well.

After the negotiation demonstration the members are asked to select other issues they wish to work on. A number of negotiations may go on simultaneously, the consultant being involved at the request of any party to any negotiation. All agreements are published to the entire group, however, and questioned by the consultant and the other members to test the good faith and reality orientation of the parties in making them. Where agreement proves impossible, the consultant and other group members try to help the parties find further incentives (positive or, less desirably, coercive) which they may bring to bear to encourage agreement.

This process is, of course, not so simple as the bare bones outlined here. All kinds of difficulties can occur, from bargaining in bad faith, to refusal to bargain at all, to escalation of conflict. In my experience, however, group members tend to be rather wise about the issues they can and cannot deal with, and I refrain from pushing them to negotiate issues they feel are unresolvable. My aim is to create a beginning to team development with a successful experience which group members will see as a fruitful way of improving their effectiveness and satisfaction. I try to go no further than the members feel is reasonable.

Follow Up

At the conclusion of a team development cycle as outlined above, I suggest that the group test the firmness of the agreements they have negotiated by living with them a while before trying to go further. We can then get together later to review the agreements, renegotiate ones which have not held or which are no longer viable, and continue the team development process by dealing with new issues. Hopefully, the group will eventually take over the conduct of the Role Negotiation activity and the consultant's role will wither away. This can occur when the group has developed sufficient control over the dangers, avoidances and threats involved in the negotiation process that they no longer need third party protection or encouragement. However, I do not claim any unusual success in freeing clients from dependence on my services. What I do find is that there is less backsliding between visits in teams I have worked with using this method than when I have applied more interpersonally oriented change interventions. The agreements obtained through Role Negotiation seem to have more "teeth" in them than those which rely on the softer processes of interpersonal trust and openness.

The Dynamics of Role Negotiation

Role Negotiation intervenes directly into the relationships of power, authority and influence within the group. The change effort is directed at the work relationships among members. It avoids probing into the likes and dislikes of members for one another and their personal feelings about one another. In this it is more consonant with the task oriented norms of business than are most other behavioural approaches. I have found that groups with whom I have had difficulty working when I focused on interpersonal issues dropped their resistance and turned willingly to problem solving when I shifted my approach to Role Negotiation.

When I first developed the technique, I tried it out on a client group which was proving particularly hard to work with. They were suspicious and mistrustful of me and of each other and said quite openly that talking about their relationships was both "irrelevant to our work problems" and "dangerous; it could split the group apart". When I introduced Role Negotiation to them they saw ways they could deal with things which were bothering them without getting into touchy emotional confrontations they could not handle. They dropped their resistance dramatically and turned to work with a will which surprised and delighted me.

I have repeated this experience more than once. Clients seem more at home with problems of power and influence than they do with interpersonal issues. They feel more competent and less dependent upon the skill and trustworthiness of the consultant in dealing with these issues and so they are ready to work sooner and harder. I also find my own skill not so central to the change process as it is when I am dealing with interpersonal issues. The amount of skill and professional training which is required to conduct Role Negotiation is less than for more sensitive approaches.

That is not to say that Role Negotiation poses no threat to organization members. The consultant asks participants to be open about matters which are often covert in normal life. This requires more than the normal amount of trust and confidence. If it did not, these matters would have been talked about before the group ever got to the Role Negotiation.

There seems also to be some additional discomfort involved in *writing down* the changes one would like to see another make in his work behaviour. Several times clients have questioned the necessity of doing this, and I suspect that some have avoided Role Negotiation altogether because this aspect made them uneasy. It is perhaps that one feels so *exposed* when his concerns are written out for all to see, and there is the fear that others will think them silly, childish or odd (though this never seems to happen). If the matter comes up, I point out that one need not write down *all* concerns he has, but only those he would like to work on with others at this time.

Of course, Role Negotiation threatens people in one basic way it shares with any other process which really changes relationships. People are never quite sure they will personally be better off after the change than before. In the case of Role Negotiation, most of these fears are around losing power and influence, or losing freedom and becoming more controlled by others. There is particular resistance to talking openly about issues where one is trying for his own advantage to manipulate another, or when he feels that he might want to do this in the future. I think this is the main reason clients in Role Negotiation so often try to avoid the step of writing down their agreements. They feel if things aren't down in black and white it will be easier later on to ignore the agreement if it becomes inconvenient. Also, writing down agreements is contrary to the aura of trust and good fellowship which some groups like to create on the surface and under cover of which they engage in quite a lot of cutthroat competition.

Role Negotiation is of course no panacea for power problems in groups and between people. People may bargain in bad faith; agreements once reached may be broken; circumstances and personnel may change so that the work done becomes irrelevant. About all that can be said in reply is that these problems can exist in any group or organization. What Role Negotiation does is to try to deal with the problems directly and to identify and use constructively those areas of *mutual* advantage where both sides can benefit from discussion and agreement. These areas are almost always larger than people think they are, and when they find that they can achieve something *for themselves* by open negotiation which they could not achieve by covert competition, then the more constructive process can begin to grow.

The Economics of Role Negotiation

One disadvantage of most behavioural approaches to team development is that the level of skill and experience demanded of the consultant is very high indeed. Managers are not confident in dealing with these issues. Because they feel at risk they reasonably want to have as much safety and skill as money can buy. The demand for skilled consultants on inter-personal and group processes has created a shortage and a meteoric rise in consulting fees. It seems unlikely that the supply will soon catch up with the demand.

The shortage of highly skilled workers in team development argues for deskilling the requirements for effective consultant performance. I see Role Negotiation as a way of reducing the skill requirements for team development consultation. Preliminary results by internal consultants using the approach have been promising. For example, one Management Development Manager teamed up with a colleague to conduct a successful Role Negotiation with his own top management. He reported that the main problem was getting up the confidence to take on the job. The team development session itself went smoothly. I cannot say whether this experience was typical; I suspect it was not. It does lead me to hope that Role Negotiation will prove to be practical for use by internal consultants without professional training in the behavioural sciences.

Summary

The following comments highlight the aspects of Role Negotiation which I believe commend it for use in team development and other face to face consulting situations in business.

Role Negotiation focuses on work relationships: what people do, and how they facilitate and inhibit one another in the performance of their jobs. It encourages participants to work with problems using words and concepts they are used to using in business. It avoids probing to the deeper levels of their feelings about one another unless this comes out naturally in the process.

Role Negotiation deals directly with problems of power and influence which may be neglected by other behavioural approaches. It does not attempt to dethrone the authority in the group, but other members are helped to explore realistically the sources of power and influence available to them.

Also in contrast to some other behavioural approaches to team development, Role Negotiation is highly action oriented. Its aim is not just the exposing and understanding of issues as such, but the achievement of commitment to changed ways of working through mutually negotiated agreements. Changes achieved through Role Negotiation thus tend to be more stable and lasting than where such a commitment procedure is lacking.

All the procedures of Role Negotiation are clear and simple if a bit mechanical, and can be described to clients in advance so they know what they are getting into. There is nothing mysterious about the technique, and this reduced clients' feelings of dependency upon the special skill of the consultant.

Role Negotiation actually requires less skill from the consultant than some other behavioural approaches. I believe it is suitable for use without lengthy special training by internal consultants who are not themselves behavioural scientists. It can therefore be a moderate cost approach to organization change.

One final comment on the relationship between Role Negotiation and other behavioural approaches is in order. As mentioned above, my own development as a consultant was in the tradition of sensitivity training and other "soft" approaches to organization change. I believed then and still do that work groups can be effective and achievement oriented and at the same time can support open and deeply satisfying interpersonal relationships among the members. What I do not now believe is that approaches at the interpersonal level can work well unless the ever present issues of power and influence are first resolved to a reasonable level of satisfaction for the members. Role Negotiation was not designed as a substitute for interpersonal approaches, but rather to fill this gap and provide a sound and effective base upon which to build more satisfying relationships. As a first or "basic" approach to team development, I think it is more appropriate than the more interpersonally focused methods. But I would hope that client groups would develop that commitment to their own growth and development which will eventually move them beyond Role Negotiation into deeper exploration of their own creative potential for integrating work and relationship.

EXHIBIT 1

Issue Diagnosis Form

MESSAGES FROM **Jim Farrell**   TO **David Sills**

1. IF YOU WERE TO DO THE FOLLOWING THINGS *MORE* or *BETTER*, IT WOULD HELP ME TO INCREASE MY OWN EFFECTIVENESS.
    "Be more receptive to improvement suggestions from the Process Engineers.
    Give *help* on cost control (see 2).
    Fight harder with the G.M. to get our plans improved."
2. IF YOU WERE TO DO THE FOLLOWING THINGS *LESS*, OR WERE TO *STOP* DOING *THEM*, IT WOULD HELP ME TO INCREASE MY OWN EFFECTIVENESS.
    "Acting as judge and jury on cost control.
    Checking up frequently on small details of the work — asking for so many detailed progress reports."
3. THE FOLLOWING THINGS WHICH YOU HAVE BEEN DOING HELP TO INCREASE MY EFFECTIVENESS, AND I HOPE YOU WILL CONTINUE TO DO THEM.
    "Passing on full information in our weekly meetings.
    Being available when I need to talk to you."

EXHIBIT 2

Summary of Messages to James Farell from other Group Members

MORE OR BETTER	LESS OR STOP	CONTINUE AS NOW
Give information on project progress completion date slippage — Bill, Tony, David.	Let people go to other good job opportunities — stop hanging on to your good engineers — Tony, Bill.	Training operators on preventive maintenance — Henry.
Send progress reports on Sortair project — Bill.	Missing weekly planning meetings frequently — Jack, Henry, David.	Good suggestions in meetings — Tony, Henry.
Make engineers more readily available when help needed — Jack, Henry.	Ignoring memos and reports re cost control — David.	Asking the difficult and awkward questions — Tony, Jack.

EXHIBIT 2 (Continued)

MORE OR BETTER	LESS OR STOP	CONTINUE AS NOW
Keep better informed re plans and activities — David.	Setting aside my priorities on engineering work — Henry, Jack	Willingness to help on design problems — Bill, Jack.
Enforce safety rates on engineers when in Production area — Henry.	Charging time on Sortair to other accounts — David.	Good quality project work — Bill, Henry, David, Jack.
Push harder for the Sensitex project — David, Henry, Tony, Jack.	Over-running agreed project budget without discussing beforehand — David.	

EXHIBIT 3

Final Written Agreement between James Farell and David Sills

Jim agrees to let David know as soon as agreed completion dates and cost projections look as though they won't be met, and also to discuss each project's progress fully with David on a biweekly basis.

In return David agrees not to raise questions about details and completion dates, pending a trial of this agreement to see if it provides sufficient information soon enough to deal with questions from above.

NOTES

1. Of course this is not true of all behavioural approaches without exception. One in particular which has influenced my own thinking in the development of role Negotiation is the Confrontation Meeting developed by Richard Beckhard some years ago.

SECTION III

MANAGING CONFLICT

EDITORS' OVERVIEW

Social conflict cannot be treated with indignation, as something that should not happen. It cannot be submerged under polite conversation, and it cannot be legislated against. To deal effectively with social conflict we need to understand its dynamics and to develop appropriate social technology.

In this section several techniques for conflict management will be examined. Readers should recognize that the term "conflict management" is not meant to be synonymous with "conflict elimination." The latter is a Sisyphean goal, and even if it were not, it would still be an undesirable one. Conflict has functional as well as dysfunctional consequences. It is an inevitable and necessary feature of organizational life. This section includes an examination of social technology which can *transform* conflict from a deadly and destructive process to a lively and constructive one.

Understanding the dynamics of social conflict is an essential prerequisite to diagnosing conflict and selecting an appropriate social intervention. For additional reading on the dynamics of social conflict, readers are referred to Deutsch (1965) and Walton and McKersie (1965). Deutsch has identified several characteristic differences between cooperative and competitive relationships that alter the way in which conflict is resolved: differences in—

1. Communication (open and honest in cooperative relationships, withholding and misleading in competitive ones).
2. Perception (Persons in a cooperative relationship tend to focus on their similarities and common interests and to minimize their differences; those in a competitive relationship focus on differences and threats and minimize similarity. Also, when persons are competitively linked, they tend to perceive one another's behavior as malevolently, rather than benevolently, intended. The opposite is true with cooperative relationships.)
3. Attitudes toward one another (trusting and willing to risk in cooperative relationships, suspicious and guarded in competitive ones).
4. Task orientation (In cooperative relationships people tend to (a) define *conflicting interests* as mutual problems requiring collaborative solution, (b) recognize the legitimacy of each other's views, (c) limit conflict size, and (d) limit influence attempts to persuasion and other "legitimate" means of conflict resolution. In competitive relationships people tend to (a) define conflicting interests as insoluble, except by a win-lose outcome, (b) minimize the legitimacy of each other's views, (c) expand the conflict size, thereby increasing the emotional involvement as well as the commitment to defeating the other, (d) use influence attempts such as threat, coercion, oppression, and other "extra-legal" means of conflict resolution.)

The articles in this section describe several techniques that can be used to lessen the costly consequences of social conflict. They fall into two groups. First are the techniques for managing the *processes* of conflict, including protagonists' feelings, attitudes, and behavior. The first article outlines one such technique, a laboratory in which the two opposing sides, management and union, came together with two behavioral scientists to analyse themselves and their differences. The second paper suggests a wide range of process approaches a manager can take to deal with differences among his subordinates.

The other group of techniques for conflict management, which focuses on *techno-structural conditions* and includes such measures as proposing compromise solutions for the substantive issues, changing protagonists' job descriptions, and submitting to third party analysis (the subject of the final article in this section), is probably the more commonly used in organizations. There are no precise guidelines for determining when to use which approach. Social conflicts rarely, if ever, involve *only* attitudes, perception, and feelings, or *only* goals, priorities, and job demands. Commonly both kinds of problems are involved, or become involved, as time passes. Selecting the appropriate intervention depends upon a good diagnosis, a wide repertoire of conflict management technology, and an OD practitioner's intuition.

REFERENCES

DEUTSCH, M. The effects of cooperation and competition upon group process. In H. Proshansky and B. Seidenberg (Eds.) *Basic Studies in Social Psychology*. New York: Holt, Rinehart & Winston, 1965. Pp. 552-576.

WALTON, R. E. and McKERSIE, R. B. *A Behavioral Theory of Labor Relations*. New York: McGraw-Hill, 1965.

THE UNION-MANAGEMENT INTERGROUP LABORATORY: STRATEGY FOR RESOLVING INTERGROUP CONFLICT

Robert R. Blake, Jane Srygley Mouton and Richard L. Sloma
Scientific Methods, Inc., Austin, Texas

Behavioral science concepts and theories are rapidly finding increased application in business, government, and other organizations and institutions.

The following article is a description of a recent step in applying behavioral science theories and research findings to a concrete organization situation. Described is a systematic approach for confronting the intense intergroup hostility between a management and an international union and moving the relationship toward a sound problem-solving one.

Following a brief description of the setting in which this intergroup situation is embedded, a "blow-by-blow" accounting of the events that occurred during a Union-Management Intergroup Laboratory is presented. The attitudes, assumptions, values, misunderstandings, and goals of each group are brought into bold relief as they jointly examine their present relationship. Through a series of systematic steps, the two groups, working independently and jointly, examine their relationship in depth. Specific or concrete issues are set aside to focus underlying barriers that are causing eruption of conflict at the surface level.

The Intergroup Laboratory permits groups in conflict to come together to work through tensions and frictions that have built up over an extended period of time. Confrontation at this level permits group representatives to get beneath the issues separating them. Once areas of misunderstanding and sources of tension have been identified and resolved, it is possible for the two groups to more effectively deal with the day-to-day operational problems shared by them.

This is a story about conflict—raw, heated, vengeful conflict. The conflict that is the subject matter of study is the invidious, vitriolic, self-destroying kind too often found in the ongoing lives of unions and management.

How an actual management and an international union came to grips with the intense conflict that existed between them is to be described. In the first part is a sequence-by-sequence account of an actual union-management intergroup laboratory. The quality and character of the intense hostility separating the international and management gradually unfold as the description moves from one sequence of events to the next. Like a surgical instrument, the description lays bare the raw flesh of an intergroup situation that has become malignant through festering win-lose competitiveness. It is not a pretty picture. It is a true one.

The basic design of the intergroup laboratory, which is a prototype of the model used in the present application, has been tested in numerous experimental situations.[1] It is based on behavioral science research regarding intergroup win-lose conflict and cooperative intergroup problem solving. The approach has been tested in a variety of industrial and governmental intergroup conflict settings.

THE BACKGROUND

The background against which this intergroup laboratory took place and certain events preceding it are described before presenting the actual events of the laboratory.

The Setting and Events Leading to the Union-Management Laboratory

The plant employs nearly 1,000 managers and over 3,000 wage and salary personnel. It is one of several locations that make up the complex of a large publicly-owned corporation.

The wage membership is represented by four major unions. The international union involved in the present application is the bargaining agent for a highly specialized and skilled group, representing approximately 10 percent of the total wage force. Membership in this local is 95 percent of those eligible. It has been the certified bargaining unit for 25 years. At present, it is one of two international unions representing wage personnel. The other unions are independent.

A History of Chronic Union-Management Conflict

Chronic long-term hostility typifies the relationship between management and this international local. No one seems to know clearly today how the conflict began. At the time just prior to the introduction of the union-management laboratory, there was no inclination to seek constructive solutions in either the union organization or among managerial personnel. Grievances had been on a steady rise. A rather large number of arbitration cases were pending. Only the financial expense involved in pushing issues through to arbitration had prevented many of the pending grievances from going all the way. Day-by-day frictions between representatives of both groups became sharper and more heated. The last round of contract negotiations had been characterized by accusation and counter-accusation. The eventual contract agreement represented a "no victory" result. Strike threats had become relatively commonplace. The union seemed to be moving in this direction as the basis for trying to achieve what it regarded as its inevitable right.

Origin of the Laboratory

Several events, but one in particular, triggered the union-management laboratory.

Local Plant Improvement Efforts. For a period of three years, the management organization had been engaged in intensive study and application of a laboratory-seminar organization development effort. The strategies and details of the behavioral science laboratory-seminar methods of organization development are presented elsewhere.[2] The significance in this connection is the fact that each member of management participated in such a laboratory-seminar. The curriculum of each laboratory-seminar included an experiment concerned with intergroup conflict and cooperation. Also included was the examination of behavioral science theory regarding the conditions for achieving sound relationships between two groups in conflict.[3]

In later organization improvement steps, management had applied the concepts and methods for conflict resolutions in the work situation. These application steps had brought about the restoration of problem solving between contending groups in a number of settings that involved friction between managerial components. In each of the applications substantial improvement was visible. These successes encouraged management to hope that the concepts and methods might find utility in the international union and management application.

A Decision To Experiment. Hardly a management meeting went by without the "question" of the international union coming up for discussion. Animosity toward the union was visible as management reacted to each new union "move."

An organization development specialist, who was auditing the development effort, was present at one such typical meeting. Following a review of the usual complaint, this specialist intervened with the following questions: "Why not experiment with the situation toward searching out a solution for it? Rather than continually complaining about the unsavory state of affairs, why not try to solve the basic problem rather than search for ways of defending against what you regard as inappropriate union behavior? Why not find ways to get to the root of the problem rather than engage, as you have done, in actions which appear to me to have the purpose of antagonizing the union?"

These questions took management members by surprise. Up to this point, their thinking and planning had been from a win-lose orientation. The intervention served as the basis for considering what the impact of such a union-management laboratory might be and how such consultaton might be brought about.

Acting from the notion that such an effort could do no harm, though with low expectations that it would be of any substantial help, management personnel concluded that it would be worth a try.

Agreement Reached—With Reservations. The assistant general manager arranged a conference between himself and the international business representative. A proposal for the laboratory was discussed. The meeting concluded on the note that the business agent would convey the proposal to the officers of the local for their reactions and decision. He did so. An agreement was reached among union officers to the effect that the other's offer could not properly be turned down, even though they were reluctant to accept it. The reluctance to meet with management stemmed from two sources. One was in the union's conviction that management's intention was "to get them, one way or another." Thus, the question was, How could such a meeting be of any real merit?

The other reluctance on the part of the union stemmed from fear that the proposal might involve some invisible gimmick. They suspected a management strategy that could result in the union's being caught in an even more difficult position. Other sources of reservation included the possibility that the methods involved would result in some kind of brainwashing and "softening up" of the union. Nonetheless, it was agreed that a two-day laboratory should be scheduled.

Union Representatives

Those attending the union-management laboratory to represent the union included the international's business agent; Jones, the local president; Smith, the secretary; the vice-president; and others in the union hierarchy. In all, nine union members participated.

Management Representatives

An equal number of plant management personnel participated. The nine included the assistant general manager, the head of administrative services, the employee relations manager and his field representative, a general foreman, two unit supervisors, and two first-line supervisors.

Participation of Behavioral Scientists

Two behavioral scientists conducted the laboratory. One met with the management group; the other with the union. Both attended all the joint sessions. The behavioral scientists familiarized themselves in advance with the situation of intergroup conflict that existed between the two participating groups.

These, then, are the conditions and background considerations against which the following description is cast. The international union and management came together—tentatively and under conditions of great mutual suspicion—for the purpose of testing each other. There was little real belief in either party's mind that the laboratory would be of any constructive help. On the other hand, there was genuine, unstated hope that they might be able to force the other over into capitulation.

DESCRIPTION OF THE UNION-MANAGEMENT INTERGROUP LABORATORY

Steps in Its Conduct

The eight steps that were involved in the sequence, the content or activity involved in each step, and the amount of time allocated to it are shown in Table 1. Each step will be briefly described, its rationale discussed, and the reactions of both parties reported.[4]

TABLE 1

Sequence of and Time Devoted to the Phases of the Two-Day
Union-Management Intergroup Laboratory

Phase	Activity	Time (Hours)
1	Orientation	½
2	Intragroup development of own image and its image of the other	5
3	Exchange of images across groups	1
4	Clarification of images	2
5	Intragroup diagnosis of present relationship	4
6	Exchange of diagnosis across groups	3
7	Consolidation of key issues and sources of friction	2
8	Planning next steps	1

Phase 1—Orientation of Participants to the Laboratory (½ hr.)

At the outset, management and the union convened in one location for a brief orientation. The behavioral scientists in charge of the laboratory pictured the purpose, ground rules, and background considerations involved.

The senior behavioral scientist began by saying, "The last decade has seen some very important experiments in problem solving between groups that have become locked in an intergroup win-lose orientation. A great deal is now known about intergroup conflict and cooperation. The union-management situation, in particular, is very prone to becoming an intensely hostile, win-lose relationship; although its genuine purpose should be a problem-solving one.

"During these next two days, what we wish to explore are problems that are blocking the relationship—to identify them and, if possible, to plan constructive steps for their elimination.

"Therefore, we are not concerned with issues of bargaining, with specific problems of grievance handling, or with attitudes about problems that currently are under arbitration. Nor are we concerned with personalities, as such. Rather, the key concern will be with the *character* of the relationship between your two groups and with the strategies of the orientations that have characterized the two of you in the past."

It was further emphasized that this two-day intergroup laboratory might be regarded as a first activity in a sequence of events rather than as an interaction which was likely, in and of itself, to bring about a resolution of the differences.

Phase 2—Intergroup Development of Self-Image and Counter-Image (5 hrs.)

Following this brief orientation, the two groups received their initial two-part task assignment. First, each group, meeting separately, was asked to develop a written description—an image—of how it saw itself, particularly in its relationship with the other group. Second, management and the union were each asked to develop an image of how they saw the other group's behavior. As these images emerged, they were to be recorded on large newsprint sheets for use in reporting back when the two groups reconvened.

Rationale for Image Development

Organized groups do have characteristics of behavior and conduct that are visible sometimes only to members themselves. But more frequently, there are characteristics that are more clearly visible to outsiders who observe such groups. The review and exchange on an ingroup level of perceptions of how that group performs—how its behavior is motivated, what its conduct has been, what its intentions, purposes, and goals are—can do much to bring to an explicit level the assumptions, attitudes, and feelings that exist among members. It is likely that these will be areas of behavior which have never previously been exchanged and understood. The very process of doing so, indeed, frequently has been observed to result in ingroup members' coming to recognize that what they *thought* they had in common was not, in fact, widely agreed upon. Group members find it far easier to develop an image of the counter-group than to develop an image of themselves. The conduct, purposes, and so on of the counter-group are seen in the minds of ingroup members in a clearer and more vivid way than are similar aspects of their own group. The development of self-image versus the development of an image of the counter-group constitutes in itself a significant learning experience. Members on either side of the group cleavage are thus made more aware of themselves and of the fact that they, many times, are not clear regrading their own behavior, conduct, intentions, purposes, and goals.

The Union's Reaction to the Task. Union members had great difficulty in understanding the assigned task. Their initial reaction was one of floundering. A false start took them into a discussion of issues surrounding a recently completed bargaining session. The session began by the business agent's exercising strong leadership, with support coming from the union secretary.

After several minutes the behavioral scientist intervened. He redefined the task for them: "The present task is aimed at describing the *character*, the quality, of the relationship—that is, typical behavior and attitudes. The task is *not* to debate technical and legalistic issues."

At the beginning, then, the union did not have the concept of examining the process of behavior—to examine and discuss actions, feelings, and attitudes. Their initial thinking pattern was so deeply ingrained on the *content* side that they, literally, did not have a process orientation. To step back from content to and to take a process approach proved to be very, very tough for the union. Eventually they were able to do so.

The intervention by the behavioral scientist led to a proposal by the secretary who, addressing the business agent, said, "I think we should caucus before we go any further!"

This proposal was interrupted by the behavioral scientist. "Look, if the matters cannot be discussed in my presence, then there is little hope that anything will be achieved in the next two days."

This intervention was followed by several moments of silence. Several union members exchanged glances, but no one spoke. Finally, the business agent began again. Gradually, tediously, the discussion shifted toward a detailed picturing of the union's behavior and attitudes in their relationship with management. Participation became more widely spread among all members.

Management's Approach to the Initial Task. Management launched into this first task with a feeling of confidence. In contrast to the union, management *had* the process orientation. This is not to say that process examination came easy for them but only that after three years of laboratory-seminars they did have the concept.

Management decided to develop its own image first, and here they ran into trouble. Their antagonistic relationship with the union was of such duration and embedded with such intense feelings that discussion of their own image repeatedly slipped into a discussion of the union. They spoke of union personalities. They accused the "clique" in the next meeting-room of being the source of all their frictions. One member of management said, "Basically, the union membership is made up of good, solid citizens. It's a shame five or six power-mad guys are running things for them."

A first-line supervisor said, "I've got some of the best, hard-working guys in the plant under me that are members of this union. We really work together. But I can't even talk with these guys. I just 'see red' and clam up every time I see one of them coming. Jones (the president) began stirring up trouble the day he joined the union. That was 15 years ago. I was president of the union myself at the time."

At this point, the behavioral scientist who was meeting with management intervened. "As I understand it, the plan you set for yourselves was to develop your own image first, and then to develop that of the union. Obviously, you are having difficulty in doing this. Your own image is repeatedly forgotten, and union behavior and personalities keep coming into the picture. Everyone seems to have something he wants to get off his chest. Let me offer this suggestion. You might table your own image for the time being and begin on that of the union. Having done this, you may find it easier to talk about your own behavior.

"Maybe it would be best at this point to summarize what has been said so far and to post it on the newsprint. Again, let me re-emphasize what we said earlier in the general session. The purpose is to identify behavior, actions, feelings, and attitudes as you see them, not to place blame or to locate problems in 'personalities.' "

This intervention caused management to pause and examine how it was working. Black, the employee relations manager, spoke up. "Let's admit it. They are no damn 'angels,' but neither are we. Let's get a mirror up here where we can see ourselves, and let's put down what we see, whether we like it or not."

Someone volunteered to record. The assistant plant manager summarized key points he thought should be in their own image. Management decided to continue with its own image. This time they stuck with it.

Phase 3—Management and the International Exchange Images

Each group presented its self-image for examination by the other group. It also presented its image of the counter-group as the basis for enabling the counter-group to compare its own self-image with its observed characteristics, as seen from the outside.

Rationale

Each group quickly recognizes that the counter-group is more readily able to picture its opposing member than itself. The images evaluated from an ingroup point of view, and from an outgroup point of view, rspectively, many times are grossly different. The sheer contradictions that they contain many times identify the hidden causes for much of the surface antagonism that makes problem solving difficult. The exchange results also in the identification of those areas of behavior and conduct, intentions, purposes, and goals where group members of the two groups do see themselves accurately. These correct perceptions may be intensely negative from the standpoint of establishing sounder intergroup relations. For example, one group may be dead set to maintain warfare. This perception from an outgroup point of view and valid recognition from an ingroup point of view, is sufficient to indicate that the approach to intergroup relationships therapy being involved here is without merit. In other words, where one or both parties are committed to continue fighting, there is then no basis for exploring how mutual problem solving might be achieved. If, on the other hand, the perceptions by the counter-group conform in many respects to those developed on the ingroup plane, and they are not of the kind that insures perpetuation of the conflict, then each group is substantially encouraged that the underpinnings of an improved relationship are present.

Results. It was easier for both management and the union to discover and discuss negative aspects of the other's attitudes and behavior than of their own. On the other hand, the "goodness" of one's own

TABLE 2

"Self" and "Other" Images Developed by Management and the International Union During Phase 2 of the Union-Management Laboratory

Management's Image

Of Itself	By the Union
1. Concerned with running the business effectively	1. . . . . (an issue not considered)
2. We show equal concern for production and people	2. Management is concerned only with production
3. Autonomous, decentralized decision-making body	3. They follow all of headquarters' policies and dictates
4. Want to learn to work better with international	4. Opposed to all organized labor
5. Prefer to deal with independent unions	5. Prefer to deal with independent unions
6. Strive continually to upgrade supervision	6. . . . .
7. Goal is to establish problem-solving relationship with the international	7. Their goal is to drive us out of the plant
8. Maintain flexibility in areas concerning our "rights to manage"	8. Management wants power and control over every aspect of a worker's life— they are "fatherly dictators"
9. We are inconsistent in how we treat independents and the international	9. They treat the independents one way and us another
10. Honest and aboveboard in our dealings	10. They are underhanded and they lie

The Union's Image

By Management	Of Itself
1. Little concern shown for the profit picture of the company	1. Concerned primarily with *people*
2. They are skillful and have intense pride	2. Proud of our craft and skills
3. Controlled by a scheming professional leader and a minority clique	3. We are governed by the will of the total membership
4. Legalistic and rigid in interpreting contract	4. Approach problems and contract with open mind
5. The union pushes every grievance to the point of arbitration. When they want to establish a precedent, they want to arbitrate	5. Do not want to have to arbitrate every grievance. We want to work them out with management
6. They want to prove they can "win"— they don't care what, just so it is something	6. We want good relations and to solve our problems with management
7. They want to co-manage. They want a say in every decision we make	7. We want a voice in those areas that directly concern us
8. The union wants the training of their people back under their control	8. We want joint control of the training and apprenticeship program
9. The union does not communicate internally. Their people don't know what is going on	9. Our people always know what is going on and what important union business is coming up
10. Union is concerned only with seniority. They are not concerned with our problems	10. We want greater consideration for our skills and what we can contribute to the plant

intentions and the "rightness" of one's attitudes came out quite easily. Despite such unevenness, there were areas of agreement in the images and counter-images developed by the two. However, misinterpretations and misunderstandings were frequent and deep. The lists prepared by the two groups are shown in Table 2.

Management's Image of Itself

Management's image of itself stressed especially:

1. We are running an aggressive, competitive, "hard-nosed," growing business.
2. We are competent at managing.
3. We are upgrading our supervision.
4. We are willing to be more fair in dealing with the international, to treat it as well as the (previously favored) independent union; we desire to get to the bottom of this running battle we have been having over the years.
5. We need to prevent loss of power to unions, to preserve our freedom to act, our right to manage things in the best interests of the business.
6. We are fair and honest in meeting our obligations.

Union's Image of Management

The local's business agent spoke for the union. Contrasted with management's self-image, the union's image of management was short, crisp, and to the point. Even then, the major points the union made could have been summed up in one simple statement: "This company is opposed to organized labor in any form, shape, or manner!"

More specifically, the union charged:

1. Management, under pressure from headquarters to cut costs, would like nothing better than to throw out the international.
2. Management gives us a "run around" with every grievance case. You try to make the union look bad by failing to settle. You try to force arbitration because you know we haven't the money to arbitrate every single case.
3. Management is a fatherly dictator. You think you are three stories taller than the worker who really makes this plant run. You want to tell us, as you do children, what is "best" for us.
4. Management took over the apprenticeship program and wrecked it.
5. Management has been chipping away at our membership for the past five years. Wherever possible, you have changed the class and scope of work that used to be under us. More and more work is contracted. You get people from the outside to do our work and pay them a dollar and a half less. You have already run one international out. We are the only sizable one left, and you are trying to starve us out.

6. Production and profits are Number One on your list. They have to be—that is your job, and headquarters won't let you forget it. That's why we have to take steps to keep you from running over our people. You're interested in a man for what you can get out of him.
7. Management is two-faced. In spite of everything headquarters and plant management have said and done, they deny publicly that they are against unions. You try to paint a different picture in the public's eye. From top to bottom, management talks out of both sides of its face at the same time.

Comparison of the Two Views of Management

Already it can be seen that deep differences have come to the surface. However, embedded in these differences are similarities neither party sees, particularly the union with respect to management's image. These differences and similarities will become sharper as we move through the images of the union. At this point, though, the union does not "see" or "hear" of management's interest in people. Yet, like the union, management says it *is* concerned with people. All the weight of the union's interpretation of management is given to management's *production* concerns. And the union sees much of this being "pushed" down from company headquarters. They do not see management as being autonomous—free to deal with the union in any way other than in an anti-union way. The international and management agree on management's past preference for independents. But the international sees this as meaning that management is openly against internationals.

Union's Image of Itself

1. We are people-oriented. That's our job—to see that our workers get a fair shake and everything that is coming to them.
2. We do our work; we are craftsmen; we do a job in the best and most skillful way it can be done; we return a fair day's work for a fair day's pay; we recognize our responsibility to the company and to the community.
3. We would like better relations with the company; that's why we are here today; but if you start to lean on us, we'll push back.
4. We are locally run; unlike management, we don't have to follow a "party line" from headquarters; we don't make decisions without going to our membership. (At this point, management objected that only about 10 percent of members turn out for meetings.)

"I don't know out of what hat you pulled your figures," the union secretary returned, "but our regular attendance is well above that. At the last wage discussion, over 75 percent were there. Our people are always there when something important is going on."

The behavioral scientist suggested at this point, "Both of you are banging at each other and this could go on and on, but no real understanding will come from this. Let's move ahead."

5. The business agent continued: "The union wants more recognition. Management has never given us the recognition our skills and craftsmanship merit. To you, it's just another job. You wouldn't recognize a good piece of work if it were staring you in the face. We contribute a lot to the operations of this plant. And, much more could be contributed by us with half a chance. The international should have a voice in those things that affect our work and our livelihood. We don't want co-management. We want the recognition we deserve, and a chance to contribute."

Management's Image of the Union

1. The union is controlled by a small minority; it doesn't truly represent the membership; the business agent is a career man looking for a higher job in the international; he and a few rabble-rousers keep the membership stirred up; most members don't know what's going on and don't care; they are proud and skilled craftsmen, but are run by a small clique.
2. The union is a tough bargainer; you fight us every step of the way; all you really care about is winning; you don't care what is won, just so it's something; union leaders want to demonstrate to the membership that they are "successful"; you use more force and pressure on us in bargaining than any of the other unions; every point in the contract is given a rigid, legalistic interpretation; you never are willing to compromise.
3. Union rules on seniority hurt the business; we can't move up the men with the best skills.

Comparison of the Two Views of the Union

The union spokesmen see themselves as democratic agents of the membership; management sees the membership as "sound" but misled by union leaders. The union is proud of skillful work but feels management fails to recognize this. The union wants to be more involved in the operations of the plant, and management has expressed the same desire; but neither sees this as a common interest at this point.

A wide gulf separated the union's and management's views of each other at the outset of the laboratory. At this point, there is perhaps even less confidence on both sides, than initially, that the two would be able to achieve any degree of understanding or a resolution of their differences.

There, then, were the "raw materials" participants had to work with during the night and day remaining in the laboratory.

Phase 4—Clarification of Images (2 hrs.)

Each group asked questions of the other to insure understanding of what had been said. The aim was to clarify rather than to belittle or attack.

Rationale

The purpose of this step is to insure that there is a complete and full understanding of the impressions, attitudes, feelings, and facts presented by each group. Less than full understanding can result in continued erroneous thinking concerning the goals, attitudes, and feelings of the other. At this point, interventions by the behavioral scientist can become critical. Frequently, without an outside observer to focus what is taking place, it is easy for the discussion to slip into one of charges and countercharges as each side seeks to defend itself against attack. Such actions and reactions, however, only tend to reinforce the beliefs each holds regarding the other's "intentions."

Results. The next two hours were spent in a joint session over the images each had developed and presented. Neither side could believe the other could be so "wrong" about it. At times the discussion, designed to clarify, became heated and sharp. Each side quickly forgot its good intentions to work in a problem-solving manner. Renewed tensions and old sources of friction bubbled at the surface. Without interventions by the behavioral scientists to focus what was taking place, it is likely the discussion would have slipped onto the more typical win-lose exchange of vindictive accusations.

"Little will be gained," one of the behavioral scientists said by way of intervention, "at the present rate. All I can hear is one side 'explaining' to the other why it is 'right' and the other is 'wrong.' The purpose of this session is to *clarify* what has emerged in your images. This is to insure that both of you understand clearly the behavior, attitudes, feelings, and intentions of the other. If common understanding is not achieved at this level, then it is likely both of you will continue to misinterpret each other's intentions and actions. Rather than discovering a common basis on which to build, differences and resulting antagonism will keep you apart."

However, the need to "bang" one another was too strong. For example, the international continued to hammer at its point that management intended to slowly drive them from the plant. "Look at what you have done," the business agent said at one point. "You've taken jobs away from us and assigned them to the independents. You have gradually shifted the class and scope of our work. More and more you contract work we should be doing."

Also, the union kept returning to grievances. "You have headquarters' answers for every grievance that comes to you. And that is because you go along with their policy of no affiliated unions in the organization. You've yet to review a case solely on merit. You force us into arbitration in order to break us. You deal with us in bad faith. Regardless of what you say, you insist on a different arbitrator so it will cost us more. The only question in our minds is, What will you think of next?"

Management in turn answered with denials and counter-charges. "It is not we who are controlled from 'upstairs.' I know of no such policy, written or otherwise, that says we are to force the international out of this plant. You file a grievance over every little thing that happens. You want to show your membership how good you are. The truth is, they don't know what is going on because this little group sitting right in here makes all the decisions. Look how you raised the dues last time. You called a meeting, just you guys showed up, and you voted to raise the dues. No one else had a chance to vote otherwise.

"During the last wage issue with another international, you gave your people a bunch of bum facts to make us look bad. You people are the union, not the 170 that are supposed to be."

At this point, one of the behavioral scientists again intervened. "It still appears that little is being 'heard' because people are so preoccupied with defending what they say and denying what others are saying. Here is a suggestion. Make sure you understand what each has said up to this point. Disregard whether you agree or not. The kinds of questions you ask should be ones that will insure that you fully understand each point that both groups have made, If one of you says 'the moon is made of blue cheese,' then the other wants to be clear that he said 'blue' cheese and not Swiss or something else. Whether you agree with this description of the moon is not what we want to accomplish at this time."

Several guarded questions were asked following this intervention, and it was obvious that most were suppressing the urge to move back to the attack. Not wanting openly to resume their previous line of "questioning," yet not knowing how and not trusting themselves to seek futher "clarification," members from both groups waited for the other to make the next move.

The behavioral scientist again intervened with the following suggestion. "If it is felt no further clarification is needed at this point, then for the remainder of the evening and for, let's say, the first two hours in the morning, more might be accomplished if both groups devote themselves to answering fully the following questions: One, what is it we do (the union or management) that has contributed to the image the other group has of us? Second, what is it in our *own* beliefs and actions that leads us to the conclusion we have reached about ourselves? To do this, take with you the images on newsprint that the other group developed. In this way, you can focus on the issues and characteristics described by the other group."

Phase 5—Intragroup Diagnosis: Self-Insight and Understanding (4 hrs.)

Although participants attempted to restrain themselves during the exchange of images, the clarification session ended on a note of "charges" and "countercharges." Each side sought to defend itself against the other. This only tended to reinforce the belief each held about the other's "intentions."

Rationale

Phase 5, self-diagnosis, is a pivotal point in the union-management laboratory. The need at this point is for both sides to look "inside" themselves and underneath surface tensions to discover *why* the relationship has become what it is.

Both groups, meeting separately, spent the evening and part of the following morning in (1) self-analysis and (2) diagnosing the "why" of their own actions. Although still far from any real degree of mutual trust or understanding, the door at least was open for both management and the union to see what actions would need to be understood and shifted if a sound problem-solving relationship were to be achieved.

Management's Approach to the Diagnosis. Initially, upon returning to their meeting-room, the management group launched into berating the union's "gross misunderstanding" that they had just heard.

One manager remarked, "I told you! Anything he (the business agent) said, the others would back him up. Those guys don't even know what is fact and what is fiction."

"How could they be so wrong?" others chimed in.

"They have always used this tactic," said the first man. "We are always the 'scheming' ones and *they* are the 'innocent' ones. The business agent has been to the international's school. They taught him all the tricks."

This line of self-justification continued for several minutes before the behavioral scientist who was meeting with management intervened with the following: "What you are doing now is not likely to move you toward better understanding of your relationship with the union. First, you are disregarding your initial commitment to work during the laboratory in a problem-solving manner. This will defeat why you are here and any progress that may have been made up to this point. Second, working through the present task, as it is intended, can help both you and the union to move toward the 'nub' of what it is that has brought about such wide differences between you."

At this, the employee relations manager made the following proposal. "Let's take their image of us as it is on the newsprint and just start listing everything we can think of under each one of their points that could possibly lie behind how they interpret us."

The proposal was picked up and management went to work.

The Union's Reaction. Meanwhile, the union reacted in a similar fashion. Management, as far as they were concerned, had demonstrated to the union's satisfaction that they (the union) had been right all along.

"How can they honestly think that we are a clique running our organization?" the president asked.

"The whole problem," the business agent answered, "is that they are still living in the Nineteenth Century. They can't understand that unions are here to stay. They have no concept of the ideology of unions."

But gradually union members were beginning to get a feel for process examination. They moved more rapidly this time into digging into their attitudes and feelings and into their reactions to the images developed by management.

Both groups worked on this task until past ten in the evening. They picked up again at eight the next morning and completed their tasks around ten.

Phase 6—Exchange of Diagnoses: Meshing Insights (3 hrs.)

Following the individual diagnosis of its own behavior and its "contributions" to the relationship, management and the union came back together to exchange the results of their analyses. Most of the day was devoted to exchanging and then debating through the results of both groups' diagnoses.

Management's Diagnosis of the Union's Image of Management

In its diagnosis, management had taken the seven characteristics of itself as the union had listed them.

Under each item, management had listed contributions (past events and actions) that it felt it and the company had made to this image. This list was quite full—so full, in fact, that management did not get to diagnosing the union's image of itself, except as it happened to relate to the management's image. The union, on the other hand, was more brief, but had studied both its own and management's images.

The assistant plant manager, as he had done in the earlier exchange (during Phase 3), began the interchange in this session. The first item he discussed was the Number One issue so far as the union was concerned, namely, "The company is opposed to international (affiliated) unions." Management was able to cite a number of instances where it could have left such an impression in the union's mind. However, it was pointed out that management did not see this statement to be an accurate description of its present thinking.

"We looked around," the assistant plant manager said, "in the whole organization, as well as in the plant, to see what it was in the past that could lead you to think we, here at the plant, are against affiliated unions. I'd like to cite a few instances. But before I do, let me say again, as clearly as I can, we *prefer* independent unions; but this does not mean that we are opposed to internationals.

"What are some of the examples? For one, Mr.————, the now retired president of the company, made a public statement several years ago to the effect that we preferred company unions, and that the company would do all it could to keep internationals out. Of course, as you know, in 1959 the 'X' International was voted in. At that time, Mr. ————, the plant manager, issued a letter to all employees, stating he was sorry to see this swing, and that it was management's hope that the independent would get back in. However, he did not say that we would not cooperate with the 'X' International, as long as they were in.

"More close to home, we feel many of our own and the company's economy moves have not been seen as such. Rather, these moves have been interpreted as efforts to get rid of the international. Our recent layoff falls into this category. The closing of a nearby plant by the company is another. Most employees have the impression that head-quarters would not make investments or expansions of our plant as long as the international were in."

The international's business agent interrupted to ask, "And isn't this true? The company hasn't made any investments in the plant in over four years. They have at others. We think this is a big reason why you go right along with the policy of 'no affiliated unions!' "

"But you are still saying there is no difference between what head-quarters thinks and what we here at the plant think," the assistant plant manager returned.

"We make no distinction whatsoever," the business agent replied. "You can't afford to do anything else. It figures. Take another of our points. In order to maintain your public image, you deny opposition to affiliated unions, but that doesn't square with the facts. You said it yourself. The company has demonstrated it prefers independents."

"But this is still not to say we are opposed to internationals. We only say we prefer independents," The employee relations manager interrupted. "You are here now, have been for over 25 years, and we expect you to be here for a long time to come. We want to work with you, but it is awfully hard when you think the opposite. I think it is true that, in headquarters, in many ways there has been opposition to interna-tionals which the company has tried to cover up. But even this is not so true at headquarters today. And it certainly isn't true here at the plant."

"Maybe a couple of points we came up with can clarify what we are saying here," the assistant plant manager said. "We think you get this impression through our omission to support or reject internationals, particularly in the recent case of the 'X' International. You will recall that we took no stand during the certification election. We publicly said we were not going to support either the independent or the inter-national. Our silence, we think, is what gives you the impression that we deny our opposition to unions."

"Do you deny that you weren't pleased when the independent won out?" the union president asked.

"No. I can't help saying that we were honestly pleased. But, had the international won, we would have continued to bargain in good faith with them and to fulfill our obligations. Right up to the election, we were still negotiating with them."

"You were just going through the motions to maintain the false image you were trying to project," the business agent said. "In the background, though, you were doing all you could to make the interna-tional appear incompetent to its membership. Your 'foot was in the aisle' all the while. This is what you are doing to us. And you were getting your orders straight from headquarters. Look at the wage issue. You offered a ridiculous amount, way below the straight rate, just to embarrass the international. We think local management would have offered them a just amount if you had been free to do so. But the whole problem is that you were not free. How can you say you work to bargain and deal with us in good faith and to cooperate with us when you *cannot* because of headquarters, even if you wanted to?"

"Let me answer that," the assistant plant manager continued. "At our 'Y' plant, the 'X' Union was offered the straight rate because to do so did not put plant 'Y' out of line in their area. We offered less because to do otherwise would have put us way out of line with the rates in our area. We were among the top 'five' at that time. Even then, we offered the 'X' Union an increase that would have put us above everyone. All this is to say that headquarters' position with respect to wages is that plants *should* exercise local responsibility to keep rates in line. Their policy is *not* to use wages to punish unions.

"We don't think we can answer why you feel we are, as you say, 'out to get you.' We don't know really how to answer your belief that we lack local autonomy any further except by denial and to say in the most honest way we know that we make our own decisions. And as far as this concerns this union, our decision is that we want to work with you in a sound manner."

"I wish we could believe that," the business agent said. Others nodded.

The assistant plant manager went on to cite other events the management group felt contributed to the union's belief that management had long-range designs to abolish affiliated unions. Included here were a recent reduction in rolls, the abolishment of two departments in which the employees were represented by international unions, contracting of work, and the movement of certain work performed by this union into areas represented by independents.

"That last one is a good example of why we say you do not act in good faith," the union secretary said. "Look at the change you made in the toolroom. You said you were only making some physical changes, but before we knew it the change resulted in different jobs. This was not what you led us to believe."

"We did not say there wouldn't be any changes in the jobs affected," a member of the management group returned. "You only assumed this."

"But it's always the same thing," the business agent countered. "You deal in half-truths—you don't tell the full truth. What we say is, that if you really wanted to work with us, you would not always be so evasive. We think you should face the issues squarely and operate on the table with trust. We want to be treated with respect. We can disagree and bargain and still act with trust and in good faith. But we cannot disagree with respect when management is evasive and does not act aboveboard.

"I'll give you another example," he continued, "and this probably is the biggest problem area we know. Again, it's the way in which you deal with grievances. Rather than giving us a straightforward answer to issues you take a legalistic approach. Now this is what you accused us of earlier. But I'm saying that if things are legalistic it is because you have made them this way. This kind of legal approach stifles openness and straightforward answers. But we feel this is only a minor part of the problem. What we see you doing is hiding your real motives in the language of your written grievance decisions. And getting back to the point of respect, your interpretations of our grievances are stated in such a way as to make us look childish even to have raised a grievance in the first place."

A Step Toward Understanding

Both groups now were more openly exchanging their feelings and interpretations on a variety of events in their history. For this reason, the behavioral scientists did not intervene when the discussion slid into the union's picturing its analysis of management's counter-image. It was felt that, in this way, overlapping issues could be productively discussed as they were encountered. The interplay from this kind of interchange seemed to generate greater understanding for the moment than mechanically completing one group's presentation before moving to the next.

The Union's Summary of Its Diagnosis

"While we have been talking all this time," the business agent said during a lull, "we have covered a number of the points we had to make with respect to your image of us. However, there are still a number of things we want to lay out on the table. So, unless there is more management has to add from their newsprints, I would like to summarize the remainder of our points now."

Management responded that they thought this would be good. They said, though, that they would like to keep it loose, the way it was. Management wanted to be able to interrupt and return to some point if something the union said triggered a thought in their minds.

This approach was agreeable to the union.

"There is one point," the business agent began, "that we think is a basic, fundamental, ideological breach in the thinking of our two groups. We are not sure this can ever be patched—that is, your over-riding preference for independent unions. I don't want to get into, *again,* whether this means management is 'opposed' to internationals or not. But, I don't see how we can interpret so many arrows in this direction in any other way. Anyway, here is what we see. In many companies, and especially this one, *independent* unions are set up to *deny* workers the freedom to bargain. When people do not have the freedom to select between an international or an independent, then we feel that, actually, they do not have the freedom of choice they should have. And people in *this* plant *don't* have that choice."

The plant manager reacted to this one. "People in this plant have the right, 'freedom of choice' in your words, to be represented by either an independent or an international. I don't see why you say they don't. We can't keep an international out. Employees can join an international whenever they want. If that isn't freedom, I don't know what you mean by freedom."

"And what if they did?" the business agent asked. "You prefer an independent. Would you treat them in the same way? No! You wouldn't. That's my point. People have no choice but to stay with independents."

The assistant plant manager responded, "I don't think we would be that different. Maybe we would. But they still have freedom of choice."

"That's like asking a man whether he wants to be shot or hanged."

The question of "freedom of choice" was kicked around at greater length, with neither management nor the union able to agree on whether or not employees did have a "free choice." Management and the union seemed to be sparring, each testing for an opening.

"Decentralization is another anti-international strategy of the company," the business agent said as he shifted the topic somewhat. "It serves to spread us so thin that we can't be effective. That's the whole strategy behind scattering plants from one end of the country to the other. You say we misinterpret economic moves you make. And we say that headquarters' real motive is to get rid of international, not just to 'pinch' a few of the pennies they so dearly love."

The Union Operates Democratically. "One of your points that we really can't understand is that 'the union is run by a clique.' Nothing could be further from the truth. We think management has this impression because they don't understand how we operate. You have never been to a union meeting. Well, let me change that to say only Joe and Pete, who were once in the union, have been to union meetings. You guys ought to attend one to see what really happens. And you ought to read our by-laws to learn how we operate. Our organization is more democratic than yours."

The employee relations manager interrupted to say, "What the by-laws say and what really happens can be completely different. Didn't you just recently pass a dues rise when only a minority—the usual 10 percent—were present?"

"I don't know who your 'stool-pigeon' is," the union president shot back, "but he sure gave you some bum information."

"This is a good example of how little you know about how we operate," the business manager said. "Let us tell you the procedure we have. It's in our by-laws." He went on to describe how action must be taken. "If we take a position in bargaining, it is because we have discussed it with our people and that's what they want. And don't be too sure our people wouldn't strike if you pushed us into it."

The business agent went to his last point. "You also said we were not interested in production—that we were not concerned with your problems. The truth is, you don't want us to be interested; that is, not beyond the point of doing what management wants. This kills any incentive and any concern for management's viewpoint."

"You know what management's attitude is?" the union vice-president asked. "It is, 'Look, you are supposed to do *what* you are told *as* you are told to do it. We are not interested in your ideas.' With that kind of attitude, how can you expect us to act differently? Management at this plant still hasn't caught up with the idea that employees today want to be more autonomous and make a real work contribution. And that doesn't mean through some 'corny' coin-your-idea program.''

The employee relations manager, who had been listening intently all this time, stood up with a look of disbelief on his face. He didn't seem to realize he was on his feet. "Do you mean to say you people are really interested in *production*?'' He had listened to the union say this for two days, but he had just "heard" it for the first time. His next question was a simple one, but it triggered an hour-long discussion. He asked, "What could management do to use people more effectively?"

A Period of Progress

The earlier period of self-analysis and this exchange made it possible for both to "hear" better what the other was saying. In turn, being able to "hear" made it possible for both sides to communicate their attitudes and feelings more openly—more honestly. Some points of agreement and similarities in thinking came to the fore as differences were examined, put into perspective, and understood.

Progress was made and better understanding achieved during this latter exchange, yet under the surface underlying tensions still remained. Neither side was "owning up" any more than the other. Old "bargaining" habits still permeated the exchange between the two. On many points, one side was unable to see why the other felt or thought as it did. Often members yielded to the temptation to explain to the other side why they were "wrong."

Over-all, though, both sides were "listening" better to each other. Although not always agreeing, they were hearing each other out. As the session continued, questions and replies gained the quality of clarifying rather than of attacking or defending.

The remainder of the day was spent thrashing through the many points of differences that had been uncovered in the early development of images. Both the union and management were able to get many things off their chests.

Phase 7—Consolidation of Key Issues (2 hrs.)

Although the two sides were far from having talked out their differences, the last part of the day was devoted to identifying those issues which seemed critical in the relationship between the union and management. Working with the behavioral scientists, union and management jointly identified, as barriers, those issues that would require more examination, discussion, and resolution if relations were to be improved. They were summarized as follows:

1. *Lack of Mutual Trust and Respect.* This was tagged as a key element in the relationship by both groups. The general feeling was that once

genuine trust and respect between the two were achieved, many of the other things would fall into place. Management's preference for independents, despite its position that it wanted to learn to work with the international, was cited as an issue "that needed better understanding."

2. *Ideological Differences.* Both agreed there existed wide differences in matters of purposes and principles. Common purposes would need to be identified if joint problem solving were to become a reality.

3. *Inadequate Knowledge and Understanding.* During the exchanges it became clear to both sides that many factual matters about each other were not known. Both the union and management felt that neither of them really understood how the other operated—how decisions, regulations governing their behavior, long-range plans, traditions, and so on, were handled at either level.

4. *Attitudinal Differences.* Differences in attitudes toward each other, plant operations, and the management of business affairs, existed between the union and management. Part of this was recognized as a difference in perspective—part was seen as due to different levels of knowledge and to past experiences and relations.

5. *Need for More Effective Use of People.* Both agreed there should be more participation and involvement of wage people in the operations of the plant. "We don't want to co-manage," the union said, for example, "but there are some areas where we have high stakes. In these matters we want to be consulted. We think we can contribute to the effectiveness of operations if management will involve us more."

6. *Better Understanding of Rights and Obligations.* Union and management, they felt, need to understand better and to respect the rights and obligations each has toward the other. There existed a need for better understanding and acceptance of each party's role in the bargaining process. Included here was the feeling that a better understanding of the mutual expectations each held for the other was needed.

7. *Better Communications.* It was also felt that management and the union need to communicate more openly, more freely, and more honestly with each other. Both felt that communication barriers precipitated many of their problems.

8. *Better Listening.* Along with a need for better communications, it was felt that both sides needed to listen more and "better" to the other. For example, the union pointed out that employees were concerned with and wanted their views heard on the economic health of the plant. One union member had remarked, "I know right now how to save the plant $10,000, but I haven't found anyone who will listen to me yet. I gave up trying a long time ago."

Phase 8—Planning Next Steps (1 hr.)

Based on the above summation, the final period of time was devoted to debating what follow-up steps, if any, should be taken to the two-day laboratory. It was agreed that many tensions and a residue of hostility still existed. Much remained to be talked out. It was felt that the two groups were not yet ready to tackle their operational problems. It was concluded that a lot of "air stills needs to be cleared" before the two sides would be able to sit down together and work in an effective manner.

It was proposed and accepted that the two groups spend some time in considering what they had learned during the laboratory. Both wanted to talk among themselves about what had come out of the session and to consider what the next best step would be. Each wanted to report to its other group members the progress that had been made, to get their reactions, and then to make a tentative proposal of what they felt needed to be done next. With this, the union management laboratory ended.

Summary of Issues. The union showed great concern for and tested, throughout the two days, the degree of local autonomy in management. There was a considerable amount of anxiety over what they saw as corporate ideology and implementation of an anti-international objective. The real question to the union, although they were not able to focus it, was not whether or not management had local autonomy, but the *degree* of autonomy management had.

The union was convinced that management was "dollar-oriented" all the way, without values with respect to people. Therefore, the union felt bound to counteract this "inhumanity" they saw in management.

Management again and again demonstrated extreme suspicion regarding the anti-democracy of the union and the "clique" qualities of the union leadership. Management genuinely felt that the union leaders did not represent the people.

Management's attitude was that the union was an institution with intrinsic goals of protecting and building itself. Management felt strongly on two points: (1) that the union had no concern for productivity and (2) that actually they had only an administrative concern for people, *i.e.,* wage rates, seniority, class and scope of work, security, and the like. In other words, management saw the union's concern for people to be an institutional one.

Similarities Not Seen. Several points of similarity were not observed by either management or the union because of their concern for the *differences* between them. For example, management saw itself as *production-oriented.* The union also saw this. But management also had a *human* interest which the union did not recognize.

On the other hand, the union saw itself as having a *people* obligation. This, in turn, management recognized in the union. The disparity here was that management did not see the same weight being attached to productivity by the union.

What the two groups shared in common, then, they were not able to recognize. More importantly, what they shared in common they saw as differences.

CONCLUSIONS

Intergroup conflict undergirds much of modern, complex organization life. More than ever, there is greater interdependence among the functions of groups. This interdependence can aid organizations to take giant strides forward toward the accomplishment of mutual goals. Or, this same interdependence can breed the most hostile and disruptive of conflicts. Once conflict erupts, it is difficult to bring it under control. It can consume everything and everyone it touches.

We have presented a view of the misunderstandings and misperceptions generated out of a long history of antagonism between an international union and the management of a large industrial plant. Both sides were weary from "battle," but neither knew how to alter the course of the conflict.

Based on behavioral sciences concepts, an educational-laboratory approach to the resolutions of the conflict was proposed. Leaders of the international and management met for a two-day period to confront the conflict between them. The differences between them, uncovered by the two groups, were presented in detail. These differences became the foundation on which the two groups began tediously to work toward a more healthy relationship. Through self-analysis and an exchange of views, management and the union moved slowly toward a better understanding of the relationship between them.

After the laboratory, much tension and distrust still existed and remained to be worked through. But by confronting each other squarely with the issues involved, the way was open for building a more cooperative and productive relationship for the future.[5]

One should not expect that a single, brief confrontation such as that described will cause a repeal of the past. It is unlikely that well-established conditions will be greatly influenced, if at all.

The greatest impact will become evident when *new* issues and different problems arise in the relationship. At that time, the parties will be able to apply themselves in a more problem-solving manner. In other words, the background of conflict does not dissolve. Rather, it remains to color and influence old issues born in that era. However, new issues, with no anchorage in the past, do not have the same "tug" in the directions of old norms and past practices. Members in both groups are not "bound" by old expectations. Instead, they are now free to explore jointly for new solutions with the other group under the more collaborative conditions produced by the laboratory sequence.

Correcting a situation of long-term, chronic hostility requires continuous and diligent follow-up efforts. As much as a five-year span may be needed before the root system that produced the original animosities can be replaced by a new and healthier root system—one that can cause the relationship to flourish.

ENCORE

"The idea persists that there is something materialistic about natural science and that morals are degraded by having anything seriously to do with material things. . . . For the

neglect of sciences that deal specifically with facts of the natural and social environment leads to a side-tracking of moral forces into an unreal privacy of an unreal self. It is impossible to say how much of the remediable suffering of the world is due to the fact that physical science is looked upon as merely physical. It is impossible to say how much of the unnecessary slavery of the world is due to the conception that moral issues can be settled within conscience or human sentiment apart from consistent study of facts and application of specific knowledge in industry, law and politics. . . .

"It is not pretended that a moral theory based upon realities of human nature and a study of the specific connections of these realities with those of physical science would do away with moral struggle and defeat. It would not make the moral life as simple a matter as wending one's way along a well-lighted boulevard. All action is an invasion of the future, of the unknown. Conflict and uncertainty are ultimate traits."

"In quality, the good is never twice alike. It never copies itself. It is new every morning, fresh every evening. It is unique in its every presentation. For it marks the resolution of a distinctive complication of competing habits and impulses which can never repeat itself."

JOHN DEWEY. Human Nature and Conduct. New York: The Modern Library, 1922. Pp. 10-12, 211.

NOTES

1. For a review of relevant experimental work, see Blake, R. R., & Mouton, J. S. Over-evaluation of own group's product in intergroup competition. *J. Abnorm. Soc. Psychol.*, 1962, 64, 237-283; Blake, R. R., & Mouton, J. S. Comprehension of points of communality in competing solutions. *Sociometry*, 1962, 25, 56-63; Blake, R. R., & Mouton, J. S. Comprehension of own and outgroup positions under intergroup competition. *J. Conflict Resolution*, 1961, 5, 304-310; Blake, R. R., Mouton, J. S. Loyalty of representatives to ingroup positions during intergroup competition. *Sociometry*, 1961, 24, 171-183; Blake, R. R., & Mouton, J. S. Perceived characteristics of elected representatives. *J. Abnorm. Soc. Psychol.*, 1961, 62, 693-695; and Blake, R. R., & Mouton, J. S. Reactions to intergroup competition under win-lose conditions. *Mgmt. Science*, 1961, 7, 420-425.

   Also, for a review and discussion of the prototype intergroup experiments, see Sherif, M., Harvey, O. J., White, B. J., Hood, W. R., & Sherif, C. *Intergroup Conflict and Cooperation: The Robbers Cave Experiment.* Institute of Group Relations: Norman, Oklahoma, 1961; Sherif, M. Superordinate goals in the reduction of intergroup conflict. *Amer. J. Sociol.*, 1958, 43, 349-356; Sherif, M., & Sherif, C. *Outline of Social Psychology* (rev. ed.). New York: Harper, 1956; and Sherif, M., & Sherif, C. *Groups in Harmony and Tension.* New York: Harper, 1953.
2. Blake, R. R., & Mouton, J. S. *The Managerial Grid.* Houston: Gulf, 1964, Chapter 12.
3. Blake, R. R., Shepard, H. A., & Mouton, J. S. *Managing Intergroup Conflict in Industry.* Houston: Gulf, 1964; Blake, R. R., & Mouton, J. S. The intergroup dynamics of win-lose conflict and problem-solving collaboration in union-management relations. In M. Sherif (Ed.), *Intergroup Relations and Leadership.* New York: Wiley, 1962, 94-140; Blake, R. R., & Mouton, J. S. Union-Management relations: From conflict to collaboration. *Personnel*, 1961, 38; and Blake, R. R. & Mouton, J. S. *Group Dynamics—Key to Decision Making.* Houston: Gulf, 1961.
4. For a review of intergroup laboratory applications in other than union-management relations, see Blake, R. R., Shepard, H. A., & Mouton, J. S., *op. cit.*, 1964; Blake, R. R., & Mouton, J. S. Headquarters-field team training for organizational improvement. *ASTD J.*, 1962, 16, 3-11; Blansfield, M. G., Blake, R. R., & Mouton, J. S. The merger laboratory: A new strategy for bringing one corporation into another. *Train. Directors J.*, 1964, 18, in press. Additional relevant discussions contained in Blake, R. R. Psychology and the crisis of statesmanship. *Amer. Psychologist*, 1959, 14, 78-94. Also in W. G. Bennis, K. D. Benne, & R. Chin (Eds.), *The Planning of Change.* New York:

Holt, Rinehart, & Winston, 1961, 466-477; and Blake, R. R., & Mouton, J. S. Intergroup therapy. *Int. J. Soc. Psychiat.*, 1962, *8*, 196-198.

5. For a description of another format for reducing tension between a union and management, see Muench, G. A. A clinical psychologist's treatment of labor-management conflicts. *Personnel Psychol.*, 1960, 12, 165-172; and Muench, G. A. A clinical psychologist's treatment of labor-management conflicts: A four-year study. *J. Humanistic Psychol.*, 1963, *3*, 92-97.

MANAGEMENT OF DIFFERENCES

Warren H. Schmidt and Robert Tannenbaum

WARREN H. SCHMIDT is Director of Conferences and Community Services, University of California. ROBERT TANNENBAUM is Professor of Personnel Management and Industrial Relations, UCLA.

—How to Diagnose An Issue And Its Causes.
—How to Decide On The Best Course Of Action.

The manager often experiences his most uncomfortable moments when he has to deal with differences among people. Because of these differences, he must often face disagreements, arguments, and even open conflict. To add to his discomfort, he frequently finds himself torn by two opposing desires. On the one hand, he wants to unleash the individuality of his subordinates in order to tap their full potential and to achieve novel and creative approaches to problems. On the other hand, he is eager to develop a harmonious, smooth-working team to carry out his organization's objectives. The manager's lot is further troubled by the fact that when differences do occur, strong feelings are frequently aroused, objectivity flies out the window, egos are threatened, and personal relationships are placed in jeopardy.

TOWARD EFFECTIVE MANAGEMENT

Because the presence of differences can complicate the manager's job in so many ways, it is of utmost importance that he understand them fully and that he learn to handle them effectively. It is the purpose of this article to assist the manager to manage more effectively by increasing his understanding of differences among the people he works with, and by improving his ability to deal with others.

A large part of what follows will focus, for simplicity of exposition, on the differences which occur among a manager's individual subordinates. However, we would like to suggest that the principles, concepts, methods, and dynamics which we discuss throughout much of the article apply to intergroup, to interorganizational, and to international differences as well.

Our basic thesis is that a manager's ability to deal effectively with differences depends on:

- His ability to diagnose and to understand differences.
- His awareness of, and ability to select appropriately from, a variety of behaviors.[1]
- His awareness of, and ability to deal with, his own feelings— particularly those which might reduce his social sensitivity (diagnostic insight) and his action flexibility (ability to act appropriately).[2]

There are two basic assumptions underlying our approach to this problem. Let us examine them before going any further:

1. *Differences among people should not be regarded as inherently "good" or "bad."* Sometimes differences result in important benefits to the organization; and sometimes they are disruptive, reducing the overall effectiveness of individuals and organizations.

2. *There is no "right" way to deal with differences.* Under varying circumstances, it may be most beneficial to avoid differences, to repress them, to sharpen them into clearly defined conflict, or to utilize them for enriched problem solving. The manager who consistently "pours oil on troubled waters" may not be the most effective manager. Nor is the manager necessarily successful who emphasizes individuality and differences so strongly that cooperation and teamwork are simply afterthoughts. We feel, rather, that the effective manager is one who is able to use a *variety* of approaches to differences and who chooses any specific approach on the basis of an insightful diagnosis and understanding of the factors with which he is faced at that time.

DIAGNOSING DISAGREEMENTS

When a manager's subordinates become involved in a heated disagreement, they do not tend to proceed in a systematic manner to resolve their difference. The issues often ramain unclear to them, and they may talk *at* rather than *to* one another. If a manager is to be helpful in such a situation, he should ask three important diagnostic questions:

1. What is the nature of the difference among the persons?
2. What factors may underlie this difference?
3. To what stage has the interpersonal difference evolved?

Nature of the Difference

Now, looking at the first of these three important questions, the nature of the difference will vary depending on the kind of issue on which people disagree. And there are four basic kinds of issues to look for:

● *Facts.* Sometimes the disagreement occurs because individuals have different definitions of a problem, are aware of different pieces of relevant information, accept or reject different information as factual, or have differing impressions of their respective power and authority.

● *Goals.* Sometimes the disagreement is about what should be accomplished — the desirable objectives of a department, division, section, or of a specific position within the organization.

● *Methods.* Sometimes individuals differ about the procedures, strategies, or tactics which would most likely achieve a mutually desired goal.

● *Values.* Sometimes the disagreement is over ethics — the way power should be exercised, or moral considerations, or assumptions about justice, fairness, and so on. Such differences may affect the choice of either goals or methods.

Arguments are prolonged and confusion is increased when the contending parties are not sure of the nature of the issue over which they disagree. By discovering the source of the disagreement, the manager will be in a better position to determine how he can utilize and direct the dispute for both the short- and long-range good of the organization. As we will indicate later, there are certain steps which are appropriate when the differences are about facts, other steps which are appropriate when the differences are over goals, and still other steps which are applicable when differences are over methods or values.

Underlying Factors

When people are faced with a difference, it is not enough that their manager be concerned with what the difference is about. The second major diagnostic question he should ask is *why* the difference exists. As we try to discover useful answers to this, it is helpful to think in terms of:

- Whether the disputants had access to the same information.
- Whether the disputants perceive the common information differently.
- Whether each disputant is significantly influenced by his role in the organization.

These questions involve informational, perceptual, and role factors. Thus:

Informational factors exert their influence when the various points of view have developed on the basis of different sets of facts. The ancient legend of the blind men and the elephant dramatizes this point as vividly as any modern illustration. Because each of the men had contact with a different part of the elephant, each disagreed violently about the nature of the animal. In the same way, when two persons receive limited information about a complex problem, they may well disagree as to the nature of that problem when they come together to solve it.

Perceptual factors exert their influence when the persons have different images of the same stimulus. Each will attend to, and select from the information available, those items which he deems important. Each will interpret the information in a somewhat different manner. Each brings to the data a different set of life experiences which cause him to view the information through a highly personal kind of filter. The picture which he gets, therefore, is unique to him. Thus it is not surprising that the same basic "facts" may produce distinctive perceptual pictures in the minds of different individuals.

Role factors exert their influence because each of the individuals occupies a certain position and status in society or in the organization. The fact that he occupies such a position or status may put certain constraints on him if the discussion is related to his role.

The concepts we have been discussing can be best illustrated by a concrete case. Such a case is presented in detail in EXHIBIT I.

EXHIBIT I

Hypothetical Situation Illustrating a Difference

The Facts

There is a disagreement over whether a company should introduce automated record keeping to replace its present manual system. The company's expert on office methods favors immediate introduction of such a system. The head of accounting is opposed to it. Some of the bases of disagreement and possible reasons for this disagreement are represented below.

Nature of the Difference

	Over facts	Over methods	Over goals	Over values
Expert on office methods	"Automation will save the company money."	"The new system should be installed fully and at once."	"We want a system that gives us accurate data rapidly — whenever we want it."	"We must be modern and efficient."
Head of accounting department	"The new system will be more expensive to install and operate."	"Let us move slower — one step at a time."	"We need most a flexible accounting system to meet our changing needs — managed by accountants who can solve unexpected and complex problems."	"We must consider the welfare of workers who have served the company so loyally for many years."

Reasons for the Difference

	Explanation of position of methods expert	Explanation of position of head accountant
Informational (Exposure to different information	He has studied articles about seemingly comparable companies describing the savings brought about by automation. Representatives of machine companies have presented him with estimates of savings over a 10-year period.	He has heard about the "hidden costs" in automation. He has priced the kind of equipment he believes will be necessary and has estimated its depreciation. This estimated cost is much higher than the salaries of possible replaced workers.
Perceptual (Different interpretation of the same data because of differing backgrounds, experience, and so forth)	He regards the representatives of the machine company as being alert, businesslike, and knowledgeable about the best accounting procedures. He feels that their analysis of the company's needs is dependable and to be trusted.	He sees the representatives of the machine company as salesmen. Their goal is to sell machines, and their report and analysis must be read with great caution and suspicion.
Role (Pressure to take a certain stand because of status or position)	He believes that the company looks to him as the expert responsible for keeping its systems up-to-date and maximally efficient.	He feels responsible for the morale and security of his team in the accounting office. He must defend their loyalty and efficiency if it is ever doubted.

Stage of Evolution

Important conflicts among people ordinarily do not erupt suddenly. They pass through various stages, and the way in which the energy of the disputing parties can be effectively directed by the manager depends to some extent on the stage of the dispute when he enters the picture.

One way of diagnosing a dispute — the third major question — is to identify it as being at one of these five stages in its development:

Stage #1 — *the phase of anticipation.* A manager learns that his company is about to install new, automated equipment which will reduce the number and change the nature of jobs in a given department. He can anticipate that when this information is released, there will be differences of opinion as to the desirability of this change, the way in which it should be introduced, and the way in which the consequences of its introduction should be handled.

Stage #2 — *the phase of conscious, but unexpressed, difference.* Word leaks out about the proposed new equipment. Small clusters of people who trust one another begin discussing it. They have no definite basis for the information, but tensions begin to build up within the organization. There is a feeling of impending dispute and trouble.

Stage #3 — *the phase of discussion.* Information is presented about the plans to install new equipment. Questions are asked to secure more information, to inquire about the intentions of management, to test the firmness of the decision that has been made. During the discussion, the differing opinions of individuals begin to emerge openly. They are implied by the questions which are asked, and by the language which is used.

Stage #4 — *the phase of open dispute.* The union steward meets with the foreman to present arguments for a change in plans. The foreman counters these arguments by presenting the reasons that led management to decide to install the equipment. The differences which have heretofore been expressed only indirectly and tentatively now sharpen into more clearly defined points of view.

Stage #5 — *the phase of open conflict.* Individuals have firmly committed themselves to a particular position on the issue; the dispute has become clearly defined. The outcome can only be described in terms of win, lose, or compromise. Each disputant attempts not only to increase the effectiveness of his argument and his power in the situation, but also to undermine the influence of those who oppose him.

The power of the manager to intervene successfully will differ at each of these stages. He is likely to have the most influence if he enters the picture at stage #1; the least influence if he enters at stage #5. This range of possible behavior and action changes as the conflict passes through the various stages. For this reason, it is important for the manager not only to assess the nature of the given dispute and the forces affecting the individuals involved, but also to assess the stage to which the dispute has evolved.

SELECTING AN APPROACH

After the manager has diagnosed a given dispute (or a potential one) between subordinates, he is next confronted by the problem of taking action. And here there are two additional questions that it will be helpful to him to consider:

1. What courses of action are available?
2. What must be kept in mind in selecting the best one?

Assuming, first, a situation in which the manager has time to antici-pate and plan for an impending dispute, we suggest that the general approaches typically available to him are (a) avoidance, (b) repression, (c) sharpening into conflict, and (d) transformation into problem solv-ing. In deciding which to use, the manager's primary concern should be to select the alternative that will yield optimum benefits to the organiza-tion.

Avoidance of Differences

It is possible for a manager to avoid the occurrence of many differ-ences among his subordinates. He can, for example, staff his organiza-tion with people who are in substantial agreement. Some organizations select and promote individuals whose experiences are similar, who have had similar training, and who come from a similar level of society. Because of such common backgrounds, these individuals tend to see things similarly, to have common interests and objectives, and to approach problems in much the same way. A staff thus developed tends to be a very secure one: the reactions of one's fellows are both readily predictable and congenial to one's own way of thinking and doing.

The manager may also avoid differences among his subordinates by controlling certain of their interpersonal contacts. He can, for example, assign two potentially explosive individuals to different groups or physical locations, or he can choose not to raise a particularly divisive issue because it is "too hot to handle." But let us take a closer look:

When is this alternative appropriate? Some organizations depend heavily on certain kinds of conformity and agreement among their employees in order to get the work done. Political parties and religious denominational groups are perhaps extreme examples of this. If an individual holds a different point of view on a rather fundamental issue, he may become a destructive force within the organization. This ap-proach may be especially important if he is dealing with somewhat fragile and insecure individuals. Some persons are so threatened by conflict that their ability to function effectively suffers when they operate in a climate of differences.

What are the difficulties and dangers in this approach? The manager who uses this approach consistently runs the risk of reducing the total creativity of his staff. Someone has said, "When everyone in the room thinks the same thing, no one is thinking very much." In an atmosphere in which differences are avoided, new ideas not only appear less frequently, but old ideas also are likely to go unexamined and untested. There is genuine danger of the organization's slipping unknowingly into a rut of complacency.

Repression of Differences

Sometimes a manager is aware that certain differences exist among members of his staff, but he feels that the open expression of these differences would create unproductive dissension and reduce the total creativity of the group. He may, therefore, decide to keep these differences under cover. He may do this by continually emphasizing loyalty, cooperation, teamwork, and other similar values within the group. In such a climate, it is unlikely that subordinates will express disagreements and risk conflict.

The manager may also try to make sure that the potentially conflicting parties come together only under circumstances which are highly controlled—circumstances in which open discussion of latent differences is clearly inappropriate. Or he may develop an atmosphere of repression by consistently rewarding agreement and cooperation and by punishing (in one way or another) those who disrupt the harmony of the organization by expressing nonconformist ideas. But once again:

When is this alternative appropriate? It is most useful when the latent differences are not relevant to the organization's task. It is to be expected that individuals will differ on many things—religion, politics, their loyalty to cities or states, baseball teams, and so forth. There may be no need to reach agreement on some of these differences in order to work together effectively on the job. It may also be appropriate to repress conflict when adequate time is not available to resolve the potential differences among the individuals involved. This might be particularly true if the manager's concern is to achieve a short-run objective and the potential disagreement is over a long-run issue. The wounds of disagreement should not be opened up if there is insufficient time to bind them.

What are the difficulties and dangers in this approach? Repression almost always costs something. If, indeed, the differences are important to the persons involved, their feelings may come to be expressed indirectly, in ways that could reduce productivity. Every manager has witnessed situations in which ideas are resisted, not on the basis of their merit, but on the basis of who advocated them. Or he has seen strong criticism arising over mistakes made by a particularly disliked individual.

Much has been said and written about "hidden agenda." People may discuss one subject, but the *way* they discuss it and the positions they take with respect to it may actually be determined by factors lying beneath the surface of the discussion. Hidden agenda are likely to abound in an atmosphere of repression.

When strong feelings are involved in unexpressed differences, the blocking of these feelings creates frustration and hostility which may be misdirected toward "safe" targets. Differences, and the feelings generated by them, do not ordinarily disappear by being ignored. They fester beneath the surface and emerge at inopportune moments to create problems for the manager and his organization.

Differences Into Conflicts

When this approach is used, the manager not only recognizes the fact that differences exist, but attempts to create an arena in which the conflicting parties can "fight it out." However, like the promoter of an athletic contest, he will want to be sure that the differing persons understand the issue over which they differ, the rules and procedures by which they can discuss their differences, and the kinds of roles and responsibilities which each is expected to bear in mind during the struggle. Again:

When is this alternative appropriate? A simple answer is: "when it is clarifying and educational." Many an individual will not pause to examine the assumptions he holds or the positions he advocates until he is called on to clarify and support them by someone who holds contrary views. In the same way, the power realities within an organization can come into sharper focus and be more commonly recognized through conflict.

For example, the manager of production and the manager of engineering may develop quite different impressions of how the board of directors feels about the relative importance of their respective units. Each is sure that the board is most impressed with the caliber of the staff, output, and operational efficiency of his department. When a dispute arises over which group is to get priority space in a new building, top management may permit both departments to exert all the influence they can on the board. During the struggle, the two managers may each gain a more realistic assessment of, and respect for, the power of the other.

Another valuable thing learned is the cost of conflict itself. Almost invariably at the end of a long dispute, there is a strong resolve that "this shall not happen again," as the individuals reflect on the financial costs, tensions, embarrassments, uneasiness, and wasted time and energy it caused.

What are the difficulties and dangers in this approach? Conflict can be very costly. It not only saps the energy of those involved, but also may irreparably destroy their future effectiveness. In the heat of conflict, words are sometimes spoken which leave lifelong scars on people or forever cloud their relationship.

Because the risks involved in conflict are so great and the potential costs so high, the manager will want to consider carefully the following questions before he uses this approach:

1. What does he hope to accomplish?

2. What are the possible outcomes of the conflict?

3. What steps should be taken to keep the conflict within organizational bounds and in perspective?

4. What can be done after the conflict to strengthen the bonds between disputants, so that the conflict will be of minimum destructiveness to them and to their ongoing relationship?

Making Differences Creative

"Two heads are better than one" because the two heads often represent a richer set of experiences and because they can bring to bear on the problem a greater variety of insights. If the differences are seen as enriching, rather than as in opposition to each other, the "two heads" will indeed be likely to come up with a better solution than either one alone. For example, had the six blind men who came into contact with different parts of the same elephant pooled their information, they would have arrived at a more accurate description of the animal. In the same way, many problems can be seen clearly, wholly, and in perspective only if the individuals who see different aspects can come together and pool their information. Here, too, let us take a more specific look:

When is this alternative appropriate? When it comes to choosing courses of action for a given problem, differences among the individuals in an organization can help to increase the range and variety of alternatives suggested.

The channeling of differences into a problem-solving context may also help to deal with some of the feelings which often accompany disagreement—frustration, resentment, and hostility. By providing an open and accepted approach, the manager helps to prevent undercurrents of feelings which could break out at inopportune moments. He also helps to channel the energy generated by feelings into creative, rather than into destructive, activities. Whereas conflict tends to cause individuals to seek ways of weakening and undermining those who differ with them, the problem-solving approach leads individuals to welcome differences as being potentially enriching to one's own goals, ideas, and methods.

What are the difficulties and dangers in this approach? To utilize differences requires time. Often it is easier for a single individual (rather than two or more persons) to make a decision. Also, when a rapid decision is required, it may be easier and more practical to ignore one side of an argument in order to move into action. Finally, unless a problem-solving situation is planned with some care, there is always the risk of generating conflict which will be frustrating to all parties concerned.

ENRICHED PROBLEM SOLVING

Let us assume that the course of action decided on is the one just discussed—turning the difference into creative problem solving. Let us further assume, now, that the manager enters the picture when his subordinates are already involved in conflict. What are the things he can do if he wishes to transform this conflict into a problem-solving situation?

• *He can welcome the existence of differences within the organization.*

The manager can indicate that from the discussion of differences can come a greater variety of solutions to problems and a more adequate testing of proposed methods. By making clear his view that all parties contribute to the solution of problems by sharing their differences, he reduces the implication that there will be an ultimate "winner" and "loser."

• *He can listen with understanding rather than evaluation.*

There is abundant evidence that conflicts tend to be prolonged and to become increasingly frustrating because the conflicting parties do not really listen to one another. Each attempts to impose his own views and to "tune out" or distort what the other person has to say.

The manager may expect that when he enters the picture, the individuals will try to persuade him to take a stand on the issue involved. While each adversary is presenting his "case" to the manager, he will be watching for cues which indicate where the manager stands on the issue. It is therefore important that the manager make every effort to understand both positions as fully as possible, recognizing and supporting the seriousness of purpose of each where appropriate, and to withhold judgment until all available facts are in.

In the process of listening for understanding, the manager will also set a good example for the conflicting parties. By adopting such a listening-understanding attitude himself, and by helping the disputants to understand each other more fully, he can make a most useful contribution toward transforming potential conflict into creative problem solving.

• *He can clarify the nature of the conflict.*

In the heat of an argument, each participant may primarily focus on either facts, specific methods, goals, or values. Frustration and anger can occur when one individual talks about facts while another is eager to discuss methods. The manager, having carefully listened to the discussion, can clarify the nature of the issues so that the discussion can become more productive.

• *He can recognize and accept the feelings of the individuals involved.*

Irrational feelings are generated in a controversy, even though the participants do not always recognize this fact. Each wants to believe that he is examining the problem "objectively." The manager, recognizing and accepting feelings such as fear, jealousy, anger, or anxiety, may make it possible for the participants squarely to face their true feelings. The effective manager does not take a critical attitude toward these feelings by, in effect, saying, "You have no right to feel angry!" Rather, he tries sincerely to communicate his sympathetic feelings.

Ordinarily, we do no real service to people by encouraging a repression of their feelings or by criticizing them for experiencing fear, anger, and so forth. Such criticism—whether implied or expressed openly—may block the search for new ways out of the controversy. There is considerable evidence that when a person feels threatened or under attack, he tends to become more rigid and therefore more defensive about positions to which he has committed himself.

- *He can indicate who will make the decision being discussed.*

Sometimes heated disputes go on with respect to issues over which one or more of the persons involved has no control. When people have differing notions about the formal authority available to each, a clarification by the manager of the authority relationships can go far toward placing the discussion in clearer perspective.

- *He can suggest procedures and ground rules for resolving the differences.*

If the disagreement is over *facts*, the manager may assist the disputants in validating existing data and in seeking additional data which will more clearly illuminate the issues under dispute.

If the disagreement is over *methods*, the manager may first want to remind the parties that they have common objectives, and that their disagreement is over means rather than ends. He may suggest that before examining in detail each of their proposed methods for achieving the goals, they might together establish a set of criteria to be used in evaluating whatever procedures are proposed. He may also want to suggest that some time be spent in trying to generate additional alternatives reflecting new approaches. Then after these alternatives have been worked out, he may encourage the parties to evaluate them with the aid of the criteria which these persons have developed together.

If the disagreement is over *goals* or goal priorities, he may suggest that the parties take time to describe as clearly as possible the conflicting goals which are being sought. Sometimes arguments persist simply because the parties have not taken the trouble to clarify for themselves and for each other exactly what they do desire. Once these goals are clearly stated, the issues can be dealt with more realistically.

If the disagreement is over *values*, the manager may suggest that these values be described in operational terms. Discussions of abstractions often tend to be fruitless because the same words and concepts mean different things to different people. To help individuals become more fully aware of the limitations to which their actions are subject, the question, "What do you think you can do about this situation?" usually leads to a more productive discussion than the question, "What do you believe in?" Because value systems are so closely related to a person's self concept, the manager may want to give particular attention to protecting the egos involved. He may make clear that an individual's entire ethical system is not being scrutinized, but only those values which are pertinent to the particular instance.

- *He can give primary attention to maintaining relationships between the disputing parties.*

Sometimes, during the course of a heated dispute, so much attention is paid to the issue under discussion that nothing is done to maintain and strengthen the relationship between the disputing parties. It is not surprising, therefore, that disputes tend to disrupt ongoing relationships. Through oversight or deliberate action, important functions are neglected which sustain or further develop human relationships—for example, the functions of encouraging, supporting, reducing tension, and expressing common feelings. If a conflict is to be transformed into a problem-solving situation, these functions need to be performed by someone—either by the manager or, through his continuing encouragement, by the parties themselves.

• *He can create appropriate vehicles for communication among the disputing parties.*

One of the ways to bring differences into a problem-solving context is to ensure that the disputants can come together easily. If they can discuss their differences *before* their positions become crystalized, the chances of their learning from each other and arriving at mutually agreeable positions are increased. Having easy access to one anoher is also a way of reducing the likelihood that each will develop unreal stereotypes of the other.

Misunderstanding mounts as communication becomes more difficult. One of the values of regular staff meetings, therefore, is that such meetings, properly conducted, can provide a continuing opportunity for persons to exchange ideas and feelings.

If the manager wishes his subordinates to deal with their differences in a problem-solving framework, he will want to ask himself, "In what kind of setting will the parties to this dispute be best able to discuss their differences with a minimum of interference and threat?" He will exclude from such a setting any individuals whose presence will embarrass the disputants if the latter "back down" from previously held points of view. It will be a setting which reflects as much informality and psychological comfort as possible.

• *He can suggest procedures which facilitate problem solving.*

One of the key needs in a dispute is to separate an idea from the person who first proposes it. This increases the chance of examining the idea critically and objectively without implying criticism of the person. Techniques like brainstorming, for example, are designed to free people from the necessity to defend their ideas during an exploration period. Another facilitating action is outlining an orderly set of procedures (e.g., examining objectives, obtaining relevant data) for the disputants to follow as they seek a constructive resolution of their difference.

MANAGERIAL OBJECTIVITY

Thus far we have tended to make the unrealistic assumption that the manager is able to maintain his own objectivity in the face of a difference among his subordinates. Obviously, this does not easily happen because his feelings also tend to become involved. It is, in fact, not unusual for people to react to differences more on the basis of their own feelings than on the basis of some rational approach to the problem at hand.

A manager may be deeply concerned about the disruptive effects of a disagreement. He may be troubled about how the persistence of a dispute will affect him personally or his position in the organization. He may worry about the danger of coming under personal attack, or of incurring the anger and hostility of important subordinates or a superior. He may become anxious as another person expresses deep feelings, without really understanding why.

While sometimes personal feelings of this kind are at the conscious level, often they are unrecognized by the manager himself because they lie in the area of the unconscious. This, then, highlights the importance of the manager's own self-awareness. While we do not intend to deal with this topic here, it might be well to note some "alerting signals" to which the manager might pay attention when he confronts a difference.

Certain kinds of behavior may indicate that the manager's handling of differences is strongly influenced by his personal needs and feelings rather than by the objective interests of the organization—as, for example:

- A persistent tendency to surround himself with yes men.
- Emphasizing loyalty and cooperation in a way that makes disagreement seem equivalent to disloyalty and rebellion.
- A persistent tendency to "pour oil on troubled waters" whenever differences arise.
- Glossing over serious differences in order to maintain an appearance of harmony and teamwork.
- Accepting ambiguous resolutions of differences which permit conflicting parties to arrive at dissimilar interpretations.
- Exploiting differences to strengthen his personal position of influence through the weakening of the position of others.

Any of these kinds of behavior could, as we have already suggested, be appropriate in certain situations and actually serve the general interest of the organization. If, however, they represent rather consistent patterns on the part of the manager, then it may be worth his while to examine more closely the reasons for his actions.

There are times in the lives of most of us when our personal needs are the strongest determinants of our behavior. Fortunately, most organizations can tolerate a limited amount of such self-oriented behavior on the part of their managers. The danger occurs if an individual believes that his actions are solely motivated by the "good of the organization" when, in fact, he is operating on the basis of other kinds of personal motivation without being aware of it.

The manager who is more fully aware of his own feelings and inclinations is in a better position to diagnose a situation accurately and to choose rationally the kind of behavior which is in the best interests of the organization.

CONCLUSION

This article began with the assumption that many managers are uncertain and uneasy when differences arise. Because their own emotions and the feelings of others quickly become involved, they often deal with differences in a haphazard or inappropriate manner. We have attempted to suggest some more systematic ways to view differences and to deal with them. We believe that if a manager can approach a difference with less fear and with greater awareness of the potential richness that lies in it, he will better understand the basic nature and causes of the difference. And having done this, he will be in a better position to discover and implement more realistic alternatives for dealing with it.

Conflict . . . is a theme that has occupied the thinking of man more than any other, save only God and love. In the vast output of discourse on the subject, conflict has been treated in every conceivable way. It has been treated descriptively, as in history and fiction; it has been treated in an aura of moral approval, as in epos; with implicit resignation, as in tragedy; with moral disapproval, as in pacifistic religions. There is a body of knowledge called military science, presumably concerned with strategies of armed conflict. There are innumerable handbooks, which teach how to play specific games of strategy. Psychoanalysts are investigating the genesis of "fight-like" situations within the individual, and social psychologists are doing the same on the level of groups and social classes. . . .

I suspect that the most important result of a systematic and many-sided study of conflict would be the changes which such a study could effect in ourselves, the conscious and unconscious, the willing and unwilling participants in conflicts. Thus, the rewards to be realistically hoped for are the indirect ones, as was the case with the sons who were told to dig for buried treasure in the vineyard. They found no treasure, but they improved the soil.

Anatol Rapoport, *Fights, Games, and Debates*
Ann Arbor, The University of Michigan Press, 1960, pp. II, 360.

NOTES

1. For insightful treatments of the causes and consequences of conflict, and the alternative means of dealing with it — as well as with other expressions of difference — see Lewis A. Coser, *The Function of Social Conflict* (London, Routledge and Kegan Paul, Ltd., 1956); and Raymond W. Mack and Richard C. Snyder, "The Analysis of Social Conflict — Toward an Overview and Synthesis," *Conflict Resolution*, June 1957, pp. 212-248.
2. For definitions and discussions of social sensitivity and action flexibility see Robert Tannenbaum and Fred Massarik, "Leadership: A Frame of Reference," *Management Science*, Vol. 4, No. 1, October 1957; and Robert Tannenbaum and Warren H. Schmidt, "How to Choose a Leadership Pattern," HBR March-April 1958, p. 95.

THIRD PARTY ROLES IN INTERDEPARTMENTAL CONFLICT

Richard E. Walton*

Reprinted from INDUSTRIAL RELATIONS, Vol. 7, No. 1, October 1967.

Almost inherent in specialization of skills and differentiation of functions performed by organizational units is the development of inter-unit differences. Reward systems, communication obstacles, status incongruity, and other factors often make it harder to achieve coordination and integration. Manifest or potential lateral conflict is a fact of organizational life. The growing literature on the subject has focused primarily on the determinants and dynamics of the conflict and has given relatively less attention to how this conflict is managed in the interest of organizational effectiveness.

The following article analyzes third party roles and interventions which are designed to assist in the resolution or control of interunit conflict; the paper reviews organizational studies which have implications for such an analysis.[1]

"Lateral conflict" refers to conflict between peer units, that is, where there are no superior-subordinate relations. The conflict may involve entire groups or merely unit representatives. It may have its foundation in stereotypes and emotional reactions or in organizational roles and forces. It may reflect differences over factors, methods, or goals.

"Third party" refers to any nonparticipant in the conflict who may facilitate the resolution or control of conflict between primary departments. In terms of organizational positions, potential third parties include: a higher organizational executive, a third peer department not directly involved in the interunit conflict, a separate unit formally assigned to coordinate the activities of two primary units, or an internal or outside organizational consultant. These various types of role relationships are depicted in Figure 1.

A focus on third party control and resolution of conflict assumes a diagnosis that the particular conflict involved has more dysfunctional than functional consequences. For example, the conflict may be more debilitating than energizing for the participants. Or it may tend to obscure rather than clarify alternatives available to the organization. The purpose in controlling conflict is to decrease or eliminate some of the more negative consequences.

The discussion takes up four types of intervention: (1) to reduce or eliminate the conflict potential in a situation; (2) to resolve directly a substantive issue in dispute; (3) to facilitate the parties' efforts to manage a particular conflict, and (4) to help the parties change their

---

*Professor of Administrative Sciences, Purdue University.

conflict-prone relationship. A section follows which summarizes how and why each of these types of interventions is differentially available to superiors, peers, coordinative units, and consultants.

REDUCING CONFLICT POTENTIAL

A great many factors can contribute to interunit conflict. Frequently the conflict potential is inherent in the technology, organizational environment, or some essential administrative apparatus. In

FIGURE 1

Role Relationships Between Third Parties and Principals

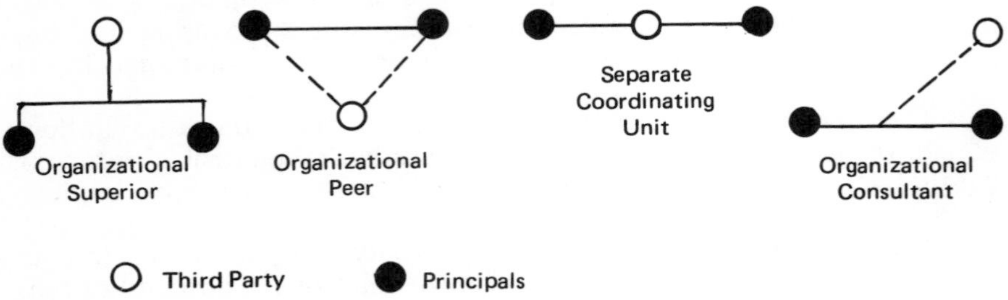

Organizational Superior   Organizational Peer   Separate Coordinating Unit   Organizational Consultant

○ Third Party   ● Principals

other cases, however, higher executives have latitude to modify the organizational structure or personnel assignment. For example:

1. Organizational superiors may adjust the allocation of rewards, status symbols, and other resources in order to ameliorate some of the sharper sources of conflict;[2] and they may decrease the specificity of those individual unit performance measures which lead to a suboptimizing orientation.[3]

2. They may reduce task load or increase capacity of units where an overload condition or task difficulty is creating bargaining or frustration among subordinate units.[4]

3. Higher executives may take steps to stabilize organizational jurisdictions for a period of time in order to decrease the ambiguity surrounding departmental status which sometimes underlies competitive interunit maneuvering. Similarly, they may make explicit rules to assign final authority for decisions on interunit matters in order to depersonalize irritating lateral influence patterns, or they may develop rules to cover an increasing proportion of interunit transactions, confining interunit decision-making to exceptional situations.[5]

4. Organizational designers may utilize mechanisms of segregation, including stricter role separation, between those organizational functions requiring affect and human relations and those requiring more impersonal social relations—because of the contradictory nature of these forms of relationship.[6]

5. Superiors may recruit, select, and assign personnel in ways that minimize the diversity of backgrounds which tends to create conflict among subordinate units[7] and that reduce the incompatibility of personalities or personal styles of unit representatives.

While the above list is not exhaustive, it includes the more important factors which both create conflict potential and are subject to the control of organizational architects or superiors.

RESOLVING SUBSTANTIVE ISSUES

By higher executives. Brown emphasizes the frequency with which interunit conflict signals the need for superiors to become involved and to contribute to the substance of the decision. Often a disputed point between managers indicates that finely balanced judgments are involved. Only a manager with broader understanding and responsibility should make the judgments. Therefore, in Brown's experience, "rapid exposure of the disagreement at the cross-over point" is necessary. The cross-over point is the first executive to whom both departments report. As an extension of the superior's own power and judgment, he may bring in an outside technical expert to evaluate the merits of the positions of the contending parties.[8]

By taking an active role on substantive issues, executives offset the tendency for subordinates either to persist in or to compromise disagreements when the final decision should be made at a higher level. This pattern also satisfies a higher manager's need to be informed.[9]

According to Brown, higher managers are more likely to play this type of third party role in a timely and appropriate way if they avoid communicating that they regard subordinate conflict as personal failure, and, rather, communicate that they see the interunit conflict as reflecting inherent executive dilemmas or poor organizational policies, or both.[10]

Taking a somewhat different position, Blake, Shepard, and Mouton argue that third party judgments in win-lose struggles simply relieve the parties from the struggle itself, but not from the problems of defeat. They find that losers tend to feel an imposed decision was unfair, to suspect the third party, and to doubt his competence or understanding of the problem. These authors also mention third party use of fate mechanisms, such as the flip of a coin, to decide interunit conflicts regarded as inevitable. Even a superior's appeal to the disputants to accept his judgment in a "good sportsman-like way" is a subtle use of a fate mechanism.[11]

Separate coordinating units. Where basic departments which are interdependent in work flow sequence are highly differentiated from each other there is a tendency to use a permanent separate unit to help achieve coordination between them. In a study by Lawrence and Lorsch, such third party units used their own substantive analysis to influence decisions.[12] The authors differentiated three principal units—research, sales, and production—on four dimensions: (1) degree of structure, i.e., tightness of rules, narrowness of span of supervisory control, and frequency and specificity of performance review; (2) members' orientation toward time, i.e., length of time perspective; (3) members' orientation toward others, i.e., openness and permissiveness of interpersonal relationships; and (4) members' orientation toward different subgoals and segments of the organizational environment, i.e., new scientific knowledge versus customer problems and opportunities versus raw materials and processing costs. Thus, for example, a sales unit compared with the production unit may tend to be less structured, to have a longer time perspective, to be more permissive in interpersonal orientation, and to be more oriented toward the market environment.

Measurements of the degree of differentiation among the three departments were applied to firms in the plastics, food, and container industries. In plastics, the research, sales, and production departments were most differentiated; all six firms used a separate coordinating unit. In the food and container industries, only one of the two firms studied used a separate unit.

What factors influenced the effectiveness of these separate third party units? If a coordinating unit had an intermediate or balanced orientation to those factors which differentiated the basic departments, it was better able to facilitate interdepartmental decision-making. The managers of the basic departments apparently believed it was especially important for the third parties to have balanced time perspective and subgoal orientation.

Technical expertise is also important if third parties are to settle substantive disputes. The coordinating units in all six plastics firms studied by Lawrence and Lorsch had considerable power relative to their counterparts in the basic departments. However, in the two plastics firms where there was great respect for the technical competence of the third party personnel, there was also a higher level of integration. The experience of the food company's integrative unit was slightly different. At first its power was perceived by the basic departments as being based on its proximity to the president; however, as the basic departments gained respect for its expertise, the integrative unit made an increasingly positive contribution to conflict resolution.

What is the relative effectiveness of using a separate coordinating unit as opposed to relying on the crossover executive to resolve differences? Lawrence and Lorsch compared the way two container firms achieved interunit integration in the areas of scheduling and customer service, both frequently the subject of disagreement. One firm utilized a formal third party unit to facilitate coordination. The other firm relied on the crossover executive alone. The second arrangement was more effective in resolving conflict and more acceptable to the basic departments. Why? Although both arrangements provided a third party with a balanced orientation, the coordinating unit lacked the power and relevant information that the crossover executive had in the second firm (see Table 1).

TABLE 1

Relative Effectiveness of Coordinating Unit and
Crossover Executive in Dispute Resolution, Two Firms

Third Parties	Attributes		
	Balanced orientation	Power	Relevant information[a]
Coordinating unit	High	Low	Moderate
Crossover executive	High	High	High

Source: Based on Paul R. Lawrence and Jay W. Lorsch, *New Directions for Organizations* (Boston: Graduate School of Business Administration, Harvard University, 1967).
[a]About plant capacity and customer requirements.

Participation of a peer department. Still another potential source of third party influence on the substance of an interunit issue is a peer department which is not essentially involved.

Zald studied the pattern of interunit conflict among teachers, social service workers, and cottage parents in five delinquency institutions. The relative influence of the three types of units varied from institution to institution. The two lower influence departments tended to be more in conflict with the high influence department than with each other. Zald suggested that these conflict patterns reflected a tendency to balance off the high power of one department.[13] Presumably the entry of a third party into an issue primarily between two units reduced unilateral decision-making and allowed the third party to exercise some substantive influence.

Dalton described the use of third party peer departments to force resolution of decisions which might otherwise represent an impass.[14] Whether or not this represents third party intervention in the sense of this paper depends on whether the third unit is interested primarily in helping to resolve the conflict or in entering into a coalition for the purpose of exchanging favors and influence.

MANAGING MANIFEST CONFLICT

The type of third party intervention described immediately above is concerned with the substance of the issues in dispute. In contrast, the interventions to help manage manifest conflict act on the *processes* of conflict and conflict management.

Influencing gross patterns of contact. It is often possible to improve conflict management processes by affecting the gross pattern of interunit contact and coordination efforts. Some of these control techniques are available to the parties through their own initiative as well as at the initiative of a third party.

Sometimes control involves constraining interunit contact. In one production-sales relationship studied by Walton, Dutton, and Fitch, certain restrictions were designed to preserve a tenuously improving relationship. Interunit business transactions were channeled through the chief liaison personnel representing each department in order to reduce the likelihood of accidents or other provocative acts. For example, salesmen were not allowed to go onto the shipping dock or directly contact the shipping clerk.[15]

Direct contact between principals is sometimes reduced by using a low status, "expendable-linker" in interface activities.[16] This person elicits less hostility and absorbs the inevitable punishment more easily as he has less emotional energy invested in the relationship. In a similar vein, buffer inventories can be used to reduce the tightness of dependency and resulting need for frequent close coordination.[17]

In other instances, collaboration can be improved between departments by promoting interunit contacts. An obvious and basic way is to increase physical proximity. As an example, the ambassador of a large overseas mission reorganized office space and dispersed many sections of the AID mission in order to bring together physically the following and other combinations: assistant director of AID, economic counselor of the State Department, and the Treasury attaché; the AID capital development office and the Commerce attaché; etc. These changes facilitated functional coordination.[18]

Brown prescribes several roles for superiors who are aware of conflict between subordinates, including (1) ensuring that they confront their conflict, with a view toward resolving it; and (2) discussing with subordinates those lateral conflicts they fail to resolve on their own. Thus, the supervisor simply adds his own pressure for continued work on the conflict to that already inherent in the issues.[19] According to the "linking pin" concept of Likert, supervisors also can play an even more positive, social-emotional role in facilitating the resolution of conflict among subordinate units.[20]

In the overseas mission referred to above, the ambassador and his staff assistant had leadership patterns which combined to promote increased interunit contact and coordination. The ambassador let it be known that he had firm expectations that the separate agencies in the mission would find ways to coordinate their affairs and collaborate where appropriate. He asked for information about friction and was willing to exercise the force at his command to bring reluctant agencies into interagency contact. His staff assistant complemented the ambassador's harsh approach by encouraging, arranging, facilitating, and reinforcing interagency contacts and instances of coordination. He did use the influence of the ambassador, but subtly enough that his interpersonal and organizational skills at facilitation were the more apparent part of his approach. Thus, the moderately high power third party who punished instances of noncooperation was complemented by the low power, socially skillful third party who could facilitate the necessary interunit contacts. Both were more effective because their third party roles were combined and coordinated.

In other cases it is unclear whether the use of process intermediaries increases or decreases the gross rate of interunit interaction. Blake, Shepard, and Mouton cite a company in which a man was employed full time at the corporate level "for the sole purpose of trying to bring competing components of the organization into some reasonable alignment."[21] Burns and Stalker refer to "liaison specialists—whose job was to move across the linguistic and functional frontiers and to act as intermediaries between the people getting on with the job."[22] The use of such intermediaries was apparently a symptom of less effective organizations in the firms they studied.

Influencing the approach to issues in dispute. A variety of distinctions have been made in how parties handle their differences. Schmidt and Tannenbaum cite avoidance, repression, sharpening into conflict, and transformation into problem-solving.[23] Blake, Shepard, and Mouton contrast a "win-lose" approach and problem-solving.[24] Walton elaborates two joint decision-making models, bargaining and problem-solving; these engagement approaches both contrast with a withdrawal posture.[25] Lawrence and Lorsch identify problem-solving, smoothing, and forcing. [26]

Common to all of these studies is problem-solving, where both parties strive toward: defining the problem in terms of underlying needs, exploring a wide range of alternatives, portraying accurately the strength of one's needs and preferences, and selecting alternatives that create the most joint gain. The outcomes of problem-solving are often integrative solutions rather than compromises. All authors appear to advocate strongly more frequent use of problem-solving, though they also acknowledge that under some conditions another approach makes sense. This general predeliction for confrontation and problem-solving appears to be justified in terms of the results of the Lawrence and Lorsch studies. The better performing firms tended to handle conflict by confronting it, rather than by smoothing it over or forcing outcomes.

Schmidt and Tannenbaum spelled out some of the third party interventions which facilitate problem-solving. The interventions are presumably available to superiors, consultants, and perhaps organizational peers.[27]

1. The third party can invite differences and stress their value in increasing the range of alternatives available to the organization. To the extent that the parties perceive value to the confrontation process, each is less likely to define success in terms of attaining the particular outcome which he preferred initially.
2. The third party can listen with understanding rather than evaluation. The conflicting parties themselves usually don't listen to one another. Each is too busy trying to be understood. By listening and understanding, the third party can contribute to the parties' understanding of each other's position. Also, the third party's listening example is frequently followed by the participants themselves.

3. The third party can clarify the nature of the issue, e.g., whether it revolves around different perceptions of facts, methods, values, or goals. Disputants themselves often depart from the original issue by chasing a tangential point or by transposing the issue. The more detached third party can perform a welcome function by helping the disputants develop a common understanding of the issue and by repeatedly bringing them back to it.

4. The third party can recognize and accept the feelings of the individuals involved. Interunit disagreements are often compounded by the irrational feelings they generate, such as fear, jealousy, anger, or anxiety. When a third party communicates to a person that he can understand and accept these feelings he assists both participants to accept these feelings and to analyze their impact on the outstanding disagreement. The risk associated with identifying these "negative" feelings is that the person who is identified with them will feel criticized and become more defensive.

5. The third party can suggest procedures for resolving differences— the particular techniques depending on whether facts, methods, goals, or values are at issue. Walton and McKersie also suggest a variety of techniques to promote problem-solving when the mixed motive nature of the issue also requires some bargaining: differentiating the two types of interunit decision processes by fractionating the issue, by interunit representatives, by time, by ground rules, etc. [28]

6. Blake, Shepard, and Mouton, who approach interdepartmental and union-management conflict in similar ways, emphasize intergroup dynamics. The third party can help the groups cope with what the authors call the "traitor threat," which involves loss of status and rejection of any representative who concedes points to the other group. The third party can influence the composition of the intergroup meeting or help regulate meeting caucuses and recesses in order to allow more continuous interchange between representatives and other members of their respective units. [29]

FACILITATING CHANGING THE RELATIONSHIP

Now, rather than analyzing interventions which act either on substance or process of conflict, we treat third party interventions which enable two units to perceive and move toward a new equilibrium—a relationship in which there is less emotional conflict and a generally improved capacity to solve differences.

In a task leadership context: interagency relations in Washington and overseas. Many different departments and agencies of the U.S. government play a role in the conduct of foreign affairs: State, Defense, Agriculture, AID, Peace Corps, Commerce, CIA, to mention merely the more important ones. The agencies are coordinated in the field missions by the ambassador and his country team. Also, interdepartmental groups, comprised of several of these departments and chaired by an assistant secretary of state, have been created in Washington to co-ordinate foreign affairs on a regional basis. However, with very few exceptions, no such mechanism in Washington exists for coordinating these agencies' interests pertaining to an individual country. Generally the separate efforts are not well integrated, considerable mutual suspicion and low regard exists among agencies, and no well developed problem-solving mechanisms exist for resolving interagency dif-ferences.

Walton studied the innovative efforts of one country director (i.e., the ambassador's counterpart in the Washington, D.C., organization of the State Department) who has tried to increase interdepartmental integration and coordination at his level.[30] Beginning in May 1966, he scheduled meetings on a monthly basis, inviting representatives from about a dozen agencies—those persons directly concerned with the affairs of the same foreign country.

The country director, who did not have the power to compel membership or attendance, relied on his own skill in managing the sessions to make discussions productive and valuable to individual members. Many meetings featured informal presentations by persons with unique knowledge about the country, followed by round-table discussions of the issues raised. His method of handling meetings included relating himself to members directly and personally; urging continuity in the personnel representing an agency, differentiating one-time observers from regular members; encouraging, accepting, and helping develop views which differed from his own; and not keeping minutes on the meetings.

By the way he managed the sessions he gradually achieved certain states that in turn improved the problem-solving and conflict resolution capacity of this interagency network. Common exposure of the agency representatives to experts and to each other, and their own mutual education and information exchange activities, decreased the likeli-hood of future interagency conflict based on differences in perceived facts and tended to break down many negative intergroup stereotypes that exist about Peace Corps, Military, CIA, and State, etc. The develop-ment of personal relationships among agency representatives in-creased their tendency to check with each other for specific advice, information, and to coordinate activities generally. Encouragement of dissent and challenge in the absence of compelling policy or action decisions was effective in setting a group norm of sharpening, accept-ing, and exploring differences—a norm which could carry over into solving specific problems. A corollary group norm was one of identifying the additional information which the group would need if it were to choose between the alternative views. The agency representatives not only achieved a better understanding from State Department officials of overall goals for U.S. relations with the country in question but also became more committed to them by virtue of a sense of identification with the interagency group. This enhanced sense of membership in the group and commitment to superordinate goals increased a member's personal discomfort whenever his agency's actions ignored the interests of other agencies.

Interagency matters pertaining to a given country are somewhat better coordinated in the field than in Washington.[31] For example, the country team, comprised of the top officials of the important agencies and headed by the ambassador, is an established concept and usually provides some integration. Nevertheless, the amount of coordination is limited by many pervasive factors: (1) interagency stereotypes; resentments about incongruities among formal status, actual influence, and privileges (such as automobile allowances and invitations to diplomatic parties); (2) an agency's fears that its programs' identities will be blurred, its personnel misused, and its program activities oversupervised.

In the overseas mission studied, the ambassador and his staff had been relatively effective in encouraging interagency contacts. The third party roles they normally played are described above. An additional important experimental device for achieving a higher and more creative level of integration of the many strands of foreign affairs activities was referred to as the "Think Tank." It was an informal weekly meeting of a group drawn from many agencies to think imaginatively about problems of concern to the foreign affairs community as a whole. The ambassador's staff assistant had played a key role in initiating the idea. The group also included a second staff assistant to the ambassador, the deputy director of AID, an assistant director of AID, two military men, and a second level official from USIS. A ground rule for members was that they were to address the problems rather than represent their respective agencies' viewpoints.[32] Generally this group included bright young men below the country team level. Apparently group meetings not only weakened stereotypes but also increased members' confidence in their similar goals and the complementary competencies of their respective agencies. At the time of the study, they had identified some new potential areas of collaboration which they intended to recommend pursuing.

The examples of the country director in Washington and the staff assistant in the overseas mission both illustrate a third party whose relationship to the other person involved slightly greater organizational power, somewhat higher status, and higher access to information. Their interventions centered on task activities which did not require immediate action outside the group, but were nevertheless immediately gratifying to members. Their critical intervention strategy was to build a social system and their process tactics ensured that the system had norms and other attributes which facilitated the productive use of differences.

In a behavioral science consulting context: an intergroup laboratory. Modifying the barriers to interunit collaboration is part of the more general problem of planned organizational change.[33] Blake, Shepard, and Mouton have utilized sensitivity training laboratory methods to improve intergroup relations in industry. Illustrative of their change strategy is the following account of their efforts which focused on the relations between headquarters and a field unit of a diversified and moderately decentralized industrial firm. This particular interunit relationship had attributes of both vertical and lateral relationships. The headquarters unit of Tennex Corporation performed staff as well as supervisory functions for the large Scofield unit.

The behavioral science consultants called in to help improve relationships first acquainted themselves with key management in both locations and the patterns of interactions, frustrations, and stereotypes in a generally deteriorating relationship.

Headquarters personnel felt the division managers were "secretive" and "unresponsive." The division was looked upon as unwilling to provide information that headquarters felt it needed. In turn, Scofield division management saw the headquarters management as "prying" and "arbitrary." For example, headquarters was critical of the labor relations practices of the division. The division management resented the criticism, regarding it as prejudiced and ill-informed. Again, headquarters felt that Scofield managers had been "dragging their feet" in implementing corporate marketing policies. Scofield felt that headquarters' demands in this area were unrealistic and that the corporate marketing group was behaving "unilaterally," and so on.[34]

The first of two basic types of intervention was training in group and intergroup dynamics. Separate three-day conferences with each group were designed to provide members with laboratory experiences which were in many respects analogous to those they face in their organizational roles. In this somewhat protected context, the consultants could identify the social dynamics while they were occurring, increase managers' awareness about how they were coping with them, and provide theory which generalized the experience and made credible its application to other situations.

. . . First, managers were able to see the headquarters-field problem in sufficient perspective to analyze the destructive consequences of the win-lose trap which had been dictating their actions. Second, an intergroup experiment and its analysis created a degree of openness within each group of managers that enabled them to review their own intragroup relationships and to develop greater mutual understanding and acceptance. This teamwork training is an important prelude to intergroup confrontation. because friction, "politics," or inability to level within each team clouds and confuses intergroup communication when the two groups are brought together.[35]

The second basic intervention was a three-day conference in which the two groups met together. This intervenion involved the following phased activities:

Phase I: meeting together the groups listed and assigned priorities to those issues they felt required joint problem-solving.

Phase II: meeting separately each group prepared a description of itself as viewed by its members, constructed a verbal image of the other group, and finally built a description of their mutual relationships. These images supplemented the previously developed list of substantive issues, by providing an inventory of existing perceptions and feelings which needed to be examined, understood, and overcome.

Phase III: each group in turn exposed its own image of itself and in turn listened to the image as perceived by the other group. By their previous interventions, the consultants had created among participants a spirit of inquiry and a desire to listen for understanding rather than evaluation. As a result, the present activity of bringing these images into the open increased the general feelings of being understood and accepted. Then the participants again reviewed the substantive issues between the units.

Phase IV: several subgroups were formed of headquarters and field personnel with corresponding functional responsibilities. They first explored interpersonal issues and then tabled the functional problems they shared.

Phase V: a review was made of the progress in subgroups and between the units as a whole, and an analysis followed of the kinds of changes required in order to bring about actual improvements. One of the results of Phases IV and V was that headquarters personnel saw more clearly the alternative of conceiving themselves as "consultants" to the field rather than as persons who "control" field operations. They also better perceived the advantages of more mutual influence on policy-making and more continuous feedback about implementation. The groups agreed to reconvene for review and evaluation after a period of implementation.

By the end of phase V the groups had increased their mutual trust, respect, and understanding. In addition, they had made a number of commitments to new ways of either preventing or handling interunit differences.

Interpersonal confrontation between key personalities. Walton has described and analyzed the functions performed by a behavioral science consulting intervention which facilitated the confrontation of differences between the officials of two interdependent units in a government agency.[36]

The confrontation occured between two program officers, whom we shall refer to as Bill and Lloyd. Bill's unit had overall project responsibility for designing an organizational system. Lloyd's unit provided many of the professional personnel engaged in the design work of the project. Lloyd himself had only recently assumed responsibility for supervising his unit's activities on the systems project. Friction had developed immediately between them. Bill decided to arrange a meeting with Lloyd specifically to review the working relationship between them and their respective units. He invited the consultant to participate as a third party. Lloyd agreed to the arrangement.

When the three of them met, Lloyd's initial statement of their difficulty stressed several intergroup issues. He asserted that his unit's personnel were being used below their capabilities and should be used more strategically. He felt that his unit had too little decision influence. He also believed that his own leadership position within his group was undermined by Bill's operating style. For his part, Bill was annoyed and harassed by what he regarded as dominating patterns of behavior by Lloyd in a combined group meeting. He objected to a similar pattern in their current interaction.

With the help of the third party they identified and discussed the issues which separated them, testing whether the differences were real or only apparent. Interestingly, as Lloyd realized that he was being listened to and understood and that the initially stated intergroup issues were being taken seriously, he began to identify more personal concerns about his own role and identity. For example, he did not feel sufficiently "connected" with the total project; moreover, he believed his own relevant experience and competence were not being recognized by Bill. It became apparent that these interpersonal concerns were an underlying part of the intergroup issues stated initially.

The confrontation was regarded by both participants and the consultant as successful. Some differences were resolved, and although other differences persisted, both principals believed they had established a basis for continuing to work on the issues. Further reports confirmed that the confrontation had been a significant factor in the improvement which occurred in their relationship and indicated that the consultant had played an important role in the confrontation.

Analysis of the confrontation suggests the functions performed by the third party. First, the consultant's presence facilitated openness in the confrontation, which enabled the parties to get the issues out and to redefine intergroup issues as interpersonal problems where appropriate. Both previously had participated in separate one-week sensitivity training workshops where high openness is normative. The consultant who was identified with sensitivity training emphasized the relevance of that prior sensitivity experience and made other attempts to invoke the norm of openness.

Second, the consultant was a synchronizing element. Arranging for the consultant's presence for a specific meeting served to create and confirm mutual expectations that they would confront their outstanding differences. Different expectations and different degrees of readiness often result in one person feeling "caught off guard" by another's attempt to raise the issues. The person who isn't prepared or doesn't recognize the other's attempt at confrontation certainly won't respond satisfactorily. Then the person whose attempt to confront is not reciprocated subsequently may well feel he overexposed himself and react by himself avoiding discussion of their issues in the future. Once Bill and Lloyd were into an exploration of their differences, the limited time availability of the consultant added further pressure to somewhat offset a natural tendency for the participants to smooth over their differences.

Third, the participants perceived the consultant as possessing behavioral skills and techniques which they could call upon if necessary. They believed that they ran less risk that the confrontation would bog down, get repetitive, and result in more frustration and bitterness. As a result, they entered into the meeting with more readiness.

Finally, the consultant both helped diagnose the underlying issues and provided an ingredient of emotional support for the participants. The third party listened to each discuss his views and feelings and sharpened what he understood to be an issue; the participants then responded in ways which tended to confirm or disconfirm that this was the underlying issue. An effort was made to state the issues in ways which made each person's position understandable, legitimate, and acceptable. One apparent effect of this was to encourage Lloyd to go on to identify the more personal concerns he had about not being involved and not being recognized as a competent person with experience relevant to the project.

ROLE ATTRIBUTES AND INTERVENTIONS: A SUMMARY

A third party may be related to the principals as an organizational superior, consultant, separate coordinating unit, or peer. These four role relationships differ in many respects, including the magnitude and types of power available to the third party, the degree of impartiality likely to be attributed to the third party, and the degree of relevant knowledge possessed by the third party. We can summarize how these and other aspects of the role relationships of a third party govern which of the four types of interventions are available to him.

Superiors. Superiors are the only third parties likely to have the organizational power to reduce conflict potential by restructuring the organization or reassigning personnel. Also, assuming that a superior's responsibility embraces both units, his view would be balanced enough to play this third party role. The main difficulty is that superiors often do not have an adequate information base or diagnostic framework by which to assess the dysfunctional consequences of conflict and the basic underlying causes. Moreover, elimination of the factors which induced the dysfunctional conflict in the first instance may not significantly reduce the conflict because of the number of self-reinforcing and regenerating processes involved in the relationship pattern.[37] Hence, structural interventions to reduce conflict potential need to be accompanied by process or clinical interventions to facilitate the change in lateral relationships.

Organization superiors can be too little or too much involved in the substance of a dispute. If deciding the issue requires unique judgment, he should be involved. He is more likely to be brought into the conflict if he tends to view inter-unit differences as based on task realities rather than arising from the emotional interreactions of line subordinates. However, substantive intervention by superiors runs the risk of creating "win-lose" reactions on the part of subordinates, especially if his action on the issue is intended merely to avoid further affects of the conflict process rather than to contribute unique knowledge.

Superiors sometimes facilitate the process of confronting and solving differences. To do this, a superior needs certain behavioral skills rather than unique knowledge about the issue in dispute. High organizational power is a mixed blessing to him in promoting problem-solving. On the one hand, he can require subordinates to change their gross pattern of interunit contact. On the other hand, his high power may inhibit the participants and discourage them from taking the personal risks associated with sharpening the issues in dispute. Similarly, high organizational power complicates a third party's attempts to create a nonevaluative social-emotional climate conducive to identifying and working through negative interunit attitudes.

Organizational consultants. The organizational consultant lacks the superior's power to modify directly the conflict potential factors or to decide the substantive issues in dispute. However, he is usually in a relatively better position to influence the interaction processes. This is true to the extent that the consultant is perceived to have little or no preference regarding the outcome of a dispute, to have both objectivity and expertise which make him a fruitful source of diagnostic insight, to be nonevaluative, to be a source of emotional support, and to have high skills in facilitating interaction processes. The consultant can be used first to help the subordinate departments identify the organizational factors contributing to the conflict. Then, in association with organizational changes designed to reduce conflict potential, the consultant third party can facilitate the change in actual relationships.

Although we have not treated the problem here in any detail, it should be noted that the interpersonal styles and institutional props which create the appropriate role identity for consultant third parties are often as important as his active interventions.

Coordinating units. Given the need for interdepartmental coordination, the more differentiated are the basic department's orientations, the more likely it is that a continuous, specialized third party can contribute to the resolution of inter-unit conflicts. If organizational differentiation is not great the interventions of a third party can reduce rather than enhance coordination.

The separate coordinative units studied were all intended to manage interdepartmental differences via substantive contributions to decision-making. The requisite role attributes for this type of intervention are balanced (or intermediate) orientation, high substantive knowledge, and moderately high organizational power (relative to the basic departments).

Peer units. There is very little evidence of peer organizational units performing neutral third party roles. Perhaps there is little reward and high risk associated with informally taking on third party functions. A peer organizational unit may have certain inherent disadvantages. First, it would not have the high power of a superior. Second, it would not have the substantive expertise of a coordinative unit. Third, typically, it would have an even more difficult time than a superior or a separate coordinative group in convincing the disputants that it had a balanced orientation. Fourth, it probably would not possess the process skills of the organizational consultant.

Ambiguous organizational role relationships. The State Department's relationship to the other foreign affairs agencies is an ambiguous mixture of the various types treated here. It is primarily a peer unit, but with legitimacy for certain supervisory and coordinative functions. State lacks authority to modify the basic structure within which the agencies deal with each other. Nevertheless, State personnel have an opportunity to design certain joint task activities and provide task leadership.

The studies reported on here focused on officials who had relatively high behavioral skill which they used to improve interagency relationships. In particular, they took advantage of slightly higher organizational power and status and high task information in order to design and lead collaborative task activities, which in turn created group membership and norms more favorable to the constructive management of interagency differences.

CONCLUSION

The present treatment is tentative and less than comprehensive in treating the range of issues involved in third party analysis. Under what conditions is it useful to intervene? What are the optimum third party role attributes for resolving types of conflicts? How are these role attributes established? By individual? Or by organization? When should an intervention be specific to a dispute? When should it treat the relationship? When should it focus on the conflict potential in the organizational context? These questions are important enough to warrant much additional research.

NOTES

1. This research was supported by AF 49(638)-1751, ARPA contract for "The Role of Third Parties in Conflict Resolution and Control."
2. James D. Thompson, "Organizational Management of Conflict," *Administrative Science Quarterly*, IV (1960), 389-409.
3. Richard E. Walton, "Theory of Conflict in Lateral Organizational Relationships," in J.R. Lawrence, editor, *Operational Research and the Social Sciences* (London: Tavistock, 1966), pp. 409-428.
4. *Ibid.*
5. Wilfred Brown, *Explorations in Management* (London: Tavistock, 1960); Henry A. Landsberger, "The Horizontal Dimension in a Bureaucracy," *Administrative Science Quarterly*, VI (1961), 298-333.
6. Eugene Litwak, "Models of Bureaucracy Which Permit Conflict," *American Journal of Sociology*, LXVII (1961), 177-184.
7. Thompson, *op. cit.*
8. Brown, *op. cit.*, p. 69.
9. George Strauss, "Work-Flow Frictions, Interfunctional Rivalry, and Professionalism: A Case Study of Purchasing Agents," *Human Organization*, XXIII (1964), 137-149.
10. Brown, *op. cit.*
11. Robert R. Blake, Herbert A. Shepard, and Jane S. Mouton, *Intergroup Conflict in Organizations* (Ann Arbor, Mich.: Foundation for Research on Human Behavior, 1964).
12. Paul R. Lawrence and Jay W. Lorsch, *New Directions for Organizations* (Boston: Graduate School of Business Administration, Harvard University, 1967).
13. Myer N. Zald, "Power Balance and Staff Conflict in Correctional Institutions," *Administrative Science Quarterly*, VII (1962), 22-49.
14. Melville Dalton, *Men Who Manage* (New York: Wiley, 1959).
15. Richard E. Walton, John M. Dutton, and H. G. Fitch, "A Study of Conflict in the Process, Structure, and Attitudes of Lateral Relationships," In Albert Rubenstein and Chadwick Haberstroh, editors, *Some Theories of Organization* (Rev. ed.; Homewood, Ill.: Irwin, 1966), pp. 444-465.
16. John A. Seiler, "Diagnosing Interdepartmental Conflict," *Harvard Business Review*, XLI (September-October, 1963), 121-132.
17. Louis R. Pondy, *Organizational Conflict: Concepts and Models* (mimeographed, Graduate School of Business, University of Pittsburgh, 1965).
18. Richard E. Walton, *Interagency Coordination in the Overseas Mission* (mimeographed, 1966).

19. Brown, *op. cit.*
20. Rensis Likert, *New Patterns of Management* (New York: McGraw-Hill, 1961).
21. Blake, Shepard, and Mouton, *op. cit.*, p. 109.
22. Tom Burns and G. M. Stalker, *The Management of Innovation* (London: Tavistock, 1961).
23. Warren Schmidt and Robert Tannenbaum, "The Management of Differences," *Harvard Business Review*, XXXVIII (November-December, 1960), 107-115.
24. Blake, Shepard, and Mouton, *op. cit.*
25. "Theory of Conflict . . ."
26. Lawrence and Lorsch, *op. cit.*
27. Schmidt and Tannenbaum, *op. cit.*
28. Richard E. Walton and Robert B. McKersie, "Behavioral Dilemmas in Mixed Motive Decision Making," *Behavioral Science*, XL (1966), 370-384.
29. Blake, Shepard, and Mouton, *op. cit.*
30. Richard E. Walton, *A Centrepetal Force in Foreign Affairs* (mimeographed, 1967).
31. Walton, *Interagency Coordination.* . . .
32. The "Think Tank" is very similar to an informal problem-solving and strategic-thinking group at Case Institute of Technology, which referred to itself as the "Hats Group" because each person was expected to leave his departmental hat at the door.
33. Chris Argyris, *Interpersonal Competence and Organizational Effectiveness* (Homewood, Ill.: Dorsey, 1962); Edgar H. Schein and Warren G. Bennis, *Personal and Organizational Change Through Group Methods: The Laboratory Approach* (New York: Wiley, 1965).
34. Blake, Shepard, and Mouton, *op. cit.*, p. 116.
35. *Ibid.*, p. 117.
36. Richard E. Walton, "Interpersonal Confrontation and Basic Third Party Roles: A Case Study," *Journal of Applied Behavioral Science* (forthcoming, 1967).
37. John M. Dutton and Richard E. Walton, "Interdepartmental Conflict and Cooperation: Two Contrasting Studies," *Human Organization*, XXV (1966), 207-220.

SECTION IV

TECHNO-STRUCTURAL

INTERVENTION

EDITOR'S OVERVIEW

When the OD specialist becomes involved in helping to plan and implement a change in the organization chart, in job requirements, or in the working environment (e.g., rearranging office furniture), he is using a techno-structural intervention. In this area of organization change there is an opportunity for a "wedding" of behavioral science to systems analysis and other related specialties. Change efforts should be facilitated because of the special abilities of each. Behavioral scientists can be useful in helping to lessen the dysfunctional concomitants of social change; systems analysts can apply their special skills to solving the more technological problems of organizational change.

Research evidence indicates that when the persons to be affected by a technological change in the organizational structure are involved in the planning and implementing process or have increased responsibility and authority in their work, their resistance to the change diminishes. The first paper in this section reports a research study in which the organizational structure and the duties, responsibilities, and authority of first-line supervisors in an aircraft organization were changed. It was found that when the supervisors received more responsbility and authority for their work, their performance increased (as well as their subordinates' performance), and the attitudes of both the supervisors and their subordinates became more positive toward their work and the organization.

The changes in responsibilities and authority are similar to what Herzberg has called "job enrichment." As mentioned in the introductory chapter, this form of change can be classified as a techno-structural intervention and fit into an overall OD effort quite easily. The second article in this section cautions that job enrichment is not always as possible or as desirable as its proponents would lead us to believe, because of differences among individuals and types of work.

The final article in this section, by Porter and Lawler, reviews recent literature concerning the relationships of various dimensions of organizational structure to the behavior and attitudes of workers. Although this article is more scholarly than practical, it helps us to understand what tends to happen when certain properties of an organization's structure are modified. The seven structural variables covered are organizational levels, line and staff hierarchies, span of control, subunit size, total organization size, tall or flat shape, and centralized or decentralized shape. For example, we learn that decentralization does not necessarily improve either job attitudes or performance. As with many other phenomena, job improvement stemming from decentralization is highly situational.

STUDIES IN SUPERVISORY JOB DESIGN[1]

Louis E. Davis and Ernst S. Valfer

Considering the critical importance with which the supervisor is regarded as the interface between management and men, it is surprising that so much contradiction exists about the design of supervisors' jobs. Too frequently job designs for most positions, including the supervisor's, are based on unrealistic and inappropriate models regarding human behavior in productive organizations founded on unsupported dogma or on popular clichés.

The design of suitable supervisor jobs is further complicated by conflicting objectives imposed on the supervisor vis-à-vis men and management, by the supervisor's uncertainties over the behaviors required of him for effective leadership of work groups stemming from conflict over perceived choice of authoritarian-participative management styles and by the implied threat to his status and effectiveness inherent in management's advocacy of participation (without support), and, lastly, by the ambiguity surrounding the discharge of his responsibility.

Managements appear to be well acquainted with the considerable body of evidence arising from organizational and behavioral studies that challenge accepted underlying organizational and job-design practices. Formidable inhibitions in the form of rigidity of policies, relationships, evaluation modes, and practices usually develop in organizations that inhibit the use of this knowledge.

The consequences are inadequate job designs and ad hoc applica - tion of piecemeal research results. The conviction still predominates that superior job performance, as measured by organizationally relevant criteria, is obtained when the technological requirements are given primary if not exclusive consideration in the design of jobs. Requirements such as communication, group formation, personality development, decision-making and control, etc. are seen as marginal at best, and at worst as opposed to the satisfaction of technological requirements. This fictitious conflict characterizes the poverty of present conceptualization of human behavior in productive organizations helping to maintain the dominance of technological requirements as exclusive determinants of job contents and relationships, and unfortunately reducing the prospect of developing an understanding of the job as part of a socio-technical system having technological, social, and personal components.

To aid in the development of models that are realistic in terms of social and personal as well as technological variables, studies of first-level supervisors' jobs were undertaken which modified both the formal organization structure as well as the structure, content, responsibility, and authority of the jobs. These were macro-level experimental studies, in that they were not directed to the study of a supervisor's personal relationships with his workers or his superior. They examined the changes in the distribution of the supervisor's activities, in the performance of the supervisor's work group as measured by total operating costs and quantity and quality of output, and in the attitudes and perceptions of the supervisor and his workers in response to their new job contents, structures, and responsibilities.

These job design studies are part of a continuing series (Davis & Valfer, 1964; Davis & Valfer, 1965; Davis, 1966), in which jobs, taken as one of the components of socio-technical systems (Emery & Trist, 1960), are examined by modifying them experimentally to test hypotheses regarding the effects of content and structure on performance effectiveness. By job design we mean specification of the content, the methods, and the relationships of jobs to satisfy the requirements, as measured by total economic costs, of the technology and the organization as well as the social and personal requirements of the job-holder. Prior studies (Davis & Canter, 1956; Davis, 1957; Davis & Werling, 1960) of worker-level jobs have provided insights into some job-design requirements having implications for the contents of supervisors' jobs and for organization structure.

In the studies reported here, modification in formal organization structure and in duties, responsibilities, and authority of some first-level supervisors were introduced into a number of shops, the basic organizational unit, by the management of the civilian industrial department of a large West Coast military establishment, as part of a planned experimental field study directed by a University of California research team. The primary function of this department was to overhaul, repair, and test military aircraft and their components. With the exception of the senior executives, all of its 5,900 employees were civilians, of whom 3,800 were employed in direct or production activities. The studies were confined to eleven shops in which sensing, power, and control accessories of aircraft systems were overhauled, repaired, and tested. The shops, ranging in size from 18 to 30 employees, were assigned to experimental or control status after matching by type of work, style of supervision, skills available, and past performance.

The experimentally introduced modifications of the supersivors' jobs were designed to test the hypothesis that: higher economic productivity (lower total costs) and greater needs satisfaction for members of a work group, including the supervisor, will result from specifying the job contents of the supervisor in the direction of increasing his authority and responsibility by including direct control over all operational and inspection functions required to complete and determine final acceptance (inspection) of the products or services assigned to his work group. In one group of two experimental shops, with two control shops, the supervisor's job design was changed to provide authority and responsibility over all functions required to complete the products processed in his shop. This is referred to as the Product Responsbilility treatment. In another group of four experimental shops, with three control shops, authority and responsibility for final quality acceptance of the products processed in his shop were assigned to the supervisor. This is referred to as the Quality Responsibility treatment. Objective criteria for evalu-

FIGURE 1 Organizational States

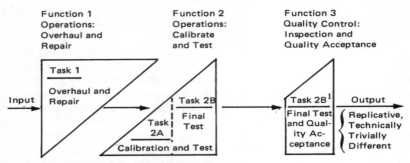

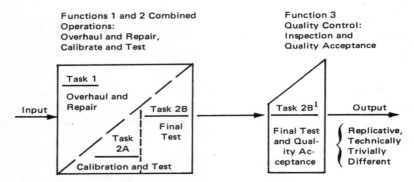

A: Organization State I: Task Contents of Work Functions for Functional Organization of Process

B: Organization State II: Task Contents of Work Functions for Product Organization with External Quality Control

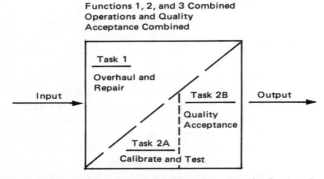

C: Organization State III: Task Contents of Work Functions for Product-Control Organization Including Quality Responsibility

ating the effects of the changes included productivity, direct costs of production (labor and materials), quality, personnel costs, and time distribution of supervisor's activities. Sources of objective data were the organization's quarterly production and cost reports, personnel records, and activity sampling. Subjective criteria in the form of changes in attitudes and perceptions of supervisors and workers were obtained by questionnaires, interviews, and ratings. Data were collected for nine months prior to the introduction of the changes and afterwards for six months for some performance measures and fifteen months for others.

The treatments introduced brought about changes in technological organization and in authority and responsibility of supervisors and workers. Beginning with shops functionally organized by process, and having divided responsibility for quality by sharing it with an inspection department, the treatments moved the shops through two additional organization states. The initial state (I) was that of functional organization by process. Introduction of the Product Responsibility treatment achieved the second state (II) in which all the processes for product completion, excluding quality control, were brought together in one shop. The third state (III) resulted from the Quality Responsibility treatment, which added quality control and product acceptance providing full product control and responsibility. The organization state changes are schematically illustrated in Figure 1 below. The difference between State I and State II was technically complex, requiring the supervisor and his workers to acquire additional knowledge and skills. The tasks added in State III were largely replicative and technically only trivially different from those already done by workers and supervisors operating in State II; the major difference lay in the status and authority to perform quality acceptance.

RESULTS

1. Changes In Jobs Of Supervisors And Workers

Under the Product Responsibility treatment, which moved some shops from State I to State II, all of the functions required to process a product were grouped and assigned to a supervisor. To accomplish this, shops were reformed, moving men and equipment. Where possible these were placed in close proximity; in a few instances large calibration equipment prevented physical contiguity. At first supervisors, acting as coordinators, worked to improve the linkages between individuals or groups carrying out the various process stages. Information feedback became internalized within each shop and informal information transfer between men began and continued to grow. With growth in supervisors' experience, they began to rotate workers and provide training so that each would eventually learn all of the tasks facilitating worker interchangeability and information feedback particularly from the final calibration stage, which provided output data, to the earlier repair and assembly stages.

When the Quality Responsibility treatment, which moved some shops from State II to State III, was introduced, the supervisors concerned assumed the inspection tasks themselves, which in short order consumed all of their time. In a short while, qualified craftsmen were certified to act as their own inspectors and the inspection activity passed over entirely to workers, becoming a regular task in their jobs. Supervisors followed up on quality problems and served as final arbiters in difficult cases. To some large extent they were involved in securing clarification of technical specifications since they and their workers had specific experience on what contributed to product quality.

2. Changes In Tasks And Time Allocation Of Supervisors

The changes introduced in supervisors' authority and responsibility were hypothesized to lead to changes in supervisors' task self-selection and time allocation. Work sampling data and task inventories with time estimates were collected from the supervisors of all eleven participating shops. Sample size was set to provide a confidence level of $90\% \pm 10\%$ accuracy. Some supervisors were transferred during the study, with the result that the available data were reduced to only eight

TABLE 1

Significant Changes in Supervisor's Time Allocation
(Activity Sampling Data)

Experimental treatments	Shops	Face-to-face communication about or with						Paperwork + phone	Non-overt activity	Meetings	Breaks, travel, unavailable
		Subordinates	Other supervisors	Higher-level supervision	Other	Control Center	Inspection				
Quality Responsibility	Experimental (4 shops)			↑			↑		↓		
	Control (2 shops)				↑ ↑			↓	↓ ↓	↓	↑ ↑
Product Responsibility	Experimental (1 shop)	↓					↑	↑			
	Comparison (1 shop)	↓							↑		

Code: ↑ Significant increase in % time allocation to an activity from pre- to post-change period per supervisor.
　　　 ↓ Significant decrease in % time allocation to an activity from pre- to post-change period per supervisor.

complete sets. The significant changes in supervisor's time allocation to his various tasks as recorded by Activity Sampling are given in *Table 1*. Significant changes in their daily task distribution attributable to the treatments as indicated by supervisors' own estimates are summarized in *Table 2*.

All changes in supervisors' time allocation to tasks that took place were predicted with the following exceptions: (1) in neither experimental treatment did the supervisors spend more time with design engineers; (2) additionally the Product Responsibility supervisors neither

TABLE 2
Supervisors' Estimates of Their Job Contents
Tasks as A Percentage of Total Day's Work

Tasks	Product Responsibility shops		
	Experimental group	Control group	Difference from comparison group
	%	%	%
1. Involved with shop personnel on production problems	34.4	17.4	16.0 more*
2. Breaks	1.25	2.5	1.25 less*
3. Involved with control center planners	21.3	12.0	9.3 more
4. General administration	20.0	20.9	0.9 less
5. Quality control	8.8	1.9	6.9 more
6. Personnel work	6.9	13.6	6.7 less
7. Meetings	3.1	12.5	9.4 less
8. Material procurement	2.5	2.5	0
9. Reporting progress to higher supervision	1.9	6.0	4.1 less
10. Reviewing technical specifications	0	6.4	6.4 less
11. Safety, house-keeping	0	3.2	3.2 less
12. Check, test equipment	0	1.3	1.3 less
	Quality Responsibility shops		
	%	%	%
1. Involved with shop personnel on production problems	29.6	46.2	16.6 less*
2. Quality control	26.2	3.0	23.2 more*
3. Reporting progress to higher-level supervision	4.5	0.7	3.8 more*
4. Involved with control center planners	12.2	16.5	4.3 less
5. Personnel work: attendance, manning	10.2	6.5	3.7 more
6. Material procurement	5.3	3.7	1.6 more
7. Review technical specifications	5.2	9.6	4.4 less
8. General administration	4.5	5.7	1.2 less
9. Safety, house-keeping	1.6	3.2	1.6 less
10. Meetings	0.6	0.8	0.2 less
11. Check, test equipment	0	4.1	4.1 less

*Significantly different.

increased their allocation of time to consultation with planners nor decreased the time they spent on quality problems. The shifts in time allocation indicated greater involvement of supervisors with shop personnel on technical management rather than personnel management problems, increased emphasis on their own technological job content, such as quality and cost control, and less dependence on other supervisors or superiors. The sum of all the time allocation changes suggests the development of more technically oriented, autonomous supervisors having less free time available.

3. Changes In Objective Organizational Performance Criteria

The objective criteria for evaluating the organizational changes included productivity, direct cost of production (labor and materials costs), quality, and personnel costs. A summary of the changes in criteria predicted by the primary hypothesis versus those achieved are as follows:

Treatments: Technical Complexity: Predicted criteria changes	Product Responsibility High	Quality Responsibility Low
	Achieved criteria changes	
a. Supported by Supervisor Objectives:		
1. Lower Total Operating Costs	No change	Significant improvement
2. Higher Quality	Significant improvement	No significant change but improvement trend
3. Lower Personnel Costs	No change	No change
b. Not supported by Supervisor Objectives:		
1. Higher Productivity .(output)	No change	No change

Actual changes in the criterion measures are shown in Figure 2.

A. Product Responsibility Treatment

Prior to the start of the study, management inadvertently introduced product responsibility organization into the shops selected to be controls. These therefore became comparison shops. Contrast between experimental and comparison shops consequently reflects the effects of complete introduction of this organizational change in a short time period into the experimental shops compared with the effects appearing toward the end of the introduction of similar changes over a much longer time period in the comparison shops.

Neither the experimental nor the comparison shops showed any statistically significant changes in productivity or costs between the pre- and post-change periods. The actual changes in productivity and operating costs were large, see *Figure 2*, but, because of high variance,

FIGURE 2 Changes in Objective Organizational Performance Criteria

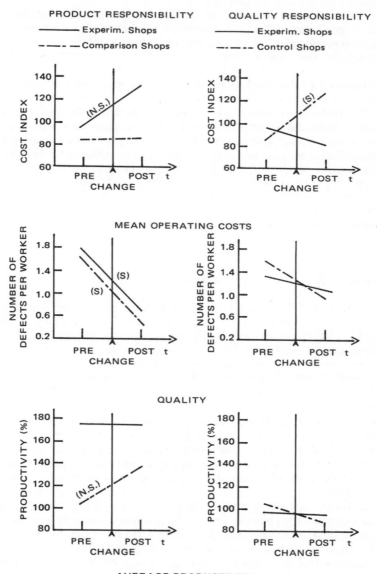

TREATMENTS:

PRODUCT RESPONSIBILITY

———— Experim. Shops

— · — · —Comparison Shops

QUALITY RESPONSIBILITY

———— Experim. Shops

—·· —·· Control Shops

MEAN OPERATING COSTS

QUALITY

AVERAGE PRODUCTIVITY

N.S. = Statistically Non-Significant Change
S. = Statistically Significant Change

the changes were not statistically significant. Despite the requirement of adjusting to the changes in organizational relationships and skills, and the introduction of new, more complex product models as the study progressed, costs of production did not increase, productivity did not decline, and quality improved.

The rise in total operating costs for the experimental shops, and their large fluctuations (high variance), while not statistically significant, are a reflection of adjustment to a rapidly introduced technically complex change. The opportunity available to the comparison shops to make their adjustment over a long time period permitted them to retain a stable cost profile and to begin to display increases in productivity, although not statistically significant as yet.

The number of defects produced per worker were reduced significantly in both the experimental and the comparison shops, while the costs of correcting defects were reduced, non-significantly, in both groups of shops. The effects of rapid introduction of change in the experimental shops did not inhibit improvement in quality. In both groups of shops, coordination between repair and testing sections improved and more consistent acceptance criteria developed internally, which led to a reduced rate of returned product items to repair stations by the calibrator-testers.

B. Quality Responsibility Treatment

Only one of the four experimental shops showed a significant improvement in productivity. When examined by product items, the experimental shops showed a slight productivity improvement and the control shops a decline. Half of the experimental shops showed significant reductions, and the remaining half showed nonsignificant reductions in total costs of production. At the same time, operating costs in the control shops increased, significantly so in one of them. The reductions in costs, which included the costs to correct defects, took place in the face of higher quality standards imposed by the supervisors of the experimental shops as a hedge against the failure to meet the added responsibility they acquired through their new authority to accept finished products. It is likely that greater decrease in production costs would have been observed had the original quality standards been maintained.

Costs of correcting quality defects increased significantly in most of the experimental shops. The identification of defects and the corresponding costs of correcting them appear to be spurious artifacts and may reflect internal changes in emphasis introduced by workers who now had control over quality. The fact is that total costs of production, including the costs of correcting defects, were lowered in all experimental shops, significantly so in half of them, even when coupled with the self-imposed more stringent quality standards.

C. Personnel Costs

Personnel costs in the form of absenteeism, lateness, grievances, transfers, injuries, etc., were unaltered by either treatment. It is difficult to evaluate whether the nonsensitivity was specific to the treatments or to response time. Historically, personnel costs were markedly low and unchanging in the organization, and this pattern continued throughout the period of the study. Relations between workers and management were cordial and cooperative. Workers were highly skilled and formally qualified as a basis for promotion. Turnover, absenteeism, and grievances were low, and such movement as took place was a result of promotions and transfers to fill needs. This remained the case in the experimental and control shops.

4. Effects Of Organizational Environment

The objective results achieved by the introduction of the changes in job content, responsibility, and authority of supervisors appear to be modest unless examined in the context of the nature of the changes and the organizational environment. Earlier it was indicated that the experimental changes were of very different complexity in the adaptation demands placed on the organization. The Quality Responsibility treatment added authority for product quality acceptance rounding out the area of control of the supervisors and workers. The expectation was that responsibility for quality would develop with authority to control and be reflected in improved quality, as indeed it appeared to be developing. The Product Responsibility treatment, however, required the supervisor, and later the workers, to acquire additional technological and organizational knowledge and skills. Adaptation to this change required more time than had been anticipated, so for most of the study period these shops were in a transient state.

The organizational environment produced a conflict in objectives between supervisors and top management. The study organization was subjected to pressures from privately owned companies seeking to acquire the work done by this and similar military industrial facilities. This led to a national and local policy on costs of operation. The stated objective of the organization's top management was to minimize costs in order to remain competitive. This was an article of faith repeatedly emphasized to all employees at all levels and reinforced by various periodic performance reviews. Everyone in the organization knew, however, that top management had only partial control over operating costs since labor-force size was in part determined by external policy decisions. As a part of the defense industries complex, the organization saw as one of its major peacetime *raisons d'être* the maintenance of a dependable core industrial system for potential emergency expansion. This was seen as requiring a good physical plant and a highly skilled labor force. The limited national supply of available workers with high skills was of special concern. Most of the employees in the study shops were in this category.

Over the years, maintenance of a balanced and skilled labor force for purposes of competing with other similar military industrial facilities and for emergency readiness was seen by all as an implicit management goal. Most of the organization's members, in fact, believed that the objective of minimizing operating costs had a lower priority than that of manpower resource maintenance. Thus, at the supervisor's level, there existed a conflict between the stated and the implicit operating objectives of the organization. The general acceptance of the implicit goal led to an essentially man-oriented organization with lip-service given to cost minimization.

A second source of conflict with stated objectives appeared to have been the application of 'lump of work' theory. Employees and supervisors saw the total demand for repair of certain existing government-owned equipment as fixed. Greater work output therefore would reduce the number of employees required. In-plant transfer of workers to less desirable positions and vaguely possible layoffs could be avoided by gearing work pace to fluctuating demands, working intensively when needed and less so otherwise. Supervisors implicitly supported this strategy to maintain their status and to retain their skilled personnel. Workers assigned to prestige shops preferred to retain their desirable position. Thus, both supervisors and workers perceived organizational stability as their own and the organization's real objective.

Stable productivity (output) may be seen as the response of supervisors and workers to satisfying their own objectives of organiational stability, which they saw as maintaining constant manpower resources. The organization's positive response in the form of lowered total operating costs may be seen as the only nonthreatening response available to supervisors and their workers given the real objectives they held.

5. Changes In Attitudes And Perceptions

Changes in attitudes, perceptions, and behavior toward others were measured by interviews and questionnaires. Two questionnaires were given to first-line supervisors before the changes in organization and two afterwards. Higher-level supervisors rated several characteristics of their first-level supervisors and the performance effectiveness of their shops. Workers evaluated both several characteristics of their supervisors and their own jobs and roles in the organization before and after organization changes were introduced. Beginning toward the end of the study and extending after its formal conclusion, interviews were conducted with all members of all groups participating in the study. The responses to the partially structured interviews essentially supported the findings of the workers' and supervisors' questionnaires and also revealed the problem of conflict in objectives between these groups and top management. Detailed information on the questionnaires and interviews can be found in the primary research report (Davis, Valfer & Pool, 1964). At the end of the study there were indications that attitudes and perceptions of workers and supervisors were still changing as they experienced and tested their roles modified by their new job designs.

The most significant changes in perceptions and attitudes of all the participants in the experimental treatments are summarized in *Table 3*. An overview of these changes may be stated as follows:

Supervisors in both treatments, after scattered initial scepticism, and some opposition, responded with mild to vigorous support and enthusiasm for the organizational changes. The most significant change in perception was in recognition of greater autonomy. The interviews indicated that this was a major source of stimulation for the supervisors toward more effective shop management. The reduction in time available for personnel management was thought by supervisors to be the greatest negative feature of the organizatonal changes. Supervisors who were technically oriented were more favorably inclined to the changes, which suggests that support for the treatments may have been a function of reinforcement of preferred style of supervision.

Workers' responses to the treatments were directly related to the degree to which supervisors transferred to workers the responsibility and authority indicated in the treatments. In the low-complexity treatment shops (Quality Responsibility) transfer of responsibilities took place rapidly and workers responded favorably. In the high-complexity treatment shops (Product Responsibility) the adjustment to the change by the supervisors was so slow that at the worker level only minor job changes such as rotation of personnel between repair and testing had been effected at the conclusion of the study. Worker attitudes toward this treatment remained relatively neutral. Intrinsic and extrinsic job content values for workers were positively correlated and increased as a consequence of the low-complexity treatment. Among the most significant changes in supervisor behavior perceived by workers were in the dimensions of 'initiating structure' and 'consideration', which were positively correlated. While increasing in the Quality Responsibility shops, they decreased in the Product Responsibility shops, which may be a reflection of the difficulties experienced by supervisors in adjusting to complex changes in their jobs and in re-establishing equilibrium between their own responsibilities and authority and those of their workers. Contrary to accepted theory, positive correlation between 'initiating structure' and 'consideration' may indicate that structuring by supervisors is seen as helpful by an organization's members.

In order of increased personal-needs satisfaction, the smallest increase was reported by Product Responsibility workers followed by their supervisors, then by Quality Responsibility workers followed by their supervisors, who reported the most pronounced increase. The generally favorable changes in perceptions and attitudes strongly suggest that, given more time, increasingly favorable responses in the objective output measures will become apparent until a steady state is

TABLE 3

Summary of Changes in Attitudes and Perceptions

Treatment	Level	Perceptions and attitudes	
		Favorable	Unfavorable
Product Responsibility	Supervisor	1. Less rigid internal structure	1. Less responsibility
		2. More contacts with shop personnel	2. Less delegation
(High Technical Complexity)		3. More contacts with higher supervision	3. Less man-orientation
		4. Greater autonomy	4. Slow shift of responsibility to worker level
		5. Greater technical orientation	
		6. Better product control	
	Workers	1. Less rigid internal structure	1. Less consideration by supervisor
		2. More responsibility	2. More pressure for lower costs
Quality Responsibility	Supervisor	1. Greater satisfaction with job tasks	1. Less man-orientation
		2. Greater involvement in job	2. Less delegation
(Low Technical Complexity)		3. Greater information flow to workers	
		4. More authority	
		5. More technical orientation	
		6. Fewer conflicts with staff groups	
	Workers	1. Greater job responsibility	1. Greater internal structure
		2. Less pressure for lower costs	2. Less work improvement effort
		3. More functional responsibilities	3. Greater emphasis on extrinsic job values
		4. More frequent praise by supervisor	
		5. Greater influence on shop operations	

reached. The Product Responsibility treatment, because of its complexity, can be expected to reach a steady-state condition later than the Quality Responsibility treatment.

CONCLUSIONS

In these field studies, some supervisory jobs were redesigned to enlarge their responsibility for product completion and others to enlarge their authority to include product quality acceptance. The consequence was an improvement in those objective organizational performances that were supported by the organizational environment at the shop level, i.e. that avoided goal conflicts for the supervisor, did not threaten achievement of his implicit objectives (seen by him to be the real goals of the organization), and avoided disincentives to him. Improvement in both objective performance and in positive attitudes was also a function of job-change complexity, developing first with low-complexity changes. Given the conflict between stated management and implicit supervisor objectives, the treatments did achieve positive changes in compatible objective criteria.

Supervisors exhibited greater degrees of autonomy and indicated greater overall personal need satisfaction as consequences of both treatments. This was also seen by the workers. These behavior and satisfaction changes would seem to contribute to an organization's viability. Further, they suggest that additional improvement in output criteria may be expected as the changes are fully implemented and the system reaches a steady state.

Both treatments resulted in a shift of supervisors' time allocation from man management to technical management. Workers responded positively to this change in managerial style. The treatments allowed better technical control and decision-making by supervisors through shortened feedback loops and product queues as well as through concentration of functional authority.

RECOMMENDATIONS FOR INDUSTRIAL JOB DESIGN

1. The design of a supervisor's job should be in the direction of including authority and responsibility for all the functions required to complete the product or service assigned to his work group, including quality acceptance. Where this appears to be technically infeasible, the technology and the organization should be subjected to detailed socio-technical system analysis to determine whether the restrictions are real or externally imposed.
2. On the basis of the results of this and previous studies, responsibility and authority for work functions should be delegated to the lowest organizational level performing the work.

NOTES

1. Supported by Office of Naval Research, Nonr 3656(04).

REFERENCES

Davis, L. E. (1957). Toward a theory of job design. *J. Indust. Engg.* 8, 5, 305.

Davis, L. E. (1966). The design of jobs. *Indust. Relat.* 6, 1.

Davis, L. E. & Canter, R. R. (1956). Job design research. *J. indust. Engg.* 7, 6, 275.

Davis, L. E. & Valfer, E. S. (1964). Supervisor job design. *Ergonomics:* Proceedings of 2nd International Congress on Ergonomics, 517-24.

Davis, L. E. & Valfer, E. S. (1965). Intervening responses to changes in supervisor job designs. *Occup. Psychol.* 39, 171-89.

Davis, L. E., Valfer, E. S. & Pool, K. (1964). *Supervisory job control.* Berkeley: University of California. Institute of Engineering Research.

Davis, L. E. & Werling, R. (1960). Job design factors. *Occup. Psychol.* 34, 2, 109.
Emery, F. E. & Trist, E. L. (1960). Socio-technical systems. In M. Verhulst & W. Churchman (Eds.), *Management Sciences, Models and Techniques,* Vol. 2.

BIOGRAPHICAL NOTES

LOUIS E. DAVIS occupies a chair in the Graduate School of Business Administration and is a Research Associate of the Institute of Industrial Relations at the University of California, Los Angeles. Since 1958 he has acted in an advisory capacity to a number of governmental and academic bodies in Europe and the U.S.A. He has recently spent six months as a Visiting Research Fellow at the Human Resources Centre, Tavistock Institute, participating in a programme of socio-technical field studies in Norway and Britain and in a project for their theoretical development supported by the Social Sciences Research Council.

ERNST S. VALFER is Head of the Management Sciences Staff, U.S. Forest Service, Pacific Southwest Experiment Station, Berkeley, California. His former appointments were as Research Director, Port of San Francisco Study, National Academy of Sciences—National Research Council and as Head of Industrial Engineering, U.S. Naval Air Station, Almeda, California.

JOB ENRICHMENT

H. Roy Kaplan and Curt Tausky
University of Massachusetts, Amherst, Massachusetts
Bhopinder S. Bolaria
University of Maine, Orono, Maine

Reprinted from PERSONNEL JOURNAL, Volume 48, Number 10, October 1969

On the job, the worker experiences a myriad of stimuli many of which may affect his motivation and job performance. Research points to the conclusion that all workers are neither motivated by the same factors nor for the same reasons. This article suggests that the utility of job enrichment programs predicated on the development of increasing intrinsic job elements, and down-grading attention to extrinsic factors, is questionable, at best.

In a recent article, Frederick Herzberg extolled the virtues of the Motivation-Hygiene theory of job satisfaction, and the efficacy of introducing programs of job enrichment in organizations in order to promote stronger motivation among employees.[1] This article will analyze the various assumptions inherent in this approach, along with the ramifications and utility of employing it in work organizations.

To obtain a comprehensive understanding of the Motivation-Hygiene theory and its consequent job enrichment, a discussion of Maslow's need hierarchy is relevant since it forms the conceptual foundation for much of the current research on employee motivation.

In Maslow's earlier statement of his theory, he conceptualized human needs as arranged in a hierarchy of prepotency. The emergence of a higher-order need usually is dependent upon the prior satisfaction of another, more basic prepotent need. The theory depicts man as a perpetually wanting animal and maintains that no need or drive can be treated as if it were isolated or discrete. According to Maslow, every drive is related to the state of satisfaction or dissatisfaction of other drives.[2] At the base of the need hierarchy, and taking precedence over all the others, are the physiological needs which are followed in order of importance by the safety, love, esteem and self-actualization needs. However, it is only after the satisfaction of a lower level need that the next higher level need gains focus. As Maslow stated:

It is quite true that man lives by bread alone—when there is no bread. But what happens to man's desires when there is plenty of bread and when his belly is chronically filled? At once other (and higher) needs emerge and these, rather than physiological hungers, dominate the organism. And when these in turn are satisfied, again new (and still 'higher') needs emerge and so on.[3]

The highest needs, then, are those which Maslow termed self-actualization needs. These represent the highest strivings of a man to be what he is. As Maslow put it: "A musician must make music, an artist must paint, a poet must write, if he is to be ultimately happy. What a man can be, he must be." [4]

Taking a cue from the work of Maslow, and after completing a review of the literature and concluding a study of job satisfaction among a sample of accountants and engineers, Herzberg and his associates formulated the Motivation-Hygiene theory of job satisfaction. It was hypothesized that contrary to previous beliefs about job satisfaction, which held that the absence of a satisfaction producing factor would cause dissatisfaction, two separate sets of factors operated independently to produce satisfaction and dissatisfaction. One set of factors was related to the intrinsic aspects of the job and was thought to be composed of satisfaction producing factors. These were labeled "motivators." The other set, which was related to the extrinsic aspects of the work and nonwork environment, was labeled "hygienes." The unique element of this theory rests on the assumption that these are two dichotomous sets of factors having their own *different* effects on worker satisfaction and motivation. The presence of "motivators" at satisfactory levels in the employee's job will lead to job satisfaction. However, the absence of "motivators" will not lead to job dissatisfaction. According to this theory, the opposite of job satisfaction is not job dissatisfaction, but no job satisfaction. It is the "hygienes" whose absence from satisfactory levels of fulfillment on the job may lead to job dissatisfaction; but the presence of satisfactory fulfillment of "hygienes" in the job situation will lead not to job satisfaction, but to a neutral state. As Herzberg *et al.* stated:

> Poor working conditions, bad company policies and administration, and bad supervision will lead to job dissatisfaction. Good company policies, good administration, good supervision, and good working conditions will not lead to positive job attitudes. In opposition to this, as far as our data has gone, recognition, achievement, interesting work, responsibility, and advancement all lead to positive attitudes. Their absence will much less frequently lead to job dissatisfaction. [5]

The logical extension of this theory was to link it with Maslow's need hierarchy—which emphasizes the strivings of man toward self-actualization—and apply it to a program of job enrichment which emphasizes the development of achievement, creativity, and independence among workers. It is assumed that only through intrinsic involvement in one's work can a person truly obtain satisfaction. Thus, the job must allow for self-actualization if work motivation is to be internally generated, rather than continually prodded by extrinsic controls and rewards.

Although the proponents of the Motivation-Hygiene theory cite studies supporting their position, an extensive review of studies by the present writers has definitely not yielded the unanimous support for the theory which is often claimed for it. Indeed, it was found that particular methodological approaches to studies of job satisfaction often yielded evidence disconfirming the theory. Figure I contains a chronological inventory of these studies. It can be seen that the majority of studies

FIGURE 1

Review of Studies Relating to Motivation-Hygiene Theory

Name of Investigator(s) *	Support of Theory	Use of Herzberg's or Similar Methodology
Schwarz	Yes	Yes
Hahn	Yes	Yes
Harrison	Yes	No
Gibson	Yes	No
Anderson	Yes	Yes
Walt	Yes	Yes
Clegg	Yes	Yes
Schwartz et al.	Yes	Yes
Friedlander	No	Yes
Lodahl	Yes	Yes
Saleh	Yes	Yes
Myers	Yes	Yes
Friedlander	Yes	Yes
Friedlander and Walton	Yes	Yes
Ewen	No	No
Herzberg	Yes	Yes
Gendel	Yes	Yes
Friedlander	Yes	Yes
Friedlander	No	No
Gordon	No	No
Malinovsky and Barry	No	No
Lindsay	No	No
Ott	No	No
Halpern	Yes	No
Dysinger	Yes	Yes
Burke	No	No
Drake	No	No
Wernimont	No	No
Graen	No	No
Ewen et al.	No	No
Hinrichs and Mischkind	No	Yes
Dunnette et al.	No	No
Hulin and Smith	No	No
Bloom and Barry	No	No
Montgomery	Yes	Yes
Brant	Yes	Yes
Randall	Yes	Yes
Kaplan	No	Yes
Levine and Weitz	No	No

*See Appendix A for citations to these studies.

supporting the theory employed the same or similar methodology as the original study conducted by Herzberg and his associates. Of the twenty-one confirming studies, seventeen used the same or similar methodology, while fifteen of the eighteen disconfirming studies employed different methodological approaches. [6]

In addition to the question of the validity of the Motivation-Hygiene theory, there are several points which should be carefully considered by a management before the decision is made to implement a program of job enrichment designed to increase the opportunities of employees to attain self-actualization through achievement and responsibility.

The key word in our analysis of problems which may be generated by the pursuit of a program of job enrichment is "differences." It is with "differences" that the Motivation-Hygiene theory and job enrichment which is derived from it do not sufficiently concern themselves. That is, they do not address themselves to: differential interpretations which workers may attach to particular job situations, the varying desires and aspirations of different levels of workers, differences in values among workers, and the differing degrees to which jobs lend themselves to enrichment programs.

Although these are rather distinct problems, they derive from common origins. An appropriate starting point for discussion of the origins of these differences lies in answering the following questions: Is the desire for the attainment of self-actualization universal among all workers, and to what extent do differences in job content affect the opportunities of workers to attain self-actualization? Specifically, do *all* workers seek and desire achievement, advancement, independence and recognition in their work? Do all workers have the same amount of interest in work? Do all jobs possess those elements which lend themselves to job enrichment? What may be the costs of introducing programs of job enrichment?

One wonders if the proponents of programs based upon self-actualization and the Motivation-Hygiene theory have inadvertently infused their own value judgments into their conceptual perspectives. As Strauss has noted, these theories were originally created and developed by members of academia for whom the opportunities to attain self-actualization are more readily found then in other segments of the population.[7] Consider also the high value attached to creativity, individuality and achievement which are part of the general academic milieu. It is erroneous to deny the existence of a desire to self-actualize among *some* people, but one can see the logic and the likelihood for a preponderance of such desires, and opportunities to obtain it, in those occupations which lend themselves to the satisfaction of higher level needs. Indeed, a case can be made that differences in interests among workers can be seen to occur when comparisons are made between occupational levels. For example, studies by Centers and Bugental, Friedlander, Pellegrin and Coates, Morse, Bloom and Barry, Kaplan and Bolaria, Friedlander, Centers, and Tausky[8] have shown a preponderance of high level, professional employees as being more interested in intrinsic aspects of their jobs than low level, non professional employees. The latter tend to exhibit greater concern for extrinsic job factors such as security, salary and fringe benefits.

Explanations of motivational differences have been attributed to the diverse structure and content of work, and the influences of socialization, that is, influences on outlook arising from a worker's social class and non-job environment. In regard to the first of these explanations, the question arises as to whether complex organizations, with their emphasis on specialization of tasks and prescribed modes of behavior, can provide the opportunities to satisfy the higher level needs of all workers. The response to this question has created a dialogue among many behavioral scientists known as the "personality versus the organization" debate. Among the writers who have maintained that conflict between person and organization is in fact the case are Argyris, Maier, McGregor, and Davis.[9] These investigators have argued that healthy individuals desire an organizational environment which can satisfy their higher level needs. It is maintained that people want to be given responsibility so that they may use their intellect, be creative, and express their individuality. Our contemporary complex organizations are, however, depicted as stifling individual initiative and creativity and fostering conformity, dependency, immaturity and subsequent alienation of employees from their work.[10] Although an analysis of the impact of structure and content of the job on worker motivation has merit, the "personality versus the organization" position, as well as its theoretical antecedents, the Motivation-Hygiene and self-actualization theories, can be challenged. Consider the alternative explanation regarding the impact of social class on employee attitudes and desires, and the previous questions raised concerning these theories.

The "personality versus the organization" position smacks of the flavor of an overemphasis on a particular segment of workers, the high level and professional employees, who are for the most part members of the higher social strata in our society. Perhaps a more meaningful approach to the factors affecting the motivation of workers lies in the exploration of class differences as they affect men's life chances to engage in a particular type of work. Is it difficult to visualize a preoccupation among the manual workers in our society with job security, salary, and fringe benefits? Several studies have shown the existence of such attitudes toward work which appear, indeed, to be prevalent among blue-collar men.[11] This does not challenge Maslow's need theory. In fact, it supports it. A preoccupation with security, salary and similar extrinsic job elements in the context of pursuit of satisfaction of lower level needs can be interpreted as an attempt on the part of an individual to satisfy those more prepotent physiological and safety needs of which Maslow writes. However, in their haste to encapsulate all worker motivations within a single approach, the advocates job of enrichment have frequently overlooked this fundamental point. Continued involvement with the pursuit of lower level needs may lead to a conditioning of the individual which emphasizes these items to the *exclusion of all others.* Due to circumscribed life chances, which is a prevalent condition among the unskilled and semi-skilled workers in our society, an individual's prospects for obtaining a job which affords him an opportunity to stop worrying about satisfying these lower needs are fairly limited. Therefore, he remains in a permanent state of relative deprivation and want. It is reasonable to assume that a great many workers have adjusted their expectations and aspirations to the reality of their life situations. In fact, it seems plausible that many workers seek those jobs which offer the promise of security, "good" salary, and fringe benefits. To conclude, as some advocates of the "personality versus the organization" position and Motivation-Hygiene theory have, that people who seek "hygiene" factors have poor mental health is, in view of the above, grossly misleading. It seems more appropriate to suggest that many people never *learned* to seek those things which are conducive to the attainment of self-actualization, due to the necessity of preoccupation with the satisfaction of lower level needs. This may explain the findings of several studies that workers often *did not want* their jobs enlarged with the concomitant opportunities for achievement, creativity and independence.[12]

There is also reason to believe that introducing changes into already established work routines may create ill-ease. There is the possibility that anxiety derived from real or imagined fears of incompetence to perform a newly designed task will be generated among workers. In addition, hostility may be exhibited by workers who may resent the intrusion of management into *their* normal work routine. The basis for this may lie in the fact, as previously mentioned, that some workers do not *wish* or *expect* more responsibility in their jobs; or there may be pressures exerted on the worker by his work group which militate against any changes that might lead to a disruption of established work routines. This point is significant and merits elaboration.

It is evident from the findings of the many studies which have investigated the interactions and social processes of work groups, that informal work group norms pertaining to the manner in which work is to be performed and the behavior of the individual on the job, have significant influences on the attitudes of the workers and his motivation on the job. It is apparent that in addition to the socializing effects of social class, the pressures generated by a work group can also have a significant effect on motivation. There is also evidence to show that informal work group norms do not always coincide with the expressed goals of the organization. The classic illustration of this phenomenon is the "Bank Wiring Room" study conducted by Elton Mayo and his associates.[13] Subsequent studies have repeatedly confirmed the existence of informal work group norms among all levels of workers, some of which negatively influence the productivity of the work group, as in restriction of output.[14] However, these norms do not always function to the detriment of organizational goals. In addition to the effect they have on facilitating workers' adjustment to the job environment (a particularly important contribution among workers performing monotonous types of work), there are studies which show these norms sometimes contribute toward increased productivity among workers.[15]

There is the possibility that the introduction of a job enrichment program, with its emphasis on individual initiative and achievement, may produce results opposite to those intended. If the job serves as a primary source of interest for the worker, greater job responsibilities are no problem. The level and type of work performed must obviously be taken into consideration. On the basis of our previous discussion, we suggest that higher level and professional personnel evidence a stronger interest in their work and the work place than lower level nonprofessional personnel. The logic of this hypothesis is related to the previous discussion of the differential opportunities for the attainment of self-actualization afforded to workers in different jobs, and their prior socialization. Some evidence in support of this hypothesis can be found in the following illustration.

In a study of a large research organization recently conducted by the senior author, significant differences were found to exist between the professional scientific personnel and the nonprofessional, nonscientific personnel in regard to reported satisfaction-producing aspects of the job. Specifically, the professional scientific personnel expressed satisfaction with the work itself, and the opportunities for achievement, advancement, and freedom on the job. The nonprofessional, nonscientific personnel expressed interest and satisfaction with job security, salary, and working conditions. It is not difficult to grant the significance of divergent interests among workers in a situation where some raise mice and clean their cages, while others conduct experiments with the mice in an attempt to discover the relation of cholesterol to heart disease. [16]

Further support for this hypothesis can be found in a comparison of the studies of Dubin and Orzack. In Dubin's study, a sampling of attitudes among industrial workers disclosed that although they exhibited a sense of attachment to their work and the work place, they did not indicate a commitment to it. [17] However, utilizing the same methodology on a sample of registered nurses, Orzack obtained contradictory results and was led to conclude that for these nurses, work and the workplace was a major, if not dominant interest. [18] (It is noteworthy that a recent trend in organizational research focuses on an analysis of technological differences in organizations as they affect structures, attitudes and motivations within them). [19]

In view of the above, management would be wise to accept the reality that all jobs do not lend themselves to enrichment. Can one appreciably enrich the work of assembly-line workers? What would be the costs to the organization (monetarily) and to the employee (psychologically) of redesigning his job? As Strauss has asked, is it in the best interests of management that workers on an assembly-line use creativity and imagination? [20]

One may ask whether we should accept the status quo and welcome the prospect of increased "small jobs" in the work situation? Our answer is that we should not accept the creation of unnecessarily meaningless work any more than we should tolerate the existence of a lower class culture which influences the abandonment of higher education for the pursuit of short-range goals, while denying individuals those experiences and opportunities to obtain jobs which can be appreciated for the intrinsic elements of the work itself. What we are suggesting is that management take into consideration the human factors discussed here when designing new tasks or contemplating the introduction of a job enrichment program. This is particularly relevant to those large numbers of people who currently hold jobs which are not amenable to enrichment.

Such considerations do not require a large expenditure of energy or resources on the part of management. The data required in order to assess the prospects of success of a program of job enrichment in a given organization can be secured from the analysis of information already available to the organization in the form of job applications and material accumulated in employee files. In addition, it would be helpful if the organization engaged in a program of attitude sampling among the workers in various levels of the organization for the purpose of ascertaining their opinions about proposed changes in their work.

It is apparent that there are many factors which act upon the individual and groups of workers which may significantly affect worker motivation and the response to job enrichment programs. Unfortunately, the proponents of job enrichment have at times neglected these diverse factors in their attempt to supply an answer to the problem of worker motivation which appears to be most applicable to high level and professional employees.

APPENDIX A

Paul Schwarz, *Attitudes of Middle-Management Personnel*, (Pittsburgh: American Institutes for Research, 1959); Clifford P. Hahn, *Dimensions of Job Satisfaction and Career Motivation*, (Pittsburgh: American Institute for Research, 1959); Roger Harrison, "Sources of Motivations in Manager's Job Attitudes," *Personnel Psychology*, XIII (Winter, 1960), pp. 425-434; Wayne J. Gibson, "Sources of Job Satisfaction and Dissatisfaction as Interpreted from Analyses of Write-In Responses," unpublished Doctoral dissertation, Western Reserve University, 1961; Frederick Anderson, "Factors in Motivation to Work Across Three Occupational Levels," unpublished Doctoral dissertation. University of Utah, 1961; Elizabeth Walt, "Motivation for Women to Work in High Level Professional Positions," unpublished Doctoral dissertation, American University, 1962; Denzil Clegg, "The Motivation of County Administrators in the Cooperative Extension Service," Unpublished Doctoral dissertation, University of Wisconsin, 1963; Milton Schwartz, *et al.*, "Motivational Factors Among Supervisors in the Utility Industry," *Personnel Psychology*, XVI, (Spring, 1963), pp. 45-53; Frank Friedlander, "Underlying Sources of Job Satisfaction," *Journal of Applied Psychology*, XLVII (August, 1963), pp. 246-250; Thomas M. Lodahl, "Patterns of Job Attitudes in Two Assembly Technologies," *Administrative Science Quarterly*, VIII (1964), pp. 482-519; Shoukry D. Saleh, "A Study of Attitude Change in the Preretirement Period," *Journal of Applied Psychology*, XLVIII (October, 1964), pp. 310-312; M. Scott Myers, "Who Are Your Motivated Workers? *Harvard Business Review*, XLII (January-February, 1964), pp. 73-78; Frank Friedlander, "Job Characteristics as Satisfiers and Dissatisfiers," *Journal of Applied Psychology*, XLVIII (December, 1964), pp. 388-392; Frank Friedlander, Eugene Walton, "Positive and Negative Motivations Toward Work," *Administrative Science Quarterly*, IX (1964), pp. 194-207; Robert B. Ewen, "Some Determinants of Job Satisfaction: A Study of the Generality of Herzberg's Theory," *Journal of Applied Psychology*, XLVII (June, 1964), pp. 161-163; Frederick Herzberg, "The Motivation to Work Among Finnish Supervisors," *Personnel Psychology*, XVIII (Winter, 1965), pp. 393-402; Howard L. Gendel, "The Motivation to Work in Hospital Housekeeping Workers," unpublished Doctoral dissertation, Western Reserve University, 1965; Frank Friedlander, "Relationships Between the Importance and the Satisfaction of Various Environmental Factors," *Journal of Applied Psychology*,

XLIX (June, 1965), pp. 160-164; Frank Friedlander, "Comparative Work Value Systems," *Personnel Psychology*, XVIII (Spring, 1965), pp. 1-20; G. G. Gordon, "The Relationship of 'Satisfiers' and 'Dissatisfiers' to Productivity, Turnover, and Morale," paper read at meeting of American Psychological Association, Chicago, September, 1965; Michael Malinovsky, John R. Barry, "Determinants of Work Attitudes," *Journal of Applied Psychology*, XLIX (December, 1965), pp. 446-451; Carl A. Lindsay, "Job Satisfaction: An Examination and Test of a Modification of the Herzberg Theory." unpublished Doctoral dissertation, Pennsylvania State University, 1965; D.C. Ott, "The Generality of Herzberg's Two-Factor Theory of Motivation," unpublished Doctoral dissertation, Ohio State University, 1965; Gerald Halpern, "Relative Contributions of Motivator and Hygiene Factors to Overall Job Satisfaction," *Journal of Applied Psychology*, L (June, 1966), pp. 198-200; Dale W. Dysinger, "Motivational Factors Affecting Army Research and Development Personnel," Report AD 640-390, American Institutes for Research, May, 1966; Ronald J. Burke, "Are Herzberg's Motivators and Hygienes Unidimensional?" *Journal of Applied Psychology*, L (August, 1966), pp. 317-321; Charles A. Drake, "A Sociological Investigation of the Factors Related to Job Satisfaction," unpublished Master's thesis, University of Maine, 1966; Paul F. Wernimont, "Intrinsic and Extrinsic Factors in Job Satisfaction," *Journal of Applied Psychology*, L (February, 1966), pp. 41-50; George B. Graen, "Motivator and Hygiene Dimensions for Research and Development Engineers," *Journal of Applied Psychology*, L (December, 1966), pp. 563-566; Robert B. Ewen, et. al., "An Empirical Test of the Herzberg Two-Factor Theory," *Journal of Applied Psychology*, L (December, 1966), pp. 544-550; John R. Hinrichs, Louis A. Mischkind, "Empirical and Theoretical Limitations of the Two-Factor Hypothesis of Job Satisfaction," *Journal of Applied Psychology*, LI (April, 1967), pp. 191-200; Marvin D. Dunnette, et al., "Factors Contributing to Job Satisfaction and Job Dissatisfaction in Six Occupational Groups," *Organizational Behavior and Human Performance*, II (May, 1967), pp. 143-174; Charles L. Hulin, Patricia A. Smith, "An Empirical Investigation of Two Implications of the Two-Factor Theory of Job Satisfaction," *Journal of Applied Psychology*, LI (October, 1967), pp. 396-402; Robert Bloom, John R. Barry, "Determinants of Work Attitudes Among Negroes," *Journal of Applied Psychology*, LI (June, 1967), pp. 291-294; Jason P. Montgomery, "The Application of Herzberg's Motivation-Hygiene Theory to High School Students," unpublished Master's thesis, Kent State University, 1967; James S. Brant, "The Relationship Between Work-Process and Work-Context Factors and Job Satisfaction and Dissatisfaction Among Scientists and Systems Programmers," unpublished Master's thesis, University of Maine, 1967; Richard J. Randall, "A Sociological Study of Hospital Personnel," unpublished Master's thesis, University of Maine, 1967; H. Roy Kaplan, "Job Satisfaction Among Scientific and Non-Scientific Personnel in a Research Organization," unpublished Master's thesis, University of Maine, 1968; Edward L. Levine, Joseph Weitz, "Job Satisfaction Among Graduate Students: Intrinsic Versus Extrinsic Variables," *Journal of Applied Psychology*, LII (August, 1968), pp. 263-271.

A good counselor, like a good signpost, doesn't tell the inquirer which way to go; he tells where the traveler will likely arrive if he takes a certain road.

From When Your Advice Is Asked
J. Gustav White

NOTES

1. Frederick Herzberg, "One More Time: How Do You Motivate Employees?" *Harvard Business Review*, XLVI (January-February, 1968), pp. 53-62.
2. Abraham H. Maslow, "A Theory of Human Motivation," *Psychological Review*, L (July, 1943), p. 370.
3. *Ibid*, p. 375.
4. *Ibid*, pp. 381-382.
5. Frederick Herzberg, et al., *The Motivation to Work*, (New York: John Wiley and Sons, 1959), p. 82.
6. For an extended methodological analysis of the Motivation-Hygiene theory see: H. Roy Kaplan, Bhopinder S. Bolaria, Donald A. Tennant, "The Motivation-Hygiene Theory of Job Satisfaction: Empirical Evidence and Methodological Considerations," unpublished paper, Department of Sociology, University of Maine, Orono, 1968.
7. George Strauss, "Some Notes on Power Equalization," *Readings in Organization Theory*, Walter A. Hill, Douglas Egan, eds., (Boston: Allyn and Bacon, 1960), pp. 380-381.
8. Richard Centers, Daphne E. Bugental, "Intrinsic and Extrinsic Job Motivations Among Different Segments of the Working Population," *Journal of Applied Psychology*, L (June, 1966), pp. 193-197; Frank Friedlander, "Comparative Work Value Systems," *Personnel Psychology*, XVIII (Spring, 1965), pp. 1-20; Roland J. Pellegrin, Charles H. Coates, "Executives and Supervision: Contrasting Definitions of Career Success," *Administrative Science Quarterly*, I (1956-1957), pp. 506-517; Nancy C. Morse, *Satisfactions in the White-Collar Job*, (Ann Arbor: University of Michigan, Institute for Social Research, 1953); Robert Bloom, John R. Barry, "Determinants of Work Attitudes Among Negroes," *Journal of Applied Psychology*, LI (June, 1967), pp. 291-294; H. Roy Kaplan, Bhopinder S. Bolaria, "Job Satisfaction Among Scientific and Non-Scientific Personnel," *Indian Sociological Bulletin*, VI (October, 1968); Frank Friedlander, "Importance of Work Versus Nonwork Among Socially and Occupationally Stratified Groups," *Journal of Applied Psychology*, L (December, 1966), pp. 437-441; Richard Centers, "Motivational Aspects of Occupational Stratification," *Journal of Social Psychology*, XXVIII (November, 1948), pp. 187-217; Curt Tausky, "Occupational Mobility Interests," *Canadian Review of Sociology and Anthropology*, IV (November, 1967), pp. 242-249.
9. Chris Argyris, *Personality and Organization*, (New York: Harper and Brothers, 1957), pp. 66-75; Norman Maier, *Principles of Human Relations*, (New York: John Wiley and Sons, 1952), pp. 1-18; Douglas M. McGregor, *The Human Side of Enterprise*, (New York: McGraw-Hill, 1960), pp. 45-57; Keith Davis, *Human Relations at Work*, (New York: McGraw-Hill, 1962), pp. 20-34.
10. For an extended discussion and critique of the "personality versus the organization" position see: George Strauss, *op. cit.*, pp. 374-402.
11. Herbert H. Hyman, "A Social Psychological Contribution to the Analysis of Stratification," *Class Status, and Power*, Reinhard Bendix, Seymour M. Lipset, eds. (second edition; New York: The Free Press, 1966), pp. 488-499; William H. Form, James A. Geschwender, "Social Reference Basis of Job Satisfaction: The Case of Manual Workers," *American Sociological Review*, XXVII (April, 1962), pp. 228-237; LaMar T. Empey, "Social Class and Occupational Aspirations: A Comparison of Absolute and Relative Measurement," *American Sociological Review*, XXI (December, 1956), pp. 703-709; E. H. Galler, "Influence of Social Class on Children's Choices of Occupations," *Elementary School Journal*, LI (April, 1951), pp. 439-445; Richard Centers, Hadley Cantril, "Income Satisfaction and Income Aspiration," *Journal of Abnormal Social Psychology*, XLI (1946), pp. 64-69; S. M. Miller, Frank Riessman, "The Working Class Subculture: A New View," *Social Problems*, IX (Summer, 1961), pp. 86-97; Allison Davis, "The Motivation of the Underprivileged Worker," *Industry and Society*, William F. Whyte, editor, (New York: McGraw-Hill, (1946), pp. 84-106; Richard Centers, *The Psychology of Social Classes*, (Princeton: Princeton University Press, 1949); Robert Blauner, "Work Satisfaction and Industrial Trends in Modern Society," *Labor and Trade Unionism: An Interdisciplinary Reader*, Walter Galenson, Seymour M. Lipset, editors, (New York: John Wiley and Sons, 1960), pp. 539-560;

Alex Inkeles, "Industrial Man: The Relation of Status to Experience, Perception and Value," *American Journal of Sociology*, LXVI (July, 1960), pp. 1-31; Ely Chinoy, "The Tradition of Opportunity and the Aspirations of Automobile Workers," *American Journal of Sociology*, LVII (March, 1952), pp. 453-459; Ruth Gould, "Some Sociological Determinants of Goal Strivings," *Journal of Social Psychology*, XIII (1941), pp. 461-473; R. A. Katzell, et. al., "Job Satisfaction, Job Performance, and Situational Characteristics," *Journal of Applied Psychology*, XLV (April, 1961), pp. 65-72; Milton R. Blood, Charles L. Hulin, "Alienation, Environmental Characteristics, and Worker Responses," *Journal of Applied Psychology*, LI (June, 1967), pp. 284-290; A. N. Turner, P. R. Lawrence, *Industrial Jobs and the Worker: An Investigation of Response to Task Attitudes*, (Boston: Harvard University, Graduate School of Business Administration, 1965); William F. Whyte, *Money and Motivation: An Analysis of Incentives in Industry*, (New York: Harper, 1955).

12. James E. Kennedy, Harry E. O'Neill, "Job Content and Workers' Opinions," *Journal of Applied Psychology*, XLVII (December, 1958), pp. 372-375; M. D. Kilbridge, "Do Workers Prefer Larger Jobs? *Personnel*, XXXVII (September, 1960), pp. 45-48; A. C. MacKinney, et. al., "Has Specialization Reduced Job Satisfaction?" *Personnel*, XXXIX (January-February, 1962), pp. 8-17. For a perceptive analysis of factors influencing the attitudes of workers toward job enlargement see: Charles L. Hulin, Milton R. Blood, "Job Enlargement, Individual Differences, and Worker Responses," *Psychological Bulletin*, LXIX (1968), pp. 41-55.

13. For a description and analysis see: Fritz J. Roethlisberger, William J. Dickson, *Management and the Worker*, (Cambridge: Harvard University Press, 1939).

14. See the folllowing studies for data pertaining to the effects of work group norms on restriction of output: Orvis Collins, et. al., "Restriction of Output and Social Cleavage in Industry," *Applied Anthropology*, V (Summer, 1946), pp. 1-13; Donald F. Roy, "Efficiency and 'Fix': Informal Intergroup Relations in a Piecework Machine Shop," *American Journal of Sociology*, LX (November, 1954), pp. 255-266; Donald F. Roy, "Quota Restriction and Goldbricking in a Machine Shop," *American Journal of Sociology*, LVII (March, 1952), pp. 427-442.

15. For example see: Roethlisberger and Dickson, *loc. cit.*; see also the report of "Century Company (A) - (I)," in Clark, *op. cit.*, pp. 199-208; Paul Pigors, Charles H. Myers, *Personnel Administration, A Point of View and Method*, (New York: McGraw-Hill, 1956), pp. 642-647.

16. H. Roy Kaplan, "Job Satisfaction Among Scientific and Non-Scientific Personnel in a Research Organization," unpublished Master's thesis, University of Maine, Orono, 1968.

17. Robert Dubin, "Industrial Workers' Worlds: A Study of the 'Central Life Interests' of Industrial Workers," *Social Problems*, III (January, 1956), p. 140.

18. Louis H. Orzack, "Work as a 'Central Life Interest' of Professionals," *Social Problems*, VII (Fall, 1959), p. 129.

19. For a review of the assumptions involved in this approach the reader is referred to the following: Joan Woodward, *Industrial Organization: Theory and Practice*, (London: Oxford University Press, 1965); Charles Perrow, "A Framework for the Comparative Analysis of Organizations," *American Sociological Review*, XXXII (April, 1967), pp. 194-208; James D. Thompson, F. L. Bates, "Technology, Organization, and Administration." *Administrative Science Quarterly*, I (1957-1958), pp.325-343; Edward Harvey, "Technology and the Structure of Organizations," *American Sociological Review*, XXXIII (April, 1968), pp. 247-259.

20. Strauss, *op. cit.*, p. 383.

PROPERTIES OF ORGANIZATION STRUCTURE IN RELATION TO JOB ATTITUDES AND JOB BEHAVIOR [1]

Lyman W. Porter
University of California, Berkeley
Edward E. Lawler, III
Yale University

Psychological Bulletin 1965, Vol. 64, No. 1, 23-51

This article reviews the results of empirical field studies that have investigated the relationships between properties of organization structure and job attitudes and job behavior in business and industrial organizations. The following 7 structural properties were examined: organizational levels, line/staff hierarchies, span of control, subunit size, total-organization size, tall/flat shape, and centralized/decentralized shape. At least 5 of these 7 variables (with the possible exceptions being span of control and centralized/decentralized shape) were found to be significantly related to one or more attitude or behavioral variables. Implications of these findings for organization theory and future research are discussed.

All organizations are structured, in the sense of having positions and parts which are systematically related to other positions and parts. Since organizations vary in their structure, it is appropriate to examine the question of whether differences in the structure of organizations are related to differences in the attitudes and behavior of their members. The purpose of this article is to review the results of published research (prior to 1964) relevant to such relationships existing in business and industrial organizations.

Although organizations have been the focus of research and interest in sociology since the time of Weber's first writings on bureaucracy in the 1920s, and in industrial psychology since the time of the Hawthorne studies in the early 1930s, it has been only in the past decade or so that intensive and concentrated attention has been given to organizations in the bahavioral sciences. The major development in this area in psychology over the past 10 years has been the advent of so-called "modern organization theory." Such theory as developed by Likert, Haire, McGregor, Argyris, and others, has been advocated as a contrast with, and improvement on, so-called "classical organization theory" as developed by Fayol, Urwick, Taylor, and others. Whereas the classical theorists, with their discussions of chain of command, specialization of function, span of control and so forth, placed heavy emphasis on factors related to organization structure, the modern psychological theorists, such as those mentioned previously, have paid relatively little attention to the structural aspects of organizations. Bennis (1959) aptly summed up this point several years ago when he pointed out that classical theorists talked about "organizations without people," while modern theorists often seem to talk about "people without organizations." Instead of emphasizing the structure of organizations, latter-day theorists have advocated supervisory human relations training, T groups, attention to the nonfinancial needs of the employees and the like, as methods for improving organizational administration and leadership. The efficacy of such methods, however, may well be reduced by failure to take into account the structural characteristics of organizations.

Not only have organization theorists tended to ignore structural variables, but also so have many of the researchers in this area. Despite the apparent lack of concentrated empirical efforts to understand the effects of structural variables (other than the variable of workgroup size), there are, nevertheless, a number of studies in the psychological, sociological, and management-science literature that are pertinent to a consideration of structure. Although many of these studies were not conceived by their authors as investigations pertaining to structure as such, they do provide relevant and important evidence and thus will be included in this review.

For the purposes of this paper, structure has been defined to mean the positions and parts of organizations and their systematic and relatively enduring relationships to each other. Thus, we are referring to the formal structure of organizations as might be indicated, in a superficial way at least, in the formal "organization chart." Within the boundaries of this broad definition of structure, we have identified the following seven structural properties or variables:

Suborganization properties
1. Organizational levels
2. Line and staff hierarchies
3. Span of control
4. Size: subunits

Total-organization properties
5. Size: total organizations
6. Shape: tall or flat
7. Shape: centralized or decentralized

The first four variables above can be considered as suborganization properties of structure inasmuch as they permit comparisons of positions or parts contained within organizations with other positions or parts, either contained within the same organizations or within other organizations. The last three variables can be considered total-organization properties of structure because they require comparisons among organizations as complete entities. This sort of distinction between suborganization and total-organization types of properties will be shown to be especially crucial in the discussion of the effects of "size." It is also important to stress that these seven properties or dimensions of structure should not be considered mutually exclusive. For example, "span of control" has an obvious connection to the variable of "tall/flat" shape of total organizations. Although such variables are not clearly distinct from each other, we have discussed them separately since they are typically considered separately in both the research and textbook literature on organizations.

In essence, for this review these seven properties of organization structure will be regarded as the "independent" variables. Since almost none of the studies reviewed were experimental studies in the strict use of the term "experiment," any relationships found between structural variables and job attitudes or job behavior cannot be considered "cause-effect" relationships. Thus, neither the studies nor our conclusions from them can prove that the variations in structure cause the particular attitudes or behavior. However, the structural properties are referred to as the independent variables in the sense that if there are any cause-effect relationships present they probably are due to either to the variation in structure causing the variation in attitudes or behavior, or else to some third variable determining both the structure and the attitudes and behavior. Although it is conceivable that the kinds of attitudes or behavior usually investigated in these studies could determine the structure of organizations, this seems unlikely (at least in a direct fashion) in most cases.

Turning now to our "dependent" variables, job attitudes and job behavior, we have used the term "attitude" in its broadest and loosest sense of "opinion concerning some object," in this case jobs or aspects of jobs. Included under job-attitude studies would be the typical morale study, where the specific attitude questions are concerned with opinions about the organization, the supervisors, the working conditions and other factors directly connected with the job situation in which the employee operates. Excluded from the review are studies focusing on attitudes toward the self, such as self-description and vocational-interest studies, on the assumption that they are more likely to describe what groups or types of people are like rather than what positions or parts of organizations are like.

Considered under the heading of job behavior are studies that were (with a few exceptions) concerned with the following types of information: performance and output rates or ratings, turnover rates, absenteeism rates, accident rates, and employee-grievance rates. In this review the problem of the relationship between job attitudes and these various indices of behavior have not been dealt with; these have merely been considered to be two categories of dependent variables that are of interest to social scientists studying organizations.

Finally, the three major criteria for the inclusion of studies reviewed can be listed:

1. Studies of industrial and business organizations. The review is purposely restricted to studies dealing with these types of organizations—rather than also including other kinds of organizations such as governmental agencies, military units, schools, churches, and the like—in order to keep the discussion reasonably focused and delineated.

2. Comparative studies. Only those studies which have dealt with at least two (preferably, three or more) positions or degrees of structure along a given property or dimension are included. Thus, for example, a

study of only foremen's attitudes would not be included in the section on organizational levels since such a study did not compare foremen's attitudes with those of employees at some other organizational level. Likewise, a study of only small companies would not be included in the section on studies of total size, since no comparisons within that study are possible between small organizations and other-sized organizations. Under this criterion, case studies of single organizations were also excluded.

3. Empirical studies. With very few exceptions, only those studies providing empirical data are included. Articles based wholly or mostly on the opinions of the author unsupported by actual data have been excluded. In addition, articles based on casual observations where it seemed unlikely that the procedures could be easily repeated by other researchers have also been excluded.

The sections of the review to follow are arranged in the same order as the previously-listed set of seven properties of organization structure. Thus, we first take up properties permitting suborganization comparisons, followed by properties concerned with total-organization comparisons.

ORGANIZATIONAL LEVELS

For many years social scientists interested in industrial organizations have tended either to ignore the effect of organizational levels or else to concentrate on the simple dichotomy between managers and workers. In the 1940s most textbook writers in the area of human relations, following the lead of the Hawthorne investigations, spotlighted the plight of workers vis-à-vis managers in terms of the types of physical, social, and psychological conditions they had to endure. The emphasis was almost completely on the worker-management comparison. This tradition carried over into the 1950s when the "modern" management theorists, such as Argyris (1957), Haire (1956), Leavitt (1958), Likert (1961), and McGregor (1960), continued to focus, for the most part, on the relationship of managers to nonmanagement subordinates.

This relative lack of attention to the effects of differentiation among levels within management is somewhat surprising when one considers the amount of interest that industrial psychologists and sociologists have shown in the effects of division of labor. Almost always, however, division of labor has been studied as it occurs along a horizontal dimension at the rank-and-file worker level. The fact that there is not only a division of labor horizontally but also vertically within industrial organizations has frequently been neglected. The importance of paying closer attention to this vertical dimension of structure has been well stated by Pfiffner and Sherwood (1960) when they point out that:

[The] differentiation of task between echelons is of more significance to the selection and training of leaders at the several levels than may be indicated by the attention accorded it in the past. The psychological adjustment necessary when one goes from one level to another is often difficult because of the tendency to continue former behavior patterns . . . . At first glance this might appear to be a problem of human relations rather than of formal organization, but such a conclusion would be only partially true. Good job descriptions should reflect task differentiation at the various echelons. It is a matter of tasks combined with behavior . . . [p. 139].

In surveying the literature pertinent to organizational levels and their impact on, or relationship to, job attitudes and behavior, we encounter several difficult boundary or definitional problems. The first such problem concerns the question of whether studies of *occupational* levels should be included in the review. For our purposes, since the focus is on *organizational* structural variables, such occupational level studies will be generally omitted on the basis that they ordinarily investigate levels in a societal or cultural setting rather than levels within an organizational setting. A second problem in defining studies of organizational levels is posed by the investigation directed toward superior-subordinate relationships. Although in one sense these are studies that compare two different organizational levels, they in fact seldom provide data that contribute to our knowledge of the effects of the vertical dimension of structure. This is because such studies are usually concerned with implications for superior-subordinate authority relationships and not with implications for attitudes or behavior that may be differentially required or exhibited at various *job levels* within organizations. Most such studies, therefore, will not be covered in this review.

Within these broad limits, this section of the review will analyze the results of studies containing two or more organizational levels as the independent type of variable and one or more categories of directly job-related attitudes or behavior as the dependent type of variable.

Attitudes

Job Satisfaction and Morale. The first studies to be considered will be those that compare management with nonmanagement employees; after that, studies dealing with comparisons among levels within management will be reviewed.

Herzberg, Mausner, Peterson, and Capwell (1957) have summarized the literature through 1954 relevant to job satisfaction attitudes associated with organizational levels. They conclude that "one unequivocal fact emerges from the studies of job satisfaction; the higher the level of occupation, the higher the morale [p. 20]." It is clear from this statement that their review included studies of occupational level. The problem of drawing conclusions from these studies is that frequently the occupational level categories include people who do not work in industrial or business organizations (e.g., professional people included in a category of "executive and professional"). Nevertheless, the Herzberg review does cite studies "in which the morale of workers was compared to that of their supervisors (Ash, 1954; Browne & Neitzel, 1952; Campbell, 1948; Hull & Kolstad, 1942, Kolstad, 1944)." The study by Browne and Neitzel was actually based on different supervisory levels and will thus be reviewed below. The other four studies, however, did show greater job satisfaction among supervisory personnel when compared to workers.

In a study not included in the Herzberg review, Morse (1953) reported on the satisfactions of 61 supervisory personnel compared with 600 workers in a single company. She found that:

The supervisors are considerably more satisfied with their jobs and with the company as a place to work. They are somewhat less satisfied than the employees with their salaries and are about equal in satisfaction with the employees regarding the advancement they have received in the company [p. 98].

Thus, Morse's conclusions are in general agreement with the other studies cited above, although, as she points out, first-level supervisors may not be as satisfied as the rank and file with the specific aspect of wages.

Since the publication of the Herzberg review, only one study (Handyside, 1961) has appeared that has focused on management versus nonmanagement differences in job satisfaction. This study involved 30 managers and supervisory personnel and 467 production workers and found that "median satisfaction" (toward jobs) was higher for managerial personnel.

In recent years the content of job satisfaction studies of different organizational levels seems to have shifted from an exclusive focus on comparisons of supervisory personnel versus rank-and-file workers to comparisons among different levels of management within organizations.

A major point at issue in these studies of levels within management seems to be whether satisfaction increases with each higher level of management, or whether middle levels may have poorer morale than either lower or upper managerial levels. In their review of the literature through 1954, Herzberg et al. (1957) state that: "In large concerns, middle levels of management often have very poor morale [p. 23]." Their review refers to two articles relevant to this point (Benge, 1944; Fortune, 1950), but neither article presents enough data on either the samples of respondents or the results to draw any meaningful conclusions. Thus, there seems to be no substantial basis in the literature prior to 1954 to support this conclusion.

Recent studies, plus one appearing prior to the Herzberg review, seem to be nearly unanimous in concluding that job satisfaction or morale does increase monotonically with increasing levels of management, and that therefore middle managers are more satisfied than those below them in the organization but less satisfied than those above. The first such study, by Browne and Neitzel (1952), found that morale scores for three levels of supervision were "positively related to the echelon level of the supervisors [p. 90]." In 1961 two articles reporting on different levels of management appeared (Porter, 1961; Rosen, 1961a). Rosen's study, which was concerned with satisfaction with conditions of work, presented findings for three levels of management within a single plant. He found that the top managers in the plant and the middle managers did not differ significantly from each other in satisfaction, but both groups of managers were significantly more satisfied than first-level supervisors. Rosen also noted, however, that there was a similarity of profiles of satisfaction among the three levels of management, such that there were high rank-order correlations (ranging from .67 to .93) between each pair of levels in terms of the degree of satisfaction with the 24 items.

In Porter's study (1961), two levels of management, were surveyed in three different types of companies with a questionnaire designed to tap satisfaction of different types of needs relevant to a Maslow hierarchical classification of needs. The results showed that the higher of the two management levels generally reported greater satisfaction and, as was the case in Rosen's investigation, the pattern of need satisfactions tended to be similar between the two levels.

Subsequent to these 1961 studies by Porter and Rosen, Porter has completed a large-scale investigation of managerial need satisfactions across all levels of management, from first-level supervisors to company presidents. This study (Porter, 1962, 1964) sampled more than a thousand managers from a wide variety of different types and sizes of companies located throughout the country. The results were in general agreement with those from the previous Porter and Rosen studies. Satisfaction increased with each higher level of management for three of five needs (esteem, autonomy, and self-actualization needs), and profiles of satisfaction were generally similar across levels. (For security and social needs, satisfaction was roughly equal across all levels of management.) It should be emphasized that satisfaction in this study was measured by the difference between obtained and expected fulfillment. This is important because it means that for at least three types of needs lower-level managers were not just getting less fulfillment, as might be obvious, but there was a larger difference between their expectations and their fulfillment than was found at upper levels of management.

Much of the same sort of results were reported in a study published by the Opinion Research Corporation (1962). Attitude data were collected from 1,200 managers showing that the percentage of unfulfilled needs decreased from lower to middle to top management. For almost all of the specific questions asked of the respondents there were no reversals wherein a higher level of management expressed greater dissatisfaction than a lower level.

Finally, in a study as yet unpublished in detail, Haire, Ghiselli, and Porter (1963) found that a cross-cultural investigation of managerial attitudes in 14 countries, higher levels of management on the whole reported greater degrees of need satisfaction in their jobs than did lower-level managers. It thus appears that the phenomenon of increased job satisfaction with increasing level of management is not confined to the situation existing in American companies but tends to be a worldwide fact of industrial organizations.

To summarize briefly at this point, it can be stated with some degree of assurance that the available literature on job satisfaction across different levels of organizations shows increasing job satisfaction at each higher level. This is true both for nonmanagement versus management comparisons and also for comparisons with the management parts of hierarchies. In addition, one other finding appears with some consistency: Patterns of satisfaction are roughly similar across different organizational levels, at least within management.

Other Attitudes. A number of studies have been concerned with the relationship of organizational levels to attitudes other than degree of satisfaction. However, such studies are somewhat difficult to classify and summarize since they cover a great diversity of types of attitudes.

There are, nevertheless, several groupings that are reasonably discernible. The first of these comprises studies of the relative importance of different types of needs and motives at different organizational levels. Two studies (*Fortune*, 1947; Kahn, 1958) have made direct comparisons between nonmanagement and management levels with regard to the importance of different motivating factors. The two studies seem to present somewhat conflicting results for these comparisons. Kahn's findings indicated that both workers and their supervisors attached high importance to security, but that supervisors attached less importance to high wages than did the workers. The *Fortune* study, on the other hand, indicated that when security was pitted against high wages in an "either-or" choice situation, high-level executives chose the high wage situation. It is obviously difficult to compare the two sets of findings since both the samples and the procedures differed. What is clear is that we need considerably more evidence from a wide variety of types of organizations before we can make any broad generalizations concerning manager-worker differences in the importance attached to different motivating factors.

Several studies in the past 5 years have made comparisons of the importance attached to different needs and conditions of work among different levels within management. The first of these studies was by Rosen and Weaver (1960) who studied the degree of importance attached to 24 conditions of work by three levels of management within one plant. They found high rank-order correlations (ranging from .76 to .90) between each pair of levels with regard to the degree of importance attached to each of the 24 items. In terms of overall importance, the first-level supervisors attached generally more importance to most of the items. Subsequent to the Rosen and Weaver study, Porter published two articles dealing with the importance attached to different psychological needs by different managerial levels (Porter, 1961; 1963a). Both studies confirm one aspect of the findings of Rosen and Weaver; namely, different managerial levels tend to be similar with regard to what they consider most important. However, the later and more comprehensive of the Porter studies differed in one respect from both the earlier Porter study and the Rosen and Weaver study. It showed that higher-level managers tended to attach somewhat more rather than less importance to various needs, whereas the earlier studies indicated that higher managerial levels regarded most needs or conditions as less important compared to lower levels. The difference in these findings may lie in the fact that in the later Porter study the degree of formal education of the respondents was about equivalent across management levels, while in the earlier studies the degree of education was either not controlled or else the lower-level respondents had less education. It is conceivable that employees with less education may be more prone to consider everything as important, whereas those with greater formal schooling may be somewhat more discriminating in attaching importance to different needs and conditions. Therefore, it may be necessary to control for differences in formal education when comparing different management levels with regard to the importance attached to different psychological needs or conditions of work.

Finally, the cross-cultural study by Haire, Ghiselli, and Porter (1963) showed that for almost all of the countries in their sample there was again a strong similarity between upper-level and lower-level managers in the relative importance attached to different needs.

Turning to a different area of job attitudes, we find a small group of studies that can be put under the general heading of role perception studies (Coates & Pellegrin, 1957; Porter & Henry, 1964a; Rosen, 1961b; Triandis, 1959b). Although each of these studies was in some way concerned with role perceptions, it should be noted that they were addressed to rather different aspects of role perceptions, they utilized different types of samples, and, particularly, they employed quite different methods to obtain their data. For instance, Triandis (1959b) utilized the semantic differential technique to study the "differential perception of certain jobs and people" by upper-level managers, lower-level managers, and clerks and workers from one company. He concluded that "the most significant variable in the perception of jobs is the *level* of the job [being perceived; p. 224]." In addition, he also found that managers made finer discriminations among their job perceptions than did workers. Rosen (1961b) investigated how three levels of management in a particular company ranked 16 "role prescriptions." His findings showed that managers at the two lower levels tended to be similar in how they evaluated their role as supervisors, but each level differed somewhat from the highest of the three levels. Porter and Henry (1964a) studied the perceptions of managers in terms of the type of behavior each level believed was most important for jobs at their particular level, and found that at each higher level of management increasing emphasis was put on "inner-directed" (as opposed to "other-directed") personality traits. Coates and Pellegrin (1957), in a study directed primarily toward self-perceptions, found that both supervisors and subordinates tended to "be aware of the rewards, penalties, and sacrifices associated with high-level roles. Such an awareness differentially influences achievement desires on the two levels (p. 220)."

An overall look at these diverse studies of role perception among different organizational levels reveals that again the variable of level seems to have a strong relationship to these types of perceptions, just as it did to perceptions of need and job satisfaction.

Two investigations have compared the factorial structures of attitudes of lower-level personnel versus those at higher levels. Baehr (1954), factoring the Science Research Associates (SRA) Employee Inventory for a "high-status" group of managers and white collar personnel and a "low-status" group of factory workers and routine clerical personnel, found considerable, but not complete, similarity in the factors emerging from the two groups. What differences there were indicated that the factors of the high-status group tended to be more concerned with the overall functioning of the organization while those of the low-status group were more relevant to specific aspects of the immediate work situation. Triandis (1960) factored the semantic job structures of managers and supervisors in a manufacturing plant and compared these with the factored job structures of workers in the same plant. He found even greater factorial similarity between the two groups than did Baehr and concluded that: "Management and workers, one might expect, will differ in their factorial structures when the domain of jobs is considered. The answer is that this is not true. The factor structures are surprisingly similar [p. 300]." It appears, therefore, from these two studies, that organizational level does not have a strong relationship to the structure of job attitudes.

The salience of different features of jobs and jobholders appears to be related to the level at which a person is working in an organization. Two studies which demonstrate this are another article by Triandis and one by Pellegrin and Coates. Triandis (1959a) found that upper-level managers focused on such "expressive" categories of description as "graciousness" and "polish," while lower-level managers and workers emphasized "instrumental" categories such as "intelligence," "skill," and "dependability," in describing different groups of employees. Likewise, he also found differences associated with the three levels of respondents when they were describing different jobs. The two managerial groups tended to use the criterion of the "nature of the work" to distinguish among different jobs, whereas the workers made their distinctions among jobs primarily on the basis of job requirements, particularly intelligence. Pellegrin and Coates (1957), in interviews with a sample of 50 "top-level" executives and 50 "first-level" supervisors, found that the former emphasized the intrinsic features of their jobs whereas the latter viewed their jobs more as means to off-job rewards. This may indicate, in the terms of Herzberg, Mausner, and Synderman (1959), that managers in higher-level positions focus more on "motivating" aspects of their positions while supervisors in lower-level jobs are oriented more toward concern with the "hygienic" conditions of their positions.

One other area of job attitudes in relation to organizational levels has received some attention, namely, types of leadership attitudes at different levels. The Ohio State studies (e.g., Fleishman, 1953; Fleishman, Harris, & Burtt, 1955) have demonstrated that attitudes about how supervisors should behave in relation to their workers vary depending on the organizational level of the respondent. For example, Fleishman's (1953) article showed that the higher the level of a manager, the less likely he was to believe that a supervisor should show "Consideration" attitudes toward his subordinates and the more likely he was to think a supervisor should put emphasis on "Initiating Structure" in dealing with subordinates.

Behavior

Studies of the relationships between organizational levels and individuals' behavior are relatively infrequent. The nature of five such studies that were located in the literature, including the sizes of their samples, is indicaed in Table 1. This table shows that the sampling, in terms of both individual subjects and organizations, is extremely limited. Any conclusions emerging from these studies, therefore, must be regarded with great caution. One other point should be noted in Table 1. These five studies dealing with behavior in relation to organizational level are not concerned with rates of production, absenteeism, safety, turnover, and the like. Instead, they concentrate on interpersonal interaction patterns, types of decisions, and types of functional activities performed by the individual in his job. The reason these studies do not focus on the types of behavior usually studied in the typical field investigation is that they are all concerned with differences in behavior between or among levels of management. Thus, output or production in the usual sense is not easily measured. Also, it is probably assumed that turnover, absenteeism, and accident rates are so negligible at managerial levels that there would be little or no variation in these indices from level to level.

Keeping in mind the severely restricted nature of the samples in these five studies, there are several conclusions that seem to be supported by the data so far obtained:

1. Informal Communication (Informational) Patterns. Davis' (1953) study of the grapevine operating in the management sector of a particular company indicated that higher-level managers are much better informed on informal communication(as well as, presumably, on formal communication) items than lower-level managers and super-

TABLE 1

Studies of Relationships of Organizational Levels to Job Behavior

Investigators	Type of behavior	N of individuals	N of levels	N of companies
Burns (1954)	Interactions and activities	4	3	1
Davis (1953)	Communications (grapevine)	65	6	1
Dubin & Spray (1964)	Interactions and activities	8	2	3
Martin (1959)	Decision making	?	4	1
Shartle (1956)	Activities	14	2	7

visors. Davis stressed the fact that, in this company at least, first-level supervisors were the most isolated from news traveling through the informal communication channels.

2. Interpersonal Interaction Patterns. Three major types of interaction variables have been examined in several studies: (a) The ratio of upward (or superior) contacts to downward (or subordinate) contacts—the three studies (Burns, 1954; Dubin & Spray, 1964; Martin, 1959) that deal with this variable present contradictory findings. Burns' data (as pointed out by Dubin, 1962) show that the ratio of superior to subordinate contacts decreases the higher the level of management; Dubin and Spray's data seem to indicate the opposite; Martin's results show no changes in the ratio of relation to level. (b) Percentage of peer contacts—both Burns' and Martin's findings indicate that the relative number of contacts with peers decreases the higher the level of management. Dubin and Spray's data are inconclusive on this point. (c) Percentage of contacts with individuals outside the organizational unit (e.g., factory, office, or company)—the data of both the Martin and the Dubin and Spray studies show a definite trend for such outside contacts to increase the higher the level of management, as one might expect. Burns' study indirectly supports this point, as does one by Shartle (1956), who found that the heads of seven organizations spent a greater proportion of their time on public relations activities than did their immediate assistants. (d) Percentage of direct (face-to-face) contacts—Martin found the proportion of face-to-face contacts decreasing at higher management levels.

3. Types of Decisions. Martin's study is the only one of the five studies to focus on the differences in the types of decisions made at different levels of management. In his investigation of four levels (from works manager down to shift foreman) within a single plant, he found that the higher the managerial level, (a) the greater the "duration" of the decision (i.e., increase in time between the inception of the decision process and the actual implementation of this decision and the verification of its corrections or incorrectness), and hence the greater the increase in the "riskiness" of the decision, and (b) the more abstract the decision (i.e., an increasing lack of "structure" of the data relevant to the decision).

4. Types of Activities (e.g., planning, coordinating, production, etc.). Data concerning differences in patterns of activities at different levels of management are so meager that generalizations cannot be made in this area, even though several studies (Burns, 1954; Dubin & Spray, 1964; Shartle, 1956) have attempted to collect such information.

Summary

A review of the relevant literature demonstrates that organizational levels are strongly related to both attitudes and behavior. The evidence shows that perceived job and need satisfactions increase not only from rank-and-file positions to managerial positions, but also from lower management positions to middle- and upper-level positions. Thus, level seems clearly to be related to what individuals think they are receiving from their jobs. Level also seems to show a relationship to what employees think they must put into their jobs, in terms of the behavior they perceive to be required by their jobs. On the other hand, it should also be stressed that level does not necessarily affect all types of job attitudes. For example, it seemed to have only a slight relationship to the relative importance attached to different kinds of needs.

In terms of behavior that is actually exhibited by employees, especially within managerial ranks, level seems to affect the amount of information a person receives in his job, the types of interpersonal relationships he has on his job, and the types and nature of the decisions he must make in his position. However, the evidence concerning these behavioral variables in relation to level is limited, and hence conclusions concerning them must be regarded as tentative at the present time.

The major research trend in this area in recent years, both in studies of attitudes and of behavior, seems to be a shift toward an increasing focus on the differentiation of organizational levels within management in contrast with the former (almost complete) concentration on management versus nonmanagement differences. Eventually, it may be possible to describe organizational differences in major aspects of attitudes and behavior for at least four discrete points along the heirarchical or level dimension of structure; rank-and-file positions, first-line supervision, middle management, and top management. To date, however, we have no major sets of attitudinal or behavioral data from a specific study that adequately sample these four levels across different kinds of industrial or business organizations.

Future research on organizational levels will need to focus on the question of what it is about different levels that seems to create different job attitudes and job behavior. In other words, "organizational level"is merely a convenient label for other, more fundamental, variables that must be operating in the situation. An understanding of the nature of these other variables and how they are distributed along the vertical dimension of structure is a research task for the future in this area.

Future research will also need to focus on the necessity of disentangling the effects of individual-difference variables from the effects of organizational-level variables. Practically all of the studies so far carried out in this area have failed to consider the fact that individuals at different organizational levels may vary systematically in intelligence and/or personality traits. To what extent the obtained differences in attitudes and behavior are a function of these types of differences relative to differences due to job level is an open question. It is a question that will require sophisticated research for an answer.

LINE AND STAFF HIERARCHIES

The distinction between line and staff hierarchies is an old one in the study of formal organizations. Traditionally, positions concerned with the main operations of the organization and within the direct chain of command have been considered part of the line hierarchy, while positions concerned with auxiliary services and outside the direct chain of command have been considered part of the staff hierarchy. The staff's function is to provide specialized aid to the line, which is composed of "generalists." Recently, this traditional distinction has received attention from two sources. One group of writers (Brown, 1954; Fisch, 1961; Leavitt & Whisler, 1958; McGregor, 1960) has contended that the distinction between these two parallel hierarchies is disappearing under the impact of modern technology. A second group of writers has dealt with the type of relationships that exist between line and staff managers. Both Dalton (1959) and Whyte (1961) have illustrated the type of conflicts that can develop between managers in these two hierarchies existing within organizations.

Attitudes

The evidence available concerning the amount of satisfaction provided by line and staff positions is consistent in showing line managers to be more satisfied than staff managers. Three studies by the Opinion Research Corporation (1959) reported that engineers and scientists in staff positions were less satisfied with their jobs than engineers and scientists in line positions. In more recent studies using broader samples of managers, Rosen (1961a) and Porter (1963b) found that line managers reported a greater incidence of desirable conditions of work and perceived greater need satisfactions, especially in esteem and self-actualization need areas.

Three studies compared line and staff managers on the amount of importance they attached to job-related factors and needs, and all three found essentially no differences between the two groups of managers. Rosen and Weaver (1960) found that managers in line and staff positions did not differ substantially in their ratings of the importance of 24 desirable conditions of work. Porter (1963b) found that there were no line-staff differences in the importance attached to four of five need areas; only on the need for autonomy did the two groups differ, with staff managers feeling this need was more important. Lawler and Porter (1963) found no differences between the two types of managers in the importance attached to pay.

In a study involving a somewhat different type of attitude, Porter and Henry (1964b) asked line and staff managers to rank five other-directed and five inner-directed personality traits on the basis of how important they are for success in their management positions. The results showed that staff managers, as Whyte (1956) and others might have predicted, felt they have to show more other-directed behavior to succeed in their jobs than line managers.

Behavior

Only three studies were located that permitted comparisons of line and staff personnel on behavioral indices. A frequently cited study by Dalton (1950) found that staff managers in three plants had a turnover rate between two and four times that of line managers. Davis (1953), in a study of one company, reported that staff managers were better informed than line managers. He attributed this superior knowledge on the part of staff managers to their greater mobility.

Staff executives in such areas as personnel and control found that their duties both required and allowed them to get out of their offices, made it easy for them to walk through other departments without someone wondering whether they were 'not working,' to get away for coffee, and so on—all of which meant they heard more news from the other executives they talked with [p. 47].

Burns' study (1954) also appears to support the notion of greater communication flexibility for managers in staff positions.

Summary

Since the studies that have compared the attitudes and behavior of employees in line and staff positions are all relatively recent, it is impossible to determine if the amount of difference between the two types of hierarchies has been decreasing over the long term, as some writers have suggested. The validity of this contention probably will not be established until we have strictly comparative data on line-staff differences from different time periods. In the meantime, however, the available evidence indicates that differences in conditions between the two types of positions are still large enough to produce significant differences in both attitudes and behavior. Staff managers derive less satisfaction from their jobs, feel they have to be more other-directed, and exhibit different patterns of behavior. The only area that failed to produce consistent differences was the degree of importance attached to various job-related factors and needs. Apparently this type of attitude was little affected by organizational conditions surrounding line and staff jobs.

The evidence on the attitude and behavior differences between managers in line and staff positions presents a picture of several factors that may be responsible for line and staff conflicts. The staff manager's position, for instance, requires him to be knowledgeable about his specialty and spend considerable time with a variety of types of executives; yet it provides him with little opportunity to use his knowledge for decision making unless he usurps the authority of the line. The line manager's position, on the other hand, places him in a situation in which he is expected to take advice, on decisions for which he has responsibility, from a man who frequently is younger and has been with the company a shorter period of time and who is not supposed to know the whole picture as he is. This is not a situation that lends itself to harmonious line-staff relations. The fact that managers in line and staff hierarchies see different traits being required for success and report different levels of satisfaction suggests that one way of easing some of the potential line-staff conflicts may be to take into account the psychological demands of the two different types of jobs in the selection and placement of manager.

SPAN OF CONTROL

Span of control is defined as the number of subordinates a manager is responsible for supervising. Since the early days of classical organization theory (Urwich, 1935), writers have prescribed what they felt to be an optimum span of control. In most instances, the classical theorists have assumed that a small span of control (few subordinates) is a "good thing" for any organization. Typical prescriptions have recommended spans of control between three and six (Dale, 1952). However, classical organization theorists generally have failed to consider what factors might call for a change in the size of the span of control. Recognizing this, Fisch (1963) has recently argued that such factors as level of management, company product diversification, and the personalities of the managers should be considered in determining the optimum span of control.

A vigorous dissent from the classical approach to the span of control was made by Worthy (1950). His radical suggestion was that a large span of control is good since it provides better communication and greater opportunities for individual growth and initiative. With this statement by Worthy, the battle line between the two approaches to organization theory was clearly drawn. However, researchers have not been quick to join in the fray, and as late as 1960 Pfiffner and Sherwood stated: "There has been relatively little, if any, empirical study of span of control(p. 156)." The majority of the research that has been done on the topic has been concerned with discovering variables that are related to the size of the span of control found in existing organizations. Entwisle and Walton (1961), for example, found that the size of the organization and the function of the organization were both related to existing spans of control. This type of research undoubtedly represents a necessary first step in determining which conditions favor a large span of control and which favor a small span of control, but it does not provide data on relationships to job attitudes or performance. In fact, only one such study was located in the literature.

Attitudes

No empirical studies were found that attempted to determine the relationship between span of control and employee job attitudes. Worthy (1950) did report that in one company a large span of control had been found to be positively related to high morale; however, he presented no published data to support this point, and thus it is difficult to evaluate his claims.

Behavior

A study by Woodward (1958) found a relationship between the size of the span of control at the first level of supervision and company performance when several English companies were viewed. The companies were divided into three groups based upon the method of production used—unit (e.g., production of unique units to customers' orders), mass (e.g., production of large numbers of identical units by assembly-line techniques), and process (e.g., production of chemicals, etc., by continuous processing). For each of the three types of production, the most successful companies were those that were near the median span of control for that production type. These median spans of control (23 for mass, 49 for process, and 13 for unit) for the successful companies were substantially larger than those suggested as optimum by the classical theorists. Woodward's study thus gives at least tentative support to Worthy's point that a large span of control can produce high performance. However, it is important to remember that Woodward's study was concerned with the span of control of first-line supervisors, and although a relatively large span of control may have proved to be optimum at this level, there is no reason to believe the same necessarily will be true of the upper levels of management. Perhaps the most significant point about the Woodward study is that the method of production was found to be an important variable in determining which span of control at the first level of supervision was optimum for producing high performance.

Summary

The lack of research makes it impossible to state that any particular span of control is best for producing high performance or positive job attitudes. What data there are suggest that it is not reasonable to expect any one span of control to be ideal for all organizational situations. Level of management and type of production appear to be two variables that influence the optimum span of control for a given situation, and undoubtedly further research will uncover other variables that are important.

SIZE: SUBUNITS

For the purposes of this review, any grouping of the members of a business organization that systematically excludes part of the membership of that organization is considered an organization subunit. Primary work groups, departments, and factories (in multifactory companies)

have been frequently studied organization subunits. Previous summaries of the research evidence on the relationship between organization subunit size and job attitudes and performance typically have concluded that small organization subunits are superior on all counts (e.g.,
Strauss & Sayles, 1960; Viteles, 1953). Morale, absence rates, turnover
rates, accident rates, and productivity are all considered to be better in
small than in large organization subunits. An example of the broad
statements supporting small organization subunits is Viteles' conclusion that "The size of the work group affects output and attitudes, which
both tend to be better in smaller sized groups (p. 146)."

Recently several articles (Herbst, 1957; Indik & Seashore, 1961)
have contained theories attempting to explain the beneficial effects of
small organization subunits. Undoubtedly the appearance of these theories is due to the aforementioned widespread acceptance of the belief
that the experimental evidence conclusively supports the proposition
that smaller organization subunits are always beneficial. Virtually ignored in the rush to accept this simple picture of the effects of subunit
size and completely ignored in theoretical attempts to explain this picture has been the effect of two other variables: job level within the
organization subunit, and type of organization subunit (e.g., work
group, department, factory). These variables may well function to limit
the degree to which it is possible to generalize about the beneficial
effects of small organization subunits. For example, increasing the size
of a department may raise the absence rate among the department's
production workers, but it is doubtful that it will also increase the
absence rate of the department's management force. Likewise, increasing the size of a primary work group may cause lower morale in that
work group, but increasing the size of a factory by adding more small
work groups may very well not decrease the morale of the total plant.
Thus, before we accept the conclusion that all types of large subunits,
regardless of job level being considered, are always inferior to small
ones, it may be well to see if the evidence justifies such a conclusion.

Since there are a relatively large number of studies that have
investigated the relationship of subunit size to both attitudes and behavior, Table 2 was constructed to summarize most (but not all) of these
studies. This table will serve as the basis for most of the subsequent
discussion in this section on subunit size.

Attitudes

Job Satisfaction and Morale. As Table 2 indicates, there is little
doubt that subunit size is significantly related to differences in job
attitudes. The evidence is strong that workers in small departments and
work groups are better satisfied than workers in large departments or
groups, as six of the seven studies reviewed show results in this direction. However, the evidence does not yet support the sweeping conclusion that all types of employees in smaller organization subunits are
more satisfied than those in larger subunits, since no studies were

TABLE 2

Studies of Relationships between Organization Subunit Size
and Job Attitudes and Job Behavior

Attitude or behavior studied	Investigators	Type of subunit considered	Relationship found*
Job satisfaction	Talacchi (1960)	Factories	Negative
	Kerr, Koppelmeier, & Sullivan (1951)	Departments	Negative
	Indik & Seashore (1961)	Departments	Negative
	Katzell, Barrett, & Parker (1961)	Departments	Negative
	Campbell (1952)	Work groups	Negative
	Worthy (1950)	?	Negative
	Indik & Seashore (1961)	Automobile dealerships	Zero
Absenteeism	Revans (1958)	Gas works	Positive
	Revens (1958)	Factories	Positive
	Revans (1958)	Factories	Positive
	Acton Society Trust (1953)	Factory	Positive
	Baumgartel & Sobol (1959)	"Plants" (airline locations)	Positive
	Research Council for Economic Security (Baumgartel & Sobol, 1959)	Plants	Positive (?)
	Hewitt & Parfitt (1953)	Departments	Positive
	Indik & Seashore (1961)	Departments	Positive
	Kerr, Koppelmeier, & Sullivan (1951)	Departments	Positive
	Metzner & Mann (1953)	Work groups (blue-collar)	Positive
	Argyle, Gardner, & Cioffi (1958)	Work groups	Curvilinear
	Metzner & Mann (1953)	Work groups (white-collar)	Zero
Turnover	Indik & Seashore (1961)	Automobile dealerships	Positive
	Kerr, Koppelmeier, & Sullivan (1951)	Departments	Positive
	Mandell (1956)	Departments	Positive
	Argyle, Gardner, & Cioffi (1958)	Work groups	Zero
Accidents	Revans (1958)	Mines (Britain)	Positive
	Revans (1958)	Factories (Britain)	Positive
	Revans (1958)	Departments (Asia)	Positive
	Revans (1958)	Mines (U.S.A.)	Curvilinear
	U.S. Department of Labor (Revans, 1958)	Factories (U.S.A.)	Curvilinear
	National Safety Council (Revans, 1958)	Factories (U.S.A.)	Negative
Labor disputes	Cleland (1955)	Factories	Positive
	Revans (1958)	Mines	Positive

TABLE 2 (Continued)

Attitude or behavior studied	Investigators	Type of subunit considered	Relationship found*
Productivity	Katzell, Barrett, & Parker (1961)	Company divisions	Negative
	Indik & Seashore (1961)	Departments	Negative
	Marriott (1949)	Work groups	Negative
	Revans (1958)	Mines	Curvilinear
	Revans (1958)	Retail stores	Curvilinear
	Herbst (1957)	Retail stores	Curvilinear
	Indik & Seashore (1961)	Automobile dealerships	Zero
	Argyle, Gardner, & Cioffi (1958)	Work groups	Positive

*A positive relationship indicates a trend for the attitude or behavior to become more frequent as size increases. A negative relationship indicates a trend for the attitude or behavior to become less frequent as size increases. A curvilinear relationship indicates a trend for the middle-sized subunit to exhibit the greatest or the lowest frequency of the attitude or behavior.

located, for example, that compared managerial job attitudes in different size organization subunits. Thus, it is impossible to reach any conclusion about the relationship between subunit size and the job satisfaction of managers.

Talacchi (1960) studied the level of job satisfaction among employees in 41 plants that were subunits of five larger organizations. His results showed a strong trend (r's ranging from —.42 to —.81) for job satisfaction to decrease as plant size increased. Kerr, Koppelmeier, and Sullivan (1951) found that for 894 workers in 29 departments in two electronics plants job satisfaction was correlated —.46 with size of department. Indik and Seashore (1961) measured the amount of intrinsic job satisfaction expressed by workers in 32 package delivery departments, varying in size from 15 to 61, and found that increased size led to lower satisfaction. Likewise, Katzell, Barrett, and Parker (1961) found a significant trend for workers in large warehouses to express lower job satisfaction than workers in small warehouses (with 23 out of 23 correlations being in this direction). Campbell (1952), in studying workers' satisfaction with incentive pay plans as a function of the size (from under 20 to over 100) of the work group to which they belonged, found that workers in the smaller groups felt they had better knowledge of how their pay plan operated and were more satisfied with their pay. Finally, Worthy (1950) reported: "Our researches demonstrate that mere size is unquestionably one of the most important factors in determining the quality of employee relationships: the smaller the unit the higher the morale, and vice versa [pp. 172-173]." Regrettably, Worthy failed to document this strong statement with any published data on the size of the units studied, the type of employees studied, or the measure of morale used.

The only study that failed to show a negative relationship between subunit size and job satisfaction was one reported in the previously mentioned publication by Indik and Seashore (1961) which concerned employee job satisfaction in automobile dealerships. Since these dealerships were relatively autonomous, and perhaps not completely accurately classified as subunits, the failure to find a strong negative relationship in this particular instance is probably not too significant.

Other Attitudes. Three studies (not shown in Table 2) investigated the relationship between organization subunit size and job attitudes other than those concerned with satisfaction. Hemphill (1950) found that as group size increased, members expressed attitudes of greater tolerance for leader-centered direction of group activities. In addition, Hemphill (1956) found that small groups were better characterized by attitudes of high intimacy, high hedonic tone, and low control than were large groups. It should be noted that both studies by Hemphill employed subjects from very diverse types of groups (ranging from industrial work groups to members of a sorority), and thus it is difficult to assess their relevance for industrial organizations.

Seashore (1954) studied the relationship between group cohesiveness and size of work group for more than 200 groups in a large industrial organization. The results showed a general trend for feelings of cohesiveness to decrease with increasing subunit size. However, there was also a tendency for the smallest size groups to fall at the two extremes of cohesiveness; that is, they were either extremely high or extremely low in cohesiveness. Nevertheless, Seashore's general conclusion was that group size is negatively related to group cohesiveness attitudes.

Behavior

Absenteeism. The greatest amount of evidence demonstrating a relationship between organization subunit size and job behavior appears on the topic of absence rates. As shown in Table 2, 10 of the 12 studies reviewed found positive linear relationships between absence rates and the size of subunits. This finding appeared for factories, departments, and primary work groups. Again, however, the finding is limited to absence rates among employees at the blue-collar level, since the only study that separately looked at white-collar workers' absences found no relationship between subunit size and absence rates.

Revans (1958) has provided an excellent review of much of the data on the topic of subunit size in relation to absenteeism. He reported that in five randomly chosen gas works,[2] ranging in size from 67 to 3,430 employees, the duration of absence due to accidents and the log of the size of the works were correlated + .91. In addition, size of works was correlated + .62 with absence rates due to sickness and other factors. Revans also reported two further studies dealing with size of factory in multifactory organizations. Each study found significant positive correlations between log size of factory and absence rates. A study by the

Action Society Trust (1953) reported a correlation of + .44 between size of factory (ranging from under 100 employees to more than 1,000) and absence rates. Baumgartel and Sobol (1959) did a well-controlled study on the relationships between the size of work locations or "plants" of an airline and absenteeism and found a strong tendency for absenteeism to increase with size of the work location. These investigators also cited the report on Prolonged Illness Absenteeism rates. And Metzner and Mann for Economic Security, which showed that smaller-sized plants had lower prolonged illness rates than medium-sized plants. However, the same report indicated that there was not a consistent linear relationship between plant size and illness. Several other studies, Hewitt and Parfitt (1953), Indik and Seashore (1961), and Kerr, Koppelmeier, and Sullivan (1951), have all found that larger departments of a company have higher absenteeism rates. And Metzner and Mann (1953) found that among blue-collar workers small work groups (seven and under) had fewer absences than did large work groups (over seven).

Only 2 of the 12 studies dealing with subunit size and absenteeism failed to show positive relationships between these two variables. Argyle, Gardner, and Cioffi (1958) reported that they found a curvilinear relationship between absence rates and work-group size (ranging from 1 to 20+), with the lowest absence rates occurring in the middle-sized groups. Metzner and Mann, in their above-cited study (1953), found an insignificant relationship, although in the expected direction, between absence rates and work-group size for white collar workers. (It should also be noted that in the previously cited Baumgartel and Sobol study of airline locations, the effects of location size were less for white-collar workers than for blue-collar workers.)

Turnover. Table 2 shows that three of four studies found that turnover is greater in large units compared to small units. However, none of the studies compared the turnover rates of different-sized factories, and none of the studies considered turnover rates among managerial personnel. Indik and Seashore (1961) found that more employees were terminated in large than in small automobile dealerships. Kerr, Koppelmeier, and Sullivan (1951) found a significant relationship between turnover and department size ($r = +.49$). Likewise, Mandell (1956), in a study of 320 companies, found that large offices tended to have higher turnover rates than did small offices. On the other hand, Argyle, Gardner, and Cioffi (1958) did not find any relationship between subunit size and turnover.

Accident Rates. Revans (1958) has thoroughly reviewed the literature on the relationship between accident rates and organization subunit size. As the six sets of data covered in his review indicate, there is not a consistent pattern of relationship between these two variables. In fact, three different patterns were found: positive, curvilinear, and negative relationships. A review of the evidence cited by Revans leads to the conclusion that accident rates may be dependent upon the type of industry considered and upon the technological development of the country in which a study is carried out. At the present time it seems wise to speak only of the type of relationship that exists for a given industry in a given country, and not for industry in general. For example, as shown in Table 2, the evidence is fairly convincing that for United States industry large size is not associated with high accident rates, while for British industry large size does appear to be associated with increased accident rates.

Revans' analysis of the accident rate for British coal miners and quarriers in 1950 showed a strong positive relationship between mine size and number of accidents. Likewise, the Annual Report of the Chief Inspector of Factories for 1956 (cited by Revans) showed that the compensable accident rate rises steadily with the average size of factory for British industrial firms. Also reported by Revans was a strong positive correlation (+.47) between accident rates and department size for steel companies operating in Asia.

Turning to the data for American industry, Revans cited three studies that indicated either a curvilinear or negative relationship between subunit size and accident rates. The data for American mines, in contrast to similar data for mines in Britain, showed the highest accident rates occurring in middle-sized mines employing 100 to 300 workers. Data for United States factories were provided in two studies which showed somewhat different results from each other. Bulletin 1164 of the United States Department of Labor (cited by Revans) on "Work Injuries in the United States during 1952" points to a curvilinear relationship in the following quotation:

The larger establishments, which can afford trained safety engineers and which conduct intensive safety programs, generally have the lowest rates. Usually the medium-size plants have the highest rates, and the smallest establishments show rates somewhat below the medium-size plants but above the average for the industry [quoted by Revans, 1958, p. 209].

In a report from the National Safety Council on 3,500 United States manufacturing plants, Revans cited data showing a strongly declining accident rate with increasing plant size.

Labor Disputes. Data contained in two sources (Cleland, 1955; Revans, 1958) show a positive relationship between subunit size and labor disputes. Cleland's data demonstrated that as plant size increases, the probability of an industrial strike rises significantly. Similarly, Revans noted that British coal miners in larger mines were more sensitive to nonmonetary issues (although not to monetary issues) than were miners in smaller locations. On the basis of these two reports it is tempting to conclude that small subunits are more likely to have fewer labor problems than larger subunits. However, one must be cautious in making this interpretation, since it is not size of operation, as such, that affects the number of labor disputes, but rather the type of technology that is associated with size (see Summary at the end of this section).

Productivity. As Table 2 shows, the studies on the relationship between performance and organization subunit size do not present a clear-cut picture. Thus, the available evidence does not support the widely believed assumption that small subunits are superior to large ones in terms of job performance.

Three studies found better performance in smaller subunits than in larger units. For example, Katzell, Barrett, and Parker (1961) found that product value, productivity, and profitability were all lower in the large divisions of the company they studied. Indik and Seashore (1961) found a negative correlation between the size of delivery organizations and rated overall performance of these units. Marriott (1949), in a widely cited study of the relationship between work-group size and production in two automobile factories, concluded from his data that: "Low, but significant correlations were obtained which demonstrate an inverse relationship between output and size, the smaller sized groups showing consistently larger output in each factory [p. 56]."

In contrast to the results from the above three studies, were the findings from five other studies and reports; three of them found curvilinear relationships between subunit size and production, one found essentially no relationship, and one a positive relationship. Revans (1958) reported that data gathered by the National Coal Board in Britain for Years 1948-53 showed a curvilinear relationship between mine size and output per miner, with the highest output being obtained in middle-sized mines where 1,500 to 2,000 men were employed. Revans (1958) and Herbst (1957) both present data on sales of retail sales units, and both report curvilinear relationships to size, with the middle-sized units again performing best. Indik and Seashore (1961), on the other hand, reported a lack of significant relationship between size of automobile dealerships and job performance, and Argyle, Gardner, and Cioffi (1958) found a slight tendency for larger work groups to achieve higher productivity than smaller groups.

Summary

The literature on subunit size shows that when blue-collar workers are considered, small size subunits are characterized by higher job satisfaction, lower absence rates, lower turnover rates, and fewer labor disputes. The evidence does not show, however, a consistent relationship for blue-collar workers between accident rates and subunit size. Furthermore, none of the studies reviewed investigated the relationship between mangers' job attitudes and job behavior and organization subunit size.

Future research might well consider the problem of assessing the relative impact on attitudes and behavior of the side of the different organization subunits of which an individual is a member. A typical worker is a member of at least three organization subunits: a primary work group, a department, and a factory or office. Although the evidence indicates that large-sized subunits are associated, for example, with high absenteeism, it is impossible to know on the basis of past studies if it is large size in the primary work group, department, or

FIGURE 1

Hypothesized Effects of Subunit Size

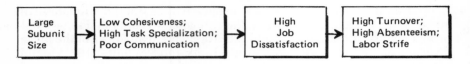

factory that is crucial in this relationship. Previous investigators have failed to control for variation in the size of the other types of subunits of which an individual is a member while they are studying the effects of size of one type of unit. For example, no study has compared absenteeism among work groups that are part of the same size departments and factories. Similarly, we do not know if factory size is related to absenteeism when all factories considered have the same size departments and work groups. It may well be that absenteeism is determined by work-group size but because large work groups are found in large factories and departments a spurious relationship exists between absenteeism and department size and between absenteeism and factory size.

At the present time, the weight of the evidence clearly suggests that small-sized subunits are desirable for a number of reasons. Although small-sized units may not improve job performance directly, the fact that they are associated with low turnover and low absenteeism argues strongly for their value. The question then arises as to why small subunits seem to have certain advantages over large units in affecting attitudes and behavior. Figure 1 presents a diagram that offers a possible explanatory model for the effects of organization subunit size on satisfaction, turnover, absenteeism, and labor strife. As subunits increase in size, it is probably increasingly difficult to maintain high cohesiveness and good communications. Further, task specialization may be more prevalent. The factors of low cohesiveness, high task specialization, and increased communication difficulties might tend in turn to lead to high job dissatisfaction. As Brayfield and Crockett (1955), among others, have pointed out, there is good reason to believe that dissatisfaction leads to higher turnover and absenteeism rates. Also, labor strife logically would seem to be affected by increases in job dissatisfaction.

On the basis of the diagram presented in Figure 1, there is no necessary reason for large units to lead directly to decreases in productivity. Although the model does predict that large units will be characterized by, among other things, higher job dissatisfaction, reviews of the literature have not found that job dissatisfaction is associated with low productivity. Nor is there evidence that task specialization, low cohesiveness, and communications problems must necessarily lead to lower productivity. It is not surprising, therefore, that the evidence on the relationship between productivity and subunit size is inconsistent.

SIZE: TOTAL ORGANIZATIONS

All of the studies discussed in the previous section were concerned with the relationships between size of some type of organizational subunit and attitude and behavioral indices. In the present section we will review only those studies that have dealt specifically with the total organization as the unit of size. It will become evident that the number of such studies on total organization size is much lower than the number of studies on subunit size.[3]

The distinction between subunit size and total-organization size has seldom been made clear either in previous empirical studies dealing with size or in various interpretations of these studies presented in textbooks concerned with organizational behavior. It is conceivable, for example, that although working in a large subunit has disadvantages (as demonstrated by the evidence in the preceding section), working in a large total organization might have advantages as long as the subunits within the organization are relatively small. Therefore, it seems necessary to keep the subunit/total-organization distinction clearly in focus because the effects of one type of size (e.g., total organizational size) may be confounded by the effects of the other type of size (i.e., size of subunits within total organizations).

The absence, in most previous studies of size, of a distinction between subunits and total organizations has been compounded by the failure to take into account the job level of the employees. As was pointed out in the previous section, organizational level may interact with size such that conclusions pertaining to lower-level employees may not hold up when applied to higher-level personnel. This possible interaction effect of level could presumably influence results both for studies of subunit size and for studies of total-organization size. With the foregoing considerations in mind, we now turn to a review of the few studies that have been concerned with total-organization size.

Attitudes

At the rank-and-file worker level, two articles have appeared in the literature that seem to be concerned with the relationship of total-organization size (rather than subunit size) to job attitudes. The first of these two articles was by Benge (1944). Apparently sampling from a number of different companies and using the "composite attitude of employees in each company toward the boss" as an index of morale, he found that "morale of employees of small companies is appreciably better than that in larger companies [p. 104]." These results are extremely difficult to evaluate, however, since neither the number or type of respondents nor the number of companies on which the results were based was specified in the article.

The second study that seems to be concerned with the relationship of total-organization size of job attitudes of rank-and-file workers is one reported by Talacchi (1960). The study is described as an investigation involving 93 "organizations"; however, as one of the tables (Table 2 in the article, p. 411) indicates, at least 45 of the 93 organizations are in reality "plants" that comprise parts of only five companies. Thus, most of the findings reported in this article are difficult to interpret if one is interested in the effects of total-organization size, since the distinction between subunits and total organizations has been completely blurred. Nevertheless, it appears that the article does present some evidence bearing on the effects of size of the total organization on employee job satisfaction. The key result reported in Talacchi's article was a correlation of — .67 between organization size and the overall index of employee satisfaction as measured by the SRA Employee Inventory. Employee dissatisfaction was, therefore, apparently greater within large organizations (which ranged up to a maximum size of 1,800 employees). Aside from the limitations in the study that have already been point out, this finding must be interpreted cautiously because it is possible that the larger organizations contained larger subunit work groups. In other words, it is possible that what seemed to be an effect of organization or, at least, plant size may have been due to work-group size.

At the management level of organizations, several recent articles by Porter (1963c, 1963d, 1964) examined the relationship between three types of job attitudes and the size of company for which each manager worked.[4] In this questionnaire study of more than 1,500 managers, respondents were placed into one of three size-of-company categories: small (companies of under 500 employees), medium (500—4,900 employees), and large (more than 5,000 employees). One part of the data dealt with need satisfactions and indicated that the effects of size were modified by the level of management being considered. At the lower and lower-middle management levels, managers from smaller companies were more satisfied than those from larger companies. At the upper-middle and vice-president levels, the reverse was true, with the managers from the larger companies indicating greater satisfaction. With respect to a different area of perceptions, when respondents were asked to rank 10 personality traits in terms of their importance for job success, it was found that managers from larger companies place more emphasis than did managers from smaller companies on innerdirected or non-organization-man traits compared to otherdirected or organization-man traits. When respondents (across the intermediate three levels of management) were asked to use semantic differential scales to describe their jobs, managers from larger companies were slightly more likely to apply the terms "challenging," "interesting," and "competitive" to their jobs than were small company managers. (For both the personality trait and job-description results, management level did not seem to affect the findings. In other words, the effects of size were fairly consistent from one management level to the next.) These latter findings were interpreted as indicating that large companies place no more emphasis, perhaps even less, on conforming, organization-man type of behavior than do smaller companies.

Behavior

With the exception of one quite limited area of investigation, there are almost no studies that specifically compare large total organizations or companies to small total organizations on behavioral measures other than attitude data.[5] Undoubtedly the major reason for this lies in the difficulty of obtaining a sample of organizations (as compared to a sample of individuals or a sample of subunits within organizations) in sufficient quantity and with sufficient variation in total size.

The one type of behavior that has been investigated in relation to total-organization size concerns the rate of managerial succession into top-level jobs. The first such study, by Grusky (1961), utilized *Fortune's* annual list of the 500 largest United States companies to select two groups of organizations differing on total size. His results indicated that the frequency or rate of succession was positively related to size such that there was more rapid turnover in the uppermost management positions within larger-sized companies. A study by Kriesberg (1962) seemed to confirm Grusky's findings. However, a later study by Gordon and Becker (1964), which involved a reanalysis of the data used by Grusky, showed very little relationship between size and rate of managerial succession. Thus, the possible effects of size on this particular variable of organizational behavior remain obscure at this point.

Summary

A review of relevant journals shows that very few studies have been carried out on the relationship of size of total organization to either job attitudes or job behavior. Two studies of worker attitudes that seem to fit in this category of investigations indicated that job satisfaction and morale were lower in larger organizations. However, both studies were reported in such a way that it is difficult to draw accurate or meaningful conclusions concerning the effects of organization size. At the managerial level, Porter (1963c, 1963d, 1964) found no overall advantage for either large or small organizations in relation to need satisfactions; he did find, however, that managerial jobs in larger companies were seen as requiring a somewhat greater emphasis on inner-directed behavior and as having a slightly greater amount of challenge and interest when compared to similar managerial jobs in smaller companies.

Overall, the findings relating total-organization size to job attitudes do not present as clear a picture as is the case for findings dealing with subunit size. It is entirely possible that the negative effects of large subunit size on job attitudes may not extend to large total-organization size. As has been suggested,

An increase in the total size of an organization—with the consequent technological advantages of large-scale operation—will not necessarily reduce the morale and job satisfaction of employees as long as intra-organization work units are kept small [Porter, 1963d, p. 61].

This is a hypothesis that could be fairly easily confirmed or disconfirmed by future studies. Further research on total-organization size should also take into account the possibility that size of the total units may have one kind of effect on attitudes at the rank-and-file level, but a reversed effect at managerial levels, especially the higher levels. Again, this possibility would not be too difficult to test with additional research.

In the area of behavior, there is almost a complete lack of information on the effects of total-organization size. It would seem that future studies on size could, among other things, attempt to obtain measures of absenteeism, turnover, and similar rates in relation to total-unit size just as past studies have obtained this kind of data in relation to subunit size. At the moment, at least in the psychological literature, we do not even know whether the United States Steels, the Standard Oils, the General Motors, etc., have higher or lower turnover or absenteeism rates throughout their total organizations than do the local Acme or Ace manufacturing companies. (Again, it must be emphasized that if such comparisons of total organizations are to be meaningful, the effects of differences in the sizes of various subunits among the organizations must be partialed out and job level controlled.) Perhaps total-organization size will turn out to be an irrelevant variable in affecting such behavioral indices. At any rate, it would seem worthwhile to know whether this is the case or not.

SHAPE: TALL OR FLAT

Tall and flat organization structures are generally distinguished on the basis of the number of levels in the organization relative to the total size of the organization. A flat organization structure is one where there are few levels relative to the total size of the organization and a tall organization structure is one where there are many levels relative to the total size of the organization. Another way of stating this is to say that the degree to which a structure is tall or flat is determined by the average span of control within the organization.

Attention has been focused on the relative merits of these two types of structures since 1950, when Worthy published his widely cited article on "Organizational Structure and Employee Morale" (see Gardner & Moore, 1955; Viteles, 1953; Whyte, 1961). Worthy's (1950) basic conclusion was that: "Flatter, less complex structures, with a maximum of administrative decentralization, tend to create a potential for improved attitudes, more effective supervision, and greater individual responsibility and initiative among employees [p. 179]." Although Worthy published no empirical evidence to support his statements, and although his observations were based upon his experience in a single company, his opinions are frequently cited by other authors to support their contention that flat organization structures produce better performance and better job attitudes than do tall ones. Worthy's opinions represent direct contradiction to those put forth by the classical organization theorists (e.g., Graicunas, 1937) who contend that a tall organization structure improves performance by allowing for close supervision and therefore complete understanding by the supervisor of the subordinate's activities.

Despite the fact that this significant disagreement about the relative advantages of tall and flat organization structures has provoked considerable comment in the literature, the topic did not generate any empirical research until 1962.

Attitudes

Three studies have compared the job satisfactions of employees in tall organizations with those in flat organizations. Meltzer and Salter (1962) published a study that reported on the job satisfactions of 704 physiologists (in nonuniversity organizations). They classified their questionnaire respondents by size of company (fewer than 20 professional employees, 21-50, and 51 or more), and by number of levels of administration within the organization (1—3 levels, 4—5, and 6 or more), and found generally insignificant relationships between tallness or flatness and job satisfaction. Their results, therefore, did not confirm Worthy's theory about flat structure producing better job attitudes. However, it should be noted that Meltzer and Salter studied research organizations of extremely small size, and hence their results may have limited generality.

A study by Porter and Lawler (1964) investigated the relationship between the need satisfactions of over 1,500 managers and the type of organization structure in which they worked. As in the Meltzer and Salter study, managers were classified as working in either a tall or flat organization structure based upon the number of levels in the organization relative to its total size. The results showed no clear overall superiority of flat over tall organizations in producing greater need satisfaction among managers. However, two qualifications to this general finding were noted: First, organization size seemed to have some effect on the relationship between type of structure and the degree of need satisfaction. In companies employing fewer than 5,000 people, managerial satisfaction was greater in flat rather than in tall organizations. For companies with 5,000 employees and over, the picture was reversed with a tall type of structure producing perceptions of greater need satisfaction. The second qualification was that the effects of organization structure on need satisfaction appeared to vary with the type of psychological need being considered. A tall type of structure was associated with greater satisfactions in the security and social need areas, whereas a flat structure was associated with greater satisfaction in the self-actualization need area.

Porter and Siegel (1964) have replicated the Porter and Lawler study with one essential difference—the sample. The Porter and Siegel sample of close to 3,000 managers was an international sample representing middle and upper levels of management in a wide variety of sizes and types of companies in 13 countries. The results of the newer study generally agreed with those found by Porter and Lawler. Porter and Siegel found that for companies of less than 5,000 employees, flat structures produced greater managerial need satisfaction, whereas for companies of 5,000 and over, there was no difference between tall and flat structures in producing managerial need satisfactions.

Behavior

Meltzer and Salter's (1962) study was the only empirical investigation that compared the job performances of individuals working in organizations with tall and flat structures. They found generally insignificant relationships between tallness and flatness and job performance (as measured by the publication of research articles). Only in large-size organizations did they find a significant trend and there it was in the direction of greater productivity in tall than in flat organizations.

Summary

The evidence does not support Worthy's (1950) sweeping generalization that a flat organization structure produces greater job satisfaction and improved job performance. The evidence points to organization size as one of the factors affecting the relative advantages of tall and flat organization structures. Two of the studies reviewed found that in relatively small organizations a flat organization did appear to be advantageous in terms of producing managerial job satisfactions. However, for relatively large organizations one study found that tall organization structures produced greater job satisfaction, and one study found that tall organization structures fostered greater productivity. Thus, it appears that the advantages of a flat structure not only decrease with increasing organization size, but that in relatively large organizations a flat structure may sometimes even be a liability.

One explanation for the tendency for the advantages of a flat organization structure to decrease with increasing organization size can be found in the characteristics generally attributed to tall and flat organization structures. Advocates of flat organization structures claim that because of the large average span of control subordinates will have greater freedom and autonomy to make decisions. As a result of this relatively greater freedom and autonomy, individuals are supposed to contribute more to the organization and receive greater satisfaction from their jobs. On the other hand, a tall structure increases supervisory controls and allows superiors to better coordinate the activities of their subordinates. In a small organization problems of coordination and communication do not tend to be severe, simply because the organization is small. Thus, in a small organization there would be little advantage in a tall structure and, in fact, since it tends to amplify the disadvantages associated with tight managerial control, a tall structure probably is a liability in a typical small organization. In large organizations, on the other hand, problems of coordination and communication are complex. Thus, for large organizations a taller type of structure may be needed to overcome these problems and allow managers to supervise their subordinates more effectively.

Future research will undoubtedly show that other variables such as type of company—for example, retail trade versus manufacturing firms—will have an important bearing on which type of structure is more advantageous in terms of job attitudes and job performance. Worthy (1959) himself has pointed out that different degrees of flatness may be desirable depending upon the type of organization considered.

SHAPE: CENTRALIZED OR DECENTRALIZED

The contemporary trend in large-scale organization is toward decentralization, but we must realize that decentralization is several things to different people. There are those who view it entirely in terms of decision-making; others see it from the standpoint of geographical dispersion of plants and installations; and still others approach it as a philosophy of corporate life, a set of organization values with sociological, psychological, and spiritual facets [Pfiffner & Sherwood, 1960, p. 190].

There is no reason to believe that these different types of decentralization produce similar effects on job attitudes and performance. Thus, the first point that should be considered about any study concerned with the effects of decentralization is the measure of decentralization that is used.

According to Chandler (1956), the movement to decentralization can be dated to the 1920s and the management policies of Alfred P. Sloan, Jr., at General Motors. That the topic of decentralization is currently in the air is clearly demonstrated by the great number of recent articles that have dogmatically set forth plans for a decentralized corporate way of life (see Cordiner, 1956; Ginzberg & Reilley, 1957; Lawrence, 1958; Smith, 1958). Most writers have claimed that by offering increased autonomy for the individual regardless of his level within the company, decentralization improves both job attitudes and performance. Since the topic of decentralization has received considerable attention for the last forty years, it is not surprising that there has been a certain amount of research on the topic. However, most of the research on the effects of decentralization has been of the case study variety (e.g., Drucker, 1946; Given, 1949; Selznick, 1949), and therefore not within the scope of this review. In fact, only four studies were found that compared the job attitudes and behavior of employees in centralized and decentralized companies.

Attitudes

A study by Baker and France (1954) compared the attitudes of managers in centralized and decentralized industrial relations departments. Their classification of centralized or decentralized departments was based upon the level at which decisions relative to industrial relations were made. When they asked managers which type of structure produced the best intramanagement relations, managers who worked in companies with centralization favored centralization, and managers who worked in companies with decentralization favored decentralization. Baker and France further found that companies with decentralized industrial relations departments revealed no greater satisfaction among their plant managers than did those companies with centralized industrial relations departments. Although this latter finding does not support the claims of those who favor decentralization, it is important to remember that the study was concerned with decentralization in only one type of department, and the attitudes of only one level of management. Thus, it is impossible to know if the findings of Baker and France are applicable to the effects of decentralization on a company-wide basis.

Litzinger (1963) has compared the attitudes of bank managers who were under centralized management with those who were under decentralized management. His results indicated no clear attitude differences between the centralized and the decentralized groups of managers. However, the results are difficult to interpret because it is not clear from the article what measure of decentralization was used.

Behavior

Two studies were found that compared the behavior of employees in centralized companies with the behavior of employees in decentralized companies. Carlson (1951) found that executives in decentralized companies spent only 6.3% of their time "taking decisions, " while executives in centralized companies spent 14.6% of their time "taking decisions." He further found that executives in decentralized companies spent less time giving orders (6.8% versus 13.8%) than did executives in centralized companies. Carlson's finding that executives in decentralized companies gave fewer orders and made fewer decisions supports the claim that decentralization can lead to greater autonomy at the lower levels of the organization. However, there is a problem with this study that makes the results difficult to interpret. It is not clear what Carlson used as his criteria for classifying organizations as centralized or decentralized. Thus, it is impossible to know which particular type of decentralization Carlson's findings support. His findings are further limited by the fact that he had only nine managers as subjects in the study.

Weiss (1957) studied the relationship between centralized and decentralized organization structures and several measures of behavior. He classified 34 companies as either centralized or decentralized based upon their answers to a 22-item questionnaire about the level at which decisions were made in the company. Weiss found no significant differences between centralized and decentralized companies on any of the following variables: turnover rate, number of grievances, number of white collar workers, absenteeism, accident frequency, accident severity, and age of managers. It should be pointed out that although Weiss found no statistically significant differences, the trend on each of the factors considered was favorable to decentralized organizations.

Summary

The studies reviewed offer no clear support for the proposition that decentralization can produce either improved job attitudes or performance. Thus, Pfiffner and Sherwood's (1960) conclusion that decentralization must be accepted partially on faith seems completely justified. The fact that two of the studies reviewed obtained a few significant results and that another showed interesting trends suggests that the topic is a meaningful one for research. Perhaps the chief obstacle to research in this area, though, is the lack of an adequate method for measuring the degree of decentralization that exists in an organization. Until such a measure is developed the research evidence gathered will undoubtedly remain difficult to interpret.

It is doubtful that future research will ever prove that any of the three types of decentralization mentioned earlier are superior to centralization in all situations. Marschak (1959) has presented a model graphically illustrating that the efficiency of decentralization of decision making varies greatly depending upon the type of business in which the company is engaged. Sloan (1963) has made a similar point by stating that different degrees of decentralization appeared to be optimum for DuPont and General Motors because of their different product lines. Thus, for companies in a business where there is a high degree of complementarity among the members' actions (e.g., airlines or railroads), such that one member's action depends directly upon what his fellow employees are doing, a high degree of centralization is crucial. However, for companies in a business where there is a great deal of independence among the action of the members (e.g., chains of retail stores), such that one member's action does not depend on what his fellow employees are doing, increased decentralization may be desirable.

CONCLUSIONS

In this final section, two broad questions will be considered: First, what is the status of our current knowledge concerning the possible effects of structure? Second, where should future research efforts in this area be directed?

With respect to the first question, a review of the literature demonstrates the following:

1. Five of the seven properties of organization structure (span of control and centralization/decentralization being the two possible exceptions) have been shown to have some kind of significant relationship to either job attitudes or job behavior, or to both of these

types of variables. However, as we stressed in the introduction, experimental "proof" of cause-effect relationships between structure and employee attitudes and behavior is elusive and almost nonexistent.

2. Certain structural variables seem to have stronger relationships to attitudes and behavior than other structural variables. On the basis of the evidence to date, the two properties of structure that have the strongest relationships with, or effect on, the two types of "dependent" variables are two suborganization properties: organizational levels and subunit size. Level was shown to have a definite connection with several types of attitudes, and subunit size was found to be associated strongly with both job satisfaction attitudes and several types of behavior. Three other properties—line/staff type of position, total-organization size, and tall/flat shape—accounted for some significant relationships to several of the dependent variables, but the strength and clarity of their relationships were not as great as was the case with organizational levels and subunit size. Each of these three former variables has not been researched as extensively as have the latter two variables, and hence it is possible that future results will show them to have somewhat stronger relationships than appears to be the case at the moment. The other two variables, span of control and centralization/decentralization, have so far not been found to be significantly related to attitudes or behavior. Again, however, relatively little research has been carried out on these two structural variables and they may yet be found to have more important influences on employees than seems apparent at the moment.

3. Certain dependent variables are more highly related to properties of structure than are other kinds of dependent variables. For example, indices of need satisfaction seem to be much more strongly correlated with structural properties than are indices of need importance. This makes good sense logically and psychologically, in that satisfactions presumably should be determined more by environmental factors (e.g., the degree of job responsibilities, supervisory behavior toward subordinates, size of work group, etc.) than by personal factors (e.g., degree of extroversion), whereas employee wants and desires are likely to come about more from personal factors than from aspects of the work environment. On the behavioral side, absenteeism and turnover seem somewhat more clearly related to structural factors than does employee output per se. The reasons why this should be so probably revolve around the fact that output or performance rates seem to be much more complexly determined phenomena than are absenteeism and turnover rates. That is, the latter types of behavior are within the employee's repertory of potential actions; however, all levels of output are not within his repertory of actions both because of personal limitations and because of possible environmental factors such as work-group pressure and equipment limitations. Therefore, if structure affects various aspects of behavior largely through its influence on employees' motivations,

absenteeism and turnover rates will be more directly affected than will output levels.

In general, the impact of structural variables appears to be clearer on attitudes than on behavioral variables. However, this conclusion should be interpreted with caution because a search of the literature reveals that for most of the structural properties somewhat more research has been carried out on their relationships to attitudes than to types of behavior.

4. The direction of relationships of certain structural variables to certain dependent variables seems clear. The following directional relationships seem to be well supported by the research evidence to date: (a) organizational levels—positive relationship between height of level and degree of job and need satisfaction, positive relationship between height of level and perceived necessity for innerdirected type of job behavior; (b) line/staff hierarchies—positive relationship between line type of position and degree of need satisfaction; (c) subunit size—negative relationship between size and degree of job satisfaction, positive relationship between size and absenteeism rates, positive relationship between size and turnover rates.

For certain other structural variables, the direction of their impact on certain dependent variables is not clear, even though particular studies found statistically significant relationships. Thus, it is not at all certain whether a flatter type of organization structure is always associated with greater employee satisfaction compared to a taller structure, or that a smaller total organization results in greater employee satisfaction than does a larger total organization. As will be pointed out below, the direction of relationship in each case seems to be affected by the interaction of some second structural variable. Also, the evidence on the relationship between subunit size and output shows a wide scattering of types of relationships, going all the way from negative through curvilinear to positive relationships. Thus, it may be that subunit size is an important determinant of employee productive behavior, but that the direction of its effects depends on relatively local and particularized conditions.

We now turn to our second question: Where should research efforts be directed in the future?

First, we would suggest that future research investigations in this area must be addressed to more complex questions. It seems evident that a great deal more attention has to be given to the possible interrelationships between and among different organization structural variables than has been the case so far. There is already some indication in the literature that such interactions among two or more properties or dimensions of structure are likely. For example, the available evidence indicates that in order to determine the effects of either subunit size or total-organization size, one must specify or take into account the organizational level or levels being considered. It seems probable that certain effects of size, either subunit or total, that are present when rank-and-file workers are the objects of investigation may be greatly reduced or possibly even reversed at management levels, especially middle and upper executive levels. With respect to a different structural variable, tall/flat organization shape, the available data indicate that its relationship to job satisfaction is modified considerably by the total size of the organizations being studied. In other cases there are, as yet, few data to support (or deny) a notion of interaction effects, yet logic would lead one to predict the likelihood of this kind of situation. As just one example, it appears probable that success, or lack of it, in cases of deliberate organizational decentralization may well depend upon which organizational levels are to be involved in the decentralization and upon such other intraorganizational structural variables as the spans of control and sizes of subunits created by the change.

To sum up this point, there are already enough indications in the literature to support a greater research effort to investigate the interactions among structural properties of organizations in their relationship to employees' job behavior and attitudes. Too much previous theorizing in the area of organizations has neglected such interaction possibilities, and hence there has been an unfortunate tendency to oversimplify vastly the effects of particular variables. Organizations appear to be much too complex for a given variable to have a consistent unidirectional effect across a wide variety of types of conditions.

Second, there is an obvious need for field experimental studies, as well as the more typical field comparative studies. We need, in other words, investigations where one or more structural variables are systematically manipulated in field, not laboratory, conditions. There are admittedly great practical difficulties in carrying out such investigations, yet with the study of organizations occupying such an important place in the behavioral sciences today, it is time that researchers in this area faced up to the necessities for this kind of undertaking. Perhaps this will require projects of greater scope and support than in the past, and most certainly it is likely to require a cross-discipline approach. But such projects are definitely not out of the realm of the possible. As examples, one can conceive without too much difficulty of the possibilities of manipulating such variables as span of control or size of subunit. The results of such studies would provide firm support for some aspects of organization theories, where such support is largely lacking at the present time.

Third, longitudinal studies are probably necessary to draw valid conclusions concerning certain structural variables. Results from studies so far carried out on the relationships of organizational level or line/staff hierarchies to job attitudes are subject to the limitation that any obtained relationships might in part be due to differences among types of people rather than to differences among types of positions within organizations. One profitable method of sorting out the relative effects of these two types of variables, that is, individual and organizational, would be to conduct longitudinal studies where the same individuals are followed in their careers from one kind of organizational position to another. Such longitudinal studies are conspicuous by their rarity in the literature on organization structure.

In conclusion, we feel that the importance attached to the study of organization structure is not misplaced. Increased attention in the future to research on structural properties of organizations should improve our understanding of the way people think and behave when they function in their jobs within organizations.

NOTES

1. The authors are indebted to the following individuals for their comments and suggestions regarding earlier versions of this paper: Chris Argyris, Peter M. Blau, Edwin E. Ghiselli, Thomas M. Lodahl, George Strauss, and Victor H. Vroom. We should also like to acknowledge the financial support of the Institute of Industrial Relations, University of California, Berkeley.
2. Much of the literature on the relationship between behavior and size fails to point out whether the units studied (e.g., gas works, factories, or mines) are parts of larger organizations or are separate corporations. For the purposes of this review, it was decided that unless the author specified he was dealing with separate companies or firms, all data on factories, gas works, and mines would be dealt with as data on organization subunits.
3. By the term "total organization" we mean a total operating company headed by an executive with the title "President." It is admittedly difficult at times to determine whether a "company," in the loose sense of the word, should be considered a separate total organization, in our terms, or merely a subunit of an even larger "corporation." In general, if a company has a chief executive with the title of president and if that company can sell stock independently of other "companies" all under the same corporate holding entity, we would consider it a total organization.
4. It should be pointed out that Porter also did not control for size of work groups or subunits in which an individual manager worked within his company. However, it is assumed that the concept of work group—number of individuals reporting to a single supervisor—is a less meaningful and important variable at managerial levels because of the nature of the work situation. Hence, it is probably not as necessary to control its effects in assessing the effects of total size when the employees being considered are managers. Nevertheless, it is possible that this variable did have some undetermined effect on Porter's findings.
5. The previously discussed article by Talacchi (1960) has sometimes been cited as an article that presents data on the relationship of "organization" size to job behavior, such as turnover rates and absenteeism rates, but no such data are given in the article. Instead, the findings are presented in terms of the relationship of size to satisfaction (as already noted above) and the relationship of satisfaction to turnover and absenteeism. Not only are there no data presented on the direct relationship of size to turnover and absenteeism, but also the data that are presented concerning these latter two variables involve intraorganization rather than interorganization comparisons. Thus, this article does not provide behavioral data in relation to size of total organization.

REFERENCES

ACTON SOCIETY TRUST. *Size and morale.* London: AST, 1953.

ARGYLE, M., GARDNER, G., & CIOFFI, I. Supervisory methods related to productivity, absenteeism, and labor turnover. *Human Relations,* 1958, 11, 23-40.

ARGYRIS, C. *Personality and organization.* New York: Harper, 1957.

ASH, P. The SRA Employee Inventory: A statistical analysis. *Personnel Psychology,* 1954, 7, 337-364.

BAEHR, MELANY E. A factorial study of the SRA Employee Inventory. *Personnel Psychology*, 1954, 7, 319-336.

BAKER, HELEN, & FRANCE, R. R. *Centralization and decentralization in industrial relations*. Princeton: Industrial Relations Section, 1954.

BAUMGARTEL, H., & SOBOL, R. Background and organizational factors in absenteeism. *Personnel Psychology*, 1959, 12, 431-443.

BENGE, E. J. How to learn what workers think of job and boss. *Factory Management and Maintenance*, 1944(May), 102(5), 101-104.

BENNIS, W. G. Leadership theory and administrative behavior: The problem of authority. *Administrative Science Quarterly*, 1959, 4, 259-301.

BRAYFIELD, A. H., & CROCKETT, W. H. Employee attitudes and employee performance. *Psychological Bulletin*, 1955, 52, 396-424.

BROWN, A. Some reflections on organization: Truths, half-truths, and delusions. *Personnel*, 1954, 31(1), 31-42.

BROWNE, C. G., & NEITZEL, BETTY J. Communication, supervision, and morale. *Journal of Applied Psychology*, 1952, 36, 86-91.

BURNS, T. The directions of activity and communication in a departmental executive group: A quantitative study in a British engineering factory with a self-recording technique. *Human Relations*, 1954, 7, 73-97.

CAMPBELL, H. Group incentive payment schemes: The effects of lack of understanding and of group size. *Occupational Psychology*, 1952, 26, 15-21.

CAMPBELL, J. W. An attitude survey in a typical manufacturing firm. *Personnel Psychology*, 1948, 1, 31-39.

CARLSON, S. *Executive behavior, a study of the work load and the working methods of managing directors*. Stockholm: Stromberg, 1951.

CENTERS, R. Motivational aspects of occupational stratification. *Journal of Social Psychology*, 1948, 28, 187-217.

CHANDLER, A. D. Management decentralization: An historical analysis. *Business History Review*, 1956, 30, 111-174.

CLELAND, S. *Influence of plant size on industrial relations*. Princeton: Princeton Univer. Press, 1955.

COATES, C. H., & PELLEGRIN, R. J. Executives and supervisors: Contrasting self-conceptions and conceptions of each other. *American Sociological Review*, 1957, 22, 217-220.

CORDINER, R. J. *New frontiers for professional managers*. New York: McGraw-Hill, 1956.

DALE, E. *Planning and developing the company organization structure*. New York: American Management Association, 1952.

DALTON, M. Conflicts between staff and line managerial officers. *American Sociological Review*, 1950, 15, 342-351.

DALTON, M. *Men who manage*. New York: Wiley, 1959.

DAVIS, K. Management communication and the grapevine. *Harvard Business Review*, 1953, 31(5), 43-49.

DRUCKER, P. *Concept of the corporation*. New York: Day, 1946.

DUBIN, R. Business behavior behaviorally viewed. In G. B. Strother (Ed.), *Social Science approaches to business behavior*. Homewood, Ill.: Dorsey Press, 1962.

DUBIN, R., & SPRAY, S. L. Executive behavior and interaction. *Industrial Relations*, 1964, 3, 99-108.

ENTWISLE, DORIS, & WALTON, J. Observations on the span of control. *Administrative Science Quarterly*, 1961, 5, 522-533.

FISCH, G. G. Line-staff is obsolete. *Harvard Business Review*, 1961, 39(5), 67-79.

FISCH, G. G. Stretching the span of management. *Harvard Business Review*, 1963, 41(5), 74-85.

FLEISHMAN, E. A. The measurement of leadership attitudes in industry. *Journal of Applied Psychology*, 1953, 37, 153-158.

FLEISHMAN, E. A., HARRIS, E.F., & BURTT, H. E. Leadership and supervison in industry: An evaluation of a supervisory training program. *Ohio State University, Bureau of Educational Research Monograph*, 1955, No. 33.

FORTUNE. The Fortune survey: A self-portrait of the American people—1947. *Fortune,* 1947, 35(1), 5-16.

FORTUNE. Effective morale. *Fortune,* 1950, 42(2), 46-50.

GARDNER, B. B., & MOORE, D. G. *Human relations in industry.* (3rd ed.) Homewood, Ill.: Dorsey Press, 1955.

GINZBERG, E., & REILLEY, E. W. *Effecting change in large organizations.* New York: Columbia Univer. Press, 1957.

GIVEN, W. B. *Bottom-up management: people working together.* New York: Harper, 1949.

GORDON, G., & BECKER, S. Organizational size and managerial succession: A reexamination. *American Journal of Sociology,* 1964, 70, 215-223.

GRAICUNAS, V. A. Relationship and organization. In L. Gullick & L. Urwick (Eds.), *Papers on the science of administration.* New York: Institute of Public Administration, 1937.

GRUSKY, O. Corporate size, bureaucratization, and managerial succession. *American Journal of Sociology,* 1961, 67, 261-269.

HAIRE, M. *Psychology in management.* New York: McGraw-Hill, 1956.

HAIRE, M., GHISELLI, E. E., & PORTER, L. W. Cultural patterns in the role of the manager. *Industrial Relations,* 1963, 2, 95-117.

HANDYSIDE, J. D. Satisfactions and aspirations. *Occupational Psychology,* 1961, 35, 213-244.

HEMPHILL, J. K. Relations between the size of the group and the behavior of "superior" leaders. *Journal of Social Psychology,* 1950, 32, 11-22.

HEMPHILL, J. K. Group dimensions: A manual for their measurement. *Ohio State University, Bureau of Business Research Monograph,* 1956, No. 87.

HERBST, P. G. Measurement of behavior structure by means of input-output data. *Human Relations,* 1957, 10, 335-346.

HERZBERG, F., MAUSNER, B., PETERSON, R. O., & CAPWELL, DORA F. *Job attitudes: Review of research and opinion.* Pittsburgh: Psychological Service of Pittsburgh, 1957.

HERZBERG, F., MAUSNER, B., & SNYDERMAN, BARBARA B. *The motivation to work.* (2nd ed.) New York: Wiley, 1959.

HEWITT, D., & PARFITT, JESSIE. A note on working morale and size of group. *Occupational Psychology,* 1953, 27, 38-42.

HULL, R. L., & KOLSTAD, A. Morale on the job. In G. B. Watson (Ed.), *Civilian morale.* New York: Houghton Mifflin, 1942.

INDIK, B. P., & SEASHORE, S. E. *Effects of organization size on member attitudes and behavior.* Ann Arbor: University of Michigan, Survey Research Center of the Institute of Social Research. 1961.

KAHN, R. L. Human relations on the shop floor. In E. M. Hugh-Jones (Ed.), *Human relations and modern management.* Amsterdam: North-Holland Publishing, 1958. Pp. 43-74.

KATZELL, R. A., BARRETT, R. S., & PARKER, T. C. Job satisfaction, job performance, and situational characteristics. *Journal of Applied Psychology,* 1961, 45, 65-72.

KERR, W. A., KOPPELMEIER, G. J., & SULLIVAN, J. J. Absenteeism, turnover and morale in a metals fabrication factory. *Occupational Psychology,* 1951, 25, 50-55.

KOLSTAD, A. Attitudes of employees and their supervisors. *Personnel,* 1944, 20, 241-250.

KREISBERG, L. Careers, organization size, and succession. *American Journal of Sociology,* 1962, 68, 355-359.

LAWLER, E. E., & PORTER, L. W. Perceptions regarding management compensation. *Industrial Relations,* 1963, 3, 41-49.

LAWRENCE, P. R. *The changing of organizational behavior patterns: A case study of decentralization.* Boston: Harvard University, Graduate School of Business Administration, Division of Research, 1958.

LEAVITT, H. J. *Managerial psychology.* Chicago: Univer. Chicago Press, 1958.

LEAVITT, H. J., & WHISLER, T. L. Management in the 1980's. *Harvard Business Review,* 1958, 36(6), 41-48.

LIKERT, R. *New patterns of management.* New York: McGraw-Hill, 1961.

LITZINGER, W. D. Entrepreneurial prototype in bank management. *Academy of management Journal,* 1963, 6(1), 36-45.

McGREGOR, D. *The human side of enterprise.* New York: McGraw-Hill, 1960.

MANDELL, M. M. *Recruiting and selecting office employees.* New York: American Management Association, 1956.

MARRIOTT, R. Size of working group and output. *Occupational Psychology,* 1949, 23, 47-57.

MARSCHAK, J. Efficient and viable organizational forms. In M. Haire (Ed.), *Modern organization theory.* New York: Wiley, 1959. Pp. 307-320.

MARTIN, N. H. The levels of management and their mental demands. In W. L. Warner & N. H. Martin (Eds.), *Industrial man.* New York: Harper, 1959. Pp. 276-294.

MELTZER, L., & SALTER, J. Organizational structure and the performance and job satisfaction of physiologists. *American Sociological Review,* 1962, 27, 351-362.

METZNER, HELEN, & MANN, F. Employee attitudes and absences. *Personnel Psychology,* 1953, 6, 467-485.

MORSE, NANCY C. *Satisfactions in the white-collar job.* Ann Arbor: University of Michigan, 1953.

OPINION RESEARCH CORPORATION. *The conflict between the scientific and the management mind.* Princeton: ORC, 1959.

OPINION RESEARCH CORPORATION. *Motivating managers.* Princeton: ORC, 1962.

PELLEGRIN, R. J., & COATES, C. H. Executives and supervisors: Contrasting definitions of career success. *Administrative Science Quarterly,* 1957, 1, 506-517.

PFIFFNER, J. M., & SHERWOOD, F. P. *Administrative organization.* Englewood Cliffs, N. J.: Prentice-Hall, 1960.

PORTER, L. W. A study of perceived job satisfactions in bottom and middle management jobs. *Journal of Applied Psychology,* 1961, 45, 1-10.

PORTER, L. W. Job attitudes in management: I. Perceived deficiencies in need fulfillment as a function of job level. *Journal of Applied Psychology,* 1962, 46, 375-384.

PORTER, L. W. Job attitudes in management: II. Perceived importance of needs as a function of job level. *Journal of Applied Psychology,* 1963, 47, 141-148. (a)

PORTER, L. W. Job attitudes in management: III. Perceived deficiencies in need fulfillment as a function of line vs. staff type of job. *Journal of Applied Psychology,* 1963, 47, 267-275. (b)

PORTER, L. W. Job attitudes in management: IV. Perceived deficiencies in need fulfillment as a function of size of company. *Journal of Applied Psychology,* 1963, 47, 386-397. (c)

PORTER, L. W. Where is the organization man? *Harvard Business Review,* 1963, 41(6), 53-61. (d)

PORTER, L. W. *Organizational patterns of managerial job attitudes.* New York: American Foundation for Management Research, 1964.

PORTER, L. W., & HENRY, MILDRED M. Job attitudes in management: V. Perceptions of the importance of certain personality traits as a function of job level. *Journal of Applied Psychology,* 1964, 48, 31-36. (a)

PORTER, L. W., & HENRY, MILDRED M. Job attitudes in management: VI. Perceptions of the importance of certain personality traits as a function of line vs. staff type of job. *Journal of Applied Psychology,* 1964, 48, 305-309. (b)

PORTER, L. W., & LAWLER, E. E. The effects of tall vs. flat organization structures on managerial job satisfaction. *Personnel Psychology,* 1964, 17, 135-148.

PORTER, L. W., & SIEGEL, J. The effects of tall vs. flat organization structures on managerial satisfactions in foreign countries. Unpublished manuscript, University of California, Berkeley, 1964.

REVANS, R. W. Human relations, management and size. In E. M. Hugh-Jones (Ed.), *Human relations and modern management.* Amsterdam: North-Holland Publishing, 1958. Pp. 177-220.

ROSEN, H. Desirable attributes of work: Four levels of management describe their job environments. *Journal of Applied Psychology,* 1961, 45, 156-160. (a)

ROSEN, H. Managerial role interaction: A study of three managerial levels. *Journal of Applied Psychology,* 1961, 45, 30-34. (b)

ROSEN, H., & WEAVER, C. G. Motivation in management: A study of four managerial levels. *Journal of Applied Psychology,* 1960, 44, 386-392.

SEASHORE, S. E. *Group cohesiveness in the industrial work group.* Ann Arbor: University of Michigan, Institute for Social Research, 1954.

SELZNICK, P. *T.V.A. and the grass-roots: A study in the sociology of formal organization.* Berkeley: Univer. California Press, 1949.

SHARTLE, C. L. *Executive performance and leadership.* Englewood Cliffs, N. J.: Prentice-Hall, 1956.

SLOAN, A. P. My years with General Motors—Part II. *Fortune,* 1963, 68(4), 145-148.

SMITH, G. A., JR. *Managing geographically decentralized companies.* Boston: Harvard University, Graduate School of Business Administration, Division of Research, 1958.

STRAUSS, G., & SAYLES, L. R. *Personnel: The human problems of management.* Englewood Cliffs, N. J.: Prentice-Hall, 1960.

TALACCHI, S. Organization size, individual attitudes and behavior: An empirical study. *Administrative Science Quarterly,* 1960, 5, 398-420.

TRIANDIS, H. C. Categories of thought of managers, clerks, and workers about jobs and people in an industry. *Journal of Applied Psychology,* 1959, 43, 338-344. (a)

TRIANDIS, H. C. Differential perception of certain jobs and people by managers, clerks, and workers in industry. *Journal of Applied Psychology,* 1959, 43, 221-225. (b)

TRIANDIS, H. C. A comparative factorial analysis of job semantic structures of managers and workers. *Journal of Applied Psychology,* 1960, 44, 297-302.

URWICK, L. F. Executive decentralization with functional coordination. *Management Review,* 1935, 24, 355-368.

VITELES, M. S. *Motivation and morale in industry.* New York: Norton, 1953.

WEISS, E. C. Relation of personnel statistics to organization structure. *Personnel Psychology,* 1957, 10, 27-42.

WHYTE, W. F. *Men at work.* Homewood, Ill.: Dorsey Press, 1961.

WHYTE, W. H., JR. *The organization man.* New York: Simon & Schuster, 1956.

WOODWARD, JOAN. *Management and technology.* London: Her Majesty's Stationery Office, 1958.

WORTHY, J. C. Organizational structure and employe morale. *American Sociological Review,* 1950, 15, 169-179.

WORTHY, J. C. *Big business and free men.* New York: Harper, 1959.

(Received September 22, 1964)

SECTION V

DATA FEEDBACK

EDITORS' OVERVIEW

Organizations have at their disposal information about how members feel and think about them. This information is occasionally collected formally (as in an attitude survey), but most of the time informally, by hearsay and the grapevine. When collected systematically (whether in the form of statistics, summaries of interviews, or observations) and used appropriately, such information can be a powerful force for change.

An appropriate use of organizational data as a vehicle for change has been provided by Mann in his extensive work with a technique he calls survey feedback, which was mentioned in the introduction to this book. Alderfer and Ferriss, in the initial paper in this section, suggest that a modification of Mann's survey feedback technique might make it more effective. Their evidence indicates that data feedback held with organizational peer groups prior to the feedback with family groups (a boss with his key subordinates) may help each supervisor to deal more effectively (less defensively) with his subordinates.

In the next paper, Bradford and Harvey explain that some of the information organizational members possess is in the form of myths, myths which are more often than not dysfunctional for the organization. A major objective of organization development is to surface these myths and help organizational members to destroy the dysfunctional ones. Bradford and Harvey use an open-ended interview as their data-gathering technique, followed by data feedback sessions in "family" units where myths are tested for reality. A primary contribution of Bradford and Harvey to OD technology is their explanation of how to conduct data feedback sessions in an organizational "family" setting. They also discuss how they help managers develop new, functional norms to replace dysfunctional myths.

Thus the first two articles in this section discuss the use of two different techniques for data gathering in an organization: the survey and the open-ended interview. In the final article, Jenks describes still another approach to data gathering: the Q-sort instrument. This particular instrument concentrates on organizational data in the area of interpersonal relationships. It is relatively easy to administer and, although it concentrates heavily on only one aspect of organizational life, the Q-sort provides specific and easy-to-understand data. Its major strength may be in facilitating team building.

UNDERSTANDING THE IMPACT OF SURVEY FEEDBACK [*]

Clayton P. Alderfer, *Department of Administrative Sciences*
Yale University
Ray Ferriss, *Head*
Education Department, Polaroid Corporation

[*]We would like to thank Thomas Lodahl, William Starbuck, Robert Kaplan, and Harvey Hornstein for their helpful comments on earlier versions of this paper.

Survey feedback is one relatively new method by which applied behavioral scientists help their clients to use the results of research conducted in ongoing systems. In the years since Mann's first report (1957), there have been several additional published efforts by applied behavioral scientists to document and analyze their work with this procedure (Argyris, 1965; Neff, 1965; Chesler and Flanders, 1967; and Miles et al, 1969). These reports underline the difficulties that often arise when behavioral scientists confront practicing organization members with an "outside expert's" view of their system (Mann and Likert, 1952; Ferguson, 1964, 1966).

Two of these early reports, Mann (1957) and Argyris (1965), have presented evidence suggesting that under certain circumstances the feedback of "objective data" may be followed by attitude change (Mann) and behavior change (Argyris). While neither of these studies is fully free of procedural problems—especially with regard to sensitization of the clients to the measuring instruments—they do suggest that feedback of data may be a very important tool for effecting change. The other studies, which tended to focus more on the feedback processes than on outcomes, both directly and indirectly raised a number of important practical and theoretical questions. For example, a number of authors (Mann, 1957; Neff, 1965; and Miles et al., 1969) stressed the importance and utility of involving organization members in the early phases of research design and data collection. Even if one fully agrees with this principle (and we do), there are circumstances in which the costs—especially in terms of both client and research time—of full involvement can be quite high. Consequently, one might wish to ask if there are some kinds of reactions to feedback which are more dependent on client involvement than others.

Another variable in the feedback process on which most investigators agree is the need for interpersonal competence on the part of the persons reporting the data to the clients. It may be that interpersonal competence by itself is only a beginning. For example, interpersonal competence does not directly deal with the fact that the researcher is often an outsider from a different subculture. Perhaps the formation of a competent team consisting of an insider and an outsider would aid the problems of communication across organizational boundaries.

Several other research reports assume the use of family groups (a superior with his subordinates) as the unit for feedback (Mann, 1957; Neff, 1965; Miles et al, 1969), almost as a "given." One of the answered questions is whether the design of feedback sessions might vary according to nature of the learning contained in the study. Are there times when the use of family groups may not be the best design for feeding back data?

Finally, there is the question of how rationally clients react to "objective" social science data. Much of the presumed rationale for the feedback of survey data is that it is dispassionate, capable of being studied and understood through the powers of reason. Mann and Neff (1962) have made a strong theoretical case for irrational reactions' being primarily a product of personality problems: "While it is true that some individuals react to a major change in ways which seem irrational, even when one has an understanding of the social and psychological meaning of the situation, we expect that these disturbed are relatively few." At the same time, however, both the Chesler and Flanders (1967) study and the Miles, et al. (1969) study show signs that clients can have rather mixed reactions to the feedback process. It would be interesting to study a feedback effort with an eye toward achieving greater understanding of clients' reactions to survey feedback.

The present study was undertaken with these questions in mind. It presents some systematic quantitative data on the reactions to one survey feedback attempt.

PROCEDURE

Organizational Diagnosis

An organizational diagnosis was conducted in a major division of a medium-sized corporation. At the time of the study approximately 1700 persons were employed in the division. A random sample of approximately 300 employees participated in the study. All three hundred were asked to complete a questionnaire, and a random sample of about 125 were interviewed. All jobs in the division, with the exception of the top ten positions, were studied. This top group was engaged in an independent research and consultation project while the survey of the rest of the division was in progress. This project was coordinated to the survey.

In preparing to do the study the investigator explained his purpose to all of the major department heads in the organization. At the same time he invited the managers to offer suggestions for topics to be studied and to explain the most convenient ways to schedule employees for interview and questionnaire sessions. In addition, the managers were invited to contact the investigator through a liaison man whenever problems or questions arose with regard to the study. As it turned out, the actual starting time of the study was delayed for two weeks while another series of meetings was held with lower ranking managers who wished to meet and question the investigator. These meetings themselves provided some very interesting diagnostic information (Alderfer, 1967). Throughout the study, the investigator attempted to be available for informal contacts in the cafeteria and other places so that persons having questions might find answers to them by informal as well as formal methods.

A written report of the study's findings was prepared and discussed with the top management group. Two results generated the most interest and discussion:

1. Satisfaction with respect to superiors decreased as job complexity increased. Employees in the more routine jobs were likely to perceive their superiors as easy to talk to about the job, willing to take account of their wishes and desires, giving credit for good work, and letting them know when their work needed improvement. Employees in the more challenging jobs were less likely to see these qualities in their superior.
2. Satisfaction with respect to superiors also decreased as seniority increased. The longer a person remained with the organization the more likely he was to experience interpersonal difficulties with his boss.

The Feedback Reaction Questionnaire

The questionnaire included 19 questions designed to measure the managers' reactions to the feedback: their evaluation of the study, their awareness of the interpersonal problems it had identified, whether their morale toward the company and management had changed (positively or negatively), whether they expected benefit to come from the study. In particular, we wished to provide ways for them to register mixed and complex attitudes if they should exist. Each question had a nine-point scale.

On the same questionnaire the managers were asked to identify their organizational level and to indicate how well they felt the consultants had answered their questions (a measure of perceived competence). They were also asked to indicate the content to which they participated as a respondent in the organizational diagnosis.

While we did not have specific hypotheses stated in advance, we were interested in exploring how various consultant and organizational variables were related to the feedback reactions and how the feedback reactions were interrelated themselves.

RESULTS

Table 1 presents the correlations between the consultant and organizational variables and reactions to the feedback. Managers who participated in feedback meetings with the insider-outsider consulting team were more likely to evaluate the study positively, show more awareness of interpersonal problems, expect improvement as a result of the study, and expect harm as a result of the study than managers who participated in meetings with the inside consultant alone. Those managers who felt their questions were answered more effectively by the consultants were more likely to evaluate the study positively, show more awareness of the interpersonal problems, report their morale as decreased, expect improvement, and expect harm. The managers with higher job levels were more likely to demonstrate awareness of the interpersonal problems and to indicate that their morale had decreased as a result of hearing about the study. Those managers who had participated more in the data collection were more likely to acknowledge awareness of the interpersonal problems than those who had participated less.

Table 2 presents the intercorrelations among the various reactions to the feedback. Managers who evaluated the study positively also tended to show greater awareness of the interpersonal problems, report their morale as decreased, and expect both improvement and harm. Managers who showed an awareness of interpersonal problems also tended to report their morale as having decreased and to expect harm. Those who expected more harm also tended to report their morale as decreasing, and those who expected harm also tended to expect improvement.

DISCUSSION

In discussing these results we shall first deal with the research questions raised at the outset of the paper, then turn to conceptual issues relevant to the results, and finally consider the use of these results in the practice of survey feedback.

Table 3 shows the intercorrelations among what might be termed the independent variables in this study. These relationships help one to understand the differential impact of the respective variables by computing partial correlations. The general tendency for almost all of these variables to be somewhat positively correlated with each other is primarily an artifact of the study design: higher ranking managers proportionately were more involved in the design and collection of the data and were more likely to receive feedback from the insider-outsider team.

Research Questions. The data indicate that prior involvement in the study was one of the least potent variables. It was related only to acknowledging an awareness of the interpersonal problems between superiors and subordinates. This finding suggests at least two possible explanations for the relationship between involvement and acknowledgement of problems. One explanation is that involvement was related to organizational rank; but the organizational diagnosis also showed that there were more superior-subordinate problems at the higher ranks. Perhaps involvement was related to awareness of problems only because those who were more involved actually had more problems. According to his hypothesis, involvement is only artifactually related to acknowledging awareness of problems. However, a second hypothesis would make involvement a key variable in itself, by suggesting, that a person who participated in the study and who had relationship problems with his boss would remember saying so and would therefore be more likely to agree with the general diagnostic results. To compare these two hypotheses we computed the partial correlation between involvement and awareness of problems, controlling for organizational rank. This partial correlation was .22 ($p < .05$), supporting the hypothesis that involvement itself was related to whether a person acknowledged superior-subordinate interpersonal problems.

From the results in Table 3 one would readily draw the conclusion that one of the components of perceived consultant competence was the formation of the insider-outsider team. But the "team effect" was more complicated than a mere additive phenomenon, as can be seen from a careful scanning of the first two columns of Table 1. Although the effects of the team and competence were parallel for evaluation and awareness, they were markedly different for moral change, expected improvement, and expected harm. First, although the relationship between the team and perceived competence was positive and moderately strong, these two variables had significantly different relationships to perceived morale change. The pattern of correlations between these two indpendent variables and the expectation variables readily suggests the hypothesis that the presence of the team increased the expectation of improvement regardless of competence, while the absence of the team increased the expectation of harm, regardless of competence. This interpretation was supported by the partial correlation analysis. The partial correlation between the team and expected improvement, controlling for competence, was .35 ($p < .01$); the partial correlation between perceived competence and expected harm, controlling for the team, was .33 ($p < .01$). At the same time, the partial correlation between the team and expected harm, controlling for competence, was .12 (n.s.), and the partial correlation between expected improvement and competence, controlling for the team, was .09 (n.s.).

One should be cautious in reading general conclusions from this finding because of several design limitations of this study. First, the team variable was not fully balanced since the nonteam condition consisted only of an insider other than the insider team member. There was no outsider-only condition. Second, only three consultants were involved in the study, and there is no way of controlling for characteristics unique to them which might spuriously affect the observed relationships.

Using family groups in this particular feedback was especially interesting because a major finding in the study pointed directly to problems in superior-subordinate relationships, especially for higher ranking managers. Consequently, any group participating in the feedback would be concurrently living in the meeting with the real possibility of having this very problem. From this standpoint, the correlations between problem awareness and job level and between morale change and job level deserve special attention. Since the managers with the higher ranking jobs were more likely to get feedback from the team which was perceived to be more competent, one would wonder whether they showed greater awareness of the problems because of having more problems or because of the extra resources provided by the team. The partial correlation between job level and awareness of problems, controlling both for perceived competence and for the team, was .13 (n.s.). Thus, although the study pointed to more problems at the higher levels, these managers themselves, after seeing the data and discussing it, were no more likely to acknowledge that they had problems than those at lower levels. Related to this same issue is the relationship between perceived morale change and job level. The partial correlation between job level and morale change, controlling for both perceived competence and for the team, was -.22 (p < .05).   Thus the higher level managers were more likely to report negative morale changes than the lower level managers, even though they were no more likely to acknowledge that they had more problems.

This finding suggests the possibility that the higher level managers denied their greater problems while suffering a relative decline in morale. If this denial interpretation is valid, it makes one wonder whether the family group design was a contributor to ineffective utilization of the data. Perhaps for these diagnostic results, the family group did not provide enough psychological safety for the managers to permit them to really come to terms with the data.

Many of the findings reported in this study point to the lack of rationality of the managers in responding to apparently "objective" data. For example, a person who was positive in his reaction to the study tended to report his morale changing negatively, to expect improvement, and to expect harm. Competence on the part of the consultants was related both to expecting improvement and to expecting harm. Managers for whom the diagnosis said there should be more interpersonal problems were no more likely to acknowledge these problems unless they received special consultant resources. Any person who expected improvement was also quite likely to expect harm as a consequence of the study.

Conceptual Issues. From a theoretical standpoint the lack of apparent rationality in response to data is probably the most interesting result emerging from the study. Three concepts seem especially useful for understanding this result: the therapeutic concept of resistance (Singer, 1965; Klein, 1969; Watson, 1969), Maslow's (1962) notions about the tension between the need to know and the fear of knowing, and Janis' (1958) formulation of the "work of worrying." The interrelationship of these three ideas seems relevant for the present work. Generally speaking for most students of personal and social change, the notion of a client blocking or resisting change is viewed as a natural process, present when constructive change is in process as well as when destructive change is occurring. Change or new information suggesting the possibility or desirability of change represents a potential departure from the current equilibrium, and personal and social systems require some sense of stability in order to exist. So fear seems to be part of most change processes. Especially with regard to the role of information in change, Maslow (1962) recognized that feelings about knowing are characteristically mixed:

"It seems quite clear that the need to know . . . must be integrated with the fear of knowing . . . We wind up with a dialectical back and forth relationship which is simultaneously a struggle between fear and courage."

When it comes to managing these conflicting feelings, it is helpful for both client and consultant to be able to deal with them directly. Talking about the fearful aspects of the learning and change process can be quite useful in aiding the clients' adjustments to the real or imagined turmoil he might face. Janis (1958) has coined the term "work of worrying" to characterize the process of managing these kinds of tensions. His work indicated that relationships with trusted authoritative persons aided the work of worrying for surgery, and one would expect an analogous process to aid adjustments to organizational change.

Practical Implications. For the applied behavioral scientist who might employ survey feedback, the results of this study point in two related directions. One concerns what might be termed the rediscovery and documentation of the nature of people's mixed feelings toward new information that is relevant to their lives. The second concerns the procedures one might employ in the design of survey feedback to deal effectively with the mixed feelings.

If a consultant expects to be faced with mixed feelings from his client, the likelihood of his being able to deal with these reactions constructively is probably greater than if he expects only rational reactions to his objective data. To the extent that the kinds of reactions observed here are general, the presence of mixed feelings in clients may be viewed by the consultant as a sign that unfreezing is beginning. If faced with only positive reactions, he may very well question whether he is hearing all that the client has to say. If he hears only negative reactions, he may be helped to know that positive feelings may not be far away.

Within the limits of the design of this particular study, the results rather strongly support the usefulness of designing feedback sessions to include both inside and outside consultants. We would suggest that the outsider aids the credibility of the information that is provided. (He has no ax to grind.) At the same time, the insider helps to guarantee that it will be possible to follow through on problems that may be discovered. In saying this we emphasize that the working relationship of the insider and outsider is extremely important. It is probably not enough simply to pair consultants; the pairing should be based on mutual trust and respect between the parties.

As a result of this study we would question whether the use of family groups is always the optimal way to design survey feedback sessions. To be most effective, the feedback session should probably have a mix of psychological safety and confrontation. Perhaps for some kind s of findings, such as the one reported in this diagnosis, the family group would not provide enough psychological safety for thorough exploration of the data to occur. Perhaps a design that began with peer meetings and then followed with family groups would be more effective. Related to the use of family groups is the key role of the superior in the family group. Our experience was very consistent with Mann's (1957) view that the reaction of the superior in the group is crucial in determining how the rest of the group reacts to the feedback. Discussing the feedback in peer groups first might provide each supervisor with an opportunity to prepare himself more effectively to meet with his subordinates. In addition, the consultants might thereby be alerted to situations where their intervention on a one-to-one basis might also be helpful to superiors.

TABLE 1

Correlations Between Measures of Reaction to the Feedback and Other Variables[a]

	Consultant Team	Perceived Consultant Competence[b]	Job Level	Involvement in the Study
	(n = 96)			
Positive Evaluation	.28**	.31**	.17	.14
Awareness[b]	.20	.50**	.22*	.26**
Positive Morale Change[b]	.12	−.40**	−.22*	−.12
Expect Improvement	.40**	.23*	.17	.09
Expect Harm[b]	.24*	.38**	.18	.03

[a]The consultant team was measured by assigning "b" to those managers who received feedback from the consulting team and "a" to those managers who received feedback from an internal consultant working alone.

Job level as measured in this study was based upon a coding system which has been validated (Alderfer, 1967). For the managers from whom questionnaires about the survey were obtained, the job complexity scores ranged from 27 to 40. A measure of a manager's involvement in the study was obtained from the questionnaire by asking if, prior to feedback, he: (1) was interviewed, (2) did a questionnaire, (3) talked informally with the researcher, (4) talked with people who did interviews or questionnaires, and (5) talked with members of management about the study. Each time the man answered yes to one of these questions, he was scored for one unit of involvement. Thus, a six-point scale of involvement was used.

[b]See footnote in Table 2.

*p < .05, 2 tailed test.

**p < .01, 2 tailed test.

TABLE 2

Intercorrelations Among Measures of Reaction to the Feedback

(n = 96)

	Awareness[a]	Positive Morale Change[a]	Expect Improvement	Expect Harm[a]
Positive Evaluation	.30**	−.23*	.45**	.37**
Awareness[a]	—	−.48**	−.06	.35**
Positive Morale Change[a]	—	—	−.06	−.51**
Expect Improvement	—	—	—	.39**

*p $<$ .05, 2 tailed test.
**p $<$ .01, 2 tailed test.

[a]All of the items footnoted in this table and in Table 1 were transformed prior to computing correlation coefficients to correct for their restricted range. Prior to transformation they had significantly lower standard deviations than the items not transformed (p $<$ .02). Each of these items was divided by the person's standard deviation for all of his questionnaire items. The transformation has the effect of converting a person's raw score on a given item to a score relative to his tendency to use the full range of the scales; it corrects for the response bias of people who use a narrow range of all attitude scales. We express our appreciation to William Starbuck for this suggestion.

TABLE 3

Intercorrelations Among Consultant and Client Variables

	Perceived Consultant Competence	Job Level	Involvement in the Study
Consultant Team	.38**	.27**	.14
Consultant Competence	—	.24*	.08
Job Level	—	—	.28**

*p $<$ .05, 2 tailed test.
**p $<$ .01, 2 tailed test.

REFERENCES

ALDERFER, CLAYTON P. "An Organizational Syndrome," *Administrative Science Quarterly* 12: 550-60; 1967.
ARGYRIS, CHRIS. *Organization and Innovation*, Homewood, Ill.: Dorsey, 1965.
*CHESLER, MARK, AND FLANDERS, MARY. "Resistance to Research and Research Utilization: The Death and Life of a Feedback Attempt," *Journal of Applied Behavioral Science* 3: 469-87; 1967.

FERGUSON, L. L. "How Social Science Research Can Help Management," *California Management Review* 7: 3-10; 1966.

FERGUSON, L. L. "Social Scientists in the Plant," *Harvard Business Review* 42: 133-43; 1964.

JANIS, I. L. *Psychological Stress.* New York: Wiley, 1958.

KLEIN, DONALD. "Some Notes on the Dynamics of the Resistance to Change." *The Planning of Change.* (Edited by Warren G. Bennis *et al.*) New York: Holt, Rinehart, and Winston, 1969, pp. 498-507.

MANN, F. C. "Studying and Creating Change: A Means to Understanding Social Organization." *Research in Industrial Human Relations.* (Edited by C. M. Arensberg, *et al.*) New York: Harper and Brothers, 1957, pp. 157-67.

MANN, F. C., AND LIKERT, R. "The Need for Research on the Communication of Research Results," *Human Organization* 11: 15-19; 1952.

MANN, F. C., AND NEFF, F. W. *Managing Major Change in Organizations.* Ann Arbor: Foundation for Research on Human Behavior, Inc., 1962.

MASLOW, A. H. *Toward a Psychology of Being.* Princeton: D. Van Nostrand, 1962.

MILES, M. B., *et. al.* "The Consequence of Survey Feedback: Theory and Evaluation." *The Planning of Change.* (Edited by Warren G. Bennis, *et al.*) New York: Holt, Rinehart and Winston, 1969, pp. 457-68.

NEFF, FRANK W. "Survey Research: A Tool for Problem Diagnosis and Improvement in Organizations." *Applied Sociology.* (Edited by A. W. Gouldner and S. M. Miller.) New York: Free Press, 1965, pp. 23-38.

SINGER, ERWIN. *Key Concepts in Psychotherapy,* New York: Random House, 1965.

WATSON, GOODWIN. "Resistance to Change." *The Planning of Change.* (Edited by Warren G. Bennis, *et al.*) New York: Holt, Rinehart and Winston, 1969, pp. 488-98.

DEALING WITH DYSFUNCTIONAL ORGANIZATION MYTHS

Leland P. Bradford and Jerry B. Harvey

NOTE: The authors would like to express their appreciation to Dr. David Bradford, Graduate School of Business, Stanford University, and to Dr. Allan Katcher, Atkins-Katcher Associates, Los Angeles, for their helpful comments concerning the content of this article.

An organization myth is an ill-founded and untested belief which powerfully affects the way in which organization members behave and respond. Such myths play an important part in contemporary organizations. In fact, any organization with more than a brief history has myths that do more to determine and control the behavior of its members than do all of the structural arrangements, work procedures, pep talks, counseling sessions and other managerial efforts designed to affect organization behavior.

Most of these myths are dysfunctional to the organization. Most fit into the passive, dependent, fear-of-accepting responsibility parts of the individual personality and are used as defenses. And most myths are so deeply rooted in the belief and perceptual structure of the organization that they can be located and destroyed only through intensive efforts by persons having special skills in the process.

The following examples drawn from the authors' experiences with a variety of organizations may help to indicate the character, strength, autistic quality and dysfunctional consequences of myths, as well as indicate the methods by which they are identified.

CASE 1:

It's No Use Trying Anything New

Interviewer:
   "What are some things that block you from getting your job done?"
Organization Member:
   "Well, for one thing, it's no use trying anything new here, because somebody would block it. It's just not allowed."
Interviewer:
   "Is this what others think? Have you talked to other people about this belief?"
Organization Member:
   "I'm sure everybody thinks the same thing. I've never talked to anybody about it because it's so obvious that everybody thinks the same way."

Interviewer:
"What makes it obvious?"
Organization Member:
"Well, you don't see many new things tried here."
Interviewer:
"Have you tried something different, or have you seen someone else try something new?"
Organization Member:
"Well, yes. So and so installed a whole new process of working in her department."
Interviewer:
"Did it work and was it allowed?"
Organization Member:
"Yes it did. But I'm sure that was an exception."

CASE 2:

The Boss Will Punish You If You Don't Know Everything

Interviewer:
"If you could change something around here, what would it be?"
Organization Member:
"I would cut out all the detailed files you have to keep."
Interviewer:
"What do you mean by that?"
Organization Member:
"Around here, you've got to have every fact at your fingertips or you would be in real trouble with your boss. He'd really lay it on you if you couldn't answer every question when you are asked it. Could be in real trouble. Do you know that I keep an extra clerk just to keep a JIC (just in case) file up to date?"
Interviewer:
"Do others do the same thing in other departments?"
Organization Member:
"I'm sure they do. Otherwise they would be in trouble."
Interviewer:
"Have you ever heard of anyone getting into trouble for not having everything at his fingertips?"
Organization Member:
"Oh, yes. I heard of a guy in Department X who really got clobbered by the 'old man' for not knowing the answer to something."
Interviewer:
"Did that happen recently?"
Organization Member:
"Oh, no. That happened sometime ago. The 'old man' retired in 1958."

Interviewer:
> "Has your superior ever asked you for information that you didn't immediately have?"

Organization Member:
> "Oh, yes."

Interviewer:
> "What happened?"

Organization Member:
> "He just asked me to get the information when I had time."

Interviewer:
> "Did he reprimand you? Did anything happen to hurt you later?"

Organization Member:
> "No, nothing. But it's very clear around here that you better be prepared on any issue concerning your work. It's worth the extra clerical help to be ready."

CASE 3:

Don't Ask Questions

Interviewer:
> "What could be changed to make it possible for you to do your job more effectively?"

Organization Member:
> "Make it possible to ask questions."

Interviewer:
> 'You mean you can't ask questions?"

Organization Member:
> "Hell, no. You never ask a question around here. If you do, you'll look stupid and you may lose out in a promotion later."

Interviewer:
> "Is that what others believe?"

Organization Member:
> "They sure do. You should see our staff meetings. Everybody looks wise and knowing when the boss says something."

Interviewer:
> "Is that what he wants people to do?"

Organization Member:
> "He says he wants people to speak up, to ask questions, to make suggestions, to criticize, but I'm sure he doesn't really mean it."

Interviewer:
> "Does anyone ask questions or raise issues with the boss?"

Organization Member:
> "Oh, sure."

Interviewer:
> "Does anything bad happen to them?"

Organization Member:
> "No, but I'm sure they're taking a chance."

CHARACTERISTICS OF ORGANIZATION MYTHS

As can be seen from the examples, organization myths have a number of distinctive characteristics. First, they frequently develop from events or situations that actually occurred in the past, but have been inflated by anxiety, communicated by rumor, ingrained by repetition, and passed word-of-mouth from one generation of employees to another as fact, until they have become integral parts of the belief structure of the organization.

In short, they have become myths. Thus, the new man hears from his boss:

"Keep your mouth shut, your nose clean, and don't ask questions. My boss told it to me, and I'm telling it to you. That's the way to get along around here."

The fact the foreman's admonition was an appropriate and accurate reflection of the way to get ahead in the company in 1907, not in 1970, is irrelevant for the new recruit. For like the tribal elder passing along the village mores to the young initiate, the superior passes the myth along to his subordinates, and his subordinates will pass it along to their subordinates, all to the organization's detriment.

Second, myths are assumed, but seldom tested. They tend to be believed uncritically, in the same way the ancients believed in Poseidon's control of the seas, and are accepted as adequate explanations for the way things are. But the modern manager is no less trapped than the ancient Greek. For example, McGregor[1] pointed out in his elucidation of Theory X that many managers accept the myth that only those in managerial positions behave responsibly and work hard. When managers believe this myth, they treat subordinates as if the myth were true, thus creating apathetic and seemingly irresponsible behavior which, in turn, reinforces the myth. Only when the myth is tested can its self-fulfilling nature be discovered and its dysfunctional character destroyed. But it is central to the character of organization myths that their validity is seldom questioned or doubted.

Third, individuals believing a myth frequently possess information to disprove or at least cast doubt on its validity. But they seldom really consider such data, or if they consider it, they reject it as irrelevant. Thus, the manager who believes that "the average human being has an inherent dislike of work and will avoid it if he can"[1] may be confronted with data about a worker who is extraordinarily productive and energetic. Faced with such information, he generally rejects it as being "an exception to the rule," thereby leaving the myth intact.

Fourth, organization myths are widely-held beliefs, owned by a large number of people on one or more levels of the organization. The generality with which they are held distinguishes them from myths ingrained in the personality of a single individual which are not broadly shared by other members of the organization. An individual may act on the myth that "no one with blue eyes can be trusted"; but that myth may belong to him alone and its treatment, in the "therapeutic sense," is quite different and not a subject of this discussion.

Fifth, acceptance of an organization myth permits the individual to be passive, dependent, and ultimately, irresponsible in coping with organization problems. For example, a common myth is that "the boss is unapproachable, aloof, and uninterested in what his subordinates think." (See Case 3) Acceptance of that myth, therefore, provides subordinates with an excuse for not developing ideas or solutions to problems since "the boss is uninterested." Myths, then, take a tremendous toll because they "release" organization members from responsibility and place that responsibility on others who, in turn, believe the myths and pass along the responsibility for coping to someone else. Unfortunately for organization problem-solving, that "someone else" is equally mythical, for he has no more existence than the mythical problem he is supposed to solve.

Sixth, individuals tend to believe myths about hierarchal levels above but not below, or about levels below but not above. Take the previous example. John Smith, Vice President, says: "My boss is unapproachable. He doesn't care what I think."

Question:
    "Do your subordinates find you unapproachable?"
Vice President:
    "No, I'm sure they don't. I want to know what my subordinates think."

Characteristically, the same response occurs throughout the hierarchy. To the Division Director, the Vice President is unapproachable, but he, the Division Director, is not. To the Section Head, the Division Director is unapproachable, but he, the Section Head, is not, and so on down the line, with each person thinking his superior is unapproachable but feeling that his subordinates see him as a paragon of accessibility.

Seventh, myths play the important psychological function of explaining and relieving the emotional tensions of those who believe them. Allport and Postman [2] identified this function in their classic study of rumors. The same dynamics underlie the formation and maintenance of organization myths. In brief, an anxiety-arousing situation occurs, "I don't feel very influential around here." How does one explain such feelings of impotence and, at the same time, maintain his self-esteem as a creative and competent manager? One way to do it is to look for an explanation which is rational and will also relieve the tension that comes from his feeling of helplessness. Therefore, he attributes the cause of his helplessness to someone else or to some event over which he has no control. In that way, the myth, "It's no use trying anything new," is born.

Interviewer:
    "What keeps you from presenting your idea for the new production process?"
Manager:
    "They say they are for new ideas, but they always shoot them down."

Interviewer:
"Who is 'they'?"
Manager:
"You know, all of those characters who knock down good ideas . . . they do it to everyone."
Interviewer:
"Who does it?"
Manager:
"All the bosses do. They're never interested in anything unless they think of it themselves."

Finally, and most important, myths, contrary to reality as they may be, have identifiable and dysfunctional effects on productivity, communication and problem-solving. In brief, they are humanistically destructive and economically wasteful.

FINDING AND IDENTIFYING MYTHS

Since myths tend to have long histories and to be deeply rooted in the belief and perceptual structures of the organization, they are difficult to isolate and identify, and even more difficult to root out.

As one individual put it, "Fish are the last to know that they are in water." And like those proverbial fish, persons in an organization who contribute to its myths are frequently the last to know of their existence, to understand their impact, and to see the part they play as managers in contributing to their birth and in maintaining their existence.

For that reason, myths are generally located or identified with the help of outside consultants or through hard probing by persons within the organization who have enough functional independence and autonomy to view the organization with the essential perspective of an outsider.

Once the investigator achieves the perspective of an outsider, he has a number of alternatives for carrying out his investigation. However, the method that has been most useful to the authors in identifying organization myths has been an open-ended interview survey. Such a survey requires interviewing individuals from several levels of the organization and involves systematic data feedback sessions[3] for those who contribute the data.

These interviews have two essential characteristics. First, they begin with questions designed to help the individual describe his perceptions of positive and negative features of the organization, areas where energy is wasted, and norms or controls which block him from using his personal resources to the maximum. Several specific questions are particularly helpful in eliciting such data:

1. What do you like best about this organization? Least?
2. If you could immediately change one characteristic of the organization, what would it be?
3. What blocks you from using your skills and abilities to the utmost?

The second step in the interview is of critical importance because it provides clues as to the possible mythical quality of those problems which are identified. The purpose is to collect data which either substantiate or call into question the kinds of perceptions described. Thus, the question, "Have you or others ever tried to do anything about the problem you describe?" usually provides clues as to whether the individual's perceptions reflect myth or reality.

For instance, sometimes an individual describes a norm or an issue which inhibits his performance and then follows by recounting a *single* event which occurred sometime in the past as the basis for his belief in that norm. Or sometimes he offers data which disproves the very norm he describes. Either event provides the interviewer with clues for identifying those norms and perceptions affecting individual and group behavior which show every likelihood of being mythical rather than real.

TESTING THE MYTHS' REALITY

Once data are collected from individuals about possible myths, the next step is to test them for reality. Such reality testing is accomplished by feeding back the interview results in small groups to those who contributed the data. Since many of the myths tend to focus on hierarchal relationships ("Bosses don't want to be asked questions"), reality testing and confrontation is facilitated if no more than two heirarchal levels are involved in the discussions at any one time.

Two points are important about these feedback sessions. First, the data which led to the interviewer's tentative conclusions must be fully shared with participants in the sessions, and the sharing must be done in such a way that the anonymity of those providing the data is protected. And second, the interviewer's hypotheses must be tentative. The reality and accuracy of the data, not the veracity of the interviewer, must be tested if real confrontation with the myths is to take place.

Stated differently, the data provide the confrontation and motivation for change. Such confrontation automatically occurs when it is clear there is a discrepancy between the interviewees' actual and perceived behaviors. Since the managers' own data tend to illustrate the inherent dysfunctionality of the myths, there is intrinsic motivation to eradicate them.

In sessions like this, it is not unusual for managers, particularly those at the top, to show shock and surprise when confronted with the number of myths which operate within their organization. To a considerable extent, this indicates that myths are not generally expressed or articulated except in the behaviors they induce.

Also interesting is the degree in which managers are unaware of the extent to which myths affect the behavior of individuals in the total organization. More concretely, the fact that the vice president, the division manager, the section head and the first-line supervisor all maintain JIC files as a means of protecting themselves in case their bosses call is a source of considerable surprise and consternation for all involved.

DESTROYING DYSFUNCTIONAL MYTHS

If a myth does exist, then it is important for the organization and its members to eradicate it and to develop more effective ways of coping with the problems it represents. But destroying a myth is more complex than it may appear; for a myth is symptomatic of a deeper concern, and maintaining a myth is a way of defending oneself against the tension generated by the underlying problem. And, as has been stated, although the myth may serve as a defense for the individual, it may also prevent his being responsible for solving important organization problems.

For instance, the myth, "It's no use trying anything new around here," is frequently based on a considerable amount of anxiety and concern the individual has about his competency ("If I try something new and fail, I must be incompetent") and power ("If I try something new and don't succeed, I must not be a very powerful or influential person"). Because of these deeper concerns, the individual creates an explanation which will relieve such tension: "It's no use trying something new, because someone will shoot it down." That explanation, however irrational, not only protects the individual's sense of self-esteem, it also prevents him from accepting active responsibility for solving problems, the solutions to which are, ultimately, important for both him and the organization.

It is not enough, therefore, to simply identify a myth and get rational agreement that it does exist as a way of rendering it impotent. In fact, unless new and more appropriate ways are devised for coping with the underlying problems the myth represents, it is unlikely that the myth can be destroyed. Or if it is destroyed, it is likely to be replaced by another which is equally dysfunctional to the organization.

DEALING WITH UNDERLYING EMOTIONALITY

Given the fact the organization myths are symptomatic of other issues, the first step leading to their eradication is to provide organization members the opportunity to talk about, understand, to "own up"[4] and deal with the feelings and emotional concerns (such as feelings of incompetency) the myths represent. This requires considerable skill on the part of the investigator and is frequently carried out in the data feedback sessions.

The following discussion, obviously annotated to illustrate the point, demonstrates how the process may occur:

Interviewer:
"Most people here seem to agree it is a myth that 'you can't try anything new.' Sometimes such myths reflect feelings we all have at one time or another that we may be incompetent or not very influential in how we carry out our jobs. For instance, if we

try something new and don't succeed, we may begin to doubt our competence. I wonder if that may be true for any of the persons here?"

First Manager:
"It is for me. I sure as hell don't want to try something new and have it fail. It makes me wonder about my capacity to do the job and even worse, I'm sure it makes others wonder about my ability to do the job. Let someone else take chances, not me."

Second Manager:
"That goes for me, too. I don't want people to think I can't do my job—even if I feel that way."

Third Manager:
"I don't know about the rest of you guys, but I'm very relieved to find I'm not the only one to feel that way."

Interviewer:
"Maybe it would be helpful to explore whether others would really think you were incompetent if you tried something and failed. That assumption might be incorrect."

First Manager:
"I would like to try that."

SETTING NEW NORMS

Once the process of dealing with underlying emotional issues is underway, it is possible to move into the phase of helping managers create new norms of behavior which are more effective than the mythical ones.

The interviewer can assist managers in creating such norms by legitimizing the process of exploration:

Interviewer:
"Since everyone here has agreed it is a myth that 'it's no use trying anything new,' what might be done to operate on a more realistic basis?"

First Manager:
"How about setting up a rule that each manager has to institute a new procedure at least once a month?"

Second Manager:
"Too mechanical; doesn't make sense."

Third Manager:
"Why don't we agree on a new norm: 'When you are going to try something new and risky, get with your boss and see what his reaction might be if you fail.' "

Various Managers:
"Sounds good . . . let's try it."

Again, the example is shortened for illustrative purposes. But it does demonstrate both requirements for destroying a dysfunctional myth. It solves the problem of providing a sound technical solution (a new functional norm), and it also takes into account the emotionality underlying the myth (fear of taking a risk and failing). And equally important, managers have been a part of the solution process and thus have begun to develop skills for identifying and dealing with other dysfunctional myths.

Finally, if the myth is to be truly destroyed, it is important that the reality of the myth be tested and confronted throughout the total organization. Consequently, once myths are identified, managers at each level of the organization should insure that the process of identification, reality-testing, and destruction takes place with their subordinates and peers. Failure to deal with myths at all levels and subparts of the organization, in addition to supporting continuation of the myths, invariably leads to problems. One part of the organization simply cannot act on the basis of reality without creating friction with those parts of the organization which are acting on the basis of a myth.

BUILDING MYTH-DESTRUCTION CAPABILITY INTO THE FORMAL ORGANIZATION

Given the extent of pluralistic ignorance and complex patterns of disclosure, organization myths can be uncovered only by a deliberate and systematic search. For a search to be effective, it generally requries either an outside consultant or an inside resource who, by function of his skills and his position within the organization, has not come to accept the myths.

In addition, since myths are reflected in attitudes and behaviors long exhibited but seldom tested, the search for current myths and their eradication calls for a long-term time commitment. Short, sporadic efforts are seldom effective and, therefore, are more harmful and upsetting than helpful. And acceptance, support and participation on the part of those at the top of the organization is required if the effort is to be successful.

Consequently, if an organization is to remain free from dysfunctional organization myths, it should have a Vice President for Human Resources, close to and listened to by the Chief Executive and with competence and access to the resources necessary to sense and resolve its mythical problems. Thus, myths, unknown to top management and destructive to organization resources and goals, will have less opportunity to disrupt individual efforts and destroy organization effectiveness.

ARE MYTHS EVER FUNCTIONAL?

The reality orientation of myth destruction frequently leads to the questions: Are myths ever functional? Is it not true that some myths are functional and, therefore, should not be tampered with? Isn't it sometimes better to allow people to live with illusions, even when they don't reflect reality?

The answers to the questions are clearly, "yes." In the same way that belief in Poseidon allowed the ancient Greeks to accept and cope with some of the imponderables of the sea, belief in certain organization myths undoubtedly allows us to accept and cope with some apparently inexplicable aspects of modern organizations. But in the same way that acceptance of the mythical Poseidon probably prevented the Greeks from developing as rapidly as they might have new solutions to problems of navigation and seamanship, beliefs in organization myths may quickly become dysfunctional as knowledge is developed for solving organization problems around which myths have developed.

At that point, they cease to be functional and the organization and its members need a means for relegating them to the pages of organization history in the same way that mythical characters of the past are part of an illuminating but, ultimately, dysfunctional approach to solving problems.

REFERENCES

McGREGOR, D., *The Human Side of Enterprise*, McGraw-Hill, 1960.
ALLPORT, G. W. AND L. F. POSTMAN, "The Basic Psychology of Rumor," *Readings in Social Psychology*, Henry Holt and Co., 1947, p. 160-71.
BECKHARD, R., "The Confrontation Meeting," *Harvard Business Review*, Mar.-Apr. 1967, p. 149-55.
ARGYRIS, C., *Interpersonal Competence and Organizational Effectiveness*, Irwin and Dorsey, 1962.

AN ACTION-RESEARCH APPROACH TO ORGANIZATIONAL CHANGE

R. Stephen Jenks

R. Stephen Jenks is assistant professor of business administration, The Whittemore School of Business and Economics, University of New Hampshire.

This paper is concerned with the development, testing, and application of a research instrument designed for use in organizational settings as an integral part of organization change and development efforts. The instrument fits in the category of Leavitt's (1965) so-called "people approach" because it is based on bringing about organizational change by changing the interpersonal relations of the organization's members.

Most helpful in bringing about change in interpersonal relationships are systematic data about the relationships. The organizational Q-sort instrument examined here was designed and developed to provide such systematic data for face-to-face workgroups. The development of a Q-sort instrument, which gathers and organizes data concerning perceptions of behavior and feelings regarding a particular problem facing a workgroup, is described in detail.

The application of the instrument in an organizational field setting is examined and evaluated in terms of (a) the usefulness of the instrument, (b) the extent to which it is a meaningful part of an organizational change and development project, and (c) the results obtained. The results are given both quantitatively (by means of content examination in three categories: characteristic items, uncharacteristic items, and discrepant items). The impact of the results in the organizational setting is examined. Further developmental possibilities of the instrument are mentioned.

INTRODUCTION

The purpose of this study is to develop and test the usefulness of a new action-research tool for use in organizational development work. The methods used in organizational development vary widely according to the needs of the organization and the skills and techniques of the change agent. Many times the methods used merely transfer information from the consultant[1] to the client. That is, the consultant's expert knowledge about organizational structure and/or functioning is transferred to the client, leading to some organizational changes. Often the consultant uses methods for organizational diagnosis which generally are not used by the organization for its own development. Examples are operations research techniques, clinical psychology methods, anthropology, and field study methods. Many of these methods share the prerequisite that the client have an understanding of the problem to be solved or the direction which the organization development effort should take.

Frequently, however, the client does not have an understanding of the problem nor does he know the directions in which the organization needs to be developed. Primarily, this situation occurs when both the problem and the major components of its solution lie in the area of human relations. Clients seem much better able to diagnose problems which arise in nonhuman areas such as financial planning, physical resource utilization, new product and/or market development, and so on. When problems arise in the development of human resources, clients seem less able to define the problem and much less able to solve it. Consequently, in the area of human organization development, the consultant must work closely with the client from the very first stage of problem definition.

Action-research methods currently are limited for use in organizational development consulting are limited in number and usefulness. The methods which the consultant can borrow from other areas in social science usually require the consultant to act as researcher (or therapist) and the client to act as subject (or patient), rather than being designed for their joint investigation of a problem area in which both can act as resources for diagnosis and solution. This study attempts to describe factors in an action-research approach as it is used in a particular organization development project.

BACKGROUND: RESEARCH METHODOLOGY

Great strides have been made in recent years toward the development of more precise research tools for the study of complex human behavior. Research methodology and statistical techniques have grown more sophisticated in dealing with the wide range of variables which may be causally related to various kinds of behavior. This is particularly true in the case of laboratory experimentation, where the number of variables active at any given time can be more fully controlled. Social science knowledge has grown rapidly in the last 10 to 15 years in such complex areas as attitude development and change (Green, 1954; Maccoby, Newcomb, & Hartley, 1958), small-group dynamics and functioning (Hare, 1962), and various aspects of organizational and societal behavior (March, 1965; Miles, 1964; and Zand, in press). Much of this knowledge has been gained through controlled experimentation in the laboratory situation.

At various points, however, the extent to which the laboratory situation accurately parallels real life situations is limited. Many of the factors which normally influence behavior in social settings are not present in the experimental laboratory situation, nor can they be created there. As the locus of study moves from the laboratory to the field setting, the ability of currently available research techniques to account for all of the possible independent variables declines sharply.[2] Often, reported statistical inferences about causality of behavior are only one of a number of plausible, but untested, explanations for the observed behavior. In the field setting, precise measurement of various types of behavior is more difficult. As a result, adherence to the physical science model of experimentation and inquiry becomes harder to attain.

Consequently, the research methodology used in field settings is largely based upon clinical methods, where many of the data are supplied by the researcher rather than the subject himself. Thus we have the development of interviewing, systematic observational techniques, participant observation, and various techniques where the subject must choose one of a number of predetermined responses (questionnaires, sociometric techniques, and so on). Many of these clinical or descriptive techniques have come under attack because they are not "scientific" in the physical science sense of the word. That is, they do not meet the normal criteria of the scientific method, primarily that of replicability. What is needed for field research in the social sciences is the development of some new approaches and methods of study which are specifically geared to field situations and which are more truly scientific. Research techniques need to be developed which provide systematic information about the phenomena being studied and which will provide such information to any researcher using the technique.

Frequently, the behavior required of the researcher in order to gain acceptance in the field research situation (which often is essential in gaining access to relevant data) has the effect of diminishing his ability to remain a marginal and objective observer of the phenomena he is studying. A social scientist working in a field setting must pay attention not only to the question of whether he should be involved—for that is open to little question—but in what way he should be involved. In social science, the dividing line between descriptive research (investigations into nature) and applied research (using research as a social change methodology) is unclear. Consequently, social scientists must ask themselves whether the purpose of their research is (a) to find out something, (b) to change something, or (c) to do both. Then research designs can be developed which have the most likelihood of helping social scientists reach their research goals. However, more and more researchers are discovering that research which is directed at problem solving and change also is research which yields new knowledge about the social phenomena under study.[3]

Difficulties in Development of Valid Field Research Tools

There have been difficulties in the development of field research tools which can meet two major criteria: (1) direct relevance to the problems and issues faced in the field organization setting and (2) normal criteria for validity and reliability of the research instrument. Most often these research tools meet one or the other criterion, but seldom both. One reason for the difficulties is that those research instruments which are valid and reliable tend to be applicable to field research settings in some general sense, but out of touch with specific researchable organizational problems faced by any given organization. Examples are morale surveys, indices of employee satisfaction, productivity, influence on decision making, and related areas. Each of these indices deals with a *general* problem found in organizational field settings, but none deals with *specific* organizational problems or problem-solving mechanisms.

There is another problem in the current state of organizational field research. Most research instruments are, by definition, time-bounded; that is, static. Questionnaires, which are the major means of field data collection, suffer from their inability to provide more than an instantaneous time-slice picture of an organization along predetermined variables (which may or may not still be relevant during a later administration of the questionnaire). For these reasons, field research tools which meet the usual validity and reliability criteria are frequently out of touch with the real problems needing research and subsequent organizational development work. *They are static rather than dynamic; they are general rather than specific.* One characteristic reinforces the other; the static research tools suffer because they investigate predetermined variables which, in order to be assured of relevance over time, must be of a general rather than a specific nature.

Action researchers working in field organization settings do research (and build research tools) for several purposes: (1) to demonstrate the validity of their theoretical hypotheses about organizations, (2) to obtain a diagnosis of the state of affairs in the organization on particular dimensions, (3) to test the impact of change(s) on the organization, (4) to clarify and show directions toward solution of practical problems, (5) to help the organization see directions for adaptive change and growth and to provide data on the organization's movement in those directions. The present study is concerned with purposes number two, four, and five. Often in these areas, the desire for directly applicable research data requires the development of new research instruments designed for specific purposes. This type of action research is designed to make a difference in the social system being studied. Rather than stressing researcher objectivity, the action-research model is based upon active collaboration between the researcher and the research subjects in the field setting. In effect, they become coinvestigators in the design and execution of the research. The task, therefore, is to develop research tools which will meet the following criteria simultaneously: (a) They should yield data which are specific. (b) They should deal with a particular *present* issue. (c) They should provide data which the client needs and asks for. (d) They should be fairly easy to administer, analyze, and feed back to those who give data.

DEVELOPMENT OF THE Q-SORT INSTRUMENT

The organizational Q-sort instrument has been developed to meet the needs stated above and is designed to yield some systematic data for use in making planned organizational changes. It is a descriptive instrument whose function is to collect and organize data which can be used in the diagnosis stage of an organizational development or change project. The organizational Q-sort instrument is intended to show people's impact on one another when working together. It demonstrates various types of behavior with regard to *specific* problems and also shows feelings about the behavior in regard to those same problems. In other words, the instrument is capable of monitoring individual and/or group *process* in a way which helps to make it a manageable *task* to be examined and dealt with. The instrument is related to three areas of social science application. It uses a *clinical research method* (i.e., a technique designed to yield self-descriptive data rather than predictive or normative data), has items drawn from *small-group dynamics, and is* intended to be used in *organizational problem diagnosis.*

A Q technique was chosen because it has been found to be a useful means for describing the relationships among a number of variables as they exist in a single situation (Block, 1961). Because the self-description sought by the present instrument is of an interpersonal and small-group nature, rather than of an intrapersonal or personality structure nature, the items were drawn from interpersonal relations and small-group dynamics sources. Because small face-to-face workgroups are common in organizational settings, items were chosen to represent the major interpersonal dimensions of such groups.

A list of behavioral dimensions in which groups operate was constructed from three sources. The first source was observing a number of workgroups and recording the kinds of interaction which occurred in them. Second was a synthesis of the kinds of categories used in several of the systematic observational techniques (Bales, 1950; Chapple, 1949; Carter, Haythorn, Meirowitz, & Lanzetta, 1951a,b). Third was the judgment of the author and several colleagues after examining the list which had been developed from the former two sources. From these three sources, a list of 16 dimensions was constructed as shown below.

DIMENSIONS OF BEHAVIOR AND FEELINGS IN GROUPS

Influence	Communication
Respect	Freedom-Initiation
Interdependence	Openness
Control-Dominance	Leadership
Trust	Self-Interest
Liking	Reliability
Commitment to Task	Competition
Competence	Evaluation

Individual items were selected to reflect each of these 16 dimensions and came from one of two sources: (a) items from previous questionnaires and group research instruments and (b) newly constructed items designed to tap areas for which other sources were inadequate. The items which came from previous questionnaires and group research instruments were drawn from a number of sources, including the following: *The Group Dimensions Descriptions Questionnaire* by Hemphill and Westie (1965), Analysis of Personal Behavior in Groups by Wagner (1965), FIRO-B by Schutz (1958), and several sample Q sorts given by Stephenson (1953, Chap. XI).

The items selected for inclusion in the initial version of the organizational Q sort were those which were most clear, succinct, and direct. They also had to be oriented to behaviors or feelings which occur in workgroups as opposed to other types of groups such as social groups, family groups, or therapy groups. The initial Q-sort instrument contained a total of 52 items arranged to reflect the 16 primary dimensions. Furthermore, the items were checked against two other formulations. One was Stephenson's (1953) method of designing Q sorts around interdependencies, and the other was Schutz's (1958) FIRO formulation. It was decided that if the 52 items were well dispersed in each of these formulations as they were by design around the 16 group dimensions, it would be safe to assume that at least theoretically the items covered the major aspects of group functioning.

Listed below are the Q-sort items, and Tables 1, 2, and 3 show the breakdown of the items into each of the analytic schemes, respectively. In Stephenson's (1953) formulation, the interdependencies are named and then are correlated with the levels of interdependence (i.e., positive or negative with regard to self, and positive or negative with regard to others). Schutz's (1958) theory of interpersonal behavior utilizes the three following categories: (1) Inclusion, (2) Control, and (3) Affection.

Q-SORT ITEM LIST

1. I say what I think.
2. I act on the others' ideas.
3. I accept the faults of the others.
4. I spend extra time and energy working on the problem.
5. I tell the others what they should be doing.
6. I exert pressure on nonconforming members.
7. I correct the others' mistakes.
8. I try to get my way regardless of the others.
9. I work on this problem to the extent to which I am directed to do so.
10. People are acting on my recommendations.
11. I pay a lot of attention to the others' ideas.
12. I feel free to do whatever I want in solving the problem.
13. I feel free to work on the problem or not, as I desire.
14. I am getting tired of working on the problem.
15. I find myself at odds with the group.

16. I need the resources of the others in order to solve the problem.
17. I trust the others to do their parts.
18. I am satisfied with the way in which we are working on the problem.
19. People in the group devaluate the ideas I have.
20. I am suspicious of the others' motives.
21. I communicate fully with the others.
22. I have many good ideas for solving the problem.
23. I have faith in my own ideas.
24. I could solve the problem myself.
25. Others communicate fully with me.
26. I am taking leadership on the problem.
27. I make use of constructive criticism.
28. It is easy for me to see both sides of a question.
29. I am open to new suggestions on how we should work on the problem.
30. I am working on the problem to the extent that I get credit for it.
31. I think each person is doing his part to work on the problem.
32. If I want something done right, I do it myself.
33. I never get credit for the good ideas I have.
34. I like the way I am working on the problem.
35. I prefer to work alone.
36. I dislike working on the problem.
37. I keep my ideas to myself.
38. I prefer to be told what I must do.
39. I like the way the others are working on the problem.
40. I settle differences of opinion.
41. I understand our objectives.
42. I accept our objectives.
43. I let other poeple make the decisions.
44. Other people influence my actions.
45. I am easily led by others in the group.
46. I have a lot to say in the group's discussions.
47. I hold on to my own opinion no matter how the rest of the group feels.
48. I'd rather let somebody else take the lead in the group.
49. I don't ask for help even if I'm "stuck."
50. The others can count on me to do my part.
51. I have a hard time communicating clearly.
52. I "have it in for" those in the group who don't "deliver."

Table 1 shows the dimensions which were identified through observation of workgroups and dimensions which are common to systematic observational techniques. Each dimension accounts for two or more of the items in the original organization Q sort.

Table 2 is based on Stephenson's methods of designing Q sorts. It consists of naming the interdependencies (left-hand column) and then correlating them with the levels of interdependence. In this case, the levels are broken down twice; first, as a distinction between self and others, and second, as a distinction between positive and negative. The latter distinction is made by the following definition: positive items were defined as those which were supportive of Theory Y, and negative items were defined as those which were supportive of Theory X (McGregor, 1960).

TABLE 1
Workgroup Dimensions and Associated Items

Dimension	Item Numbers			
Influence	2,	10,	44,	45
Respect	3,	11,	19	
Interdependence	16,	32,	49	
Control-Dominance	5,	6,	43	
Trust	17,	20,	31	
Liking	18,	34,	36,	39
Commitment to Task	4,	9,	14,	42
Competence	7,	22,	23,	46
Communication	21,	25,	41,	51
Freedom-Initiation	29,	12,	13,	35
Openness	1,	27,	28,	37
Leadership	26,	38,	40,	48
Self-Interest	30,	33		
Reliability	50,	52		
Competition	8,	15		
Evaluation	24,	47		

TABLE 2
Stephenson's Interdependency Model and Associated Items

Inter- dependencies	Level			
	Self		Others	
	Positive (Y)	Negative (X)	Positive (Y)	Negative (X)
Behaviors	1, 2, 3, 4	5, 6, 7, 8, 9	10, 11	43
Feelings	12, 13	14, 15	16, 17, 18	19, 20
Thoughts (Opinions)	21, 22, 23, 46	24, 51	25	44
Evaluations	26, 27, 28, 29, 50	30, 45, 47	31	32, 33, 49, 52
Preferences	34, 48	35, 36, 37, 38	39	
Other	40, 41, 42			

TABLE 3
Schutz's FIRO Model and Associated Items

Dimension	Category	Expressed	Versus	Wanted
Behavior	Inclusion	1, 4, 21, 34, 35, 37		11, 46, 50
	Control	5, 6, 7, 8, 10, 40		2, 9, 27, 29, 44, 45
	Affection	3		25
Feelings	Inclusion	15, 22, 23, 41, 42		16, 24, 28, 51
	Control	26, 30, 32, 47, 49, 52		12, 13, 38, 48
	Affection	14, 17, 18, 31, 36, 39		19, 20, 33

Items were placed in categories in Tables 1, 2, and 3 on three bases: 1. Items drawn from other instruments were placed in corresponding categories in the present instrument. 2. Items constructed for the present instrument had content designed for particular categories they were to fill. 3. The author and two colleagues pooled their judgments on item placement. The initial Q-sort instrument of 52 items was complete when the items met the criteria of the three tables, that is, when the item universe had been reduced in some areas and built up on others to satisfy the various theoretical bases for the instrument. Pilot testing then began in order to refine the instrument further to its final form.

In addition to a statistical analysis, the pilot study data were analyzed diagnostically to answer several questions which would help to determine which items could be dropped from the instrument without changing its ability to collect and organize data in the manner intended. An item-by-item correlation was performed on the data across participants. There were several highly significant correlations which indicated item redundancy.

All items which were neutral, had very low variance, or very high variance were pulled together and content analyzed to determine whether there was a pattern or particular type of item which had such characteristics. Twenty items were examined on these bases, 11 of which were finally dropped from the Q sort. The final Q sort consisted of 41 items, after the following 11 items were dropped from the initial list: 1, 3, 18, 22, 27, 28, 31, 39, 40, 42, 45.

APPLICATION OF THE INSTRUMENT TO AN ORGANIZATION

The present study was part of an organizational change and development project in a large Midwestern manufacturing corporation and covers a time period of three months from March 1966 through May 1966, during which the Personnel Department was reorganized to meet new demands and challenges arising from drastic changes in the corporation's business situation. The action-research, person-oriented approach described earlier was used in helping the Personnel Department through the reorganization and subsequently in helping the new organization begin to function smoothly. Essentially, the approach meant including the members of the organization in all stages of the "people" approach (Leavitt, 1965): problem diagnosis, planning, and implementing action steps to solve the problems. Data were collected through interviews and through the use of the organizational Q-sort instrument described above.

In March 1966, the Group Vice President, the author, and several other interested persons began to encourage the Personnel Director to reevaluate his own organization to determine ways to increase his effectiveness while at the same time decreasing the work load pressures on him and on the department. Several realignments were considered, each of which would give power and responsibility to individuals beneath the Director, and thereby would free him from some of the pressures his centrality had created. The realignment which was finally chosen divided the Personnel Department into four major functions as shown in Figure 1.

FIGURE 1

Personnel Department Realignment[4]

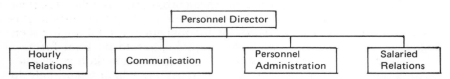

The organization shown in Figure 1 was chosen as the best of several alternatives, and the four functional heads were summoned to begin the work of reorganizing the rest of the Personnel Department under the new arrangement which was a significant departure from the past. This group began to call itself the Personnel Planning Group (PPG), and constituted the central group in the present study.

The author, as consultant to the PPG from its inception, continued to help the group develop methods of working together toward accomplishment of the tasks which it faced. As part of a large organizational development effort aimed at increasing the efficiency and effectiveness of workgroups throughout the corporation, work with the PPG was two-fold: (a) to increase the internal efficiency and effectiveness of the Personnel Department members, thus freeing them from some of the more pressing day-to-day problems and making them available as internal consultants to other parts of the line organization; and (b) to provide a methodological consulting model which would be useful in the PPG's work with others.

The problem of Personnel Department recruiting had been identified as one of the high-priority problems facing the PPG and was one which involved all the members of the PPG equally, with no indication of who had major responsibility for its solution. Moreover, the problem was in danger of being dropped or lost in the shuffle of other pressures and high-priority items. Consequently, it provided an ideal opportunity to test the organizational Q sort instrument and the theory behind it. There were several reasons why the problem and the organizational Q sort were well suited to each other in this particular situation:

1. Everyone in the PPG shared the problem.
2. There was uncertainty about how to solve the problem.
3. There had been no action to date.
4. PPG members were unsure how each one felt about the problem, or what anyone proposed to do about it.
5. PPG members were having a difficult time communicating their positions on the problem to one another.

At this point, the author suggested that perhaps the types of systematic data provided by the organizational Q-sort instrument might be helpful in obtaining diagnostic data about the problem. Then planning for appropriate action steps could be based on the data which the instrument would collect and organize. Readily concurring that the data could be helpful, PPG members agreed to provide the data by sorting the cards.

Q-SORT PROCEDURE AND RESULTS

Each member of the PPG was given two decks of cards. One deck was in the first person for self-perceptions, and the other deck was in the third person for perceptions of the Personnel Director. They were given instruction sheets, data sheets, and a Problem Card which stated the problem as follows: *How the Personnel Planning Group works on people selection for Personnel jobs.* The PPG members were asked to sort one deck of cards describing themselves and one deck of cards describing their perceptions of the personnel Director. Because of the Personnel Director's central role in the PPG and his dynamic style of leadership, it was hypothesized that a comparison between his self-perception relative to the problem versus others' perception of him relative to the problem might be essential in diagnosing it. The PPG members were asked to sort the two decks within the next few days and leave the data sheets with a secretary. They were instructed not to discuss the task with one another. The author collected the data sheets and did the visual and statistical analyses of the data in preparation for presenting a summary to the PPG at its next meeting.[5]

Most Characteristic, Least Characteristic, and Most Discrepant Items

The results were summarized and placed on charts. They were presented to the PPG at its next meeting with relatively little interpretation. Data showing the items which everyone agreed with Most Characteristic, Least Characteristic, and Most Discrepant aroused much more interest than did the correlational data, particularly when they were shown with the items everyone agreed were Most Characteristic, Least Characteristic, and Most Discrepant regarding perceptions of the Personnel Director. The correlational data mainly were useful in showing that every member in the group perceived his own behavior and feelings regarding the problem in very much the same way as did the others. The results reported to the PPG by the author-consultant were as follows:

1. *Items Everyone Agreed Were Most Characteristic of Themselves:*
   I need the resources of the others in order to solve the problem.
   I am open to new suggestions on how we should work on the problem.
2. *Items Everyone Agreed Were Least Characteristic of Themselves:*
   I tell the others what they should be doing.
   I try to get my way regardless of the others.

    I am suspicious of the others' motives.
    I never get credit for the good ideas I have.
    I keep my ideas to myself.
3. *Items on Which There Was Least Agreement:*
    I am taking leadership on the problem.
    I spend extra time and energy working on the problem.
    I work on the problem to the extent to which I am directed to do so.
    I feel free to do whatever I want in solving the problem.
    I communicate fully with the others.
    I'd rather let somebody else take the lead in the group.
    I don't ask for help even if I'm "stuck."

    A long discussion could have taken place concerning the wealth of information contained in the summarization presented above. For example, discussion of discrepant items could have been detailed and illuminating. Why did some people feel free to do whatever they wanted in solving the problem, and others not feel that way? One reason could be that people felt freedom as a result of the trust and/or full communication with the Personnel Director. Another explanation could be that people felt a lack of freedom because of dependence on the Personnel Director. Who in the group felt that he was taking leadership in working on the problem? Why will some people ask for help when they are "stuck" and others will not?

    In short, the instrument provided more information than the group basically needed to begin working on the problem. The discussion of the data centered instead on trying to determine what factors were inhibiting work on the problem. PPG members were interested to know, for example, how their perceptions of the Personnel Director differed from his perceptions of himself. After obtaining his consent to show the comparison, the data from the Personnel Director were presented.

1. *Items the Personnel Director Placed Most Characteristic:*
    I spend extra time and energy working on the problem.
    I need the resources of the others in order to solve the problem.
    I have a hard time communicating clearly.

The group quickly came to the conclusion that one of the things which was hampering progress on the problem was the fact that two of the items which they had agreed were Most Characteristic of the Personnel Director implied that he could solve the problem himself: "I have faith in my own ideas," and "I have a lot to say in the group's discussions." The Personnel Director, on the other hand, placed the item, "I need the resources of the others in order to solve the problem," as one of his three Most Characteristic items. In other words, the group began to see that perhaps each—that is, the group and the Personnel Director—was waiting for the other to take the lead in solving the problem, because no one had a workable solution in mind, but each felt that the other did. With the discovery that all agreed that they could not solve the problem alone and that everyone was open to new suggestions toward solution of the problem, the PPG began to work on it in earnest.

It should be noted that the discussion of the data gathered by the organizational Q sort on the problem of Personnel Department recruiting was originally expected to take about 15 minutes of a two-hour meeting. The group had planned then to go on to other matters on the agenda. After seeing the data summary, members actually began to work on the problem for more than two hours, pushing the other agenda items into the background. The discussion of the problem occurred because the instrument made some of the process issues, which were previously blocking work on the problem, explicit and, thereby, workable.

The Ideal Sort

In order to get some idea about how the members of the PPG would behave regarding the problem if the system were functioning ideally (as they all now hoped it would), the author also asked them to sort the cards on the same problem area at the time of the initial sorting, but with the problem stated as follows: *How the Personnel Planning Group ideally would work on people selection for Personnel jobs.* These data were collected and summarized in the same manner as before but were fed back to the group by means of a memorandum. The essential purpose of the use of the instrument in this manner was to provide a goal or direction for the PPG group in the same way that a consultant might provide direction. That is, if the group members were presented with their own *ideal* data concerning the problem area, then perhaps they would be inspired actually to behave in that way as work on the problem progressed. As was the case in the present study, when the initial data pertinent to the actual situation are reported back to the group members, they can easily see the implications of the data and begin to devise adaptive behaviors or methods of operation which *they are convinced* will improve things in the direction of *their goals.* Introducing an *ideal* sort at this point makes those adaptive behaviors explicit, and the group members can then determine whether or not they all agree that the means identified are best for moving them toward their goals.

DISCUSSION AND IMPLICATIONS

The organizational Q sort was used to gather individual perceptions about behavior and feelings regarding a problem that the Personnel Planning Group faced. The data were summarized and reported back to the group which then made some decisions regarding how it would work on the problem in the future. From this initial use of the instrument in an applied field setting, it seems clear that the instrument has value by providing relevant, helpful information to the organization using it. The information is most useful if it is gathered in relation to a particular organizational problem which is shared by all members of the subject group and which is recognized by all members of the group as an important problem to work on.

With the limited use the instrument has had in applied settings, it is difficult to assess all of its strengths and weaknesses. The primary strengths of the instrument appear to be the specificity and clarity of the interpersonal data it yields, its relevance to ongoing problems the organizational unit is experiencing, and its ease of administration and interpretation. The primary weaknesses which have appeared to date are that the instructions may focus the instrument on too specific a problem and that the instrument may be too heavily oriented toward interpersonal relations. For example, the problem around which the Personnel Planning Group sorted the cards was considered one of the high-priority problems facing the group when the initial sort was done. One week later, at its next meeting, a totally different problem facing the group had suddenly become the most important problem for members to spend time working on. In some ways, then, reporting back to the data from the instrument was seen as peripheral to that meeting because the problem to which the data were applicable was no longer so important as it previously had been. The question being raised is whether the instrument should have been designed to deal with such specific problem areas. Short-range problems can change radically or change in importance in a very short period of time. More experimentation with the instrument will provide more information on the question.

The idea of a small group's generating, analyzing, and using systematic data to guide itself is not original with the development of the organizational Q sort. The fields of group therapy and human relations training have been using a technique called instrumented or self-directed laboratories for some time (Berzon, 1964). These groups work toward greater self-awareness and insight with the frequent outcome of changed behavior and feelings. Although therapy groups and work-groups are dissimilar in many ways, the goal of change in the currrent method of operation often is similar. Instrumented laboratory and therapy groups rely on questionnaires, exercises, rating scales, and the like to provide the members of the group with data about their behavior, feelings, perceptions of others, and others' perceptions of them. The organizational Q sort provides similar data (albeit less intrapersonal) to members of small face-to-face workgroups with two important differences: (a) the data relate to a specific problem rather than generalized behavior and feelings in the group; and (b) the purpose of the instrument is to help the subjects to see directions in which behavior change would aid in solving the problem at hand rather than to increase the subjects' self-insight per se.

NOTES

1. The word "consultant" as used in this paper refers to an internal or external change agent.
2. Some of the more common independent variables which often are playing a major

determining role in subjects' behavior and which cannot easily be accounted for are such things as (a) organizational size and (b) stability of the system under study over time. Frequently, social scientists are trying to do longitudinal studies, and although the research subjects may be members of the organization throughout the entire study, some of the subjects' significant others may leave or change during the course of the study, thereby having a major effect on the subjects' behavior, such as a change in a company's top management. (c) Other factors in the exteral environment such as rise or fall in business volume often have a marked effect on many aspects of people's attitudes and behavior.

3. This viewpoint is supported by Chin (1961, p. 672).
4. The previous departmental structure had between six and eight different functions that reported to the Personnel Director.
5. However, the organizational Q-sort instrument could easily be utilized without the help of an outside consultant or researcher to administer and interpret it. A small amount of time and the ability to perform a correlational analysis of the data are the only requirements in using the instrument.

REFERENCES

BALES, R. F. *Interaction process analysis: A method for the study of small groups.* Cambridge, Mass.: Addison-Wesley, 1950.

BERZON, BETTY. The self-directed therapy group: An evaluative study. Unpublished manuscript. La Jolla, Calif.: Western Behavioral Sciences Institute, 1964.

BLOCK, J. *The Q-sort method in personality assessment and psychiatric research.* Springfield, Ill.: Charles C. Thomas, 1961.

CARTER, L. F., HAYTHORN, W., MEIROWITZ, BEATRICE, & LANZETTA, J. A note on a technique of interaction recording. *J. abnorm. soc. Psychol.*, 1951, *46*, 258-260. (a)

CARTER, L. F., HAYTHORN, W., MEIROWITZ, BEATRICE, & LANZETTA, J. The relation of categorizations and ratings in the observation of group behavior. *Human Relat.*, 1951, *4*, 239-254. (b)

CHAPPLE, E. D. The interaction chronograph: Its evolution and present application. *Personnel*, 1949, *25*, 295-307.

CHIN, R. Problems and prospects of applied research. In W. G. Bennis, K. D. Benne, & R. Chin (Eds.), *The planning of change.* New York: Holt, Rinehart & Winston, 1961.

GREEN, B. F. Attitude measurement. In Gardner Lindzey (Ed.), *Handbook of social psychology.* Reading, Mass.: Addison-Wesley, 1954.

HARE, A. P. (Ed.) *Handbook of small group research.* Glencoe, Ill.: Free Press, 1962.

HEMPHILL, J. K., & WESTIE, C. M. *Group dimensions descriptions questionnaire.* Columbus: Ohio State Univer., 1965.

LEAVITT, H. J. Applied organizational change in industry. In J. G. March (Ed.), *Handbook of organizations.* Chicago: Rand McNally, 1965. P. 1151 f.

MACCOBY, ELEANOR E., NEWCOMB, T. M., & HARTLEY, E. L. (Eds.) *Readings in social psychology.* New York: Holt, Rinehart & Winston, 1958.

McGREGOR, D. *The human side of enterprise.* New York: McGraw-Hill, 1960.

MARCH, J. G. (Ed.) *Handbook of organizations.* Chicago: Rand McNally, 1965.

MILES, M.B. *Innovation in education.* New York: Bureau of Publications, Teachers College, Columbia Univ., 1964.

SCHUTZ, W.C. *FIRO: A three-dimensional theory of interpersonal behavior.* New York: Holt, Rinehart & Winston, 1958.

STEPHENSON, W. *The study of behavior.* Chicago: Univer. of Chicago Press, 1953.

WAGNER, A.W. Analysis of personal behavior in groups. Questionnaire from unpublished doctoral dissertation. Cleveland, Ohio: Case Institute of Technology, 1965.

ZAND, D.E. Organizational development: Theory and practice, in press.

SECTION VI

TRAINING

EDITORS' OVERVIEW

Current OD technology evolved in large part from laboratory training methodology and continues to place a heavy reliance on training as an OD intervention. The three papers in this section illustrate the skillful use of training as an intervention for organizational change.

Levy provides a case study of how laboratory training became an integral part of a systematic change process. The "organizational renewal lab" has been a major training and change vehicle in his company. The lab is essentially an attempt to change the organization's norm of not examining the ways its members relate with one another in doing their jobs to a norm of continually examining these interpersonal processes.

The article by Schmuck, Runkel, and Langmeyer illustrates how training can be an effective OD intervention if designed and conducted so that the organization can make immediate use of it. Unlike the other authors in this section, who worked with manufacturing organizations, Schmuck et al. worked with a public school faculty.

The case study by Dyer, Maddocks, Moffitt, and Underwood emphasizes not only the importance of preparing for immediate transfer of learning, but also the role of the OD specialist in this process. Their paper also helps us to understand more about the use of training as an entry process for OD.

THE PROCESS OF ORGANIZATIONAL RENEWAL - ONE COMPANY'S EXPERIENCES

Seymour Levy

Historically, organizations have been confronted with the problem of optimizing relationships with their environment in order to achieve their purposes. They have been required to sense dominant trends in their environment and to develop productive responses. In more recent years, another need has been evolving: the need for organizations to develop strategies to improve their internal workings in order to utilize their resources more effectively.

The process of organization development—of improving internal problem-solving processes—as it has evolved in a particular industrial organization is the theme of this paper. The rapid escalation of organizational development suggests that it should be a dominant force in effecting social change in our society in the future. The sharing of experiences, ideas, and designs can be a stimulus to additional research and development.

The organization of this paper is as follows:

—A brief history of the initial events contributing to the organization's recognition of its need to create a process of continuous organizational renewal

—A series of beliefs and assumptions underlying the development of the concept of organizational renewal at the Pillsbury Company

—The design of an organizational renewal lab

—Some observations of the consequences of such a lab and some hypotheses regarding the conditions underlying continuous organizational renewal.

A brief description of the history of the development process is appropriate. In 1960 and 1961, attitude surveys administered to the management group revealed some major problems in coordination of effort and decision making.

An analysis suggested that some of the psychological processes underlying our major problems might be functions of the kinds of attitudes, perceptions, and values that we had with respect to people. We were more evaluative and judgmental than analytic, and more evaluative than supportive in our feelings about people. A strong emphasis was placed on individualism and individual rewards in contrast to team action and cooperation. Committees, groups, and teams were all "bad" words in our society, and themes like openness, supportiveness, and integrative conflict resolution were infrequently emphasized. Issues of trust versus suspicion were also common. All this led us to suppose that many of our company's problems might be related to our value systems. An analysis of some survey data made it possible to test and confirm this supposition and its organizational consequences in a way that clearly indicated to the top management group the relationship between value systems and organizational dysfunctioning.

The recommendation was then made to make available opportunities for relearning and reexamining value systems, using the methodologies developed by the National Training Laboratories. Shortly thereafter, a number of key executives participated in some National Training Laboratories sessions and returned with strong recommendations that we develop an internal program. After a period of outside seedings at NTL Key Executive Labs, Robert R. Blake was invited in December 1963 to present a seminar to groups of top-level managers. Subsequently a number of other managerial groups participated in a Phase I Grid Laboratory. After several Managerial Grid Labs were conducted, the Manpower Development and Training Section of our company developed its own versions of instrumented labs tailored for each of three groups: sales management, production management, and general management.

Since that time, most managers in the company have participated in an initial "orientation" lab experience as well as in an organizational renewal lab, the major subject of this paper.

The initial lab experience within the organization is considered to be a critical first step in the organization renewal process. Although the specific content of the instrumented lab designs varies for sales, production, and general management people, the major focus is the same: to examine one's own values with regard to openness, trust, and experimentation. In our view, the major purpose of the orientation laboratory experience is to give organizational legitimacy to the process of giving and receiving feedback. In addition, significant strides are taken toward developing a common language and shared meanings with respect to values that have behavioral significance, such as honesty, openness, trust, conflict, and group decision making. These orientation labs provide the platform for individual participation in the organizational renewal lab design.

THE CONCEPT OF ORGANIZATIONAL DEVELOPMENT

In discussing the organizational renewal lab and its design, some brief comments are made about the concept of organizational development and the assumptions underlying its design. In addition, a "typical" design is presented and some of the results and consequences of the organizational renewal labs are reviewed.

The concept of organizational development is of very recent origin and owes much to the thinking of Bradford, Bennis, Blake, and John Gardner. Organizations have been concerned about development in the past, but this concern has focused on the development of isolated individuals as targets of change. Modifying skills, attitudes, knowledge, and motivation were deemed to be the significant goals of a developmental action program.

The group dynamist and the social critic both emphasize the need for expanded definitions of the target of change to include not only the individual, but the small team, task force and department, as well as the total organization. The need to recognize the team or the organization as a target for change stems from social psychological conceptions of individual behavior as rooted within group membership. Moreover, the relationship between groups becomes a critical issue for improvement when one recognizes that in a sense organizations are a collection of interdependent groups.

The process of changing involves first the diagnosis and then planning action steps with the emphasis that the responsibility for change lies within the individual and the organization. With the shift in focus from the individual to groups and organizations as targets of change, there has been a corresponding shift in the definition of the changing process. Rather than defining change as the acquisition of concrete skills or knowledge, we now define it as the development of a system in which a process of continuous renewal can occur, a system that has the capacity for planned, self-corrective activities. Hence, organizational development intends to bring about change in an organization's feelings about its responsibility for effecting planned change and in its skills to maintain a process of continuous renewal.

Just as the targets of development and change have been shifting, the criteria for examining an organization have been expanding. Organizations are moving away from programmed sets of behaviors, a condition in which past achievements are used to estimate future achievements, where comparison with the past can be used as a measure of present performance, and where hard data is available for evaluating task and organizational achievement. They are moving toward a point where process criteria such as the quality of integration of effort and the quality of the decision-making process are used as criteria for reviewing an organization's performance. Thus, one definition of organizational functioning has shifted from a simple technical-economic system to a socio-technical-economic system—a much broader frame of reference—with the need to consider such variables as organizational commitment in addition to such classic variables as costs, return on investment, and shrink.

It has been our assumption that the conditions leading to an effective renewal process are also the conditions leading to an effective work performance process for individuals and groups in organizations. At Pillsbury we believe that the need to build and maintain a competence- and confidence-building system is a requirement for an effective working system.

We propose that there are two critical dimensions necessary to create effective work performance in individuals and in organizations. The effective individual or effective group possesses (a) high confidence, courage, and conviction and (b) high competence and creativity required for execution of the tasks. The concepts of confidence and competence are applicable at both the individual and team levels.

Thus, there is an emotional-motivational as well as task component variable in determining the overall productivity of an individual as well as a team. The critical issue for the organization is to create conditions under which individuals (and teams) have confidence in themselves and are willing to take risks—are able to show courage at the same time that they try to expand their own competence in their specialized tasks. The therapeutic model and the group dynamics model clearly suggest that courage and confidence have an interpersonal locus and that a basic condition for increasing task competence is to create a feedback system. Task achievement information is useful in expanding the competence dimension, and socio-emotional messages can be useful in enhancing the realistic confidence dimension.

The first step in creating an organizational climate which is confidence-and competence-building is to develop and foster a data exchange system. Valid data must become available as members need feedback, both cognitive and affective information. Since one operating assumption is that the issues that cannot be talked about are generally the ones that "hang us up," the feedback system assumes a major role in determining organizational and individual productivity.

Yet, before a data exchange system can be created, it is essential to create conditions of trust, openness, and supportiveness. It is also necessary to develop norms that support the cooperative resolution of conflict. Thus normative change is both a condition and a consequence of an effective organizational renewal lab. The virtue of doing this with a total organization at a moment in time is essentially the value of communicating the same signal to everyone and having everyone then hear the same subsequent echoes. This is in great contrast to a model of change in which executives are sent off, one by one, to outside organizational labs.

We have learned the inevitability, circularity, and interdependence between openness and trust. As openness increases, generally so does trust. As trust increases, so does openness. While we cannot manipulate trust directly, we can try to create greater openness by opening up the channels for data flow, thus increasing trust.

The feedback system then becomes the self-corrective feature necessary to maintain and improve performance. Actually, the renewal process is dependent upon the organization's creating the conditions in which individuals receive data that enable them to look at their performance and situation realistically and also become motivated and encouraged to take steps that are necessary to improve their situaton.

Another underlying assumption of organizational development is that individuals have more elbow room and freedom than they normally use and unwittingly place restraints upon their own freedom of action. Similarly, groups have more power and influence than they normally wield and unconsciously tend to place limitations upon themselves. Just as individuals and teams place some restraints on the degree to which they trust others, they also have less than complete acceptance and trust of themselves. Our objective was to create situations in which individuals and teams felt that they could rely on themselves and were expected to do so.

Another part of the conceptual framework for change is to emphasize concurrent rather than sequential developmental activities. The assumption is that the *concurrence* of diagnosis and planning by a number of groups *simultaneously* has a greater effect on the total organization than the planning done by one group at a time in a sequential fashion. There is a social facilitation effect whereby individuals recognize that others are engaging in the same process as themselves at the same moment in time and more importantly that the total organization, rather than just an isolated, independent group, is making a commitment in a particular direction.

Fear and apprehension are fairly constant companions in a hierarchially organized society where the assumption is that "he who moves up is to be valued and to be esteemed." Related to this is the assumption of a malevolent intention on the part of another group toward one's own. From a design point of view this means that one needs to recognize that fear will be higher earlier in the week than later in the week and that individuals need to move into a situation where their assumption of malevolent intent is disconfirmed or is confirmed and the issues are confronted.

Another way of viewing an organizational renewal lab is to suggest that the task of an organization is to integrate and achieve diverse goals. This includes an *integration* of individual goals with the organization's mission, as well as an integration of different department goals. Developing conditions then for achieving integration and congruency is a critical mission of the organizational renewal laboratory. The determinants of congruency basically involve the development of a communications system that fosters the exchange of clear, understood messages and also the presence of said technology that facilitates the resolution of intergroup differences in goals or choice of means to attain goals.

Below the structural as well as chronological design of an organizational renewal lab are presented. By *organization* we mean a multilayer hierarchy composed of a number of functions or departments (more than two) that need to interact with each other to accomplish an overall organizational goal. Thus a divisional group that would include the usual functional groups of sales, production, marketing, etc., would be an organization, as would an information systems department with its planning group, operations group, and operations research group.

ORGANIZATIONAL RENEWAL LAB—THE DESIGN

The lab design is based on the assumption that there are multiple targets for change—the individual, the team, and the organization as a whole. The major processes or conditions for change are the diagnostic phase and the goal-setting phase (see Figure I). The figure includes six cells which represent the major aspects of an organizational lab design.

FIGURE 1

Process and Target Design for Organizational Renewal Lab

Targets for Change

PROCESS	Individual	Team	Organization
Diagnosis	(a)	(b)	(c)
Goal Setting Planning Action	(d)	(e)	(f)

a. How do I work as a member of this team?

b. How well does this team work together?

c. How well do we integrate our efforts and how well does the top team work together?

d. What goals and plans do I need to establish to increase my own effectiveness?

e. What goals and plans do we (this team) need to increase our effectiveness?

f. What goals and plans does this organization need to increase its effectiveness?

These major diagnostic questions may be answered from multiple frames of reference. The success of the lab depends upon the ingenuity of the internal consultant in developing procedures to confront the individual, the team, and the organization with data on their own behavior.

A variety of instruments are available that can be useful, such as the Personnel Relations Survey developed by J. Hall. This instrument provides an individual with a reflection of his own reported tendencies toward giving and asking for feedback from subordinates, colleagues, and superiors. Attitude survey questionnaires can be used to provide data to teams as well as to the organization. Results from these questionnaires can be fed back to the concerned individuals, thereby providing them with frames of reference for developing insights about their own thinking. In Pillsbury we use the same basic set of questions over time. This enables us to evaluate attitudinal trends. One last word: The greatest psychological data-gathering instrument ever invented is the 3" X 5" index card, which can also be used to obtain data quickly about issues in the "here and now" environment.

Team functioning can also be diagnosed or assessed in a variety of ways: a team can look at itself and use its own frame of reference, or a team can be the object of the perceptions of the other teams that interface with it. Intergroup perceptions generally provide a very provocative and useful intervention in a laboratory. Our experience suggests that it is better to have intergroup perceptions occur before a team examines its own functioning. When a team has to cope with others' assumed views of its behavior, it truly widens and increases its own understanding of its internal organization.

In the goal-setting process we normally go through two stages: the individual or team (a) spends time formulating goals and outlining some plans to achieve them, and (b) shares its goals with others with the intent of testing the validity of each goal and the appropriateness of the plan. This public exchange has the advantage of developing a greater public commitment to the goal and a plan for its achievement.

The design of the lab resembles the notions of Blake and his specifications of a Phase II and Phase III design. In Phase II an organization examines itself through the perspective of individual teams. In Phase III Blake introduces interteam problem solving. We have found that the *concurrent* development of these activities is mutually reinforcing in terms of facilitating intrateam as well as interteam effectiveness. Teams become data-saturated and find it difficult to avoid the central issues. The wide-open data exchange is the medium and perhaps, following McLuhan, also the central message ("let's keep it open around here").

In the design of these organizational renewal labs, we have often used introductory tasks to get people interacting and reacquainted. We may have tasks dealing with listening skill, or show a film to demonstrate some concepts regarding management, or present some concepts and practices with respect to improved team functioning, or arrange a group-observing-group phenomenon, or review progress toward goals set at a prior meeting.

The group then embarks on a cycle of individual-, team-, and organization-wide diagnostic and planning activities. Figure II is a chronological outline of a fairly typical organizational renewal lab's design. After a period of orientation and introduction to some organizational data on the first day, the design focuses largely on interdepartmental relationships the second day. The third day deals with intrateam relationships and includes feedback to individuals on their competencies in carrying out their jobs. The last two days (or the fourth and fifth days) involve the development of goals and plans. Often the top team meets together to work through their working relationships while the subordinate groups develop proposals to improve interdepartmental relationships. The concluding session is the presentation of the goals and plans of each of the departments.

Results of Organizational Renewal Labs: The objective of the organizational renewal lab is to create a sustaining, mutual confidence- and task competence-building system that leads to greater individual satisfaction and organizational productivity.

Let's look at some of the changes in behavior at the individual level as reported by the supervisor as well as by the individual in light of these objectives. Supervisors report many changes in behavior of lab participants, including—

—Becoming a better listener.
—Becoming more assertive.
—Behaving with greater openness.
—Becoming more aware of needs of interdependence with others.
—Becoming less dogmatic.
—Developing plans for his own growth—recognizing need for personal development.

FIGURE 2

"Typical" Organization Renewal Lab Design

DAYS 1	2	3	4	5
MORNING				
Orientation experiences: Exercises Warmup	Development of intergroup per- perceptions of re- lationships	Within-team analysis of cli- mate and working relationships	Top team meets to ex- amine its rela- tionships .	Public ex- change of team goals and plans
AFTERNOON			.	
A review of orga- nizational achievements related to prior goal setting	Feedback of inter- departmental relationship per- ceptions	(Personal feedback (about individual (performance in (working teams ((((	Other persons are involved in across-team problem-solv- ing or develop- ment of tenta- tive goals and plans	
EVENING		((		
Feedback of survey results of organi- zational and indi- vidual data	Across-department problem-solving	((((	Individual and team goal setting	

—Becoming aware of lack of communication upward.

—Becoming more sensitive to how he or she is perceived by others.

Changes have also been measured by psychological tests of the individuals before and after labs. For example, the Rotter internal-external Locus of Causation scale, which reflects whether an individual perceives man as an agent of change or as the object of events, shows a significant increase in the degree to which managers who have partici-pated in the lab see man, (presumably themselves) as determining his own destiny. This is consistent with the expectations of increased self-confidence and feelings of personal power as a legitimate result of the laboratory process.

When managers are asked to report on changes in how the division or department may be operating, they most frequently emphasize im-provement of interdepartmental functioning, followed by better plan-ning and operating. A series of interviews was held with persons who had participated in an organizational lab three months earlier. Kinds of organizational changes that were spontaneously reported included—

—Being better informed.

—Developing better relationships with the field.

—Better understanding of the decision process.

—More sympathetic understanding of one's problems by others.
—Better relationships with other departments—more unity and coordination.
—Things "talked about" are now being done.
—Earlier involvement in projects.
—Improved understanding of the organization—who does what.
—More issues are getting on the table—the personal hangups of the other guy are getting cleared up.
—New projects have been created that involve collaboration between new people.
—Better feedback and more openness with superior.
—Improved priority setting and better managing.

We have also assessed organizational changes by administering a questionnaire similar to the one used as a prelab survey instrument. Six months after one organizational lab, the participants were posed with a questionnaire dealing with the session and were asked to reflect on the worthwhileness of the lab. The results were as follows:

Not at all worthwhile	2%
Slightly worthwhile	—%
Somewhat worthwhile	2%
Quite worthwhile	22%
Very worthwhile	48%
Extremely worthwhile	22%

Using some of the scales developed by Larry Greiner in his thesis research, we can report several significant differences between pre- and post-perceptions of individuals who participated in an organizational lab. Six months after the lab significantly more managers report that—

—Their supervisor is a person who stands behind them on important issues.
—Their work group now discusses their differences openly in meetings.
—An individual can now take the initiative in introducing new topics for discussion during the work group meetings.
—Meetings are resulting in important decisions, being worked out, and individuals are leaving meetings with a willingness to work on the decisions made in the meeting.
—There is increased approval for group members who raise sensitive problems for discussion.
—There is decreased approval for members who prefer to keep their opinions to themselves, rather than "putting their cards on the table."

Significantly, positive changes were also found in the way individuals evaluated the division in terms of "coordination between departments" and "getting decisions made." The interdepartmental coordination items are generally the ones with the greatest changes.

Other observed changes resulting from the labs involve the relationship between the individual and the organization and how the top team and other departments feel and act about the future. There is a significant rise in expectations of individuals with respect to their need to know how well they are doing and have superior performance rewarded. Individuals become more critical of the organization and how it lets them know how they are doing. My conjecture is that individuals, as a function of the organizational critique, develop greater investment in the organization and commit greater energies to it to achieve their own and the organization's goals. Concurrently they feel a need for increased concern and respect from the organization. This parallels some of the Levinson notions of reciprocity in organizations. Thus, as a consequence of greater involvement, there are greater expectations of returns and rewards from the organization, reflecting the wisdom of Billie Dawn in "Born Yesterday," who declared, "If he don't come across, I don't come across." Conversely, if I as a manager come across, I now expect the organization to come across.

Teams also often change their ways of planning and thinking about the future. From an organization renewal point of view, this is an extremely important finding. Teams become more concerned about their strategic planning responsibilities. My hypothesis is that this strategic planning issue arises as a function of the increased respect and regard the teams have for each other, which in turn is a function of the individuals' increased identification with the organization. The individual's respect for others leads him to say, "I am willing to commit myself to shape the future with these other persons." When one has little regard for one's colleagues, there is very little press to have a department or group engage in a strategic planning process. In this situation of low regard, the individual is engaging in his own solo strategic plan that may involve excess or subversion of nonconcern for the others. Interpersonal anxiety leads to a focus on the present, and individuals lose a sense of the future. Increases in cohesion lead to an increased time perspective. This suggests that strategies involving member participation and involvement create some of the conditions that underlie the development of strategic versus tactical operating plans.

These remarks should not be interpreted as suggesting that organizational labs successfully deal with all problems of organizations and hierarchies. Within an organization clearly there are different management style preferences. Some individuals are deeply committed to a team approach, and for these people organizational labs make integral sense. There are also managers who prefer to operate at a distance from their people, and from this point of view a lab with the attendant openness and frankness becomes a threatening social situation and one that is to be avoided. There are some individuals whose lack of freedom with emotional data is such that they try to suppress and deny the validity of these issues, and for them the lab may not be too fruitful.

There are some persons to whom business morality means that you do not talk about people—personalities; they find it very difficult to be asked to be candid and direct about their views of another's performance.

Not only personal styles operate against an effective organizational lab. Issues too may pose real difficulties. While the Peter Principle may be that in hierarchies each individual rises to the level of his incompetence, Levy's Law is that in hierarchies, "the higher you go, the tougher is the fighting for the next spot." Thus, there are some real issues with respect to power needs and the competition for the ultimate position in the hierarchy. In the ultimate political struggle, sometimes openness is not the best vehicle. Sometimes the political maneuvering is brought out into the open and the pressure from peers leads to finding a better resolution of the issue.

Over the years, organizational development labs have been composed of multiple team organizations ranging from as few as 12 to as many as 70. The retreat may last anywhere from two to five days. A number of groups at Pillsbury have been developing these sessions on a recurring systematic basis: one division has had four organizational retreats of four to five days duration in the last six years; another major department has its annual retreat every September.

CONTINUOUS SELF-EXAMINATION

The critical issue is to create the conditions which allow the process of organizational self-examination to become a continuous one. These conditions are not as yet fully understood. The following are hypotheses about the conditions tending to create the institutional process of continuous self-examination at Pillsbury:

1. The individual managers find learning, merit, and organizational value in the process and thus see it as worthwhile.
2. Managers see other managers as engaging in a process and thus there is some suggestion of "keeping up with the Joneses."
3. There is an attempt to try to develop a follow-up process to the goals and plans that have been developed at the meeting with the aim of trying to facilitate the achievement of these goals. Planning leads to the need for a review session.
4. Sometimes new organizational forms get created as a function of these sessions, and these forms develop their own vitality and inspire the organization to develop further critique processes.
5. As additional sessions are held, it is easier for leveling to occur and as greater leveling occurs, greater payoffs result. Thus, each review sessions is generally better than the last one and serves to raise expectations for future sessions.
6. The support of top management clearly exists. It is reflected when the chief officer publicly says, as he reflects on a complex situation, "Now if Lee Bradford (current director of NTL Labs) were here, he

would . . . ." and then proceeds to behave in the way he thinks Lee would. His internalization of this model becomes a clear signal to other members of the organization as to where the chief officer stands. This support is a very important element in establishing the legitimacy of a process that involves, for example, managers' absenting themselves from the organization for four to five days at a time.

7. On the business side, there is an emphasis upon a systematic monitoring of our economic process. The renewal lab design is consistent and congruent with this process of reviewing earnings and learnings.

CONCLUSION

We have described the history of one organization's attempt to institutionalize the process for facilitating continuous, individual, and organizational growth. In trying to create the conditions of an open, vital society, we recognize that all organizations evolve but at different rates. Our concern has been to speed up the rate of adaptive evolution that the organization requires to exist, expand, and contribute in today's society.

The change agent in the early stages of this process was quite anxious about the issue of possible imposition of his own values upon the organizational functioning. That is, were the values a reflection of the needs of the change agent or did these values in reality contribute significantly to individual fulfillment and organizational achievement?

Over the years his anxiety has disappeared with the development of a conviction that these values are functional both for individual as well as for the organization's continued growth.

IMPROVING ORGANIZATIONAL PROBLEM SOLVING IN A SCHOOL FACULTY*

(The 1969 Douglas McGregor Memorial Award-Winning Article)

Richard A. Schmuck, Philip J. Runkel and Daniel Langmeyer

The intervention detailed here was aimed at improving the flexible organizational problem solving of a junior high school faculty. It was pointed toward organizational development, not personal change. Even though the emotional reactions of faculty members were considered in designing the training events, our intervention remained fixed on organizational roles and norms and their interrelationships. We hoped to learn whether improved organizational functioning could be produced in a faculty by integrating group training in communication and problem solving with the normal business of the school. We began our intervention just prior to the academic year and returned intermittently until February.

Data evaluating the effects of the intervention support the claim that a number of salutary outcomes were at least partly due to the intervention. Movement in favorable directions occurred in a number of concrete, observable organizational changes, in verbally expressed attitudes about the principal and staff meetings, in the kinds of innovations reported, and in the changing organizational norms of the faculty. Strengths and weaknesses of the intervention are discussed.

*The research detailed here was supported by the Center for the Advanced Study of Educational Administration. CASEA is a national research and development center established under the Cooperative Research Program of the U.S. Office of Education. We wish to thank the faculty of the Highland Park Junior High School, Beaverton, Oregon, for their collaboration. This project will be reported at monographic length by Schmuck and Runkel (in press).

Richard A. Schmuck is professor of educational psychology and a research associate at the Center for the Advanced Study of Educational Administration, University of Oregon. Philip J. Runkel is professor of psychology and a research associate at the Center for the Advanced Study of Educational Administration. Daniel Langmeyer is assistant professor of psychology, University of Cincinnati.

INTRODUCTION

Like many organizations with traditional modes of operation, schools are suffering stresses to which their customary practices seem ill-adapted. When faced with massive changes in the community, there are at least two strategies a school can adopt. One is for the school to remodel itself into a form maximally adapted to the new demands of the community, e.g., the middle school, the campus school, the unitized school, and the community school. The other strategy is to build new norms and procedures that enable the school constantly to monitor the changing community, to compare the results of its own reactions with what it would accept as movement toward its goals, and to establish new forms whenever the movement toward the goals falls below a criterion. This latter kind of strategy we call *flexible organizational problem solving.* John Gardner (1963) has called it *self-renewal* and Walter Buckley (1967) has referred to it as *morphogenesis.* The purpose of this project was to improve the capability of a school for organizational problem solving.

From the point of view of research, our purpose was to test whether improved organizational problem solving could be produced in a school faculty by training in interpersonal communication skills, where the group processes to be altered and the methods of doing so were consistent with McGregor's (1967) thinking. We assumed, along with McGregor, that functions within organizations are "carried" through interpersonal interactions and that heightening abilities for organizational problem solving must commence with new norms for interpersonal openness and helpfulness. In seeking a lever with which to change group norms, we adopted McGregor's strategy:

. . . to provide opportunities for members of the organization to obtain intrinsic rewards from contributions to the success of the enterprise. . . . The task is to provide an appropriate environment—one that will permit and encourage employees to seek intrinsic rewards *at work* (pp. 13-14).

We did this by inviting the faculty to state the frustrations they encountered in the school and to practice a sequence of problem-solving steps to reduce these frustrations. This activity led to reduced frustrations and to the satisfaction of knowing that others valued the contribution one had made to outcomes highly desired by the faculty. It also facilitated changes in organizational norms by requiring staff members to behave in new ways in the actual workgroup where others could observe the new behaviors and see that their colleagues actually accepted the new patterns of behavior in the setting of the school.

In designing this intervention, we made strong use of the laboratory method (Bradford, Gibb, & Benne, 1964). The training often called for conscious observations of the group processes of the faculty; the design required actually practicing new behaviors before using them in daily work. Although the design made use of the school as its own laboratory, we made use of laboratory groups in ways very different from sensitivity training or the T Group. Personal development was not our target. We did not attempt to improve the interpersonal functioning of individuals when this occurred, it was incidental. Our targets were the faculty as a whole and several subgroups within it. We sought to increase the effectiveness of groups as task-oriented entities. We tried to teach subgroups within the school, and the faculty as a whole, to function more effectively as working bodies carrying out specific tasks in that particular job setting. This strategy of training was supported by a recent review of research by Campbell and Dunnette (1968) on the transfer of skills from T Groups to organizations. They found that a T Group, as ordinarily conducted with focus on individual growth in a setting away from the job and without guided application to workaday tasks, has had little effect on organizational development.

In comparison with other efforts at bringing about more effective organizational functioning in schools, our intervention contained a unique combination of three features. First, our training took place with actual groups from the school we sought to affect. Of equal importance, we carried on training with the entire staff of the school, including secretaries, the head cook, and head custodian, as well as all the faculty and its administrators. Finally, during the training, especially in its early parts, we rotated sizes and memberships of subgroups so that every pair of staff members interacted with each other in more than one kind of group.

TRAINING GOALS

The major training goals were developed out of a conception of flexible organizational problem solving. It was hoped that the faculty of our experimental school would establish a continuing series of activities for improving its own communication—we held this to be a minimum necessity. Further, we hoped that participation at faculty meetings as well as the initiation of attempts at influence would spread to more and more members of the faculty. We strove to help the faculty increase its discussions about interpersonal or inter-role problems and to continue to make conscious use of a sequential problem-solving technique. A related goal was that the teachers would show increased initiative in solving problems they were having with those in higher echelons and that the initiator of an idea would test his idea more frequently than previously with a lower-echelon subgroup before carrying it to the administration. By far the most significant goals had to do with structural and instructional changes in the school. We hoped that the staff would invent some new organizational forms within their school or at least borrow some from our training that would help them to confront problems continuously. Finally, we wanted the teachers to find some uses for the new forms and methods from the training that would have effects on their classroom instruction.

We supplemented these broad goals with more specific ones in designing the initial training events that centered on interpersonal skills and systematic problem solving. We hoped first to build increased openness and ease of interpersonal communication among the faculty by training them in the skills of paraphrasing, describing behavior, describing own feelings, and perception checking. We hoped that through skillful, constructive openness with one another the staff would develop an increased confidence in the worthwhile outcomes deriving from improved communication. We hoped to increase skills of giving information to others about their behaviors and of receiving information about one's own behavior. After increasing communication skills, we hoped to stimulate skill development in using a systematic problem-solving procedure and in helping colleagues to enunciate clearly ideas that might develop into practical plans for solving organizational problems.

THE INTERVENTION

We assumed that the faculty members of our experimental school would be likely to attempt new interpersonal procedures if they could first practice them away from the immediate demands of the school day. At the same time, we assumed that transfer of training to the everyday work of the building would be maximized if the faculty expected to continue problem-solving activities on their own after each training event and if the training design called for additional training some weeks and months following the first event. Within this general framework for transfer of organizational training, we made several other assumptions.

We felt that communication could be improved, that feelings of solidarity could be increased, and that power differences could be clarified if virtually every pair of persons on the faculty were brought into face-to-face interaction during the initial training period. Second, we thought that the initial input during training should pose a discrepancy between the ideal and actual performances of the faculty. Out of confrontations with discrepancies would come problem solving. We felt that applications to the work of the school building would be maximized if the faculty dealt with real organizational problems even during the first week of training. Furthermore, we thought that training in a series of overlapping small groups would help individuals to use the skills learned in one group in each of the next training groups, and subsequently, to transfer the accumulated skills to groups in which they work ordinarily. Finally, we assumed that the transfer of the communication and problem-solving skills to the school would be facilitated if the faculty members conceptualized the possible applications of the skills and made plans to try them out in the real school setting.

The training commenced with a six-day laboratory in late August of 1967. Staff members present included almost the entire building staff other than students. There were 54 trainees: all the administrators, all the faculty but two, the head cook, head custodian, and head secretary. The first two days were spent in group exercises designed to increase awareness of interpersonal and organizational processes: e.g., the NASA trip-to-the-moon exercise, the five-square puzzle, and the hollow-square puzzle. Although these excercises were gamelike, they demonstrated the importance of clear and effective communication for accomplishing a task collaboratively. After each exercise, small groups discussed ways in which the experience was similar to or different from what usually happened in their relations with one another in the school.

All staff members then came together to pool their experiences and to analyze their relationships as a faculty. Each small group chose its own way to report what it had experienced. Openness and giving and receiving feedback about perceptions of real organizational processes in the school were supported by the trainers. Brief but specific training was given in clear communication, overcoming difficulties in listening, and skills in describing another's behaviors. Selected nonverbal exercises augmented this practice.

The faculty devoted the last four days to a problem-solving sequence, working on real issues that were thwarting the organizational functioning of the school. After a morning of discussion and decisions, which also served as practice in the skills of decision making, three problems emerged as the most significant:

1. *Insufficient role clarity*, especially in the roles of principal, vice principal, counselors, and area (departmental) coordinators.
2. *Failure to draw upon staff resources*, especially between academic areas but also within subject-matter specialities.
3. *Low staff involvement and low participation at meetings* of committees, areas, and the full faculty.

Three groups formed, each to work through a problem-solving sequence directed toward one of these problems. Each group followed a procedure consisting of five steps: (a) identifying the problem through behavioral description, (b) diagnostic force-field analysis, (c) brainstorming to find actions likely to reduce restraining forces, (d) designing a concrete plan of action, and (e) trying out the plan behaviorally through a simulated activity involving the entire staff. Each of the three groups carried through its sequence of steps substantially on its own; the trainers served as facilitators, rarely providing substantive suggestions and never pressing for results.

The group concerned with clarifying roles reasoned that an ambiguous role often served as a defense and that a first step must be to increase trust among the faculty. Accordingly, this group carried out four nonverbal exercises to increase trust among the faculty. The group working on better use of staff resources set up eight subgroups, each of which was to pretend to be a junior high faculty trying to avert a crisis due to lack of texts; each group then developed curricula by drawing upon one another's resources. The group concerned with low staff involvement arranged for three groups to have discussions on role clarification, staff resources, and staff involvement. During the discussions, the more loquacious members were asked one after another to stop participating until there were only two members left. Discussions were then held in each group on feelings about involvement on the staff.

The first week of the training culminated with a discussion to highlight the resources of the staff. Staff members described their own strengths and those of their colleagues. Finally, they discussed what their school could be like if all the strengths of the faculty were used.

During the early fall, we interviewed all faculty members and observed a number of committees and subject-area groups to determine
what uses they were making of the first week of training. The data
indicated that problems still unresolved were communicative misunderstandings, role overload, and capabilities for group problem solving.

The second intervention for training with the entire staff was held
during one and one-half days in December. In this session we attempted
to increase the effectiveness of the area coordinators as communication
links between teachers and administrators, to increase problem-solving
skills of the area groups and the Principal's Advisory Committee, to help
the faculty explore ways of reducing role overload, and to increase
effective communication between service personnel and the rest of the
staff. Training activities included communication exercises, problem-
solving techniques, decision-making procedures, and skill development
in group observations and feedback. On the first day, area (departmental) groups applied problem-solving techniques to their own communication difficulties and received feedback from observing area
groups on their methods of work. Problems raised in area groups were
brought to a meeting of the Principal's Advisory Committee held the next
day in front of the rest of the staff. The staff observed the advisory
committee in a fishbowl arrangement, participated in specially designed ways, and later gave feedback on how effectively the committee
had worked and how accurately members had represented them.

The third training intervention also lasted one and one-half days
and took place in February. The main objective was to "take stock of"
how the staff had progressed since the workshop in solving the problems of using resources, of role clarity, and of staff participation, and to
revivify any lagging skills. A group discussion of each problem area was
held. Each teacher was left free to work in the group considering the
problem that most interested him. Each group discussed the positive
and negative outcomes associated with its problem. For example, in the
group discussing staff participation, the question was: "In what ways
has staff participation improved and where has it failed to improve?"
The group wrote out examples of improvements, no changes, and
regression in staff participation. The groups then focused on the negative instances and tried to think of ways to eliminate them by modifying
organizational processes in the school. Faculty members continued with
this activity in small groups during the spring without our presence.

ORGANIZATIONAL CHANGES

One source of evidence for the effects of the training came in the
form of concrete, observable changes in the behaviors of faculty and
administration in our experimental school. These data were taken
primarily from spontaneous events that were later reported to us and
corroborated by the parties involved or by disinterested observers.
These actions were not directly a part of our planned training events

and therefore constituted movements in the direction of increased flexible organizational problem solving.

About three months after the first week of training, a sample of faculty members were interviewed and also were asked to write essays on the effects of the training. From these data we discovered that at least 19 teachers were applying techniques learned in the organizational training to improve the group processes in their classrooms. Application typically involved such group procedures as "using small groups for projects," "using nonverbal exercises to depict feelings about the subject matter being studied," "using theatre-in-the-round or fishbowl formations for having students observe one another," "using a paraphrasing exercise to point out how poor classroom communications are," "using the problem-solving sequence and techniques in social studies classes to learn more about social problems," and "using small groups for giving and receiving feedback about how the class is going." As far as we know, none of these practices was used by these teachers before the organizational development laboratory.

Previous to our intervention, a group of eight teachers called the "Teach Group" was granted freedom to alter schedules, classroom groupings, assignment of teachers to classes, and other logistics in attempts to maximize their educational impact on a selected group of students. The group, made up mostly of area coordinators, received many negative reactions from other staff members. They were envied, misunderstood, and often engaged in conflict with others, with the result that their innovative ideas were more often resisted than emulated. However, the organizational training seemed to reduce the distrust, and the end of the year saw the Teach Group's type of collaboration extended to twice as many teachers. At the same time, two other teachers decided to form another team in order to gain some of the advantages of mutual stimulation and the sharing of resources.

The Principal's Advisory Committee, made up of administrators and area coordinators, was raised from advisory status to a more powerful force in the school. It became a representative senate with decision-making prerogatives. During the training event in December, the members of this group delineated and accepted their roles as representatives of their areas and as gatherers of information for the upper-echelon administrators. Later, an actual occurrence lent credence to the power of the advisory committee. Members of the mathematics area decided that they were underrepresented on the committee because their area coordinator held responsibilities in the district as a curriculum consultant. They petitioned the principal through the advisory committee for a new area coordinator and one was chosen. The primary criterion for selecting the person to fill the position seemed to be his recent improvements in interpersonal and group skills. Later in the school year, the advisory committee requested two other training events to help it clarify its role in the decision-making structure of the school.

A number of other events indicated that the quality of relationships on the staff improved because of the intervention. For instance, only two teachers resigned from the staff at the end of the school year, giving the school a turnover rate of only 3 percent. Comparative rates in other junior high schools in the same district ranged from 10 to 16 per cent. Several times during the year, faculty meetings were initiated by faculty members other than the principal. Such initiations ran counter to tradition, but nevertheless those meetings ran smoothly, with strong participation from many.

During the spring of 1968, faculty members initiated a meeting to discuss the possibility of having another group process laboratory before the next school year. Faculty members first discussed the idea in area groups and later asked to meet as a total staff to present recommendations to the advisory committee. The laboratory or workshop was to have two goals: (a) to socialize new faculty members into this "group-oriented" staff, and (b) to give teachers new skills to use with their classroom groups. The workshop actually took place, without our active participation, in August 1968.

The principal's interpersonal relationships with staff members were noticeably improved, and he became very much excited about improving further his own leadership skills. He requested funds to attend an NTL Educators Laboratory and was granted them. Later he served as an assistant trainer in a laboratory and performed with great effectiveness. That same summer six members of the faculty planned to go to a laboratory in group process and eventually did go at their own expense.

Perhaps the most dramatic changes after the intervention occurred in the school district. First, a new job was created at our experimental school; namely, vice principal for curriculum, to act as consultant on interpersonal relationships to task groups within the staff. The role also called for providing liaison between groups, providing logistic support for curricular efforts, transmitting to upper echelons in the district the proposals for curricular development originating at the school, and serving as a liaison with other junior high schools in the district concerning innovations in curriculum. This new vice principal was asked by the superintendent to maintain a log of his activities and to develop a job description for possible use in other schools. That completed, the school board granted funds for the position in several other junior high schools. The "curricular vice principal," first to hold the role, has been asked to aid the other new vice principals in learning the role. Still other schools in the district have requested funds for organizational development training for their staffs and the introduction of the "facilitator" role as a vice principalship.

COMPARISONS WITH OTHER SCHOOLS

The previous section contained descriptions of directly observable outcomes reflecting commitments to action within the school. This section reports comparisons of data taken from questionnaires administered early and late during the 1967-68 school year at the experimental school with data from six junior high schools in the New York City area and four junior high schools near the Seattle, Washington, area. None of the New York or Seattle schools was engaged in our kind of organizational training; in their demographic characteristics, too, they met some of the requirements for a control group.

The data for comparing our school with the New York schools came from two questionnaires: one dealing with the faculty's feelings about the principal's behavior, and the other dealing with the faculty's feelings about staff meetings. The data for comparing the experimental school with the Seattle schools came from questions concerning innovations adopted, readiness to communicate about interpersonal relations, and readiness to use and share the resources of other staff members.[1]

The Principal

The questionnaire used to measure the faculty's feelings about the principal contained 24 items. Twelve of the items were used by Gross and Herriott (1965) to measure the Executive Professional Leadership (EPL) of elementary school principals; the remaining 12 items were developed by the Cooperative Project on Educational Development (COPED) instrument committee to measure managerial support and social support of the principal for his staff.

The facet of educational leadership studied by EPL deals with the principal's efforts to improve the quality of performance of his staff. Gross and Herriott (1965) found EPL to be related to the morale of the staff, the professional performance of teachers, and learning by students. Hilfiker (1969) used the same instrument and found that both EPL scores and social support scores were related to school systems' innovativeness. Because of these findings we felt that the items in this questionnaire were reasonable indicators of the direction the interaction of faculty and principal would take if our training of the faculty approached its goals.

EPL was measured by asking teachers to what extent their principal engaged in activities such as the following:

Makes teachers' meetings a valuable educational activity.
Treats teachers as professional workers.
Has constructive suggestions to offer teachers in dealing with their problems.

A principal's managerial support was measured by items such as the following:

Makes a teacher's life difficult because of his administrative ineptitude.
Runs conferences and meetings in a disorganized fashion.
Has the relevant facts before making important decisions.

A principal's social support was measured by items such as the following:

Rubs people the wrong way.
Makes those who work with him feel inferior to him.
Displays integrity in his behavior.

To compare the teachers' responses to this questionnaire at the experimental school with the responses at the six junior high schools near New York City, we performed a series of chi-square analyses. For every item and every school we let the pretest results be the estimate of expected proportions against which to test the proportions obtained at the posttest—i.e., the proportions of teachers responding in one of six preferred categories. A summary of the analyses appears in Table 1, where the schools near New York City are labeled A through F.

TABLE 1

Numbers of Items Showing Significant Changes (p < .10)
Among Those in the Questionnaire on the Principal

	Exp'l	Schools A	B	C	D	E	F
Positive change	18	1	2	0	0	5	9
No significant change	6	19	17	12	13	19	11
Negative change	0	4	5	12	11	0	4

The results leave little doubt that the faculty of the experimental school changed its perceptions of the principal much more than did any of the other school staffs. At the experimental school, the teachers changed significantly (p < .10) on 18 of the 24 items; more importantly, every one of these 18 changes was in the positive and supportive direction. In contrast, in no other school, except for school F, did the teachers change on more than half of the items. Furthermore, in schools A, B, C, and D more of the changes were in a negative direction, indicating that the principal was being viewed less in accord with the EPL ideal at the end of the school year compared with the fall. The staffs of schools E and F changed more positively than negatively, but on far fewer items than at the experimental school.

Specifically, the teachers at our school were reporting that their principal was easier to get along with, made better decisions, helped them more in their own problem solving, improved faculty meetings and conferences, and treated them more as professionals after our training had been completed than before training. Staffs at junior high schools in the New York City area not undergoing organizational training did not report similar changes in their principals' behavior.

Staff Meetings

We were concerned about staff and committee meetings because they are important formal arenas in which communication and group problem solving can occur. Our early conversations with the staff at our experimental school revealed that low participation at staff meetings was viewed as an acute problem. We hoped that improvements in the conduct of meetings would occur as a result of the organizational training. To measure such change, we used a questionnaire to measure educators' responses to the meetings in their schools developed by the COPED instrument committee and reworded in minor ways by us. The questionnaire contains 37 items and has yielded excellent reliability.[2] The total score and subscale scores from this instrument have been found to be related to a school system's innovativeness (Hilfiker, 1969).

The 37 items describe specific behaviors; teachers are asked to rate each in one of six categories of frequency of its occurrence at staff meetings. The following are sample items from the instrument:

When problems come up in the meeting, they are thoroughly explored until everyone understands what the problems are.
People come to the meeting not knowing what is to be presented or discussed.
People bring up extraneous or irrelevant matters.
Either before the meeting or at its beginning, any group members can easily get items onto the agenda.
People do not seem to care about the meeting or want to get involved in it.
People give their real feelings about what is happening during the meeting itself.
When a decision is made, it is clear who should carry it out, and when.

In a manner identical to the questionnaire dealing with the principal, pretest responses for each item and from each school were used as expected frequencies for evaluating shifts in posttest data. Data about staff meetings were available only from three of the six comparison schools, namely, schools A, C, and D. Table 2 summarizes the chi-square analyses applied to these data. Like the results on the changed perceptions of the principal, the results on staff meetings also show major

TABLE 2
Numbers of Items Showing Significant Changes (p < .10)
Among Those in the Questionnaire on Staff Meetings

		Schools		
	Exp'l	A	C	D
Positive change	21	3	2	6
No significant change	14	30	32	23
Negative change	2	4	3	8

differences between the changes at the experimental school and the changes at the comparison schools. Among 37 items, our school showed significant positive change in 21, school A in three, school C in two, and school D in six. Changes at our school were almost entirely in the positive direction; among 23 significant changes (p < .10), only two were negative. In contrast, changes in the comparison schools could hardly have been more evenly balanced between positive and negative. The nature of the items on the questionnaire permits us to conclude that members of the experimental school reported that they could be more open, had improved the conduct of their meetings, dealt with problems more completely, had more commitment to the meetings and observed more solutions emerging from meetings, and felt that meetings were more worthwhile after completing our organizational training.

Innovations

The experimental school and four junior high schools from two cities near Seattle were administered an instrument as part of a larger project. One of the questions in the instrument read:

How about recent changes that could have useful effects on your school? Have there been any innovations, any new ways of doing things, that began during the last year or two that you think could have helpful effects in the school? If so, please describe each very briefly below. If none, write "none."

Teachers' responses to this item were coded into 14 categories according to the nature of the innovations they mentioned; for this report, we have gathered these categories into the four types shown in Table 3. "Packaged" innovations include curricular changes, establishing new jobs or duties, acquiring equipment, and adopting methods of evaluating programs. We describe these as "packaged" because some tangible set of materials or instructions usually goes along with the innovation such as teaching materials, specifications for a new job, TV equipment, or instructions for a bookkeeping method. Moreover, innovations under this heading can usually be put into effect by training *individuals*; it is not often necessary to establish delicate new role relations or new modes of group problem solving for innovations of this type to be successful. Packaged innovations were mentioned more frequently in three of the schools near Seattle (labeled *W* through *Z* in Table 3) than in the experimental school.

Another cluster of innovations contained those *instrumental* in achieving new forms of organization and new methods of solving organizational problems. Here we included relations between teachers and students, sharing power among the faculty, and changes in frequency

TABLE 3
Numbers of Teachers Mentioning Four Types of Innovations

Type of Innovation Mentioned	Exp'l Dec. 1967 N = 46	W N = 30	X N = 30	Y N = 34	Z N = 44	Exp'l May 1968 N = 39
"Packaged": curriculum, new jobs, equipment, program evaluation	18	25	11	36	22	15
Instrumental in achieving new forms of organization	9	0	3	1	1	16
New methods of problem solving or new organizational structure	21	1	1	0	1	17
Nonspecific improvements and vague answers	6	0	0	0	0	6

NOTE: Schools W, X, Y, and Z answered the questionnaires in January 1968.

or content of communication, as well as new training of any kind and new attitudes without mention of accompanying actions in organizational arrangements. Although the total number of responses in these categories was generally low by comparison with the first set of packaged innovations, mentions from the experimental school were more frequent than mentions from any of the other four junior high schools.

Innovations of primary importance to our training goals were new *methods of solving problems* or making decisions and *new organizational structure* such as committees, channels, and conference groups. Table 3 shows that teachers at the experimental school reported many more innovations in this area than the other junior high schools.

Norms About Interpersonal Communication

We asked the faculty at the experimental school and the faculties at the four junior high schools near Seattle to answer a set of seven questions about their readiness to talk about feelings. Three of the seven questions follow:

Suppose a teacher (let's call him or her Teacher X) disagrees with something B says at a staff meeting. If teachers you know in your school were in Teacher X's place, what would most of them be likely to do? Would most of the teachers you know here seek out B to discuss the disagreement?

( ) Yes, I think most would do this.
( ) Maybe about half would do this.
( ) No, most would *not*.
( ) I don't know.

Suppose you are in a committee meeting with Teacher X and the other members begin to describe their personal feelings about what goes on in the school; Teacher X quickly suggests that the committee get back to the topic and keep the discussion objective and impersonal. How would you feel toward X?

( ) I would approve strongly.
( ) I would approve mildly.
( ) I wouldn't care one way or the other.
( ) I would disapprove mildly.
( ) I would disapprove strongly.

Suppose Teacher X feels hurt and "put down" by something another teacher has said to him. In Teacher X's place, would most of the teachers you know in your school be likely to avoid the other teacher?

( ) Yes, I think most would.
( ) Maybe about half would.
( ) No, most would *not*.
( ) I don't know.

Taking those respondents who did not skip the question or answer "I don't know," we analyzed the responses to these seven items.[3] We found that the faculty at the experimental school reported that more teachers would (1) seek out another person with whom they had a disagreement, (2) tell another teacher when they had been hurt by the other teacher, (3) be less approving of a teacher who tried to cut off talking about feelings in a committee meeting, and (4) be more approving of a teacher who shared his own feelings at a faculty meeting than would teachers from the four schools near Seattle, according to their report. There was no significant difference between the teachers at the experimental school and other teachers in (5) their estimation of the proportion of teachers who would keep a disagreement to themselves (most teachers in all schools felt the majority would do so).

On the other hand, many more teachers in the schools near Seattle than in our school claimed that their fellow teachers would (6) not avoid another teacher and would (7) not tell their friends the other teacher was hard to get along with if the other teacher had hurt them or "put them down."

On balance, we believe these results indicate that after our intervention the faculty members at the experimental school, to a greater degree than the faculties near Seattle, were more open in their interpersonal communication and were more willing to talk about their feelings.

Norms About Sharing Ideas and Helping Others

Along with items reflecting norms about interpersonal communication, 12 items in the questionnaire concerned the faculty member's readiness to ask for help from other staff members and give help to them. Here are three examples:

Suppose Teacher X develops a particularly useful and effective method for teaching something. In Teacher X's place, would most of the teachers you know in your school describe it briefly at a faculty meeting and offer to meet with others who wanted to hear more about it?

( ) Yes, I think most would do this.
( ) Maybe about half would do this.
( ) No, most would not.
( ) I don't know.

Suppose Teacher X develops a particularly useful and effective method for teaching something. If X were to describe the method briefly at a faculty meeting and offer to meet further with any who wanted to know more, how would you feel about it?

( ) I would approve strongly.
( ) I would approve mildly.
( ) I wouldn't care one way or the other.
( ) I would disapprove mildly.
( ) I would disapprove strongly.

Suppose Teacher X wants to improve his classroom effectiveness. If X asked another teacher to observe his teaching and then have a conference about it afterward, how would you feel toward X?

( ) I would approve strongly.
( ) I would approve mildly.
( ) I wouldn't care one way or the other.
( ) I would disapprove mildly.
( ) I would disapprove strongly.

The faculty at the experimental school reported that they would (1) expect other teachers to report useful and effective teaching methods at faculty meetings, (2) seek administrative support to disseminate these methods, and would (3) approve in a significantly greater degree teachers who engaged in such activities than would faculties of the schools near Seattle. Several items concerned a teacher's attempts to improve his classroom effectiveness. The faculty at our school reported that teachers (4, 5) would ask others, including the principal, to observe their teaching and have a conference afterward, (6) would ask to observe a colleague's teaching to get new ideas, and (7, 8) would approve a teacher who did these things in significantly greater numbers than the faculties of the other schools. The remaining four items showed no significant differences. These results indicate that teachers at the experimental school were willing to share new ideas to a greater extent than in those schools where no organizational training had taken place. Furthermore, teachers at the experimental school were willing to take greater risks to improve their teaching effectiveness.

LESSONS FOR CONSULTANTS

In this section we discuss what the consultant can learn from this project that will help him in designing interventions to improve the organizational functioning of school faculties.

Special Nature of This Intervention

The training events in our intervention were aimed at improving the organizational problem solving of a school faculty. The feature that most sharply sets this intervention off from other laboratory training events is that natural workgroups—not individuals—were trained to be more effective. The intervention attempted to influence ways in which the entire faculty or its subgroups carried out their job-related tasks in the context of the school. This was, in other words, a training intervention pointed toward organizational development, not personal development. At the same time, it is an inescapable truism that role-occupants are persons and that the trainees are persons. It is only an abstraction, a way social scientists conceptualize things, to say that roles are different from the persons in a particular organization. Persons sometimes invest so much of their personal existence in a role (and this is perhaps particularly true of educators) that strong emotional reactions enter into organizational change of any kind. But even though the emotional reactions of persons always must be considered in designing even *organizational* development, our target remained fixed on roles and norms and their relationships. Organizational training as we conceive it aims at rearranging, strengthening, or in some way refurbishing the relationships among people in various positions in the school.

The Research Evaluation

From the point of view of research, we hoped to learn whether improved organizational problem solving could be produced by carefully integrating training in communication and problem-solving skills within the context of the living school and by beginning the training just prior to the opening of school and continuing intermittently for some months. We interpret the data to support the claim that a number of desirable outcomes were at least partly due to our intervention. Many teachers began using a greater variety of more effective group techniques in their classrooms. Collaborating subgroups of teachers increased in strength and number. The Principal's Advisory Committee became more potently and specifically representative rather than merely advisory. Faculty turnover decreased well below the rates at the other junior high schools in the district. Additional training in organizational development during the summer following our intervention was initiated by the faculty; and a number of staff members, including the principal, sought training for themselves in communicative skills and group dynamics. The district established a new variety of the vice principalship, modeled after a role fashioned at the school following our intervention; the definition of the role included skills in group development and problem solving.

These definite changes in organizational practice and structure were accompanied by changes in verbally expressed attitudes about the principal and staff meetings; the nature of reported innovations within the school; and norms concerning interpersonal openness, sharing of influence, and use of staff resources. These changes were found in the school where we conducted our organizational training, but not in other junior high schools not engaged in organizational training.

Strengths of the Summer Workshop

These outcomes indicate that improvements occurred in the school, and we believe that the summer workshop was crucial in getting the project off in a productive direction. Aspects of the design for a training activity like this one can be divided into macro- and micro-aspects. Macro-aspects are the design's overall structure and outline, its sequence of parts, and the general forms through which the individual activities flow. Micro-aspects refer to the specific activities played out during any limited period. We feel confident in offering the following features as the most successful macro-aspects of the summer workshop.

1. *Including all members of the faculty.* Almost the entire staff was included in the training right from the beginning. This meant that everyone learned about the goals of this training at the same time, that all were in the same circumstances *vis-a-vis* coping with the training activities, and that it was easy to transfer what was learned during the week to the school situation because staff members could remind one another

of what happened at the workshop. The importance of everyone's attending was underscored later when the two members of the staff who could not attend posed significant barriers to the staff's further development.

Even a few days' difference can create distance and set up barriers between the trained and the untrained. Perhaps the main reason is that one can feel a threat when others, especially those in roles comparable with one's own or those in roles that are removed only by one hierarchical level, develop skills or procedures that they might "use on you."

The faculty of a not-too-large elementary school or junior high school has no more than three levels of hierarchy: administrators, teachers, and nonprofessional personnel. For many purposes, there are only two layers, with the administrators comprising one layer and the teachers and nonprofessional personnel the other. Such an organization is closer to a primary group than it is to a bureaucracy. In a primary group, where role-takers relate to one another with more emotionality and individuality (in contrast with a more formal bureaucracy), there is no reasonable or legitimate way in which some can be chosen for special training while others are left out.

2. *Structured skill activities.* The macro-design called for a sequence of training events that started with games and structured skill activities and moved to first steps in solving real organizational problems. This sequence appears to have worked well in two ways. First, we think that faculty members who attend a training event as a duty rather than by self-selection find their ways into new interpersonal modes more easily via structured skill exercises than through less structured experiences demanding more personal commitment such as the traditional T Group probably would have led into considerations of particular interpersonal relationships within the staff; these, we believe, would have set the stage for personal development orientations and would have led away from a focus on organizational problems. Second, the results of the exercise led rather naturally into back-home problem solving and seemed to set the stage for the choices of increasing role clarity, using staff resources, and increasing staff participation at meetings. Unstructured activities probably would have led into work on relationships between certain persons and led away from our goals of working at the organizational level.

3. *Rotating subgroup membership.* The macro-design called for staff members' rotating through groups of different sizes and compositions during the first few days. This was done to increase the potential network of workable relationships on the staff and to decrease the possibility of an in-group/out-group pattern's emerging. Another goal of such rotating was to increase staff members' identification with the staff as a whole. We felt that some degree of identification with the whole would be necessary for the motivation that would be needed to carry the project through the year, and rotating subgroup memberships appears to have increased the cohesiveness of the faculty.

4. *Equal treatment to all ranks.* The design was consciously contrived to reduce status differences on the staff. No member of the staff was singled out for any special treatment. Rotating the staff through various groups brought teachers and administrators together as well as nonprofessional personnel, teachers, and administrators. The exercise emphasized that persons within groups carry out tasks and that one attempts to do the best he can on a given task regardless of who happens to be in his group. Such an assumption brought staff members closer together—a prerequisite to achieving more openness and clearer communication.

5. *Exemplifying new organizational forms in the training.* Group processes, new group forms, and procedures for problem solving were introduced in the design with the assumption that the use of such procedures by staff members would lead to new organizational structures. New structures were expected to arise out of problem solving, and we believe that the macro-aspects of the design encouraged that to happen.

Several micro-aspects of the design for the summer workshop warrant special attention because of their positive effects on the faculty.

a. *The fishbowl.* The fishbowl arrangement, in which a group on the outside of a concentric circle observes a group in the inside working, became especially useful to this faculty. The arrangement used most often called for two or three empty chairs left in the inside group. Members of the outside group were invited to enter the inside when they chose to communicate something to the insiders. During the summer workshop, this pattern was used in the problem-solving phase late in the week. Later, in a follow-up session when the Principal's Advisory Committee met in front of the rest of the staff, the same group formation was used. We learned that the faculty spontaneously employed such a formation several times during the school year to increase communication flow and participation between groups.

b. *Two-way communication.* In several activities during the training we emphasized the importance of two-way communication. The impact on the faculty was great indeed, for it especially affected the shape of the area coordinator's role. Area coordinators were encouraged by their colleagues to serve as communication links between the Principal's Advisory Committee and the area groups. This was an instance when learning about new processes motivated structural change. The new structure was similar to the *link-pin* organizational structure described by Likert (1961). Likert's link-pin structure uses small face-to-face groups as multiple-path communication channels in themselves; work units are organized across hierarchical levels, and members participate in group decisions at levels both above and below their own. In our school, the area coordinators were to represent their area colleagues in the Principal's Advisory Committee and to communicate actions of that advisory committee back to the members of their area.

c. *Systematic problem solving.* Working through the problem-solving process step by step was another important micro-element. We returned to this problem-solving sequence many times. It became a convenient mnemonic device for staff members. They could easily keep the stages in mind and, in fact, made use of several of them spontaneously during the next school year.

Strengths of Training During School Year

Next we wish to describe the things which we believe went especially well during the remainder of the period of intervention. Five training activities stand out as crucial aspects of the training during the school year. One was the fishbowl technique which we have already mentioned. The other forms were as follows:

1. *Interviews after summer training.* The interviews brought our training staff psychologically closer to the faculty and gave us a number of key ideas for designing training events during the school year. We interviewed staff members during the hour set aside for them to prepare for their teaching. We interviewed some in groups and others individually. Where we seemed to get contradictory comments, we tried to probe for clarity or to go back to a person who had been previously interviewed to ask a few more questions. We tried to keep the interview process open to easy surveillance. All staff members knew that we were at the school on the day of the interviews, the interviews were held in accessible spots in the school such as the teachers lounge, and staff members were invited to sit in or nearby while others were being interviewed.

2. *Problem solving in natural groups.* During the first follow-up training session, we set up meetings of the area groups and asked them to carry out the problem-solving procedure. This simulation of a real meeting was a significant force in transferring learnings about problem solving to new group procedures in the area groups during the school year.

3. *Review of progress before departure of trainers.* A significant contribution to the total design occurred during the February follow-up session when the staff reviewed how far it had progressed toward solving its basic problems of role unclarity, low use of resources, and lack of participation at meetings. The session had three helpful effects: (a) It encouraged continuing discussions and collaborative problem solving that had just begun to emerge. (b) It helped faculty members to recognize that already they had accomplished many positive things. (c) It helped set the stage for a graceful departure of the training staff without also indicating that the project was over.

4. *Final unstructured session.* A significant event in the total design was the unstructured session, in the manner of a T Group, held for a complete day with the Principal's Advisory Committee. Members of the

committee originated the session, involvement on the part of most was very high, and the results led to a strengthening of the group.

Weaknesses in the Summer Workshop

Certain features of our design were noticeably weak. We mention below some features we think could be bettered in another application.

1. *Making specific plans.* First, we believe that we should have encouraged the faculty to commit themselves to more specific and concrete action steps at the end of the summer workshop to be used in specific problem-solving processes back home. In essence, the problem solving was learned as a process and used rather well later in the year, but more gains in terms of concrete actions could have come from the problem solving if the faculty had been enabled to use action steps started at the workshop as a springboard.

2. *Dealing with absent persons.* The two staff members who did not attend the summer workshop never were brought into the training psychologically. One attempt was made to bring one of the noninvolved persons in by conducting a discussion about the workshop with that person together with three of her closest associates. At that meeting, events of the workshop were interpreted to the absent person, and feelings within the group appeared to be supportive and positive. However, little improvement seemed to occur after that meeting. In retrospect, we feel that a session should have been designed in which the problem of informing those who were not present would be dealt with openly and skillfully.

3. *Information-gathering techniques.* The problem-solving sequence lacked attention to concrete techniques for diagnosing organizational processes. The training could have included some diagnostic tools in the form of self-report questionnaires, brief but systematic interview schedules, and categories for observation that staff members could have used during the year to diagnose their own organization.

Weaknesses of Training During School Year

Three circumstances may have had adverse effects during the school year.

1. *Demands on personal energy.* Many teachers came to the training sessions after a difficult week of teaching. The training events constituted additional burdens for thèm to bear. We are now considering ways of arranging training episodes within the context of the school day itself, and we are having some success with meetings during free periods and by using substitutes part of the time. We are also making use of parts of vacations and the weeks immediately before and after the school year.

2. *Changing trainers.* Only two members of our training staff remained throughout the project. At times, the faculty was not sure who

were our staff and who were not. Some of our own confusions probably sent confusing messages to the faculty.

3. *Lack of clarity of expectations among trainers.* Along with our own staffing difficulties, it should also be pointed out that our training plans often were not extensive and at points not sharply enough defined. This led to uneven performances, especially in subgroups within the faculty, when different trainers were involved. We tried to correct for this by rotating trainers continuously.

In conclusion, this project was salutary for a school faculty and contains valuable lessons for consultants or change agents. For us, it serves too as a preface to a series of forthcoming interventions in schools with different structures.

NOTES

1. The data from the junior high schools near New York City were kindly provided by the Cooperative Project on Educational Development (COPED). Some of the questionnaire items used with the schools near Seattle were adapted from items used by COPED; some others were adapted from items kindly suggested by Ray Jongeward and Michael Giammetteo of the Northwest Regional Educational Laboratory. For a description of COPED, see Watson (1967).
2. The total test was analyzed by Warren Hagstrom using Frank Baker's test-analysis package at the University of Wisconsin. Using a sample of 625 school professionals, including both teachers and administrators who described a wide variety of meetings and types of meetings, a reliability (Hoyt analysis-of-variance method) of .96 was found for the total score.
3. Schmuck and Runkel (in press) present analyses of frequencies of "I don't know" answers and omissions.

REFERENCES

CAMPBELL, J. P., & DUNNETTE, M. D. Effectiveness of t-group experiences in managerial training and development. *Psychol. Bull.*, 1968, *70*, 73-104.

BRADFORD, L. P., GIBB, J. R., & BENNE, K. D. (Eds.) *T-group theory and laboratory method: Innovation in re-education.* New York: Wiley, 1964.

BUCKLEY, W. *Sociology and modern systems theory.* Englewood Cliffs, N.J.: Prentice-Hall, 1967.

GARDNER, J. *Self-renewal: The individual and the innovative society.* New York: Harper and Row, 1963.

GROSS, N., & HERRIOTT, R. *Staff leadership in public schools.* New York: Wiley, 1965.

HILFIKER, L. R. *The relationship of school system innovativeness to selected dimensions of interpersonal behavior in eight school systems.* (Technical Report No. 70.) Madison, Wis.: Research and Development Center for Cognitive Learning, 1969.

LIKERT, R. *New patterns of management.* New York: McGraw-Hill, 1961.

McGREGOR, D. *The professional manager.* New York: McGraw-Hill, 1967.

SCHMUCK, R. A., & RUNKEL, P. J. Organizational training for a school faculty. Eugene, Ore.: Center for the Advanced Study of Educational Administration, University of Oregon, in press.

WATSON, G. (Ed.) *Change in school systems.* Washington, D.C.: National Training Laboratories, associated with the National Educational Association, 1967.

A LABORATORY-CONSULTATION MODEL FOR ORGANIZATION CHANGE

William G. Dyer, Robert F. Maddocks, J. Weldon Moffitt,
and William J. Underwood

William G. Dyer is program director, NTL Institute for Applied Behavioral Science, Salt Lake City, Utah. Robert F. Maddocks is manager, Training and Professional Development, RCA Staff, Camden, New Jersey. J. Weldon Moffitt is professor of psychology, Psychology Department, Brigham Young University. William J. Underwood is administrator, Training Design and Application, RCA Staff, Camden, New Jersey.

Behavioral change agents engaged in management and organization development efforts recognize as crucial solutions to the recurring problems of entry and transfer. The major feature of the project reported here and still underway is the attempt to optimize both entry methods and transfer activities by a single developmental approach which includes the unique feature of using laboratory training to build a consulting relationship between internal consultants and their operating managers in an industrial organization.

The essential elements of the total design included: (a) laboratory training as an initiating vehicle, (b) the use of internal Trainer-Consultants, (c) the use of data collection and feedback, and (d) a single framework was used to overlay prelaboratory, laboratory, and post-laboratory activity. Data about each of the 25 participating managers were collected from peers and subordinates prior to the laboratory. The laboratory allowed each manager to receive data from other participants, to receive data from backhome work peers and subordinates, to establish a working consulting relationship with internal consultants, and, with them, to begin to formulate a plan of action for back-home application.

Initial results from back-home application within the organization indicates that these design features have reduced the entry and transfer problems experienced in utilizing laboratory learnings in organization development. However, certain problems still exist in transfer of learning, namely: uneven skill on the part of the managers to implement laboratory learnings, some lack of skill on the part of the Trainer-Consultants to intervene effectively, and the existence of certain organization conditions that do not support change.

With the increasing number of organizations turning to management and organization development as avenues for increased effectiveness, two difficult problems have arisen as a real challenge to those engaged in such endeavors.

The first problem is mainly the result of organizations which place management and organization development in staff functions and hence confront the staff manager with the task of entry into the line organization. This problem of appropriate entry and responsibility is a recurring one for behavioral change agents.

The second and broader problem is that of the transfer of laboratory learnings to organizational improvement. Most of the attempts to do so can be subsumed under three models.

1. *The training model.* Managers can be sent to training programs geared to develop a motivation and conception for organizational improvement. Popular examples are Grid seminars, NTL Institute laboratories and company-sponsored programs.
2. *The survey-feedback model.* Data can be collected about the organization and fed back to management as a basis for initiating problem solving. Examples are Beckhard's (1966) or Blake's (1965) confrontation designs and much of the survey action-research work of The University of Michigan (Mann, 1957).
3. *The process consultation model.* A consultant can engage directly with a management group and use their ongoing business activities as a vehicle. Much of the development work at Esso R & E and Union Carbide Corporation serves as examples.

THE ORGANIZATIONAL SETTING PRIOR TO THE CHANGE PROGRAM

Recently, a method of combining desirable features from all three models into a single approach for initiating an organizational improvement project was completed by the Radio Corporation of America (RCA) training group in conjunction with two external consultants. The enthusiastic response of management and the training group suggests its usefulness to those working in the organization field as well as to those more specifically concerned with the issue of transfer of training.

RCA is a large international organization of some 120,000 employees engaged in manufacturing a variety of products and providing services primarily in the field of electronics. The organization has a highly successful business image in terms of growth and financial return.

In the company there are two organization development persons at the corporate staff level, and out in the divisions are six experienced staff persons and five others who are less experienced. This makes a total staff of 13 persons available for OD work in the company, but only eight staff members considered experienced in OD.

There was no sense of urgency in the company on the part of management of the OD staff for beginning immediately an organization change program. Certain conditions were identified as pushing for change, but the desire was to build an OD model carefully with thoughts toward long-range results rather than some immediate transformations.

Previous Work of the OD Staff

Prior to the beginning of the organization change program, most of the internal OD staff were thought of as trainers (i.e., persons who diagnose management and organization needs, design a training program for certain personnel, and then conduct the program). The strategy for change was the hope that such training programs would lead to a change in management performance and perhaps in some organization change. It was felt by the staff that the training programs they were conducting were not producing adequate transfer into the organization, and that a different model of change was necessary—including a different way for the OD staff to work with managers. Although the staff felt competent in training and felt comfortable with their knowledge of new methods of OD, they lacked experience in carrying out new OD programs, e.g., consulting, team building, intergroup building. The image that the managers saw in the OD staff was a trainer image—these were people who conducted training programs but did not work regularly and consistently in the organization with the manager. It was felt necessary to change this image.

FEATURES OF THE CHANGE PROGRAM

For this project, laboratory training was chosen as an initiating vehicle. However, the problems of entry for the internal training group and connecting the laboratory learnings with the organization were critical design issues. Recognizing the continuing problem of transfer of training, the authors knew that some organizations provide internal consultants to serve as an application resource to their managers who attend residential laboratories while others use the "family" concept of composing the training group of managers who have ongoing working relationships.

It was within these experiences that the authors designed the RCA project and attempted to optimize both entry and transfer by a single approach. The essential elements of the design included: (a) the use of internal Trainer-Consultants, (b) the use of a single management and organization conceptual framework, and (c) the use of data collection and feedback.

Internal Trainer-Consultants

The key factor in the total design was the utilization of a corps of full-time internal Trainer-Consultants (presenting the trainer image mentioned above). The individuals used were RCA division training staff who carried the training responsibility for managers in their organizations. This group was to be the major link between the training laboratory and back-home organizational application. The Trainer-Consultants (hereafter called T-Cs) had been attempting to establish a working consulting role with management as a supplement to their normal training activities; however, at the time this project was conceived, the consultant-manager relationship had not been fully developed. It was decided that this project would be used to build such a relationship and that this relationship would be the instrument for back-home application. The Trainer-Consultants would be expected to follow their managers back into their organizational units and to continue to find ways of transferring laboratory learnings into the organizational setting.

It was decided, therefore, that the laboratory would be restricted to only those managers who would be willing to come to the program with their respective internal T-C and who would commit themselves to working with him prior to, during, and following the laboratory experience. A description of the proposed development project was discussed with a select group of managers who, in the past, had indicated a desire to initiate development activity within their organizational units. All 25 managers who were invited agreed to participate in the project.

It was necessary to build a set of conditions within the laboratory which would enable the consultant-manager relationship to be established. One requirement, therefore, was to bring the Trainer-Consultants and managers into contact during the laboratory in such a way as to establish an open and trustful relationship similar to the one which often develops between laboratory trainers and participants.

The design must also allow the Trainer-Consultants and managers to share the learnings of the laboratory, thereby cementing the consultant-manager relationship and avoiding the blocks that often appear when two people have to work together on issues which have not been shared in a common experience. This is particularly important since an effective consultant-manager relationship can be blocked by forces in the organization.

Since establishing a working relationship would also require that the T-Cs be seen by their managers from the beginning as being an integral part of the laboratory, the design of the project called for the internal Trainer-Consultants to do the following:

1. Collect data prior to the laboratory about each of their mangers from his subordinates and peers.
2. Consult with their managers during the laboratory regarding the experiences the latter were having in the laboratory itself and on the back-home data which were given to the managers at a precise time during the laboratory.
3. Develop the kind of relationship with their managers which would carry over to the organization.
4. Continue to work with their managers within their organizational units after the laboratory to design and implement a plan of action to move the laboratory learnings toward organization application.

Unifying Conceptual Framework

A second major design feature was the decision to provide a single unifying framework to the total project which would provide a cognitive map for the learning taking place in the laboratory and for relating laboratory learnings to the organizations of each of the participating managers.

The idea of a cognitive framework is not new. "We should always be sure in designing learning experiences that they have both confrontation and a support for current orientations built into them. Cognitive models have particular value in the analysis of problems of transfer of learning" (Harrison, 1965).

The idea of using a single framework to overlay prelaboratory, laboratory, and postlaboratory activity is new. We wanted to avoid the fairly typical response to laboratory learning, "I think I learned a lot, but I really can't say what it is or how it applies;" or the condition stated as, "Laboratory values are so different from the values of most organizations that if the individuals learned well while at the laboratory, they would probably tend to conclude that they should not use their new learning back home except where they have power and influence" (Argyris, 1966). The choice of a single framework for simplicity and understanding but which was broad enough to avoid oversimplification was seen as critical. Likert's (1961) system of organizational characteristics, which arranges several behavioral categories into a matrix with four general styles, was chosen as an appropriate vehicle.

Data Collection and Feedback

Another important project element was the use of three separate data-collecting instruments. While each was geared to a different purpose, all three were designed under the Likert conceptual framework. The instruments measured behavior along the following dimensions: leadership, motivation, communication, interaction-influence, decision making, goals, and control. Measurements of each dimension were differentiated across four broad management styles ranging from autocratic to participative.

One instrument was built to focus on the individual behavior of the manager in his organizational role. Each manager had subordinates and peers fill out this instrument just prior to the laboratory. Data were received, profiled by T-Cs, and held to be fed back to the manager at a certain point in the laboratory.

Another instrument was constructed for the dual purpose of assessing the processes of a T-Group and for assessing individual T-Group member behavior. The latter purpose provided the manager with systematized feedback on his behavior from his fellow T-Group members in the same conceptual framework used for the data gathered from his organizational subordinates and peers.

The third instrument designed for the project was cast at the organization level and built specifically to assess the processes of an organizational simulation exercise used in the laboratory.

The use of this instrumentation was expected to meet several objectives, the most important of which was to aid learning transfer. The instruments appeared to be an effective method of illustrating the operational value of the management and organizational conceptual framework. Data collected under a common framework were expected to be useful in helping the manager relate his laboratory behavior to his organizational behavior. In addition to their transfer value, the instruments were expected to aid the laboratory learning process and to illustrate for the managers the feasibility and value of collecting quantitative data about human behavior and relationship processes.

These three key elements—internal consulting resources, a single conceptual framework, and data collection—were viewed as bringing together for this project successful approaches from prior experience in the fields of training and organizational improvement.

PREPARING THE INTERNAL CONSULTANTS

For the laboratory experience and for their follow-up work prior to the beginning of the laboratory, the seven internal Trainer-Consultants were brought together to prepare them with their managers in the back-home organizational application. During the two and one-half days thus spent, part of the time was used for giving the T-Cs an opportunity to contribute to the general design elements of the laboratory since its preliminary design had been done by the outside consultants and two internal trainers. The design work completed to this point called for the internal T-Cs to have a major decision role in locating and prescribing the timing and nature of consultations which would take place between them and their managers.

The major role of T-Cs during the laboratory experience was to act as ongoing consultants to their managers. They were to observe their managers in all aspects of the laboratory—T Groups, exercises, and theory sessions. They were to interact with their managers in a consulting capacity which would help them to function more effectively during the total laboratory experience. The week was to be used to practice their consultation skills and to build the type of consultant-manager relationship which would be functional when they went back to their organizations.

The Trainer-Consultants were also briefed on the use of data. They were responsible for feeding instrumented data back to their managers. Time was spent in helping the T-Cs interpret data and in examing ways data could be fed back in usable form so that the managers could identify those characteristics in the Likert system relating to their managerial performance which required planning for improvement.

Time was also spent in talking about and role-playing the building of the consultant role. A model of the consulting process was presented which examined the various dimensions of control. The T-Cs looked at the types of requests which could be made of them by the managers during the laboratory and the ways in which varying response to these requests would result in the T-Cs' either exercising control over the managers or allowing the managers more autonomy. The Trainer-Consultant saw that his function with his manager was to help the manager increase his awareness of the processes going on around him, recognize the feedback given in the T Group, and to begin to plan more effective behaviors for himself without relying on the T-C for direction.

THE LABORATORY PHASES

By way of overview, the major phases of the laboratory design were as follows:

Preview

Phase I—2 days. Concentrated T Grouping focused on general personal and interpersonal issues. A day-long marathon was used on the first full day.

Phase II—2 days. T Grouping was combined with organizational exercises and theory sessions. The learning focus was shifted to group and organizational issues.

Phase III—1 day. The collection, feedback, and analysis of data. Managers were supplied with data from both their organizational colleagues and their laboratory colleagues. The learning focus was the manager's impact on others along managerial and organizational dimensions.

Phase IV—1 day. Participants were assigned to use this period in whatever way they considered to be important. They chose concentrated T Grouping both to process their instrumented data with others and to resolve remaining issues developed in the T Group.

Because these phases were intersected by the key elements previously described, the laboratory will now be described to illustrate the use of each feature.

Phase I

During the concentrated T Grouping in Phase I, the T-Cs took three roles. First, they acted as observers watching the behaviors of their managers as they interacted with others. Second, they met with their managers in three private consultations interspersed throughout this period. The initial consultation was used to clarify the purpose of the several consultation periods scheduled in the laboratory agenda. Generally, this was described as helping the manager obtain maximum value from the laboratory events. The remaining consultation periods in this phase were used to help the manager focus more deeply on his experiences in the T Group. The third role taken by the Trainer-Consultant was to collect, tabulate, and feed back data. During the marathon on the first day, managers completed a group questionnaire designed around the Likert format. The results, in profile form, revealed to the managers that nearly all perceived their T Groups to be operating somewhat autocratically but that each perceived himself to be operating more participatively. This brought into the design the features of the conceptual framework and data collection as well as opening up data for analysis in the T Group.

Phase II

During the focused exercises on group decision making and organizational processes in Phase II, three more private consultations were scheduled. Each of these was located immediately following either an exercise or a theory session and in turn was immediately followed by a T Group session. This scheduling gave the Trainer-Consultant an opportunity to help the manager assess his behavior in structured task work and to relate it to his behavior in the T Group. These consultations tended to open for the manager new dimensions of concern which he could then test out in the T Group.

Also during the second phase, a Likert-Type questionnaire assessing organizational processes was used during the organizational exercise. For the second time the managers were exposed to the use of quantitative data by a replication of the conceptual framework, but applied to a different context.

Phase III

Phase III was used entirely to collect, feed back, and analyze data. First, each manager completed a questionnaire on every other manager in his T Group. The questionnaire was designed within the Likert framework but geared to assess individual behavior in a T Group. After each manager had received the results from his T Group peers, he met with the Trainer-Consultant for help in analyzing the data. A T Group session following this analysis was used for processing concerns raised by the data.

The final event in this phase was particularly significant to the entire design. It consisted of the Trainer-Consultant's making available to the manager the profiled results of data collected prior to the laboratory from the manager's organizational subordinates and peers.

Thus, at this point the manager had available comprehensive data which included: (a) systematized perceptions of his management behavior in his organization; (b) feedback he had ootained from the T Group and exercise sessions of the laboratory, and the analysis of this in previous consultations; (c) systematized perceptions of his T Group behavior; and (d) the resources of a Trainer-Consultant.

The hazard of data overload was reduced by the single conceptual organization of most of the data and by allowing a considerable amount of time for processing in private consultation. The substantial impact of this event derived from the direct relatability of laboratory data to organizational data by the single framework. Plainly, the manager had considerable data about himself in relevant roles—and in what to him was management language. The T-C helped the manager relate the various pieces of data and make his own personal assessments.

Phase IV

In Phase IV the managers were requested to decide for themselves what activities would be most useful. They chose continuous T Grouping. There were, therefore, no further consultations or data collections.

APPLICATION TO THE ORGANIZATION

The first laboratory took place in May 1968. Since that time two more laboratory programs have been conducted which utilized the same design. Approximately 90 managers have gone through the change programs. After the first group, the next groups included the subordinates of those managers who had attended the first session, with the plan in mind of building a pool of persons with a common experience whom the consultant could continue to work with in the organization.

Initially, the T-Cs had no specific design for working with the participants back in the plant, except for a general notion of continuing the consulting started at the laboratory. However, it was discovered that practically all the managers felt a strong desire to reveal to their subordinates something about their laboratory experiences, including data and analysis of the questionnaire ratings which the subordinates had given them. It became the role of the T-C to help the managers plan and carry out such a communication process. Sometimes the T-C agreed to present the Likert framework in order to give the subordinates background and introduction to the data analysis.

Results of these meetings with subordinates have varied widely. Some managers presented the data, had a limited discussion, but did little follow-through for reasons to be discussed. Others used this as a base for continuing a set of problem-solving meetings to work on the issues raised by the data. As might be predicted, the meetings of a manager with his staff were characterized by the following processes:

1. *Initial Threat.* This was a unique experience for almost all of the persons involved. By and large the culture of the company did not have norms that supported such openness of discussion. People were often embarrassed and uncertain about what to say and do.

2. *Reluctance To Respond and Flight.* After the manager and/or T-C had reported the laboratory experience and data, subordinates were asked to respond. This invitation was met by reluctance and often by elements of flight behavior.

3. *Provisional Resolution.* If the units were able to deal with the first two conditions, an attempt to work out resolutions to problems raised followed. The units which decided to continue generally set up procedures and times to work on the issues raised in the early meetings. It was noted that the units that did not continue could not make decisions to work on their own staff problems. The continuing groups have gone in different directions: Some have initiated direct family T Groups; some have used data collection-feedback sessions; others have stayed with the discussion of the original laboratory-generated data.

Continued OD Efforts

Results of the program have been determined by reports coming directly from the T-Cs working with the managers; systematic research designs have not been used. The direct reporting and anecdotal data indicate that about 25 per cent of the managers who have participated in the three laboratories over a one-and-one-half-year period have *not* continued in any detectable OD efforts beyond the first meetings. Another 50 per cent are continuing to make an effort toward OD, but the results are not considered totally effective by the T-Cs who are working with them. The remaining 25 per cent have accomplished and are continuing to work on organizational change efforts that are considered significant improvements.

One manager who has been seen as particularly effective was perceived in the prelaboratory data as being very stiff and formal with his men; and since he was younger in age than most of his subordinates, some real barriers were created in working effectively with them. His organization, a staff service to a production operation, was, up to that time, widely judged to be mediocre in effectiveness. As a result of the laboratory experience, the manager and his T-C began a series of team building meetings which reduced the level of formality, rigid role differentiation, intellectualization, and one-way influence. As the manager's staff team changed, the effect spread to the other parts of the organization because of the renewed energy exhibited by his staff. Organization improvement in terms of hard data began to emerge. As the case continues, recently this manager was given an unusually substantial promotion. He was placed in charge of a sizable plant whose business is critical and which has experienced considerable difficulty. His superior acknowledge that a year before this manager would not have been considered for the new position, but the fact that he was able to change and was able to bring about an improvement in his organization gave them some confidence that perhaps he had learned how to bring about change in another problem situation.

Characteristics of Abortive OD Efforts

Where managers have not continued to develop an improvement program, it has been felt that one or a combination of negative factors has been present in the following organizational components.:

1. *The Manager.* Some managers have not seemed to benefit from the laboratory experience either for certain personal reasons or because their own anxiety about engaging in an open, leveling process with subordinates has been so high as to make further action difficult.

2. *The Organization.* It has become painfully evident that certain parts of the organization culture do not support continuing OD efforts. Sometimes the manager who went through the laboratory was faced with a boss who would not support new behaviors. Others found that work pressures requiring frequent travel, heavy overtime, and urgent time deadlines prevented the manager from moving ahead with the development meetings he would have liked holding.

3. *The Trainer-Consultant.* It must be admitted that this is no "game" for a novice. Inappropriate interviewing or mistimed or inadequately handled interventions by the T-C have undoubtedly had negative effects. This issue is so sensitive that a single fault by a T-C has in some instances permanently blocked further OD efforts for some units.

Four models are now being used to engage the participating managers in development activity. These are: (a) private consulting with the participating manager, (b) process interventions in regular business meetings, (c) direct and instrumented examination of staff teamwork in meetings established especially for this purpose both on and off plant premises, and (d) data collection and feedback from subordinates and other organizational members using a Likert conceptual framework to assess interpersonal data and as a data source for staff group action. (No Trainer-Consultant is engaged in private consulting with his participating manager as an exclusive process. Private consulting when used is being done in combination with one or more of the other processes.)

CRITIQUE

In reviewing the approach thus far, several weak and strong points can be identified. Two problems emerged during the laboratory, and another became visible during the application period.

Weaknesses

One problem concerns the number of managers worked with by the Trainer-Consultants. One T-C brought nine managers to the laboratory while another brought only one. The remaining ratios fell between these. Therefore, while the 1-to-1 ratio team could spend a given time period in individual consultation, team ratios of more than one manager were required either to reduce the individual time or work as a sub-group. Although the design was timed to provide as much balance as possible, the consensus among the training staff was that more consulting time was available than the low-ratio teams could productively use and not enough time was available for the high-ratio teams. The optimum ratio for this design seemed to be about three managers per Trainer-Consultant.

Another problem concerned the use of one of the questionnaires. It was anticipated that collecting and feeding back group process information via the Likert framework during the first-day marathon would aid group development as well as introduce the framework and the use of quantitative methods. In fact, the managers displayed very little interest in these data, and it was not observable that the method had any effect, positive or negative. It is probably that such quantitative data were too "cold" to fit the context of the personal involvement of a marathon.

Another problem has become visible during organizational application attempts. A few of the managers, while highly motivated to apply, have defined change goals more in terms of others than of themselves.

Strengths

The entire project to date has yielded several results which are considered highly valuable. It is clear that a successful relationship has been built between the Trainer-Consultant and his managers. From all observations of the T-Cs, their managers see them as useful resources, understand the nature of their role, and are desirous of utilizing them as adjuncts in the manager's back-home application efforts.

Almost all of the managers have either initiated application activity or have voiced intentions of doing so. This is interpreted as a clear indication that the project has produced an intention to apply laboratory learnings. At this point, there is every reason to believe that training will be transferred to the job in significant ways.

With respect to the laboratory features which can be judged as helpful, the following appear salient:

First-day marathon. This "up-front" period of continuous and intensive T Grouping was judged by the staff as moving the groups to a point approximating the third day of a standard laboratory design.

Single conceptual framework. The staff considered the use of a single overall framework to be quite useful. During the laboratory it provided a consistent set of dimensions which were inclusive enough to refer and relate most of the laboratory phenomena as well as organizational phenomena. This framework has continued to be highly useful as an organizing system for considering application goals and approaches.

Relating laboratory and organizational data. It was apparent to all the staff that having an opportunity to compare laboratory-produced data with data from their organizational realities was highly valuable for the managers. It provided a means of cross-validation and of relating similar concepts. It seemed a sufficient method for combating the typical tendency to compartmentalize laboratory experiences.

Cross-feed between consultations and other laboratory activities. The T Group and focused exercises provided the data source for consultations; on the other hand, the consultations had a visible effect on managerial behavior in the T Groups and focused exercises. Many a T-C observed his manager's explicit attempts in the T Groups to explore dimensions which the consultations had previously exposed and dealt with. It is difficult to assess, but the staff impression was that private consultations produced a beneficial effect on the more traditional laboratory experiences.

Application Problems

In terms of organization application it seems that the Likert framework has given an expectation for and a focus on changing an entire organization. The managers have worked at the level of their own staff—a small-group orientation. They are impatient with the length of time which is seemingly required to change a total organization. We feel it important that the laboratory gives the small-group element a greater emphasis and that it helps managers to see that the place to begin to influence the total organization is to improve group process within their own staff.

More attention needs to be given to careful selection of participants for the program. It seems there are some types of managers located in certain kinds of situations for whom the laboratory experience can only result in minimal change efforts. If these can be identified, perhaps managers can be selected in whom greater possibilities for change are present.

It is our belief also that the laboratory should focus more attention on change strategies in addition to self-insight, interpersonal, and group and organization learnings. Managers who plan to engage in change efforts need to learn more skills, e.g., how to conduct confrontation meetings, data collection and feedback sessions, process analysis of meetings, team building meetings, and so on.

CONCLUSION

The field of behavioral science interventions has developed a number of approaches to planned organizational change. The one reported here has been a systematic attempt to utilize workable features from a variety of methods. It has been shown to be possible to build a laboratory design which incorporates internal Training-Consultants, quantitative data collection and feedback, and a single general conceptual framework into the more traditional laboratory experiences of T Group, exercises, and theory input. The total approach, which has been evaluated as successfully facilitating entry into the organization and transfer of laboratory learnings into the backhome setting, hinges tightly on the continued use of an internal resource person.

REFERENCES

ARGYRIS, C. Explorations and issues in laboratory education. *Explorations in human relations training and research,* 1966, *3,* 15.

BECKHARD, R. An organizational improvement program in a decentralized organization. *J. appl. Behav. Sci.,* 1966, *2* (1), 3-25.

BLAKE, R. R., MOUTON, JANE S., & SLOMA R. L. The union-management intergroup laboratory. *J. appl. Behav. Sci.,* 1965, 1 (1), 25-57.

HARRISON, R. Cognitive models for interpersonal and group behavior: A theoretical framework for research. *Explorations in human relations training and research,* 1965, *2,* 109-110.

LIKERT, R. *New patterns of management.* New York: McGraw-Hill, 1961.

MANN, F. C. Studying and creating change: A means to understanding social organizations. In C. M. Arensberg (Ed.), *Research in industrial human relations,* Harper & Row, 1957.

COMMENTS ON THE PRECEDING ARTICLE

I. GEORGE S. DILLON

This paper impressed me very favorably. The writing is clear and precise and relatively free of technical jargon. The model described in the paper, which was intended to facilitate the transfer of laboratory training back to the job, was conceived logically and implemented carefully.

It has seemed to me that the usefulness of laboratory training in organizational development has been limited severely by the lack of a really effective transfer technique. The model described here shows exceptional promise for overcoming this limitation.

Custom requires the critic to register some complaints, however minor. I have three:

1. Were the results influenced significantly by the managerial climate from which the managers and trainers came? It would be helpful to have been able to ascertain this.
2. The research and data collection certainly was thorough. Was it not overwhelming?
3. The model seems to have provided at least a partial solution to the entry problem of the Trainer-Consultants.
   Does the entry problem really rank in priority with the transfer problem?

I trust that complaints noted will not in any way obscure for the reader my admiration for the substance of the paper and its presentation.

George S. Dillon is president, Air Reduction Company, Incorporated, New York City.

II. JAMES RICHARD

The case study "A Laboratory-Consultation Model for Organization Change" developed in the preceding pages describes a well-conceived design to cope with two of the most difficult problems of organization development.

The paper outlines a project which was implemented at RCA by two outside consultants and a team from the RCA training group. The integrated design was aimed at optimizing the entry of internal change agents into the line organization and the transfer of laboratory learnings to organizational improvement.

The report is clear and succinct but so surgical in style that it provides no flavor of the human encounters which certainly must have colored the experience. The subject is important enough to receive some warmer treatment, and reporting of some of the live experience would have enhanced the report. Literary style notwithstanding, the design which the authors describe is an important integration of some major organization development concepts.

There is more to be examined in the design, but I shall focus my comments on three major issues of the RCA model which strike me especially.

Professional organization development consultants both internal and external will recognize the perplexing dilemma of how to establish an optimum working relationship with management. Differences in personal style and varying orientations prompt consultants to try varied approaches. Since circumstances and personalities vary as widely within the organization, there is a perennial discussion among organization professionals about varieties of approach.

James Richard is visiting professor of business administration, College of Business Administration, Boston College.

The designers of the RCA experience have done well, I believe, to integrate the corps of full-time internal Trainer-Consultants into the one-week laboratory with the 25 individual managers whose divisions the trainers will serve. I like the underlying idea of Trainer-Consultants assigned divisionally; and I also like the use of outside-inside consultant teams that is implied in this report.

My experience has been that to introduce an organization development program featuring internal Trainer-Consultants requires that some extraordinary measures be taken to reinforce the internal consultant role. Operating managers have difficulty understanding how to use the internal consultant, and the traditional company system does not understand the function. The RCA model seems to me to meet this difficulty well by demonstrating the role first to the managers in a laboratory and next by connecting the laboratory to prelaboratory and postlaboratory experience.

The use of data feedback is the second feature of the design that seems well conceived. By introducing into the laboratory data which were collected from peers and subordinates of each manager before the laboratory, and then by connecting laboratory experience to subsequent back-home activity, the design provided for carryover of laboratory learning. In addition, the T-C role in this process gives opportunity for tangible experience from which the manager and trainer can build a working relationship. Further, this experience shared by the combined groups of managers and trainers should give validity and impetus to the entire organization development program in a multidivisional system.

Probably the degree of effectiveness of the data-feedback feature of the RCA model and the extent of transfer from the laboratory experience to back-home groups depend a good bit upon the working competence of the Trainer-Consultant team and the readiness of the individual managers to work on improvement in their organizations. Even if the laboratory-consultation design merely achieves some successful Trainer-Consultant entry and a measure of laboratory learning transfer, as a beginning step it can be counted a success. Significant change is a long-range procedure, and to overcome the entry problem is a crucial step.

The third interesting feature of this design is the use of a single conceptual framework. The Likert matrix, with its framework of four general styles, seems to have been especially well suited to the other purposes of this design. Other conceptual schemes might have served as well. But in any event, it is the very provision of a framework within which managers can integrate their personal experience from the T Groups and data feedback that I consider to be important. Especially in the early stages, such a framework is an asset, when the values and behavioral patterns of laboratory experience and of personal feedback are probably a high contrast to the manager's traditional experience. Even though the particular conceptual framework of the design might conceivably be outgrown by future developments, it serves well at this stage to hold the design together.

Perhaps it might be charged that the effect of introducing the three elements into the RCA experience—the inside trainer-manager teaming; the data collection and feedback featuring prelaboratory data, laboratory, and postlaboratory data; and the use of a single conceptual framework into which the entire design is integrated—was overstructuring the design. The charge might also be leveled that the managers were exposed to far more data than they could assimilate in the time span of the laboratory.

But I am not troubled by either concern. The problems of Trainer-Consultant entry and of transfer from laboratory experience into the work environment are major. The elements which this group has put together into an integrated design should go a long way toward making comprehensible for managers the processes of organization development. Hopefully the design will help to make life livable for the internal Trainer-Consultants by generating sanction and support of their work. If in several parts of the system other colleagues are working with other line managers and all from a frame of reference which they experienced together, the organization development effort should have had an auspicious take-off. With this lift off, effort can be applied to maintaining altitude and strengthening communication links throughout the larger system.

SECTION VII

EPILOGUE

EDITORS' OVERVIEW

When hearing about OD for the first time, many laymen ask, "Where's the evidence that OD really works?" The following article responds to this question by presenting impressive data from a study of a company in which OD changes made in 1962 took hold and became permanent features of the organization still readily observable eight years later.

DURABILITY OF ORGANIZATIONAL CHANGE [1]

Stanley E. Seashore and David G. Bowers
Institute for Social Research, University of Michigan

The aim of this article is to add a modest footnote to the growing literature concerning planned change in the structure and function of formal organizations. The question asked is whether changes that have been planned, successfully introduced, and confirmed by measurements, over but a relatively short span of time, can survive as permanent features of the organization. Will such a changed organization become stabilized in its new state, or will it continue the direction and pace of change, or perhaps revert to its earlier state?

This report will include a brief review of an earlier effort to change an organization, a presentation of some new data about the present state of the organization, and some first speculations about the meaning of the data for the understanding of psychological and social phenomena in formal organizations.

Background

The earlier events against which our new data are to be set are reported rather fully elsewhere (Marrow, Bowers, & Seashore, 1967). A brief review of the essential facts will set the stage.

In late 1961 the Harwood company purchased its major competitor, the Weldon company. This brought under common ownership and general management two organizations remarkably similar in certain features and remarkably different in others. Both made and marketed similar products using equipment and manufacturing processes of a like kind; were of similar size in terms of business volume and number of employees; served similar and partially overlapping markets; were family-owned and owner-managed firms; and had similar histories of growth and enjoyed high reputation in the trade.

The differences between the two organizations are of particular interest. The Harwood company had earned some prominence and respect for their efforts over many years to operate the organization as a participative system with high value given to individual and organizational development, as well as to effective performance. The Weldon company had for years been managed in a fashion that prevails in the garment industry, with a highly centralized, authoritarian philosophy and with secondary concern for individual development and organizational maintenance. The two organizations were, in 1962, rather extreme examples from the continuum vaguely defined by the terms authoritarian versus participative. Measurements in both firms in 1962 confirmed that the difference was not merely impressionistic, but was represented in quantitative assessments of the organizational processes for planning, coordination, communication, motivation, and work performance, and was represented as well in member attitudes. The two firms were also sharply contrasting in their performance in 1962, even though over a longer span of years their business accomplishments had been similar. In 1962 Weldon, in sharp contrast to Harwood, was losing money, experiencing high costs, generating many errors of strategy and work performance, suffering from member disaffection with consequent high absenteeism and high turnover. Weldon, despite its technical, fiscal, and market strengths, was near the point of disaster.

The new owners set out on a program to rebuild the Weldon enterprise according to the model of the Harwood company. The ultimate aim was to make the Weldon firm a viable and profitable economic unit within a short period of time. A rather strenuous and costly program was envisioned, including some modernization of the plant, improved layout and flow of work, improvements in records and production control methods, and product simplification, as well as changes in the human organization. The renewal program concerning the organization itself concerns us here.

The approach to organizational ch nge can be characterized briefly in three respects: (a) the conception of the organizational characteristics to be sought; (b) the conception of processes for changing persons and organizational systems; and (c) the linking of the social system to the work system.

The guiding assumptions or "philosophy" on which the change program was based included elements such as the following:

1. It was assumed that employees would have to gain a realistic sense of security in their jobs and that this security would have to arise basically out of their own successful efforts to improve their organization and their performance, not out of some bargained assurances.
2. The introduction of substanial change in the work environment requires that employees have confidence in the technical competence and humane values of the managers and supervisors; this confidence can be earned only if it is reciprocated by placing confidence in the employees.
3. In a situation of rapid change it is particularly necessary to use procedures of participation in the planning and control of the work and of the changes; such procedures are needed at all levels of the organization.
4. The rebuilding of an organization may require an input of technical resources and capital on a substantial scale—not unlike the investments required to rework a technology or control system of a factory.
5. Management involves skills and attitudes that can be defined, taught, and learned, and these skills and attitudes need not be confined to high rank staff; each member of the organization, at least in some limited degree, must learn to help manage his own work and that of others related to him.

6. Guidelines such as these are not readily understood and accepted unless they can be linked to concrete events and to the rational requirements of the work to be done and the problems to be solved.

The conception of change processes incorporated in the rebuilding of the Weldon organization emphasized the application of multiple and compatible change forces. The physical improvements in work resources and conditions were to be accompanied by informational clarity, enchanced motivation through rewards, and ample skill training and practice. That is, change was to be introduced simultaneously at the situational, cognitive, motivational, and behavioral levels so that each would support the others.

The linking of the social organization to the work system was to be accomplished through efforts, however limited, to design work places, work flows, information flows, and the like in a manner not merely compatible with but integral with the associated social organization and organizational processes.

The program of rebuilding the organization was carried out by the local management with substantial assistance and stimulation from the new owners and from a variety of consultants, including psychologists. The general planning and guidance of the program were influenced primarily by Alfred Marrow, Board Chairman of the Harwood Corporation and Fellow of Division 14. The role of the Institute for Social Research was not that of change agent, but rather that of observing, recording, measuring, and analyzing the course of events and the change that resulted.

The change program was successful in important respects. Within two years there occurred improvements in employee satisfactions, motivations, and work performance. The organization took on characteristics of an adaptive, self-controlling, participative system. The firm as a business unit moved from a position of loss to one of profit. At the end of 1964, after two years of change effort, the factory was abandoned as a research site, the rate of input of capital and external manpower into the change program diminished substantially, and the factory and its organization were expected to settle down to something like a "normal" state.

EXPECTATIONS ABOUT CHANGE

From the start of this organizational change program there was a concern about the long-run consequences of the program, and there was uncertainty about the permanence of change. The following quotations from our earlier report illustrate the intentions, hopes, and doubts (Marrow et al., 1967):

the whole organization, from the plant manager down to the production workers, were taken into an exercise in joint problem-solving through participative methods in groups, with a view toward making such procedures a normal part of the management system of the plant [p. 69].

The refreezing of Weldon in a new and more effective state is not regarded as a permanent thing, but as another stage in the evolution and continuous adaptation of the organization. Some features of the conversion plan explicitly include the provision of built-in capacities for easier change in the future [p. 232].

Will the changes at Weldon last? The only evidence we have at the present time is that the change from a predominantly "authoritative" to a dominantly "consultative" type of management organization persisted for at least two years in the view of the managers and supervisors involved. Surely there exist forces toward a reversion to the old Weldon form of organizational life; it remains an uncertainty whether they will or will not win out over the new forces toward consolidation of change and further change of the intended kinds [p. 244].

In mid-1969, four and one-half years after the termination of the intensive change program, Dr. Bowers and I invited ourselves back to the Weldon plant for a follow-up measurement of the state of the organization. This remeasurement consisted of a one-day visit to the plant by a research assistant who administered questionnaires to managers, supervisors, and a sample of the employees.[2] In addition, certain information was abstracted from the firm's records, and the views of the plant manager were solicited as to changes that had taken place and possible reasons for change. We can turn directly to a few tables and figures representing the changes and the situation as of 1969.

RESULTS

First, we present some data from the production employees. Table 1 shows selected items from our questionnaire survey bearing on the issue of whether there has occurred a decline, a rise, or a stabilization of the attitudes, satisfactions, and optimism of the employees. The table shows the percentage of employees giving the two most favorable responses, of five offered, to each question. The columns represent the results in 1962 before the change program began, in 1964 at the conclusion of the formal change effort, and in 1969.

TABLE 1

Changes in Job Attitudes

Item	1962 %	1964 %	1969 %
Company better than most	22	28	36
Own work satisfying	77	84	91
Satisfied with pay system	22	27	28
Company tries to maintain earnings	26	44	41
Satisfied with supervisor	64	54	54
Like fellow employees	85	86	85
Group cohesiveness	25	25	30
Plan to stay indefinitely	72	87	66
Expect future improvement in situation	23	31	43

The general picture is one of the maintenance of earlier gains in the favorability of employee attitudes or the further improvement in attitudes. This observation holds for seven of the nine indicators. The remaining two deserve brief special comment.

Satisfaction with supervisors declined during the period of the active change program but has remained relatively high and constant since 1964. The initial decline is viewed as a consequence of the substantial change in the supervisors' role during the active change program. During that period, the supervisors acquired substantially more responsibility and authority as well as some new activities and duties that are thought to have removed the supervisors from a peerlike to a superior status relationship with the operators, which they retain now. This interpretation is, of course, speculative but made before the 1969 data were in hand.

The decline in the proportion of employees planning to stay on indefinitely is rather difficult to assess. The rise between 1962 and 1964 can be attributed to the improvement in pay and working conditions in that period. The subsequent decline is to be accounted for, partly, by the fact of recent production expansion and the presence on the payroll of a relatively larger number of turnover-prone short-service employees. One might also speculate that rising prosperity during the period might have increased the attractiveness of marriage, child bearing, or retirement for these female employees. In any case, the decline in the percentage committed to long job tenure appears to be at odds with the general rise in job satisfactions and in the marked rise in optimism about the future improvement in the Weldon situation. We should add that the decline in percentage committed to long tenure is confirmed by the fact of a moderate rise in actual turnover rates in recent months.

Table 2 shows a few selected items bearing on the question whether the rise in satisfactions and expectations is accompanied by some loss in productivity concerns and task orientation. The data, again, are from employee questionnaire responses (except for the last line) and show changes from 1962 to 1964, and then to 1969.

TABLE 2

Change in Task-Orientation Indicators

Item	1962 %	1964 %	1969 %
Company quick to improve methods	18	24	31
Company good at planning	22	26	35
Not delayed by poor services	76	79	90
Produce what rates call for	44	67	53
Expect own productivity to improve	63	55	62
Peers approve of high producers	58	58	66
Closeness of task supervision	38	27	47
Desired closeness of supervision	57	52	64
Mean productivity (% of standard)	87	114	?

Five of the indicators reflect a rise in level of task orientation and production concern since the end of the formal change program. The remaining items are not negative, but merely indeterminate. There is clearly a rise in recent years in the percentage of employees who say the firm is quick to improve work methods, good at planning, provides efficient services (maintenance, supplies, scheduling), who report that their peers approve of high producers, and who themselves desire frequent and ready access to supervisory help. Two sets of data require special comment.

The data on productivity, three lines in the table, should be considered as a set. The numbers show that the self-report of "Nearly always producing what the rates call for" rose substantially during the active change program, and this is confirmed by the actual productivity records of the firm as shown in the last line "Mean productivity against standard." During the same period, the percentage of employees expecting a further gain in their own productivity declined, as it should have considering that more employees were approaching the firm's hoped-for level of high productivity and earnings. By 1969 there was some decline in the percentage reporting high productivity and a corresponding rise in the percentage expecting a future rise in their productivity; this pair of related changes appears to reflect the presence on the staff of an increasing number of relatively new employees not yet up to the level of skill and performance they may reasonably expect to attain. There is a crucial item of missing data in the last line of the table; for technical reasons, we have not been able to calculate the current actual productivity rate in a form that allows confident comparisons with the earlier figures. Our best estimate is that productivity has been stable with a slight decline in recent months arising from the recent introduction of additional inexperienced employees.

Attention is also suggested to the pair of lines in Table 2 concerning closeness of supervision. At all three times of measurement, these production workers desired more close supervision than they actually experienced; these employees, unlike those in some other organizations, see their supervisors to be potentially helpful in improving productivity and increasing piece-rate earnings. The decline in experienced closeness of supervision during the period 1962-64 matches other evidence to be presented later that during this period there was a substantial change in the supervisors' role that diverted the supervisors from immediate floor supervision and left a temporary partial shortage of this service to production workers. The figures show that by 1969 this supervisory deficit had been recouped and more. This sustains our general view that during the years following the Weldon change program there has been not a decline in concern for task performance among employees and in the organizational system generally but rather a further gain in task orientation.

The change in supervisory behavior mentioned earlier is shown in Figure 1. We attempted at the three points in time to measure the extent to which supervisors, in the view of employees, engaged in behaviors we

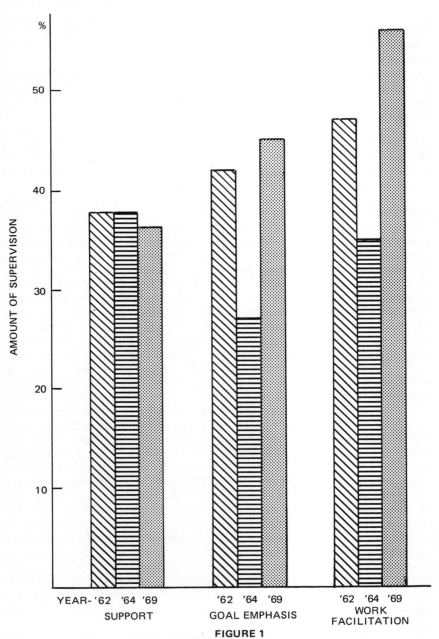

FIGURE 1
Change in three dimensions of supervisory leadership behavior.

categorize as "supportive," "goal emphasizing," and "work facilitating." (Two additional dimensions of leader behavior that we now use in describing organizations are not represented here because they were not yet identified in 1962; we chose to continue use of the initial measurement methods rather than to update them.)

Figure 1 shows that the amount of supervisory supportiveness experienced by employees remained constant during the 1962-64 period and has risen slightly since then. Goal emphasis and work facilitation both dropped during the active change program, for reasons mentioned earlier, and have since risen above their 1962 levels. These data sustain our belief that the Weldon organization since 1964 has increased its expression of concern for production goals and its provision of conditions for effective work performance, and at no cost of declining concern for employee attitudes and satisfactions.

One more set of data from the employees is pertinent here, namely, their description of the amount and hierarchical distribution of control in the Weldon organization. One of the explicit aims of the change program was that of increasing the total amount of control and of altering the distributions of control so that lower rank people—supervisors and operators—would have some added degree of control. This was accomplished during the change program period to a very limited and nonsignificant degree. Subsequent changes have been in the direction intended and more substantial in degree. The data are shown in Figure 2. In 1969, compared with the earlier periods, there is more control being exercised in total, with a notable increment in the case of the headquarters staff, a further small decline for the local plant management, and increments for the supervisors and for the employees. There appears to have been a change of modest degree, more or less as hoped for, and there has clearly not been a reversion to the original condition of concentrated control in the hands of the plant manager.

We turn now to some indicators of the state of the Weldon organization from the views of the supervisors and managers. The data presented in Figure 3 are derived from Likert's assessment instrument "Profile of Organizational and Performance Characteristics" (Likert, 1961, 1967). Most readers will have some acquaintance with this instrument and the theory and research data that it expresses, but a brief characterization might be helpful. The instrument used is a 43-item graphic-scale rating form that allows the respondent to describe his own organization as it presently functions and as he ideally would like it to function. The items are so chosen and arranged that the respondent may report a syndrome of organizational characteristics that locates the organization on a scale ranging from "authoritative" to "participative." Likert discerns four regions of this scale, named Systems 1, 2, 3, and 4, with word labels ranging from "Authoritarian" through "Benevolent Authoritarian" and "Consultative" to "Participative." The conception is analogous to McGregor's "Theory X" and "Theory Y" scale, and also to Blake's two-dimensioned matrix. To put it somewhat disrespectfully, the bad guys are thought to have and to prefer System 1

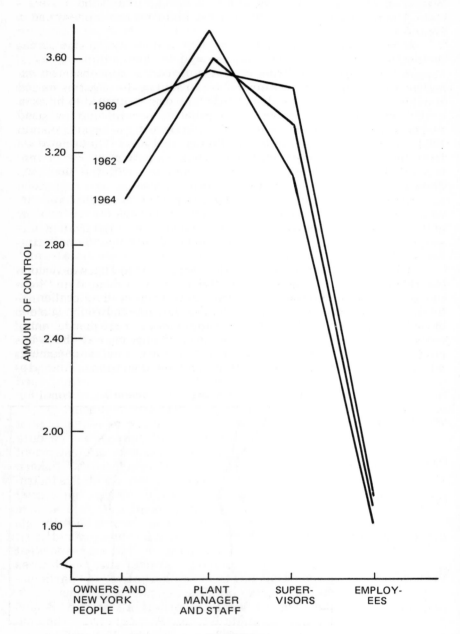

FIGURE 2

Change in amount and hierarchical distribution of control.

organizations while good guys aspire to and approach the System 4 state. The results for Weldon, 1962, 1964, and 1969 are represented in Figure 3.

At the left of the field are two graph lines showing the state of the Weldon organization in 1962, first as rated by the Institute for Social Research research team from interview protocols and observations, and next and somewhat more favorably as rated by the supervisors and managers on the scene. Weldon at that time was described to be auto-cratic—in some respects rather harshly autocratic and in some respects more benevolently autocratic. The state of the organization in 1964 and in 1966 is represented in the next two lines. These data are from supervisors and managers; they indicate a pattern of change that is substantial in magnitude and wholly compatible with the intentions embodied in the Weldon change program. There was no regression toward the earlier state during the 1964-66 period. The right-hand line represents the results of our 1969 assessment; it shows that in the view of the managers and supervisors at Weldon, the organization has progressed still further toward their ideal of a participative organiza-tional system.

A final remark should be made about measured changes in Weldon before we turn to a consideration of the meaning of these data. Some readers will be interested in business outcomes as well as in the atti-tudes and behavior of the members of the organization. Briefly, Weldon moved from a position of substantial capital loss in 1962 to substantial return on investment in 1964; this direction of change in profitability has continued through 1968, the last year of record. Employee earnings which rose substantially between 1962 and 1964 have been sustained at

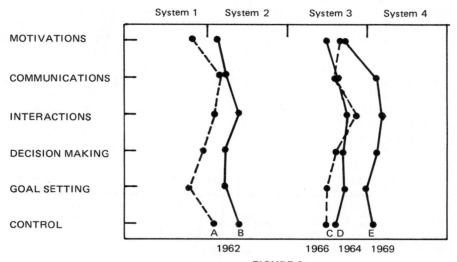

FIGURE 3
Change in profile of organizational characteristics.

a relatively high level. During the period since 1964 there have been substantial gains in efficiency and volume for the factory as a whole. New products and work methods have been introduced. By such business indicators, Weldon is a successful organization.

DURABLE CHANGE

The evidence we must weigh, although somewhat mixed and with a few contrary elements, appears to sustain the conclusion that the Weldon organization, far from reverting to its prior condition, has during recent years made additional progress toward the organizational goals envisioned by the owners and managers in 1962, and envisioned as well by supervisors and production employees at a somewhat later time. This outcome invites speculations about the psychological and social forces that are at work.

We confess a brief regret that there was not an opposite outcome, for we are rather better equipped with ideas about organizational stability and regression than we are with ideas about organizational change and continuing development. For example, before the data became available, we were prepared to make some remarks about the "Hawthorne effect"—about the superficiality and transient quality of organizational and behavioral changes induced under conditions of external attention and pressure; but it boggles the mind to think of a "Hawthorne effect" persisting for over eight years among people half of whom were not on the scene at the time of the original change. Similarly, we were prepared to make wise remarks about cultural forces, habits, and the natural predilection of managers for nonparticipative methods; these we thought would help explain a reversion to the prevailing conditions in organizations. We were prepared to assert that in the absence of contrary environmental forces, external influences, and purposive continuing change efforts of a vigorous kind, an organization would migrate back to some more primitive form of organizational life.

Clearly we need to appeal to other ideas than these. We are, all of us, ill prepared to do so. Two recent and fairly comprehensive reviews of organizational change strategies (Leavitt, 1965; Shepard, 1965) say nothing about the permanence or continuation of change processes except for a remark by Shepard that "change in the direction of collaboration-consensus patterns [participative patterns] . . . facilitates growth, change and adaptation to new environmental challenges and opportunities [p. 1141]."

A first explanatory idea rests on the possibility that the heavy investment of external talent, money, and effort that characterized the original change period at Weldon has been continued during the subsequent years. We are assured that this is not the case. There has indeed been some additional use of external consultants, but at a modest rate that is considered normal and permanent. There has indeed been further improvement and change in the work system and the production facilities, but at no more than a permanently sustainable rate. There has indeed been a continuation of certain organizational activities introduced as part of the original change program, but these are regarded as normal operating procedure and not as special change efforts. Economic conditions have been favorable to the firm, but they were also favorable at the distressed time preceding the change of ownership in 1962.

We believe that there are three other lines of explanation that do bear scrutiny. These thoughts about the Weldon experience are not offered with any sense of great insight or of conceptual innovation. They are offered only as suggestions for lines of inquiry and emphasis in future organizational research. The first concerns the provision of "lock-in" devices that make difficult the reversal of the original change.

It was mentioned earlier that the original change program contained some notions of seeking mutually reinforcing change actions across the psychological, organizational, and technological domains. A central idea was to make structural changes in the organization that matched the work system and that did not violate reasonable assumptions about the values and motives of individual members. For example, the revitalized piece-rate pay system was viewed to be viable only if sustained by the provision of assured services that allowed high earnings, a revision of the record and information flow system that assured instant supervisory response to low earnings, and a moderating of the prior job assignment system so that a production employee could become skilled in the work assigned. The idea of systemic consistency is surely an elementary one, no more than common sense—a habit of thought for those who have learned to view the factory as a total system in which all elements are interdependent. The interdependence of elements tends to preserve, to enhance, and to "lock in" the central characteristics of the system and thus to prevent retrogression.

A second factor in Weldon's continuation of intended change might lie in the earlier legitimation of concern about organizational processes. This is speculative, for we have no ready way to assess the extent to which there was implanted the habit of deliberate and self-conscious examination of the potential side effects of the many policy and operating decisions, usually technical or economic in origin, that arise daily. One of the fragmenting features of many organizations is the tendency to isolate problems, to treat them as if they could be optimally resolved without reference to their broader context. An organization habituated at all levels to think about, discuss openly, and to weigh properly the full range of elements in the organizational system might well have unusual capacities for self-maintenance and self-development.

A third possible explanation of the maintenance of the changes at Weldon and their further development under conditions of limited continuing external influence might lie in the inherent merit of the participative organizational model. Could it be that people who have experienced a taste of it get hooked, know what they want, and lend their effort to maintaining it? A glance at the newspaper headlines on almost any day will suggest that some of our fellow citizens do not like what they are experiencing in formal organizations and have thoughts of having something better, by force if necessary.

NOTES

1. Presidential Address by Stanley E. Seashore presented to the Division of Industrial Psychology (Division 14) at the annual meeting of the American Psychological Association, Washington, D.C., September 1969.
   Requests for reprints should be sent to Seashore, at the Survey Research Center, Institute for Social Research, University of Michigan, Ann Arbor, Michigan 48106.
2. The assistance of Edith Wessner is acknowledged.

REFERENCES

LEAVITT, H. J. Applied organizational change in industry. In J. G. March (Ed.), *Handbook of organizations*. Chicago: Rand-McNally, 1965.

LIKERT, R. *New patterns of management*. New York: McGraw-Hill, 1961.

LIKERT, R. *The human organization*. New York: McGraw-Hill, 1967.

MARROW, A. J., BOWERS, D. G., & SEASHORE, S. E. *Management by participation*. New York: Harper & Row, 1967.

SHEPARD, H. A. Changing interpersonal and intergroup relationships in organizations. In J. G. March (Ed.), *Handbook of organizations*. Chicago: Rand-McNally, 1965.